AFRICA FROM EARLY TIMES TO 1800

Readings in African History

Edited by P. J. M. McEwan

AFRICA FROM EARLY TIMES TO 1800

NINETEENTH-CENTURY AFRICA

TWENTIETH-CENTURY AFRICA

AFRICA FROM EARLY TIMES TO 1800

EDITED BY

P. J. M. McEWAN

LONDON
OXFORD UNIVERSITY PRESS
IBADAN NAIROBI
1968

Oxford University Press, Ely House, London W.1

GLASGOW NEW YORK TORONTO MELBOURNE WELLINGTON
CAPE TOWN SALISBURY IBADAN NAIROBI LUSAKA ADDIS ABABA
BOMBAY CALCUTTA MADRAS KARACHI LAHORE DACCA
KUALA LUMPUR HONG KONG TOKYO

Maps drawn by Regmarad

PRINTED IN GREAT BRITAIN BY
THE CAMELOT PRESS LTD, LONDON AND SOUTHAMPTON

Preface to
Readings in African History

For the past eighty years the continent of Africa has been steadily increasing its proportion of the limelight in world affairs. There have also occurred, during the same period, a general educational awakening and a dramatic refinement of the techniques available for the advancement of knowledge. The coincidence of these developments has led to African studies, social, political and economic, past as well as present, becoming a recognized part of a balanced university curriculum.

The history of Africa holds a special position as a subject worthy of study. In the first place, it is that part of man's heritage which most strongly captures the interest of modern African men and women. The long-run contours of African history are rich in content and often revealing in their illumination of the present.

African history has, indeed, the same claims to be studied as British history or American history, and just as its role in Africa is much the same as the role of British history in British schools and universities, or American history in American schools and colleges, so is its role in these countries similar to that which the study of British and American history has to play in Africa.

But in addition to the intrinsic importance of the subject, it has a further significance within Africa itself. It provides a context of man's development into which many of the problems and aspirations of the present can be meaningfully placed, thus stimulating a broader sense of tradition and a deeper pride of achievement which lend natural and legitimate support to the growth of nationhood.

In the second place, the rapid growth of African influence and importance in the world, together with previous neglect of its history, give to the study unusual significance. For too long, and with increasing incongruity, nations have studied and taught, often exclusively, the history of their own people. As the world shrinks and the extent of national interdependence expands, our knowledge of other civilizations and other continents becomes commensurately more necessary.

There is a third, more technical, reason for the importance of African history. This is the direct relevance to it of other disciplines, principally archaeology, ethnography and comparative linguistics, and the further problems raised by oral tradition. The nature of their respective associations and the issues that each separately raises, brings the student of history in continuous contact with these other studies, making him more responsive to their application and value.

African historians have tended to fall into two groups. There are those who seek to identify common factors in disparate regions of space and differing periods of time and who, perhaps mindful also of the practical need for comprehensive texts, write in unifying and comparative terms of tropical Africa as a whole. There are others who prefer to narrow the focus so that it embraces one selected area or a single nation. The former provide the condensation necessary for comparative study and for a more complete understanding of those developments, such as partition, which have been trans-continental in character and origin. The latter, on the other hand, provide the detail and depth necessary for detailed understanding. As time goes by and our knowledge extends so may the more intensive studies increasingly outnumber the continental histories. For the present, however, there is room for both.

In addition, there are a number of historians who concentrate still more intensively, writing only in learned journals.

Where, in this scheme of things, does the present work stand? The aims of the three volumes are several. First, their essential aim is to provide the student of African history with a comprehensive but detailed understanding, through writings by recognized authorities, of the major events and developments in their subject. Whether the readings are studied on their own or in conjunction with one of the several general histories now available, the reader will have at his disposal the most significant events and movements as recorded and interpreted by leading historians.

A second aim, and a corollary of the first, is to provide a

necessary adjunct to general history texts. It is impossible to deal adequately with even the most influential sequences of events in Africa's past within the confines of a single volume. It is difficult to do so even in a regional history. The present volumes will allow the student to undertake a closer examination of the more important of these developments. It also offers a useful corrective against the bias of a single author when dealing with such discursive material as, for example, partition, or the rise of nationalism, making direct comparison possible between different points of view.

A third important objective has been to bring together definitive writings which are not generally available, either because of inadequate library facilities or because of their original appearance in a comparatively obscure publication, perhaps in a language other than English.

A book of readings is inevitably susceptible to the sins of omission and commission. Selections always invite criticism not only for the subjects chosen but for the writings chosen to cover them. The present work can be no exception. In determining what to include, the following criteria have been employed. With regard to design, three volumes were decided as being the least possible number to allow adequate treatment of the major themes. In order to follow the flow of history and to draw appropriate comparisons, with due reference to regional and temporal inter-relations, each volume deals with a different period of time. Volume I takes the reader to the end of the eighteenth century, Volume II is concerned with the nineteenth century, and Volume III with the twentieth century. Thus, while early times are by no means neglected, there is an emphasis on the history of the last two hundred years.

Within each volume the material is presented in sections. These follow the same geographical pattern throughout, in the order: West Africa, North Africa, Egypt, Ethiopia, East Africa, southern Africa. In the sections themselves, the readings are presented in the order approximating most closely to the connection, logical and temporal, between the material they discuss. Thus, within a framework based on chronology, the readings are organized in accordance with geography as well as with time. In this way, it is hoped that convenient reference will be facilitated without sacrificing the occasional need for ignoring spatial boundaries in the interest of historical accuracy.

There are, however, a number of issues which do not fit neatly into any conventional category of either time or space. These include the spread and influence of the two great religious movements Islam and Christianity, partition, and the rise of nationalism and pan-Africanism. In accordance with their closest logical affinity, treatment of the religious questions is included in Volume I, partition in Volume II, and nationalism and pan-Africanism in Volume III. In each case, the subject is treated as a whole in its own specific section with the same geographical order of presentation, wherever this is appropriate.

There is a further subject amenable to study only in a single, continent-wide context. This is the study of pre-history, which comprises the opening section in Volume I.

As will have been observed from the geographical order of presentation, two countries have been singled out for specific reference, Egypt and Ethiopia. The long history of Egypt cannot, of course, be encompassed in a work of this nature and, in any case until the nineteenth century, Egypt was closer in her development to Asia Minor than to Africa. Since, however, our concern is with the whole continent of Africa and because the influence of Egypt had been felt to the south and west for many centuries, its inclusion was demanded. In order to account for Egypt's peculiar role in African affairs, as a nation at the crossroads of three continents, its individual role has been accordingly recognized in the text.

Ethiopia has been singled out in the same manner on account of her long history of independence and for the long periods of her isolation from outside influences. Where her development has been associated with other forces, as has occurred increasingly since the early part of the nineteenth century, these factors are discussed in the sections dealing with Ethiopia.

An examination of the section headings will indicate a slight bias towards political history and, in Volume III, towards political science. Although every effort has been made to give full attention to economic, religious and social developments, it is perhaps inevitable that the main emphasis has been on political change, on the fluctuating powers of government and on conflict. Detailed comparative studies of African economic and social history are still awaited.

There is another bias which should be mentioned. Movements and events that are discussed in the following pages have been chosen not only on account of their intrinsic importance but also because, in the majority of cases, they figure in one or more of the commoner examinations in the subject.

In spite of this consideration, it must not be thought that the readings have been streamlined to fit probable examination questions. This would be a task not only impossible but contrary to our intention of providing a comprehensive selection. Thus, for example, considerable space has been given in the third volume to the question of *apartheid*. This subject, which seldom appears in any examination, has been analysed in detail because of its importance for the whole continent, not only as national policy but as a rallying point for international opposition.

Turning from design to detailed content, it was only when the choice seemed to lie equally between two or more readings that criteria other than pure merit were introduced. Length and accessibility were then considered, the less readily accessible and the more concise being preferred. Articles were generally more suitable than extracts from books, especially if the book had just been published and was in most libraries. Articles, apart from being less widely known and more difficult to find, have the advantages of being self-contained, of paying greater attention to the general historical context of their subject matter, and of bringing a sharper focus to bear on a narrower front—all important factors for our purpose. At the same time, where there has seemed no adequate alternative, rather than have no reference to an important question, an extract has occasionally been chosen from a book, however recent, and, if unavoidable, however derivative.

There are a number of works which, although strongly criticized in their main thesis, nevertheless contain, often as an introductory chapter, a summary of an important sequence of events which in accurate conciseness is not to be found elsewhere. Such books present a problem: should the extract be included, at the risk of inviting ready criticism, or should general suspicion be allowed to drown incidental quality? In a limited number of cases, which it would be invidious to identify, where the alternative has been less than satisfactory, the editor has therefore included what has seemed to him a sound extract from an otherwise doubtful source.

One final category of choice should be mentioned. In three cases, readings have been included because of their own historic quality as classical statements on important issues, in spite of more modern treatments of the same topic. These are Professor Schapera's paper on 'Economic changes in African urban life', first published in Volume I of *Africa* (1928); Dr Gann's paper on 'The significance and suppression of the slave trade in British Central Africa', which first appeared in the *Journal of the Rhodes-Livingstone Institute* (1954); and an extract from Sir Winston Churchill's *The River War*, first published in 1899. In their contrasting ways each is a model of its kind.

Finally, a word about interpretation. History, once it passes beyond being a mere chronicle of events, becomes inevitably interpretative. Interpretation implies selection. The historian of an epoch or a movement or a personality selects his data and reaches a general conclusion. In many cases, more numerous than is sometimes appreciated, the conclusion is reached prior to the selection. The result may be accepted at once, in which event it will pass into the realm of historic fashion, or it may evoke alternative, perhaps contradictory, interpretations, firing a general dispute. Occasionally, when it is openly polemical or intentionally provoking, the bias is transparent and may therefore be easily countered. But it more often happens that the selectivity is hidden and the assumptions and personal prejudices of the historian are occluded by an aura of objectivity, and an apparently scrupulous concern with accuracy. Whether this obscuring is conscious or otherwise makes no difference to its effect, which is that the unprepared observer accepts as proven what is only hypothesis, and is left in ignorance of the existence of any solid grounds for an alternative explanation. It is true, of course, that certain subjects in history, as in other things, are more emotive than others. Subjects also vary in their degree of certitude. It is these two factors, emotion and doubt, which most often give rise to the hidden premiss and an unhinted selectivity. Thus, to mention just two examples from the study of African history, one has to be particularly cautious when considering colonialism (particularly in southern Africa), and the factors leading to partition.

In the first (emotive) case, fashions have changed, and to be implicitly anti-colonial is to be as modish as was the almost unconditional praise of the colonist by white historians in the 1900s. Thus we find writers suppressing data that reflects badly on the colonized while concentrating on evidence that reflects adversely on the colonizer.

This is not intended as a general indictment of historians but as a warning against the common academic hypocrisy of believing that in one's own work the hidden value-judgement is not only hidden but non-existent.

Faced with this situation, the aim of the present volumes has been to give expression, as far as space permits, to alternative interpretations, exposing the critical reader to more than one point of view, leaving him, with the guidance of his teachers, to make up his own mind.

Similarly, in an area of doubt, such as the principal causes of partition, where opinions are no less biased for being openly divided, there have been included alternative explanations, Stengers as well as Robinson, Hyam as well as Gallagher. The same applies to other discussions, the comparative influence of Islam and Christianity for example, wherever space has allowed and contentious selectivity demanded.

For myself, as editor, the selection of readings has been as objectively chosen as it is possible for one man to make it. My main regret is that there have not been many more African written texts from which to choose. One may be confident, however, that in twenty years' time, if these volumes should be revised or others written, then the ratio of texts written by Africans to others would be about reversed. Such is the rate of change in all things African.

Contents

Maps

Maps 6 and 7 are based on maps which appear in *A Political History of Tropical Africa* by Robert I. Rotberg (Harcourt, Brace & World, Inc. and Oxford University Press, 1965)

Acknowledgements

THESE volumes, prepared in three continents over a period of two years, would not have been possible without the co-operation of a very large number of people.

Although, of course, I am alone responsible for all the deficiencies involved in the selection and exclusion of material, I wish to express my deep appreciation for the manner in which so many scholars allowed me to consult their wisdom and consume their time. Often this was done more intensively than anyone has the right to request, but always more willingly responded to than anyone has the right to expect.

Mention cannot be made of all the help I have received, but a special word is due to Professor J. B. Hargreaves, Professor J. F. Ade Ajayi, Professor George Shepperson and Mr Anthony E. Atmore. Their constant advocacy of alternatives proved invaluable. My greatest debt in this regard, however, is to Dr Robert I. Rotberg, whose patient criticism and comments extended as fully in time as they did in detail. I am extremely grateful and I hope that the final result will not be too disappointing to him.

I would like to record my thanks to the many librarians who gave so freely of their time and who allowed me the use of their facilities, often from a distance, and to all the authors and publishers who kindly gave permission for me to include their material. The fact that only one reading has had to be excluded from a final list of 140 choices reflects the extent of their co-operation.

Dr Ian Lockerbie, of the Department of French at Aberdeen University, did a magnificent job in rapidly organizing the translation of difficult material when he and his colleagues could ill afford the time. To him and his team I am deeply grateful.

My sincere thanks to Carol Stein and Ruth Spivack who hunted countless books through countless shelves, and to Madeleine Allen, Dorothy Roberts and Florence Zamchek who spent many daunting hours establishing order out of chaos.

An immeasurable debt of appreciation is due to my wife. Without her long-term patience and encouragement through many vicissitudes these volumes could never have been completed.

P. J. M. McEwan

Boston, Massachusetts
January 1967

Introduction

THE first volume takes the reader from the earliest times of pre-history to the close of the eighteenth century.

These were centuries of conquest and migration. From the north the influence of Islam began to spread south-west across the continent. In the west and east patterns of trade began to arise and develop, across the Sahara and later, with the coming of the European explorers and slave-traders in the fifteenth century, inland and to the south.

In order to readily observe the patterning of events the reader is advised to become acquainted with the maps that have been provided. Otherwise it becomes difficult, if not impossible, to follow the history of, for example, the kingdoms of the Western Sudan, or the Arab conquests.

During the last hundred years covered by the present volume, Christianity began to make its presence felt, rivalling Islam as a system of religious belief and agent of change. Two sections have therefore been devoted to the spread and influence of these two major world religions, while a third section discusses the growth of African religious movements.

Throughout this long period of human history the emphasis of African historiography has been on political and military events. This volume remains in the tradition. But the student will realize that there is a danger of distortion in this approach. Many social and cultural changes had been taking place, art forms had been evolved, extinguished and contrived, economic cycles and other subtle changing rhythms of human existence were occurring. But the most tangible developments were the political and most writings have up to the present been primarily concerned with these. We must hope that before long it will be possible to write a social history of Africa. First, however, it is important to understand the lines of conquest and defeat, of exploitation and challenge, of tribal migration and absorption that have taken place in the continent of Africa since the dawn of human history.

For the convenience of readers a short bibliography and a list of major events, with their dates, are provided at the end of the text.

I. PREHISTORY

1. Prehistoric origins of African culture

J. DESMOND CLARK *Journal of African History* Vol. 5, No. 2, 1964; pages 163–82

. . . The earliest evidence of culture in the world occurs at the unique site at the Olduvai Gorge, the discovery of which is due to Dr and Mrs L. S. B. Leakey (as also is so much of our knowledge of the earliest history of man the tool-maker). Olduvai Gorge is situated in northern Tanganyika in the Eastern Rift, and cuts through some 300 feet of old lake sediments of Lower and Middle Pleistocene age. These beds are dated relatively in respect of the fossil faunas and cultural remains they contain, and absolutely by the potassium/argon method. Bed I is between 1½ and 2 million years old, and indisputable evidence of cultural activity has been found from top to bottom within it. The tool-makers camped round the edge of shallow open water near small lakes, and formed temporary camps on the mud flats exposed by seasonal fluctuations of the water level of the kind that can be seen at many of the Rift Valley lakes today. The surfaces on which the artifacts occur appear to have been covered fairly rapidly by falls of volcanic tuffs from the adjacent Ngorongoro crater. The skill and patience with which these occupation areas have been uncovered have permitted the making of floor plans that show beyond any question the artificial nature of the accumulations. On these floors, stones and bones are concentrated in quantity, and many of them have been artificially broken. Many stones occur which, though unworked, are not natural in the area and can only have been carried in, while many others have been intentionally flaked, and bashing stones, choppers, cores, flakes and small chunks, some utilized and occasionally retouched, occur inextricably mixed with the smashed bones of a number of different species of animal. Long bones and other bones have been broken to extract the marrow, and some of them show unmistakable marks of having been smashed with a rounded blunt object. The most famous of these floors is that in the upper part of Bed I, on which were lying the remains of the

Australopithecine *Zinjanthropus boisei*. Here the Leakeys found a concentration of highly comminuted bone some 15 feet in diameter, with larger bones on the periphery and a mass of worked stone in and among the bone. The remains represented several different antelopes, pig, tortoise, catfish, a snake, and several other small animals. A high proportion of the pig and antelope remains are from immature creatures. The most characteristic forms of tool are a chopper flaked from two directions to form an irregular and usually wide-angled cutting or chopping edge, made on a lava pebble or chunk of quartz, and a sharp flake for cutting.

The other floors are similar, but of especial interest is one only a foot or so above the lava on which the beds rest. Here the stone tools are, on an average, a good deal smaller, but they are associated with various accumulations of natural stones. It is very difficult to see how these could have got to their present position, resting on the clay, except by having been carried there. There is certainly one, and perhaps two, concentrations in rough semi-circles, and several stones rest one upon the other as if they had been purposely piled up.

These occupation floors represent the home bases—the living quarters—of early tool-making hominids who were in part carnivorous, obtaining their meat by hunting and scavenging. It is probable, however, on the analogy of modern hunter-gatherers, that quite 75 per cent of their food was vegetable, and, in this connexion, the pebble chopper may have been developed as a tool for sharpening sticks for digging.

Recent geological assessment of the climatic conditions under which Bed I was formed shows that the environment must have been very like that of the Serengeti Plains today, that is to say, semi-arid grass and parkland, with shallow pans and lakes, and forest relicts on the slopes of the adjacent volcanic masses. The relatively sparse scatter of occupation debris suggests that Lower Pleistocene hominids rarely stayed long in one place.

Artifacts of comparable age and form have been found at a few other sites, notably at Ain Hanech in Algeria, at Casablanca in Morocco, in the Albertine Rift, and at Kanam on the Kavirondo Gulf of Lake Victoria (which yielded also an enigmatic hominid jaw fragment), as well as in residual gravels in river and marine high terraces. It would seem that if it is indeed in the East African tectonic region that tool-making first developed, it was not very long before such a fundamental advance in technology spread widely throughout and beyond the continent (Figure 1).

No hominid more advanced than the Australopithecines is known from any of these Lower Pleistocene sediments. They are well represented by over 300 fossil remains. Two forms are known—a slenderer type (*Australopithecus africanus*), and a more heavily built type (*A. robustus*, known also as *Paranthropus*). Their membership of the family of the Hominidae is unquestionable on the evidence of their brains, teeth and jaw patterns,

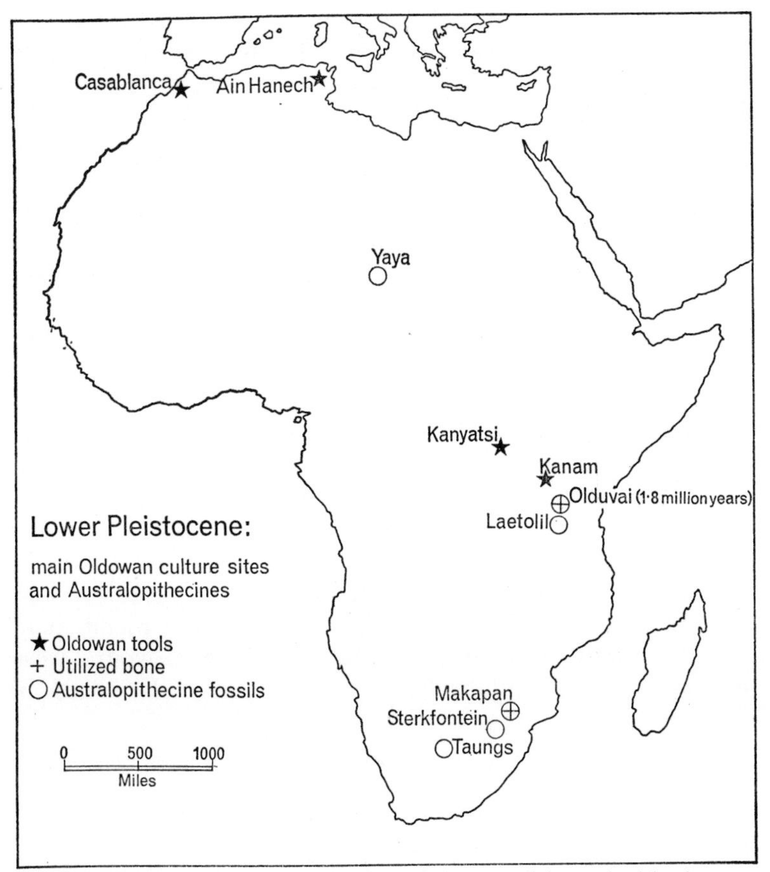

1. Distribution of Lower Pleistocene Culture and Australopithecines

and because of their bipedalism and their possession of hands adapted to tool-using. Lightly built and only some 4 feet 6 inches tall, they were nevertheless able to run fast and had arms adapted to throwing. In the small size of the brain and the massiveness of the face, however, they resembled the apes, with the result that they are sometimes known as the 'Man-Apes'. Napier's study of the hand from the pre-Zinjanthropus horizon at FLK NNI in Bed I at Olduvai shows that though primitive, it is intermediate between the hands of apes and of man, and would have been capable of clumsy tool-making.

The artifacts in the Bed I living-sites show that there can be little doubt that the East African Australopithecines were working stone for use as tools. Indeed, their Pliocene ancestors had been using tools for millions of years. The hand is the best proof of this, though another is the extreme simplicity of the technique involved in making the tools, and we must expect that at the end of the Lower Pleistocene certainly more than one form of hominid was living that was capable of making—and did make—tools.

There is no indication that the Australopithecine tool-makers lived in large groups. The small areas of the living-places rather suggest that there were unlikely to have been more than a dozen or so individuals in the band. While they seem to have been incapable of killing large animals, the concentrations of bones in the Transvaal caves (if they are indeed, as Dart claims, the food debris of the Australopithecines) would argue that they were, none the less, resourceful hunters and scavengers of medium- and small-sized animals. No doubt, also, they made capital of the necessity for the game to seek the only available surface water during the dry season, which was in the deep limestone caves where they were ambushed and slaughtered. For this some co-operation between members of the group must have been essential and, since the young were dependent on the adults for longer than were the young of apes, regular sharing of food is also implicit.

Many find it difficult to accept the wholesale manufacture of bone tools claimed for the Australopithecines by Dart in his 'Osteodontokeratic Culture', and consider that most of this material represents food debris. These caves have, nevertheless, provided fairly good, though rare, evidence of the utilization of bone, as has also one of the Olduvai floors. The most impressive of these bone tools are fragments of long bones that show shallow, highly polished groovings.

Why did stone tool-making first begin in the savannah? The answer is believed to lie in economic and social necessity. The African savannah is an environment with a long dry season in which a small and very defenceless hominid, forced to protect its hunting territory and ill-equipped biologically for digging or meat-eating, had to find some way to supplement the sources of vegetable foods that would dwindle under times of climatic deterioration. It is believed that this was one of the primary reasons why these early hominids turned to meat-eating, just as baboons sometimes do today. The use of some kind of sharp cutting tool to open the skin of an antelope, or of a bashing tool to break open long bones or the shell of a tortoise, or of a sharp tool to point a stick for digging, would have meant a regular and substantial increase in the quantity and variety of food available. The hominids would also have found these tools useful for defence.

Australopithecines have been found in South and East Africa, and now in Chad, as well as in the Far East, so that it is reasonable to suppose that tool-making, this most fundamental of human inventions, spread with remarkable rapidity.

Africa abounds with pebble tools, but the earlier claim that most of these are of Lower Pleistocene age remains as yet largely unsubstantiated, and it is probable that many of these industries belong to the earlier Middle, rather than to the Lower Pleistocene. For knowledge of the cultural pattern of these times we again rely most heavily on Olduvai, for this site preserves a unique evolutionary sequence of developing stages up to the earlier part of the Upper Pleistocene. But there are now several other sites, equally well dated, though without such a long stratigraphy (Figure 2). By the beginning of the second glaciation in the northern hemisphere, there is substantial evidence that tool-making had spread throughout all the semi-arid regions of the continent and had overflowed into other parts of the Old World. The artifacts are still predominantly choppers, chopping tools and worked flakes, but they are now more shapely, show greater variety, and are generally more skilfully made, though still remaining remarkably crude in appearance.

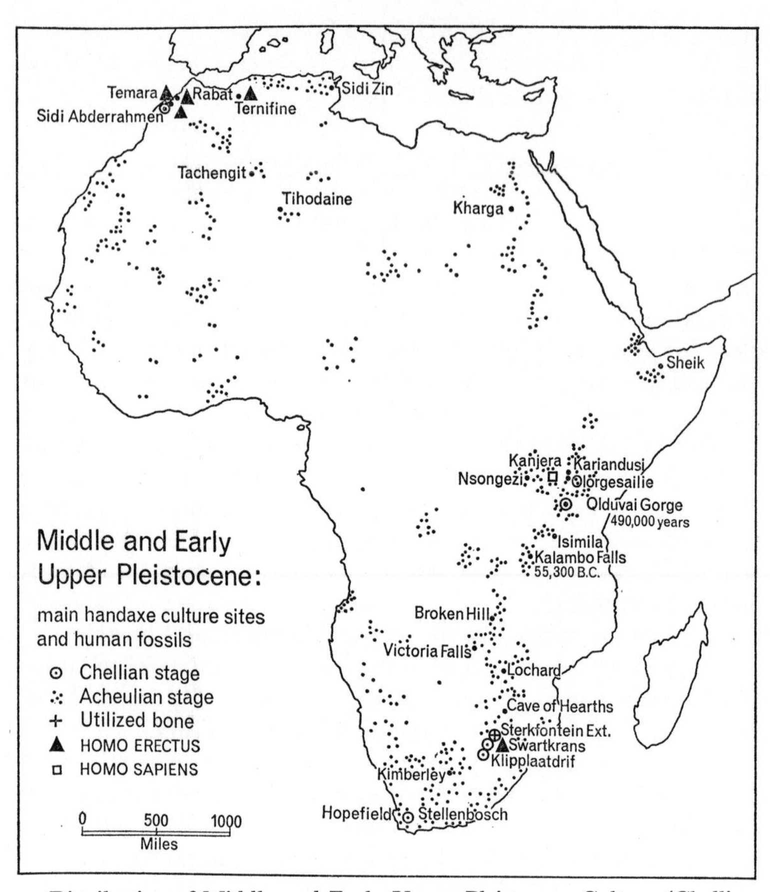

2. Distribution of Middle and Early Upper Pleistocene Culture (Chellian and Acheulian) and hominids

They represent the earliest stages of what is known as the Chelles-Acheul or Handaxe culture, the latter name being derived from the commonest type of tool, roughly the shape of a hand when seen in silhouette, though the earliest examples are very crude and rare. . . .

What do these early Handaxe cultures look like? The living-sites stratified at the base of Bed II at the Olduvai Gorge, which are now believed to date to about one million years ago, show that important changes had taken place since Bed I times. The accumulations of tools are much more extensive and there are generally many more artifacts. There are choppers, polyhedral stones and utilized flakes in quantity, together with a few pear-shaped, handaxe-like forms. But perhaps the most significant tool is a small flake or chunk that shows careful retouching to form notches and scraping edges. Some of these small, delicate, informal tools look as if they belong to the Later Stone Age, and it is obvious that the hominid that made them was fully capable of what Napier has called 'the precision grip' between finger and thumb. We do not know what these tools were used for, though they would have been effective in trimming the meat off bone, in cleaning skins or in paring wood. It is also evident that hunting techniques had undergone important changes, and now it was very often large animals that provided the major part of the meat supply. These consisted of extinct forms of elephant, giraffids, and ox- and sheep-like creatures that appear to have been driven into swampy ground or into open water and there butchered. This implies not only considerably improved hunting ability, but also reasonably efficient group organization.

The only remains of the earliest occupants of Bed II at Olduvai are two teeth, but at Sterkfontein in the Transvaal a similar industry is found in the later, brown breccia. These pebble tools are associated with teeth of *Australopithecus*, but it is suggested that they were really made by an early form of *Homo erectus*. The somewhat later and adjacent site of Swartkrans also contained tools and the large Australopithecine *Paranthropus*, but in addition another hominid is present, previously known as *Telanthropus* and now identified with *Homo erectus*.

About mid-way up in Bed II at Olduvai is a horizon known as 'the Chellean III horizon', the latest potassium/argon date for which is 490,000 years. Handaxes made by a stone technique are now much more common, though the pebble chopper still predominates. All the other types of tool occur, and there are now steep core-scraper forms besides, though full details have not yet been published. Associated with this cultural stage, Leakey found the greater part of a skull cap which falls within the pattern of the Pithecanthropoids, or *Homo erectus*, as this stock is now called. The Chellean III skull differs, however, in having a larger cranial capacity, and in anticipating in some measure the Rhodesioid type of man. There can be no doubt that the cultural, physical and intellectual developments that had taken place since Australopithecine times are inextricably interconnected, and the rapidity of the biological change could not have occurred without culture.

With this level at Olduvai we can correlate a 'Chellean' (Clacto-Abevillian) stage from an early marine level at Sidi Abderrahman, near Casablanca, as well as the lakeside site of Ternifine on the Algerian plateau. Here there is a somewhat more developed stone industry, and the usual bone debris from meals, together with three well-preserved jaws and a parietal bone. Arambourg has described these as belonging to an African Pithecanthropoid stock which he has named *Atlanthropus*. Thus the African representatives of this 'palaeoanthropoid' level would be contemporary with those from China and south-east Asia.

The second half of the Handaxe culture—the Acheulian—was a time of population movement into areas where no signs of earlier occupation by man have yet been found, and it was probably a period of population increase also. The extreme richness of Africa in the stone tools of this time points to the very favourable environment in which the Acheulian was practised. It may be inferred, though it has not yet been proved, that with the advances of the polar ice-sheets in the second and third glacials, and during the Great Interglacial, there was a more temperate environment over most of the African continent, so that many areas now desert became favourable for settlement. This was also a time of great proliferation of species among the antelopes, pigs and other African mammals, so that it is to be expected that man was also quick to take advantage of the opportunities now available to him.

The Acheulian populations were, however, still confined to the savannah and, as rainfall and temperature permitted, to the drier parts of the continent. It was only later that the tropical forest zone became permanently occupied. Moreover, man was still virtually confined in his choice of living quarters to waterside sites, probably because he had evolved no efficient means of carrying water supplies for any distance. Even more important than the richness of the stone industries of this period is the existence of a number of stratigraphically sealed and dated camping-sites, from which we can gain some idea of the manner of living of the people. Most of these occupation sites belong to later Acheulian times, from perhaps 150–50,000 years ago. There are several sites of this kind: in East Africa, at Olorgesailie, Kariandusi and Isimila; in Rhodesia, at Broken Hill and Kalambo Falls; in South Africa, at Kimberley and the Cave of Hearths; while in North Africa there are caves at Casablanca and Rabat, fossil spring sites in Egypt and the Maghrib, to mention but a few.

Acheulian man still concentrated on killing large animals, and he seems to have been much better equipped to do so than his predecessors. The handaxes are now really fine examples of the stoneworker's craft. They were made by what is known as the cylinder hammer technique, which enabled thinner and flatter flakes to be removed, and the result was most shapely tools with straight cutting edges. Another cutting tool is known as a 'cleaver', and is often U-shaped and axe-like. Balls of stone, different types of steep core-scrapers, and many varieties of small scraping and cutting tools also form an integral part of any Acheulian industry. There was already selection of raw material: the tougher, harder rocks were used for the heavy cutting and chopping tools, while the fine-grained, homogeneous rocks, capable of producing a sharp but relatively brittle edge, were used for the small tools. This must reflect differences in activity.

Some four or five variations in the cultural pattern can now be seen, though as yet no regional specialization is discernible. Sometimes industries consist of high percentages of large cutting tools and low percentages of other forms. Elsewhere the large cutting tools may be completely absent (as at Hope Fountain). At yet other sites there are roughly equal percentages of both large and small tools, or industries occur with high percentages of heavy equipment—choppers, picks, core-scrapers and the like. Finally, there are the mining-sites, where the raw materials were worked up from cobbles, boulders or outcrops. This again shows that Acheulian man engaged in a number of different activities for which he used different stone tools. . . .

It was not until the very end of Acheulian times in Africa that man became a regular user of fire. There are some three or four sites where evidence of fire is preserved, and all these probably date to between 50,000 and 60,000 years ago. One such site is at the Kalambo Falls, where charred logs and charcoals occur, and where man used fire to aid in sharpening sticks for digging, to shape clubs, or to make edges on knife-like tools of wood.

Thus fire-making, first known from second glacial times in the Far East, does not appear to have spread universally in Africa before the end of Acheulian times some 50–60,000 years ago, presumably because there was no need for it before. But now the climate became cooler and wetter, bringing about a considerable readjustment in the vegetation patterns and in the distribution of animal and human populations. Under a lowering of temperature of between 4° and 5°C., coinciding with the earlier part of the last glaciation in Europe, higher-living forest species replaced lowland tropical forest down to 600–900 metres below their present altitude range in sub-Saharan Africa, and a Mediterranean flora spread southwards to the southern borders of the Sahara. With the vastly increased potential for food getting, technical development, and living conditions made possible by a regular use of fire, man now spread into country which he had not previously occupied—the now most favourable but formerly forest-covered regions of Equatoria. Here the routes of migration into the Congo basin and the West African rain forest must have lain along the grass-covered interfluves, and man was better able to avail himself of the opportunities offered by, on the one hand, the savannah and, on the other, the forest galleries in the adjacent valleys.

This was a time of considerable population movement and of cultural experiment. It saw the fairly rapid disappearance of the old traditional forms of tool—the handaxe and the cleaver—in the higher rainfall, more heavily tree-covered parts of the continent. Here there developed many heavy chopping tools and smaller denticulated artifacts that are believed to have been associated with woodworking. The complex became dominant throughout the Congo and West Africa, spreading into East Africa west of the Eastern Rift and into south-east Africa down to Natal. It is known as the Sangoan culture. Elsewhere in southern and eastern Africa, in regions favourable for the preservation of the traditional type of habitat, the old handaxe tradition lingered on. This is known as the Fauresmith complex, and it is associated with pans and grasslands and an abundant ungulate and large-animal fauna (Figure 3).

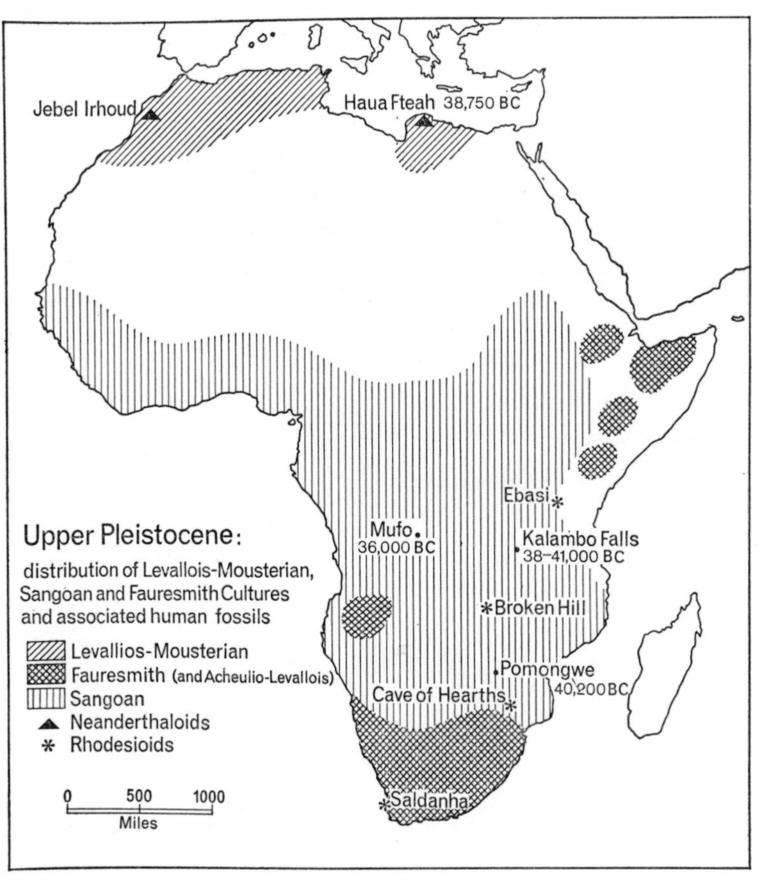

3. Distribution of Early Upper Pleistocene Culture and hominids (Fauresmith, Sangoan, etc.)

For the first time man now began to occupy caves and rock shelters as regular homes, for, with his control of fire, these provided safe and more comfortable living-quarters. Furthermore, because of the regulation of the seasonal movements of the bands and the use of efficient carrying devices, he could now afford to stay in one place for much longer. Whereas the Australopithecines with their limited technology must very quickly have exhausted the sources of food available to them, the Acheulian and, later, the Sangoan and Fauresmith peoples, who were becoming steadily more proficient and inventive in their methods of food getting, were able to exploit the available resources with ever-increasing efficiency. Increase in the size of the band, more permanent residence, and ability to live in a greater variety of habitats, previously unfavourable, must have been the inevitable concomitant of increasing technical skill and mental ability, and at this time, as the distribution maps show, there were few parts of the continent where man did not

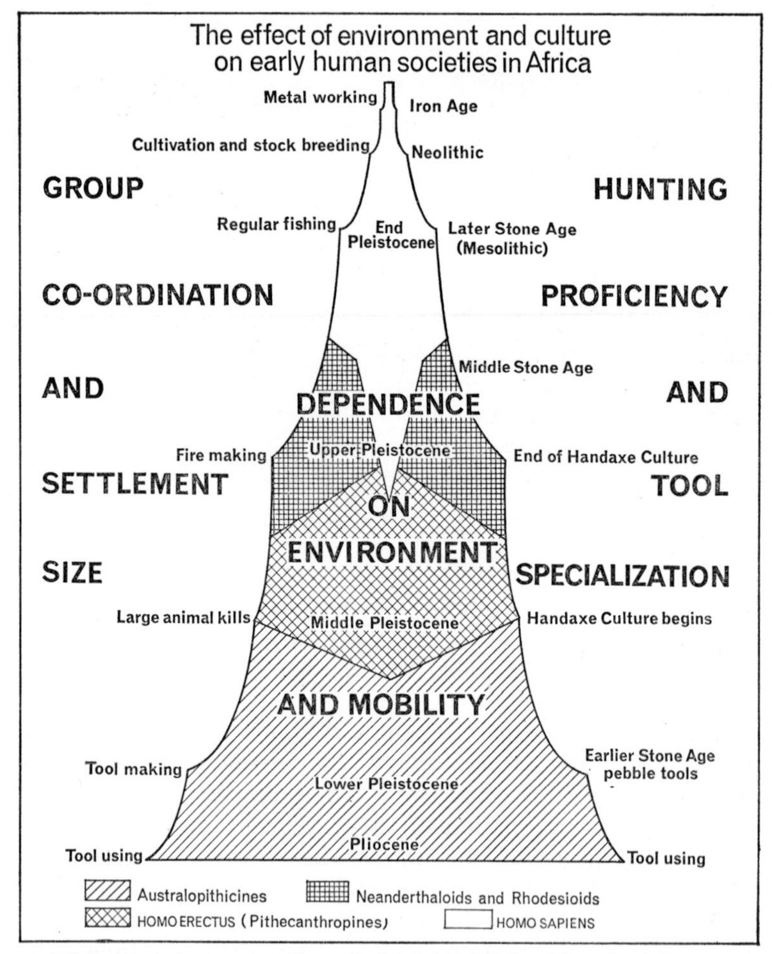

4. Diagrammatic presentation of the inter-relationship of environment, genotype and culture through time and their effect on the prehistoric societies of Africa

penetrate. Figure 4 is an attempt to show the inter-relationship of environment, genotype and culture through time, and their effect on the prehistoric societies of Africa.

After the disappearance of the Acheulian culture from North Africa, which was contemporary with encroaching desertification, there appear, from Cyrenaica to Morocco, flake industries that are closely similar to those from the Levantine coast and the Near East generally. These are known culturally as Levallois-Mousterian and they are associated with a Neanderthal physical type. From the magnificent site of Haua Fteah in Cyrenaica, and from the newly discovered site at Jebel Irhoud in Morocco, we know that the Levallois-Mousterian people were cave dwellers, competent fire-users, and specialized in making light cutting, scraping and piercing tools from fine, thin flakes.

It is an intriguing problem whether these industries and the associated Neanderthal men were the outcome of migration into Africa from the Near East or Europe, or whether they were an autochthonous evolution from the Acheulian. The evidence is equivocal. The Kanjera type of man, if he is accurately dated, could have been ancestral to both the Neanderthal and the *sapiens* forms in Africa and, so far as the industry is concerned, the prepared-core technique is also present in the late Acheulian in North Africa. Any movement could, therefore, equally well have been out of Africa as into it. On the other hand, the closer similarities with the Near East rather than with sub-Saharan Africa, and the appearance of some representatives of the Palaeoarctic fauna in North Africa, suggest that the culture and the human stock could also be intrusive. At present the evidence is, it would seem, if anything weighted in favour of the latter alternative.

Whatever the answer, it is from this time onwards that culture in North Africa becomes differentiated from the south of the Sahara, though influences spread at favourable times in both directions (Figure 5). In the Maghrib the Levallois-Mousterian evolved into a culture—known as the Aterian—specializing in the use of tanged flakes and points, while further east and as far south as the Horn the more generalized Levallois-Mousterian pattern was preserved. The Levallois-Mousterian was largely contemporary with the savannah-living Sangoan

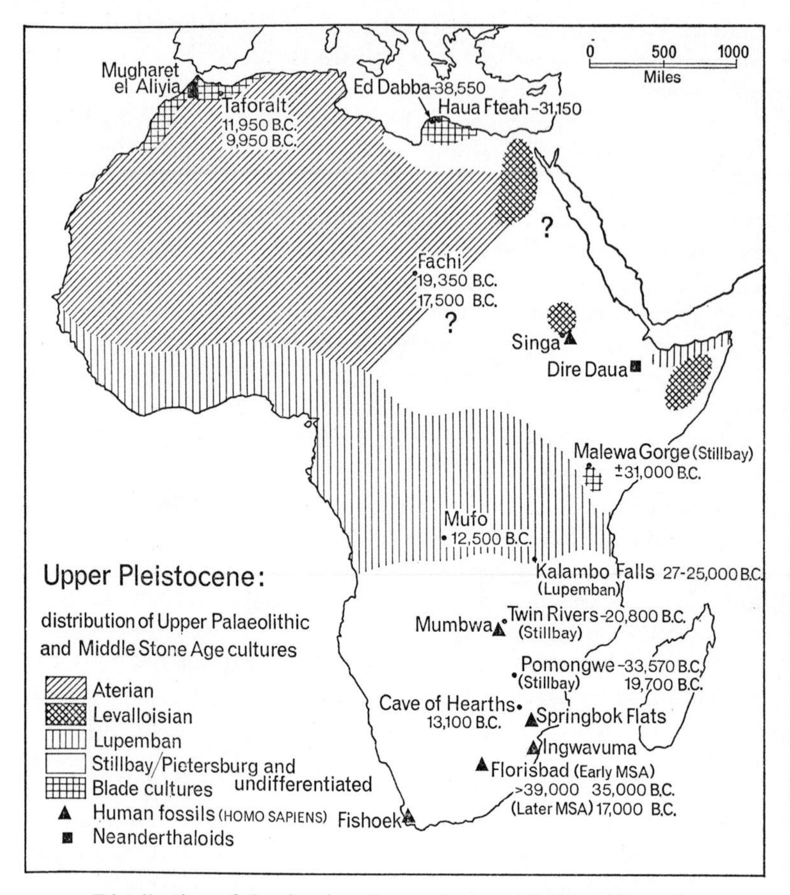

5. Distribution of the Aterian, Lupemban and Stillbay/Pietersburg

and the Fauresmith populations of the grasslands south of the Sahara, thus making the Neanderthaler of the north contemporary with the Rhodesian physical type in the south. This last represents the extreme development of the heavy-browed stock and it is known from as far apart as Broken Hill and the Cape, where it represents the makers of a late Rhodesian Sangoan (or Proto-Stillbay, since these are now known to be the same thing) and of the Cape Fauresmith.

In the earlier part of the Middle Stone Age, the Rhodesioid type began to be replaced by the more efficient *Homo sapiens* forms as a result of natural selection. The Middle Stone Age proper evolved from the Sangoan and Fauresmith after about 35,000 B.C. and ended about 8–10,000 B.C. There has for long been a tendency in Europe to refer to Africa after the end of the Middle Pleistocene as a cultural backwater. This was based initially on the fact that the earliest *sapiens* stock in Europe is associated with what we know as blade and burin, or Upper Palaeolithic, industries, which rather abruptly replaced the Neanderthal populations and the Mousterian culture there about 35,000 B.C. In Africa the prepared-core technique, Mousterian if you like, continued for a further 25,000 years, and by inference drawn from the European associations it was, therefore, considered that in Africa the Middle Stone Age was made by late surviving Neanderthalers. Radiocarbon and later discoveries show that this is not the case, and there is no evidence of any such time-lag in the genotype as had been postulated. The reason for the survival of the prepared-core tradition is obviously that it was the most efficient for producing the specialized equipment that was required by a hunting people in tropical and sub-tropical environments.

These Middle Stone Age cultures, as they are known in sub-Saharan terminology, though based essentially on the prepared core and faceted flake, differ in fact considerably in the nature of their end-products, so that a number of distinct variants can be identified and directly related to environmental specialization. Thus we find the Stillbay and Pietersburg variants in the savannah and grasslands of south and east Africa concentrating on light cutting, piercing and projectile tools of stone, while in the Congo forests, for example, the contemporary form, known as Lupemban, contains many axe and chopping elements and magnificent lanceolate knives or stabbing points. Whereas the tanged point was the speciality of the Aterian population, the foliate form in many varieties was that favoured south of the Sahara.

During the African Middle Stone Age there is the same evidence as in Europe for the appearance of religious beliefs. This is shown by the careful burial of the dead. Simultaneously there appear signs of an aesthetic sense in the use of paint and ornamentation. It would seem, therefore, that it was primarily the contrasting environments of glacial and tropical Africa that were responsible for the basic differences in the stone cultures.

Upper Palaeolithic blade and burin industries are found in two parts of Africa—on the Mediterranean littoral and in the East African Rift. The first appearance of Upper Palaeolithic culture in Cyrenaica[1] has been dated to between 38 and 31,000 B.C. It is considered that this may also be the time of its earliest appearance in East Africa, though most of the evidence there, as also in north-west Africa, belongs to later times. There can be little doubt that these industries are intrusive from the Levant, being introduced presumably by an early *Homo sapiens* stock which must inevitably have hybridized with the existing populations. No human fossils of this culture stage are as yet known, so it is not possible at present to say whether the makers could have been the ancestors of the Erythriote and Mediterranean longheads. There is quite a possibility that this might have been so, for in East Africa, certainly, the later blade and burin industries were the work of populations of this physical type, largely identified today with the Hamites.

The close of the Pleistocene about 8000 B.C. was preceded by a cooler and wetter climate of some 2000 years duration, during which there were two immigrations of Caucasoid stock into North Africa, the one of Cromagnon type, bringing the Oranian culture to the Maghrib and the other, probably of Mediterranean type, bringing the Et Tera culture to Cyrenaica. At the same time there appears evidence of blade and burin industries in the Horn, while the Aterian populations of the Maghrib were able to move down as far as the southern and eastern Sahara and the Nile. These contacts resulted, for example, in the Congo with the final Middle Stone age, in the appearance of tanged projectile heads, and in South Africa and Rhodesia in the appearance of new forms of tool made on blades. Similarly, the bifacial foliate points of the later Aterian, the transverse arrowheads and heavy lunate forms of the Mesolithic, and the bifaced axe element of the Neolithic are probably the result of diffusion

[1] A much earlier blade industry occurs in the lower levels of the Haua Fteah cave, and is probably of an age with similar industries from the Levantine coast, where they are named Amudian and intercalate with a final stage of regional Acheulian known as Jabroudian. It is not known at present whether these early blade industries represent the ancestral form from which the Upper Palaeolithic of the Near East is derived, since they are followed in both regions by the Levallois-Mousterian.

northwards from the Lupemban and Tshitolian of Equatoria. This was the second major period of cultural readjustment in Africa.

The wet phase known as the Makalian that followed the end of the Pleistocene, which lasted from about 5500 to 2500 B.C., similarly permitted free exchange between Mediterranean and Negroid populations that had both moved into the Sahara with the advance of the Mediterranean flora and the improved water supplies. It is from this time that waterside habitats take on new significance. The sea coasts, rivers and lakes were now exploited for their food sources as never before, and it was the permanent food supply provided by the fish, shellfish and other water foods that enabled man to remain permanently in occupation of areas where previously he had been only a seasonal visitor. The wide distribution of, for example, the bone harpoon, the gouge and other traits of a waterside culture throughout the southern Sahara, the Nile and the Central African lakes, shows the rapidity with which the indigenous populations in such favourable localities took the opportunity to improve their economy. It is useful to keep in mind this facility for readjustment when considering the change-over from a stone-using to a metal-working economy.

By the end of the Pleistocene, the Bush physical stock was already present in South Africa and it may be postulated that, similarly, by selective processes, the Negroid and Erythriote types had also made their appearance, though the earliest known fossils representing these types are no older than the Mesolithic or the Later Stone Age. Because of their blood group relationships, the Bushman and the Negro must be derived from the same African ancestral stock. However, only in the case of the Erythriote or Proto-Hamite does there seem to be any close tie between culture and physical stock, and it was not so much race as cultural specialization springing from long adaptation to different habitats that dictated the distribution of culture forms in the post-Pleistocene.

Since the Later Stone Age is also the period of greatest adaptive specialization, a large number of distinctive cultures can be distinguished. In the Congo basin the cultures of the plateaux differ markedly from those of the forests, though both are fairly certain to have been made by an unspecialized

Negroid ancestral type. Markedly different again are those in the Albertine Rift or the Kenya Rift. In South Africa the Smithfield of the high veld, using various forms of end-scrapers made from indurated shale, is very different from the crescent-like microliths of the Wilton culture, though both were made by Bushmen and both had a number of traits in common. This specialization of equipment and the greater use that was now made of quite small animals for food is likely to have been stimulated by population increase and a corresponding reduction in the size of the hunting territory of the band. This in turn, however, could only have become possible because of the spread of new technical advances—the bow and arrow, poison, barbed fish-spears and other devices—that raised the yield of the hunting territory.

Food production and domestication first make their appearance in the continent in the later half of the sixth or early fifth millennium B.C. in Egypt. This is, therefore, later than the beginnings of cultivation (of wheat and barley) and of animal domestication in the Near East, and there can be little doubt that in the first instance Africa derived its knowledge of these things from immigrants into the Nile Valley. It took, however, a surprisingly short time for the new economy to spread across North Africa. It was present in Cyrenaica by 5000 B.C. and throughout much of the Sahara by 3500–3000 B.C. Neolithic culture is unknown south of the Sahara, however, until later, and in fact it never succeeded at all in replacing the Mesolithic, collecting way of life throughout most of the sub-continent.

What is the reason for this cultural lag? In part it must have been geographic. But it was also, and probably more importantly, economic. Cereal crops and domestic stock in the rich environment of tropical Africa were not the necessities for permanent village life that they were in the arid and semi-arid regions in which they were first developed. This would be especially so if the primary importance of livestock was already then, as it is today in Africa, an expression of wealth rather than a source of food. The abundant vegetable and animal resources of the tropical savannah and forests provided all that was needed to maintain the Mesolithic populations at much the same level of subsistence as did the crops and stock of the Neolithic farmers, and probably with less expenditure of labour.

It was not until the Sahara began to dry up after 2500 B.C., and the consequent over-grazing forced some of the Neolithic populations there to move southwards into what is now the Sudan belt, that any serious attempt at farming could have been made, though 'vegecultural' practices round the forest margins had probably been in use for some considerable time before that. Barley and wheat, however, are winter rainfall crops, and can rarely be grown in the tropics successfully except under irrigation. The high plateau in Ethiopia is one of the exceptions, but in other parts there must of necessity have been much experimentation with local potential domesticates from ± 2000 B.C. onwards. Thus several indigenous food crops were developed—rice in Guinea, sorghum and *Pennisetum* in the Sudan, tef and *Eleusine* in those parts of Ethiopia where wheat and barley were not established. This experimentation may also have stimulated the cultivation on the forest fringes of the indigenous *Dioscoreas* and of *Ensete*.

We find Neolithic cultivators in northern Nigeria, the makers of the Nok culture, between 2000 B.C. and A.D. 200, when stone began to be replaced by metal for essential tools. Neolithic pastoralists also reached Ethiopia and the Kenya Rift about 2000 B.C., and in the latter region they were not replaced by Bantu immigrants until after the sixteenth century A.D. The only other part where Neolithic industries are known, though they are all believed to be late, is the Congo basin. The whole of the rest of southern Africa remained in the collecting stage. The reason why it did so must be due, as well as to the richness of the wild food resources, to the generally inefficient equipment of Neolithic man for clearing forest and closed woodland and his inability to maintain himself in large enough communities. It was, therefore, not until the population explosion that precipitated the Bantu movements around the beginning of the Christian era that any fundamental change in the economy was feasible. What made this possible, even then, was the development of iron-working—the iron axe and spear—and, no doubt, also the introduction of the Asian food plants.

The many investigations that are going on today are steadily tracing the history of the spread of Negroid and Bantu culture into the sub-continent, and in another decade it is certain that a firm chronology will have become available. We can already trace the spread down the Central African lakes of the earliest Iron Age immigrants, the makers of the Dimple-based and Channelled ware pottery, the earliest date for which is A.D. 100 from Machili in eastern Barotseland. We know that the copper mines of Katanga were being worked and the products traded widely by the eighth century A.D.; that central Angola had been occupied by metal-users a century earlier; that trade was coming up the lower Zambezi at the same time; that by A.D. 300 there were agriculturalists living at Zimbabwe, and that by A.D. 1100 there was a flourishing centre at Mapungubwe (Bambandyanalo) on the Limpopo. At the beginning of the sixteenth century these earlier Iron Age cultivators were joined by other more efficiently organized groups establishing powerful political confederacies, and the process of absorption of the older populations was speeded up.

One point that needs stressing here, however, is that the coming of the Iron Age mixed farmers was not, as is all too often supposed, necessarily coincident with the disappearance of the old hunting–collecting populations. Such apparent anomalies as a Bush-Hottentot physical stock with a Negroid culture, as is found at Mapungubwe or at Inyanga and a number of other places, is surely the result of some of the old hunting populations having changed their economy. In the same way the historic Cape Hottentots were a Stone Age people who had acquired stock and become pastoralists. Moreover, from the skeletal remains from Northern Rhodesia and Nyasaland it can be seen that the Late Stone Age population was already Negroid in a number of its physical characteristics, and in the Bergdama and Hadza we can probably see surviving examples of two of the Later Stone Age populations of Equatoria.

It is, therefore, probably true to say that the origins of the older Bantu populations of these countries are most likely to be found in the Stone Age, though of course the present populations must be the results of subsequent modification by hybridization with small groups of immigrants. The fundamental change is not so much in the population as in the economy, though there is of course ample evidence to prove immigration and replacement in a number of cases. The caves and rock shelters were gradually abandoned as pressures dictated, that is, by all except the unadjustable minority of the hunting populations, and the inhabitants now settled in open villages, planted crops and herded stock. Hybridization completed the transformation that economic expediency had begun.

There is increasing proof to show that this was the pattern in many of the southern and central parts of Africa following the coming of the first groups of iron-using immigrants. The consequence is to emphasize the continuity of African culture, and to show the need to study both the prehistoric populations and their culture, since here lies the clue to the understanding of the present.

At the time of correcting the proofs of this paper Dr L. S. B. Leakey has just announced that the Pre-Zinjanthropus fossils from Bed I and new fossils from the lower part of Bed II at the Olduvai Gorge together represent a new species, *Homo habilis* (so called for his tool-making ability), whose characteristics, it is claimed, fall outside the range of Australopithecine variability. This implies, therefore, that the species *Homo* had become genetically differentiated from the *Australopithecinae* at a time anterior to the deposition of Bed I rather than posterior to this time. If this is so it would also seem unlikely that *Homo erectus* represents a stage of human evolution directly ancestral to modern man. Some lively controversy can be expected when the full details of the new discovery are made available.

2. Economic prehistory

C. WRIGLEY *Journal of African History* Vol. 1, No. 2, 1960 Cambridge University Press; pages 191–4, 199–203

. . . Professor G. P. Murdock has applied botanical arguments to the problem of the origins of agriculture in tropical Africa. Pointing out that the crop plants of this region are quite different from those of the Middle East, and that many of them—notably the millets (*Sorghum vulgare*, *Eleusine coracana* and *Pennisetum typhoides*), simsim (*Sesamum orientale*), certain pulses

(*Vigna sinensis*, *Cajanus cajan*) and the Guinea yam (*Dioscorea cayenensis*)—are certainly or probably indigenous, he makes the forthright assertion that agriculture was initiated in the upper Niger area by the ancestors of the Mande-speaking peoples about 5000 B.C., and that they took this step independently of, though somewhat later than, the peoples of south-western Asia.

For such precision of date and place there does not appear to be any adequate justification. Nor is it, on the whole, likely that the starting-point of African agriculture was in the western Sudan. Murdock's main argument for this choice is based on plant distribution: certain crops, such as fonio (*Digitaria exilis*), are peculiar to West Africa. But this hardly proves his point, for such plants might well have been added by West Africans to the stock of cultigens which they had received, or brought with them, from the east. We might even turn the argument about, and ask why, if sorghum and pearl millet spread from west to east, fonio should have failed to accompany them. A secondary argument, founded on the wide extension of the 'Nigritic', or Niger-Congo language-family, and especially of its Mande branch, is even less convincing. The dispersion of Mande languages can more plausibly be attributed to empire-building and trading activities at a very much later date. The Sudanic language-family, centred on the upper Nile area, has ramifications hardly less wide than those of Niger-Congo; and it is in the region of the eastern Sudan and western Ethiopia that the birthplace of most African crop plants is probably to be sought. Botanists have long regarded Ethiopia as a major centre of agricultural evolution—not merely, as Murdock suggests, because this was the only part of tropical Africa to be visited by Vavilov, but because its wide range of soils and climates makes it ideally suited to plant variation and ennoblement.

Whereas criticisms may be made of his more specific hypotheses, Murdock's main contention, that the antiquity of African agriculture is much greater than archaeologists have been willing to concede, is surely well founded. Not only is the continent the original home of a large number of cultivated plants, but some at least of these species have proliferated into a great many different races and varieties, clearly indicating a history that cannot reasonably be fitted into the two-thousand-year span of the African Iron Age. Many of them, moreover, recur in India; and, again, the number of Indian varieties, as well as their concentration in the interior of the sub-continent, suggests that their introduction cannot have been at all recent. The most concrete evidence, however, comes from the study of the cotton plant.

The cultivated cottons of the Old World belong to two species, *Gossypium herbaceum* and *G. arboreum*. The latter, which is fairly certainly the more recently evolved, is known to have been woven at Mohenjodaro in the third millennium B.C. Varieties of the older *herbaceum* species are widely distributed in northern Africa, Persia and central Asia, but until recently its original centre was believed to have been in or near southern Arabia. It is well established that the wild ancestor of the true cottons was *G. anamalum*, a desert shrub which grows only on the fringes of the Sahara and the Kalahari. Between this plant and the most primitive cultivated plants, however, there is a morphological as well as a geographical gap. Sir Joseph Hutchinson (to whom I am indebted for much patient tuition on the subject) argued that the former could be filled only by *G. herbaceum* race *africanum*, a crude but lint-bearing cotton which is found growing wild in a belt running across southern Africa from Ngamiland to Mozambique. The geographical gap remained, and could be bridged only by one of two very improbable hypotheses. Either, as Hutchinson himself suggested, seeds of the wild *africanum* were gathered and taken home by Arabian seafarers, who must therefore be supposed to have reached southern Africa at least as early as 3000 B.C. Or cotton spread northwards across East Africa under cultivation, so that agriculture must be supposed to have been practised in *southern* Africa at an equally early date. Now, however, an alternative theory has been proposed. It is suggested that a primitive *herbaceum*, ancestral both to the *africanum* race and to the known cultivated cottons, was developed in south-west Ethiopia. However this may be, the combined evidence from cotton genetics and Indian archaeology leaves no reasonable escape from the conclusion that cotton was being cultivated in Africa before 3000 B.C.—and probably long before, since the plant had to undergo considerable evolutionary change before being used in the Indus Valley civilization. Further, although cotton may have been grown for its oil before its lint was spun, it is not likely to have been among the first African plants to be domesticated.

The theory of the high antiquity of African agriculture receives additional support—more nebulous perhaps, but also, in my view, convincing—from the linguistic configuration of the continent. The languages of tropical Africa are legion, and, apart from Bantu, there are no large groups having an indisputable common descent. Nevertheless, on the most widely accepted view, the great majority of languages do belong to three main stocks: the Hamito-Semitic family, including the Chadic and Cushitic groups; the Niger-Congo family, comprising most of the languages of West Africa together with Bantu; and the Sudanic family, occupying most of north-central Africa.[1] The Hamito-Semitic family extends over north Africa and western Asia, but the other two stocks are confined within, and clearly indigenous to, the regions south of the Sahara.[2] This configuration seems to me to be radically inconsistent with the view that until about two thousand years ago these regions were inhabited only by a few primitive hunters. Are we to suppose that peoples equipped with a knowledge of metallurgy and agriculture, and presumably multiplying and expanding with great rapidity, would everywhere have adopted the speech of the scanty groups of aboriginals whom they found in the land? Common sense forbids, and so does analogy. On the contrary, many of the surviving independent hunters—such as the Pygmies, the Ndorono and the Bergdama—speak the language of their agricultural or pastoral neighbours. Yet, if the first cultivators did not thus lose their language, the orthodox conception of African prehistory cannot be reconciled with the range of African linguistic variation. What we should expect, if agriculture were a recent innovation, would be a wide network of closely related languages. This is just what we do find in the Bantu third of Africa, but elsewhere we are confronted by wide networks of languages which are only very

[1] J. H. Greenberg, *Studies in African Linguistic Classification* (New Haven, 1955). We learn from Murdock that Greenberg now tentatively includes in the Sudanic family most of the minor groups which he formerly classed as independent.

[2] Bantu has been related, by one student or another, to nearly every language-family of the Old World, except Indo-European. These theories, however, are sheer fantasy.

remotely related. The more ambitious claims of glottochronology may or may not command conviction, but on no reasonable concept of relative linguistic distance can a period of less than several millennia be allotted to the differentiation which has taken place within the Niger-Congo and Sudanic stocks. And it seems at least a plausible assumption that this differentiation accompanied the spread of an agricultural economy.

Against these arguments are arrayed the negative inferences from archaeology. In the first place, there is the rarity in tropical Africa of assemblages that are strictly comparable with those of Middle Eastern and European neolithic sites. It is, however, not true that neolithic tools are absent, for the characteristic ground stone axe has been found sporadically in almost every part of the continent. It is admittedly possible, even probable, that neither these implements nor the more elaborate neolithic assemblages of Ethiopia and Kenya belong to a period which antedates the Iron Age by any very wide margin. On the other hand, although polished stone tools and the cultivation of the soil are so closely linked in the minds of archaeologists that the term 'neolithic' has virtually come to *mean* 'food-producing', there is in reality no universal or necessary connexion between these two techniques. Even in the last century, many thoroughly agricultural African tribes did not use either iron or stone hoes. Moreover, in the equipment of 'neolithic' Jericho there was an 'almost complete lack . . . of picks or hoes for working the soil'. An agriculture sufficiently advanced to support a town of perhaps three thousand people was apparently carried on by means of the stone-weighted digging-stick, such as was used by many prehistoric African peoples who have not been accorded neolithic status.

A much more serious difficulty is the absence of direct evidence for agriculture, in the form of actual grains or of grain-impressions on potsherds. For this reason Arkell has rejected the view that the authors of his Khartoum mesolithic culture were agriculturalists, even though their equipment included not only pottery but also large numbers of grinding-stones. He assumes that the sole function of the latter was the preparation of ochre, with which indeed many of them were stained. It is not for a layman to dispute this conclusion. Yet I am inclined to think that it should not weigh decisively against the botanical and linguistic evidence for the great antiquity of African agriculture. . . .

Whatever may be said about agriculture, it is quite certain that animal husbandry did *not* develop independently in Africa south of the Sahara where the fauna does not and did not include possible ancestors of the domestic cow, sheep or goat. As to the time and manner of their coming there is very little direct evidence. Sheep and goats were present at Shaheinab in the late fourth millennium, cattle and sheep in the Kenya Neolithic, probably not much later. Domestic animals are not attested archaeologically in other areas until quite recent times, but it seems highly improbable that, having crossed the main geographical barrier, they should not soon have spread over the remainder of the continent. The original route of entry almost certainly led from Egypt by way of the Nile valley. The other route sometimes suggested, from Arabia across the Horn, is ruled out by the absence of all but the most primitive cultures in south Arabia until the first millennium B.C. and in Somalia until the Christian era. Moreover the word for 'cow', in a great variety of Sudanese and East African languages, can be referred to the Nubian form, *ti*.[1]

Murdock makes in this connexion an extremely important and original point. Stock-keeping in Africa is by no means co-extensive with the practice of milking. In West Africa, notably, cattle are milked only by the Fulani and in areas of Fulani influence. From this he infers that the Nubians borrowed cattle from Egypt 'without the associated milking complex'. The argument might, I think, be taken further: the Nubians acquired cattle before the practice of milking had begun. It is noteworthy that the unmilked cattle of the West African forest zone and pockets of central Africa are dwarf shorthorns of the species *Bos brachyceros*. Their distribution in the least accessible parts of the continent (where they have lived long enough to acquire immunity from trypanosomiasis) implies that they were among the first, if not *the* first, arrivals. Yet *Bos brachyceros* is

[1] E.g. Moru-Madi *ti*; Interlacustrine Bantu *-te*; Mbugu *dee*; Temein *nteng*; Shilluk *dyang*; Nandi *tany*, pl. *tic*; Merarit *te*. The numerous West African forms in *ni* perhaps have the same origin. These data were kindly supplied to me by Professor A. N. Tucker and Miss Bryan, who are not responsible for the linguistic and other inferences drawn.

generally believed to have been evolved later than the humpless longhorn, *Bos primigenius*, and to have reached Egypt only in early dynastic times. These assumptions, however, may need revision. The first cattle to reach north-west Europe, in the third millennium, were shorthorns, said to bear a close resemblance to those of West Africa. Moreover, in association with the pre-neolithic Sebilian culture of upper Egypt there are bones both of *primigenius* and of *brachyceros* cattle. The Sebilians are assumed to have been a purely hunting people and the bones to be those of wild animals. But is it not possible that they were in fact the domesticators of cattle, and that tropical Africa acquired its first stock from this source in the fifth millennium or earlier?

It has generally been believed hitherto that the pastoral and agricultural economies of Africa were originally quite distinct; that pastoralism was a racial characteristic (Baumann, for instance, used cattle-herding as irrefragable evidence for the presence of his Eastern Hamites); and even, absurdly, that the pastoralists were responsible for the transmission of the elements of higher culture to the Negro peoples and for the original construction of complex political systems. Murdock's argument, as he sees, completes the work of destruction that Greenberg began when he severed the supposed link between a pastoral economy and Hamitic forms of speech. The extensive dairying of such peoples as the Fulani, the Masai and the Herero, so far from being an original trait, must be a secondary and comparatively recent development. Cattle, in Africa as elsewhere, must have been originally the property of agricultural peoples.

The innovation, moreover, was a disastrous one. The fourth chapter of Genesis is an impudent libel, for Abel, not Cain, has always been the killer. It is one of Murdock's chief achievements to have seen the herdsmen of Africa, from the Masai to the Hilalian Arabs, for the destructive barbarians that they were—chief disturbers of the peace of the continent, and, we may add, chief spoliators of its soil.

Up to the end of the Egyptian Neolithic we have assumed that tropical Africa was in tenuous contact with Egypt and, through Egypt, with western Asia. In the case of agriculture and pottery, contact is only probable, and the direction of movement uncertain. In the case of domestic animals neither the fact of contact nor its orientation can be in any doubt. Towards the end of the fourth millennium, however, the general picture undergoes a sharp, and for tropical Africa a disastrous, change. Just at the time when the northern peoples were constructing urban civilizations, characterized by large-scale social organization, metallurgy and writing, it seems that insuperable geographical obstacles arose to sunder them from the peoples of the south. For tropical Africa had no bronze or copper age; and although this deficiency might possibly be accounted for by the scarcity of the relevant mineral deposits, the most likely inference is that between the fourth and the first millennium it was totally out of contact with the north. This period of isolation, in the post-Makalian dry phase, was probably the most crucial in the whole long history of the region. It was then that it fell decisively behind North Africa and most of Eurasia, and acquired that character of technical and cultural backwardness which even the advent of the Iron Age could not entirely alter.

The technique of iron-working did succeed in crossing the Sahara without any very undue time-lag, reaching Nigeria shortly before and south central Africa shortly after the time of Christ. There seems little reason to doubt that the mediators of this technique were the people of Meroe in upper Nubia. It is, however, doubtful whether it spread directly southwards into central Africa. The tribes of the southern Sudan, who might have been expected to have experienced the earliest and most intensive influences of Nile Valley civilization, notoriously remained among the most primitive, from the point of view of material culture, in the entire continent; and it seems that the swamps of the Bahr-al-Ghazal and the arid steppes lying between the upper Nile and the mountains of Ethiopia long acted as a barrier to the passage of iron-age cultures, which were forced to penetrate southward by a more devious route.

The immensity of the area covered by the closely related group of Bantu languages calls out for explanation. Behind these vast and evidently quite recent movements there must have been a powerful dynamic. Murdock's theory, that the dynamic was provided by the acquisition of bananas, fails to account for the Bantu penetration of large areas in which the banana could have been of little or no use; and his solution of this difficulty is too involved to be readily accepted. Moreover, it could be valid only on the assumption that the banana reached central Africa from the north-west, and that it entered a land which was previously devoid of crops. I have argued, however, that bananas arrived first in south-east Africa, which is certainly not the homeland of the Bantu, and that they were adopted by people who were already cultivators. If these things are so, it might be a reasonable hypothesis that the acquisition of bananas by the Bantu when some of them were already settled in the latitude of the Zambezi might have produced important secondary migrations into favourable areas, but we must still look elsewhere for the asset which enabled the first Bantu-speakers to impose themselves and their language on these pre-existent agricultural societies. I do not see what that asset could have been unless it were the iron spear. Plausible *a priori*, this theory finds support in the fact that the early iron-using Nok culture impinges on the central Benue valley, which Greenberg has selected as the probable homeland of the Bantu. Thus I see these people, not as agriculturalists spreading out over a virtually empty land, but as a dominant minority, specialized to hunting with the spear, constantly attracting new adherents (as many east and central African traditions actually affirm) by their fabulous prestige as suppliers of meat, constantly throwing off new bands of migratory adventurers, until the whole southern subcontinent was iron-using and Bantu-speaking.

This story, however, is probably an over-simplification, for it is necessary also to account for the distinction, clearly visible in the archaeological record of southern Africa, between the peaceful, unstratified society of its Iron Age A and the complex warlike states that succeeded them. It is possible that there were two 'waves' of Bantu immigration, or that the Bantu civilization of Rhodesia underwent a profound internal change as the result of the development of the gold trade. There are, however, some indications, especially from the associated pottery, that the 'A' cultures derived from the north-east, perhaps ultimately from the 'Azanian' coast, and were therefore not Bantu. If so, the later Bantu ascendancy would be attributed, not to metallurgy as such, but to the military organization and ethos which arose from the full exploitation of the iron spear.

The coming of iron technology must indeed have brought about far-reaching changes in every branch of African life. But if there is any substance in the arguments presented in this paper there can be no warrant for the common assumption that it made for a complete break with the past, and that the history of Africa is virtually coterminous with the Iron Age—as is implied, for example, in Mr Basil Davidson's recent book.

The orthodox picture of African prehistory presents, indeed, a curiously unconformable appearance. Up to a point, the record is one of extraordinary continuity. From the first chipped pebbles to the cultures of almost modern times there is unbroken linear evolution—with one possible interruption represented by the blade-using cultures of late pluvial times. Even the Kenya Neolithic shows clear links with what had gone before. But as we approach the threshold of history this continuity is abruptly shattered. The whole of Africa's enormous past is bundled off into the Kalahari with the Bushmen, and the stage is cleared for the enactment of a new story with a new cast. First, we are told, the Negro appears from nowhere and takes possession of the land. Later, a ghostly horde of civilized Hamites, having apparently no connexion with the 'proto-Hamites', long resident in the land, marches across eastern Africa, constructing roads and terraces and irrigation systems and founding elaborate political systems. These then disappear into the mists from which they came, and their civilizations fade into the light of common Bantu day.

All this is very odd. There is really no need to make a mystery of the emergence of 'the Negro'. The various physical traits which make up this concept were presumably gradual deviations, for the most part environmentally determined, from the less specialized forms of *Homo sapiens* which occupied Africa in the pluvial epoch. (Though not visible in the archaeological record until perhaps ten thousand years ago, this evolutionary trend may have begun much earlier in the forest zone, where evidence is lacking.) Nor is there anything specially mysterious about the outburst of engineering activity that clearly took place in many parts of east and central Africa between 500 and 1500 A.D. It was the product of iron tools and of the political organization associated with the iron spear—both, I have suggested, brought thither from the west. Nor, again, need we be puzzled by the disintegration of most of the Bantu states and the dereliction of their works, or attribute these disasters to that *diabolus ex machina*, the slave trade. A 'dark age', after all, is a familiar historical phenomenon, signifying merely that organization has broken down. The cause of the breakdown here was undoubtedly again the iron spear. It is not for nothing that Ogun, god of smiths, is also god of war. Unlike Bronze Age kingdoms, whose rulers could easily monopolize the raw materials of military power, the kingdoms of the Early Iron Age are almost necessarily ephemeral, for in these conditions every young man can say with Archilochus, *mutatis mutandis*: 'My spear wins bread, my spear wins Thracian wine.' Where this is said, the centre cannot hold. The sackers of cities soon gain ascendancy over the builders. Nor was there here an active commerce such as made the dark age of post-Mycenean Greece a relatively brief interlude. Indeed, the misfortune of most parts of eastern Africa was not that they had to endure the slave trade but that they had no trade at all. Where commercial possibilities did exist, as on the coast and in the region of the Rhodesian gold-field, Bantu civilization was exceptionally vigorous and long-sustained. . . .

II. EARLY PEOPLES OF WEST AFRICA

3. The growth of centralised states in the southern Congo basin

J. VANSINA, R. MAUNY and J. V. THOMAS *The Historian in Tropical Africa* Oxford University Press for the International African Institute 1964; pages 96–9

. . . The history of this region has been dominated by the formation of a series of states struggling for hegemony which led to an important extension of trade routes and favoured the spread of some distinctive cultural complexes over a very large area.

These states cover today nearly the whole region south of the tropical Congo forest, west of Lake Tanganyika, and north of the Middle Zambezi and lowlands of Southern Angola. They seem to be derived ultimately from two to four centres of origin only: one north of the Stanleypool, one near Lake Kisale in the lake region of Katanga, and possibly one on the Upper Tshuapa within the Congo forest and one near the headwaters of the Zambezi.

Already in the seventeenth century O. Dapper mentioned that it was said that all the coastal states around the lower Congo, including those of Loango, Kakongo, Ngoi, Kongo, and Teke, were derived from a prototype north of the Stanleypool. All indications we have seem to support this thesis. Kongo was founded from Bungu, a small state north of the Lower Congo river, and Loango from Kakongo, a neighbour of Bungu. But before their foundation, even, there were chiefdoms both in the Loango and in the Kongo area, extending as far south as the Dande or the Cuanza rivers. While there is no absolute proof that these chiefdoms were founded by stimulus diffusion from the earliest kingdom reported by tradition, the kingdom of Nguunu, just north of the Stanleypool, this seems to be the most likely explanation for their origin.

The Nguunu kingdom was succeeded by the Teke kingdom of Makoko, which existed already in 1491. Moreover, all the chiefdoms and kingdoms on the lower reaches of the Kasai and

Sankuru rivers claim to derive from the Stanleypool area. They would thus be linked with the Nguunu or Teke kingdoms as well. This hypothesis must, however, remain provisional, as long as Teke and Boma history has not been studied in detail.[1]

A second main centre appears to be in the area of Lake Kisale in Katanga. The ruling classes of the first five Luba and Songye states claim to originate from places around this lake.[2] Archaeological excavation there has revealed vast cemeteries which can be dated to a period between the eighth and ninth centuries.[3] The archaeological data do not yet make it possible to determine whether the Kisalian cultures represent states, but the great concentration of population there and the testimony of the traditions suggest this. From this Kisale centre stemmed the later Luba states—the Songye, Lunda, Bemba, and the Lundaized states from the Luapula to the Kwango. The Jaga also appear to have come from there. But on their arrival in the Upper Kwango and after their foundation of the Imbangala state, the Jaga adopted features from the Kongo-type political structures and transmitted these to the Ovimbundu states which were also founded by them during the eighteenth century. The Lozi state seems to have been modelled on states of the Lunda type and could have been founded by them. The chronology of these migrations and diffusions of distinctive forms of state organization would then be as follows: between 1500 and 1600 the Second Luba Empire and the Lunda states were founded from the pre-existing states of the Kaniok, Mutombo, Mukulu, Putu, Songye states and one or more states of the Eastern Luba. During the same period the Jaga migrated westwards, and the Bemba eastwards. Around 1600 the Imbangala Cokwe, Luena, and Southern Lunda states were founded; around 1650 the Lozi state, around 1700 the Lunda states of the Kwango Kasai, and around 1750 Kazembe's state on the Luapula river. At a period before 1500, which cannot yet be

[1] We know little about the present political structure of the Teke, but the cultural and linguistic similarities enable one to put this hypothesis forward, pending better Teke data.

[2] Cf. Verhulpen, 1935, Samain, 1924. These data contradict Van Bulck's hypothesis which drives these states from the Interlacustrine and Nilotic ones.

[3] Nenquin, 1958 and 1959.

determined, migrant Luba reached the lower Zambezi, but it is doubtful whether they brought a state system with them.[1]

Two subsidiary centres of development of states must be mentioned. The Bolia of Lake Leopold II founded a state in the fourteenth century. According to their tradition, they immigrated from beyond the Upper Tshuapa. On that river they found a people with chiefs and they took over the institution of chieftainship. Having reached Lake Leopold, they in turn transmitted the institution to the Ntomba and finally to the Boma before 1640. It is possible that the first Lozi state structure was not derived directly from the Lunda but from the Mbunda, their western neighbours, who have not as yet been subject to thorough study. Evidence of a state organization independent of the Lunda model might be found there.

The evidence for several centres, from which patterns of state organization were widely extended, shows the capacity for proliferation of these state systems, but it is at the same time an indication that any assumption at present of a single ethnic source for the origins of state systems in central Africa is without support. The main centres referred to must go back, in the case of the first three, to at least the fourteenth century, and it is not likely that the earlier connexions between them will be demonstrated. On the other hand, the available data make it possible to outline coherently the political history of central Africa from the sixteenth century onwards.

The discussion above rests on some basic assumptions which should be clearly understood. First, whenever the traditions speak about a state in the past, it has been assumed that the political entity referred to possessed a centralized state structure. In some cases this assumption can be doubted. For example, Bolia political structure shows that although chieftainship exists with what could be called a state-like ideology, the other political structures seem to be very close to a segmentary lineage system. A second assumption has been that state structures spread either by conquest or by stimulus diffusion. But there is evidence of internal evolution of political structures. Did

[1] There are in some texts references to a Cewa empire of Undi and the Cewa claim a Luba origin. But recent ethnographic studies and Monteiro and Gamitto's book *O Muata Cazembe* (Lisbon, 1846) show that this was not a true state structure.

centralized state structures arise independently in many different cultures as a result of such evolution or was the step to centralized structures so original that it could only be taken independently in very few instances? This basic question is not settled yet. . . .

It must also be underlined that many of the states existing around 1900 had elaborated their structures, not only through internal evolution but under various external influences as well. Many of them cannot, therefore, be seen as the products of one diffusion only. Reality is much more complex, as even one example shows. It is thought that there were chiefdoms in Northern Angola before the arrival of the Kongo. These were later influenced by Kongo political structures, probably in the fifteenth and sixteenth centuries. In the seventeenth century one of them, the state of Matamba, incorporated with all these elements derived from Lunda tradition, so that already by 1650 its political institutions were the product of three different diffusions at least, not counting possible Portuguese influence and leaving internal developments aside as well.

4. Influence of the Mande

J. VANSINA, R. MAUNY and L. V. THOMAS *The Historian in Tropical Africa* Oxford University Press for the International African Institute 1964; pages 91–3

. . . The Mande expansion may be presented provisionally as follows. Some early waves, which are impossible to date exactly, carried early Mande-speaking groups (Toma, Guerzé) to the south (where there were perhaps already some Mande on the edge of the forest), to the east (Samo), and the north-east (Dogon); the data which support such an hypothesis are mainly linguistic and ethnographic (for example, the ritual connexions between Dogon and Bambara Mandingo). There were other later migrations. A Mande group must have settled in the Mossi–Dagomba area although there is no linguistic proof of this. The Mande (Gangara), who brought Islam to the Hausa, were in the area from the thirteenth–fourteenth centuries. On the south-west route from Hausa Katsina to Ashanti, another Mande fraction, the Bussa, settled at the crossing over the Niger. The whole course of these movements, which covered a long time, must have been very complex. Thus in the Banda area we can distinguish four successive Mande groups: a first group derived from the Southern Mande, a group of proto-Diula, a Diula group, and finally the Mandingo themselves. The second and third group were traders, the last conquerors. And the movements which are referred to here include only those of the Southern Mande and of the proto-Diula.

Before the fifteenth century, but after the early movements which have been described, further trading expansion took place. It followed or created the two main trade routes of kola, slaves, and gold: one led from the Niger bend to the gold-producing areas of Ashanti and then, after the arrival of the Portuguese, to Elmina; the other, starting from Timbuktu and from Mali, ascended the Niger and reached the coast of Sierra Leone, where subsidiary branches led to the east, following the fringes of the forest as far as the Comoë and Bandama rivers; from there it united with the first route in the vicinity of Begho, near the gold- and kola-producing areas. Another route stemming from Hausaland also ended in Banda country. It is noteworthy that the Mande group of the Bussa was located on this route, which was used by the Gangara, or the Mande of Katsina. The route from the Niger to Bandaland was used only by traders; but new populations settled along the western route and mixed with the aborigines. The path of this latter migration can be traced by toponyms, the occurrence of Mande dialects, such as Vai and Vai-Kono, and ethnographic distributions.

After the sixteenth century Mande expansions were limited mainly to infiltrations into neighbouring regions which were not organized as states. In the main they followed the trade routes. In the region of San, in Bobo and Senufo country, one finds double villages bearing two names, the one ending in the suffix *-dugu* or *-so*, which is Mande, the other in *-kwi*, which is Senufo. One village is occupied by aboriginal inhabitants, the other by Diula who immigrated from Kong at various periods from the fourteenth century. The Gonja state, which is probably Bambara in origin, derives from a late migration.

The Mande have certainly exercised a great influence on the

whole of West Africa, as far as the Voltaïc region. There their trade routes encountered the Hausa trade organizations in Gonja, in Dagomba, and even in Songhay. Their prestige was very great and was equalled only by that of the Hausa, which explains why many legends of origin stress a Mande or Hausa ancestry. This very fact should make us wary of the value of such traditions: in Gonja, for instance, a manuscript tells us that the founder of the states was a certain Naba'a whose name resembles those of the founders of the Mossi-Dagomba and Hausa states; but the oral traditions, on the contrary, insist that a certain Jakpa, a Mandingo horseman, was the founder of the states. The first source stems from the Muslims. It was important for them to see themselves as descendants of Hausa, since the latter maintained important trade contacts with Gonja; the second tradition is that of the pagan Gonja aristocracy, for whom Mande is the land of their ancestors. But excessive scepticism must be avoided and in this case, for example, many indices point to the Mande origin of the ruling class.

This Mande influence was complex: it was sometimes mainly political, sometimes predominantly commercial, and sometimes mixed. It is possible that it made itself felt more particularly in the Voltaïc region as an agent in the formation of states (Mossi-Dagomba traditions). It is also likely that extension of the trade routes towards Begho and then towards the coast of Ghana after the arrival of the Portuguese provoked the foundation of small city-states which developed later into fully-fledged chiefdoms. But it is not possible as yet to indicate every region affected, to define the period when it began, or to evaluate its importance compared with other cultural and political influences, such as those from Hausaland.

On the subject of Mali, there is a need to emphasize the distinction between working hypotheses and data which are well established. Is it, for instance, certain that 1240 is the true date of the destruction of Ghana by Sundiata, king of Mali, as all the history textbooks, following M. Delafosse, claim? And did the Soninke capital survive after 1240, since Ibn Khaldoun said that he had known the mufti of the inhabitants of Ghana in Cairo in 1393?[1] . . .

[1] M. V. Monteil points out that Delafosse calculated this date—evidently approximate—as 1240 according to Mande traditions.

5. African background in Ghana

J. D. FAGE *Ghana* University of Wisconsin Press 1959; pages 23–9

. . . For the purposes of this survey, the inhabitants of the Gold Coast forest and coastlands can be divided into two groups: a smaller group concentrated in the extreme south-east, largely in the more open country between the Akwapim-Togo hills and the sea, and a larger group, the peoples speaking languages termed Akan, who inhabit the remainder of the country, the more forested part. The smaller group comprises two sub-groupings, the Gã and Adangme of the Accra plains, and the Ewe of southern Togoland. Their languages are mutually unintelligible, but their social organisations are rather similar; what specifically political and military organisation they have seems to have been borrowed from their Akan neighbours; and their traditions of origin indicate that both groups came to the Gold Coast from the east in a number of waves, the earliest probably arriving not earlier than about the fifteenth century.

The Gã, Adangme, and Ewe traditions conform to an observable cultural and linguistic pattern, namely that the Kwa-speaking peoples are distributed about a lateral axis parallel to the coast. They would seem also to suggest that the prime centre of dispersion of this culture is in the east, among the Yoruba and the Edo, the peoples who produced the world-famous Ife and Benin brass castings. Thus the line of migration of the Ewe is remembered as Ketu-Tado-Nuatsi (Notsie); that of some of the Gã-Adangme groups ran through Nuatsi from 'Same between the rivers Efa and Kpola', a location which suggests the Niger delta, while according to a Benin tradition, the Gã left there *c.* 1300. Ketu is today the capital of one of the westernmost Yoruba states; Tado, about sixty miles from the coast on the river Mono, was the centre of dispersion for the Adja, a people akin to the Ewe, who together with the Fon or Fõ constituted the core of the great state of Dahomey, a state much influenced by the Yoruba; Nuatsi, the modern Nuatje some fifty miles north of Lome, the port and capital of French Togoland, was the Ewe centre of dispersion. Small groups of

Adangme survive as islands among the Ewe in Togoland. The Ewe name for the Gã is Gẽ, and there is a people who call themselves Gẽ in south-eastern French Togoland whose language is usually classified as a dialect of Ewe. Similarly in south-eastern Dahomey are the Gũ or Egun, and, according to Dr. S. O. Biobaku, the earliest Negro inhabitants recalled in Yorubaland were 'probably Efa or Egun peoples'.

Enough has been said to demonstrate that Gã, Adangme, and Ewe traditions are consistent with the idea of the Kwa-speaking peoples developing along a coastwise axis from east to west. But the earliest traditions as yet recovered among the much larger Akan group of Kwa-speaking peoples in the Gold Coast all indicate a dispersion not from the east, but from the *north or north-west*, from the Niger valley from Timbuctu westwards, the region of development of the empires of Ghana and Mali. It is plausible to interpret traditions among the Akan, particularly in the territory of ancient Bono and modern Gonja, as indicating that their ancestors left the Niger valley at about the time when Ghana was in decline and Mali was beginning to emerge, that is to say about the twelfth century, and some confirmation of this may be seen in traditions of the upper Niger valley.

The Negroes of Ghana and Mali were what we should now call Mande-speaking peoples; the word 'Mali' indeed is a variant form of 'Mande'. But the Mande languages are a sub-family of the Sudanic family of Negro languages quite distinct from the Kwa sub-family to which the Akan languages belong. Thus not only do Akan traditions run contrary to the east-west line of the other Kwa-speaking groups of the Gold Coast, but they also appear to be inconsistent with the linguistic evidence.

The impasse is more apparent than real, and a key to its solution is provided by the situation in Gonja. The Mande traditions of origin of Gonja, as has been seen, are not the traditions of the bulk of the people, but of a small ruling class which established its domination comparatively recently (*c.* seventeenth century), and which has not totally identified itself with the people at large. The latter in fact belong to the Kwa cultural grouping. Their language and the language of the country, Guang, is Akan, and they possess residual traditions of origin of their own, separate from those of the ruling class, which, as we have seen, can be equated with those of the Akan states. Clearly the modern state of Gonja has resulted from a comparatively small band of invaders (from Mande-land) imposing their rule on (Akan) groups already resident in the country when they arrived. Although the invaders have dropped their own language and have taken up that of the mass of the people, their conquest was too recent, and perhaps also not sufficiently positive, to result in a complete merging of the two stocks and their traditions.

The same pattern of state-formation by invaders from outside is to be seen in a much more complete form in Dagomba, and presumably also in Mamprussi, though there the evidence is less well defined. Here the process of symbiosis is more complete, but it is interesting to note that it has gone further in western Dagomba, the region first settled by the invaders from the north-east, than it has in eastern Dagomba, an area of later expansion. In western Dagomba, the invaders have totally eclipsed the original Gur kinship groups: the traditions, which are totally those of the invaders, refer significantly to the killing of the *tengdanas*, the priest-leaders of the original holders of the soil, and to marrying into their families. In eastern Dagomba, incorporated into the state only after the rise of Gonja in the west in the seventeenth century had forced the Dagomba to move the centre of gravity of their state further to the east, more of the old social structure remains. Further east still, protected by the marshes of the Oti River from the cavalry of the state-forming invaders, among the Konkomba the primitive kinship form of society has survived almost intact, and it is more than a presumption that it was people like these Konkomba groups who provided the mass of the material that the Dagomba invaders fashioned into their state.

From evidence already discusssed, it would seem that the trade route towards the Gold Coast from the north-west, from Mande-land, developed earlier than that from the north-east, from Hausaland. This may afford at least a partial explanation for the fact that the first European to visit Mossi and Mamprussi, Capt. L. G. Binger, during his journey of 1889–90, saw in their states abundant features of Mande provenance. Such features would seem less in evidence in Dagomba, the most southerly state of the Mossi-Mamprussi-Dagomba complex (which was not visited by Binger), but their common earliest traditions suggest that when the state-forming immigrants arrived from the north-east, there was already a Mande influence of some kind existent among the Gur groups, and that in Mossi certainly, and possibly in Mamprussi also, the process of social symbiosis covered Mande peoples as well as Gur-speaking autochthones.

Be this as it may, the picture we get from Gonja and Dagomba is one of comparatively small groups of invaders forming the more numerous peoples of pre-existent kinship groups into states, and in course of time merging with them ethnically and linguistically. This process of the eventual mergence of small groups of state-forming conquerors with the more numerous populations of the conquered would seem to be the key to a great deal of African history. It would seem almost certain that the Akan traditions of migration from the north or north-west are not necessarily the traditions of the bulk of the people, but more essentially those of successive waves of immigrants who organised earlier kinship groups into political states of the type being developed further north in the Sudan.

In the case of Gonja, we know that the earlier inhabitants were already what we should now call Akans; in the case of Dagomba, we can deduce that they were Konkomba or similar Gur-speaking groups. It is also known that when the Gã arrived from the east about the fifteenth century they infiltrated among and sometimes absorbed Akan groups, the Kpesi and the Afutu. Remnant groups of these peoples still survive to the immediate west of the Gã area; their languages or dialects are closely related to the Guang of Gonja. Similar languages are found in pockets north of the Gã and through the Volta gap in the Akwapim-Togo hills back towards Gonja. It has been inferred from this linguistic evidence that the first Akan migrations to reach the coast came from the north through the Volta gap in a clockwise sweep around the borders of the forest, and that the Akan penetration directly through the forest towards the sea was a later phenomenon. It may be that previously the forest was but thinly occupied, and that its settlement by the Akans does represent more of a movement en masse. However, the evidence of the Gonja and Gã migrations suggest that the first Akan settlements were appreciably earlier; with the result that, even if the Akan state-formers had not tended to eclipse earlier traditions (as has undoubtedly been the case), the formation of the first Akan states took place at too remote a period of time for us to have any idea of what the pre-state peoples were like.

In general terms, however, just as we can consider the early history of Dagomba, Mamprussi, and Gonja essentially as the impingement, into a mass of indigenous Gur- or Kwa-speaking peoples, of state-forming invaders coming down the lines of the major north-eastern and north-western trade routes which linked the Gold Coast to the great empires and commercial centres of the Sudan, so too it is permissible to think of the creators of the Akan states impinging along the north-western highway into an already existent pattern of "Kwa" kinship groups distributed along their east-west coastwise axis. This leads us to take another look at the westwards movement along this axis from what is now south-western Nigeria, in particular from the land of the Yoruba states and of Benin, of the Gã and Ewe Kwa-speaking peoples. It has already been remarked that much of the political organisation of these peoples is Akan-inspired, that is, that it derives indirectly from the north-western impulse from the Sudan of state formation. On the other hand, in point of time the Gã and Ewe movements would seem to be associated, as an end product, with successive waves of state-forming movements coming south or south-westwards from the Sudan east of the Gold Coast, in what is now Nigeria. These are the 'Kisra', 'Oduduwa', and 'Bayajidda' invasions remembered in the traditions of the people of Hausaland, Nupe, Yorubaland, and Benin. The circumstances suggest that the effects of these invasions were deflected westwards by the coast, but that the state-forming impulse itself did not proceed much further west than Ketu, or, at a second remove, to what became Dahomey. Recent work by Dr. Biobaku suggests that while the ancestors of the Gã and Ewe might derive from the earliest remembered invasion of Yorubaland from the north, the 'Kisra' invasion, their westwards emigration could be a flight from the later consequences of the second major state-forming movement, the 'Oduduwa' invasion, which produced great states like Oyo and Benin which expanded by conquest.

The general Gold Coast pattern might therefore be tentatively viewed in something like the following terms. Before about the eleventh century, the land was occupied by a number of small kinship groups. Those in the northern savanna we may call 'Gur' groups; those in the south, in or near the forest, we may call 'Kwa' groups. In remote and isolated parts of the country, such as the Oti marshes and some mountain regions of Togoland, kinship groups of these types still survive in something like their original form; the process of state-formation has not taken place at all. Elsewhere, however, this primitive pattern has been upset by the state-forming activities of relatively small groups of immigrant Negroes coming southwards as a consequence of the process of change initiated in the Sudan through the expansion of the Mediterranean peoples and their trade. The immigrants tended to approach the Gold Coast either along the north-western trade route, from the region in which Ghana, Mali, and other great predominantly Mande states emerged, or along the north-eastern trade route from the region of Hausaland and Bornu. The newcomers began to create states on the Sudanese model from among the local kinship groups on which they imposed themselves, and with whose members they eventually merged in race and language.

From the north-east came the founding ancestors of Dagomba and Mamprussi, arriving about the fifteenth century. At about the same time the Gã and Ewe began to arrive from the east, possibly as a consequence of state-forming upheavals in what is now south-western Nigeria. A number of waves arrived from the north-west, the earliest settling just north of the forest by about the thirteenth century, and then spreading eastwards round it through the Volta gap to the sea and then westwards along the coast. These early waves produced, among others, the first Akan groups of what is now Gonja and of the coastlands, and large or important states such as Bono and Banda. Later waves tended to push into and through the forest, creating there and at the coast a large number of small states, small perhaps because the difficulty of movement in and through the forest tended to break the immigrants up into small groups. The Fante states of the coast emerged from this movement, while many of the small forest states were eventually, in the eighteenth century, incorporated into the Ashanti Union.

Finally, about the seventeenth century, the creators of modern Gonja appeared, who, by the time of the arrival of the Europeans at the end of the nineteenth century, had hardly succeeded in forming the earlier Akan groups into a coherent state.

III. KINGDOMS OF THE WESTERN SUDAN

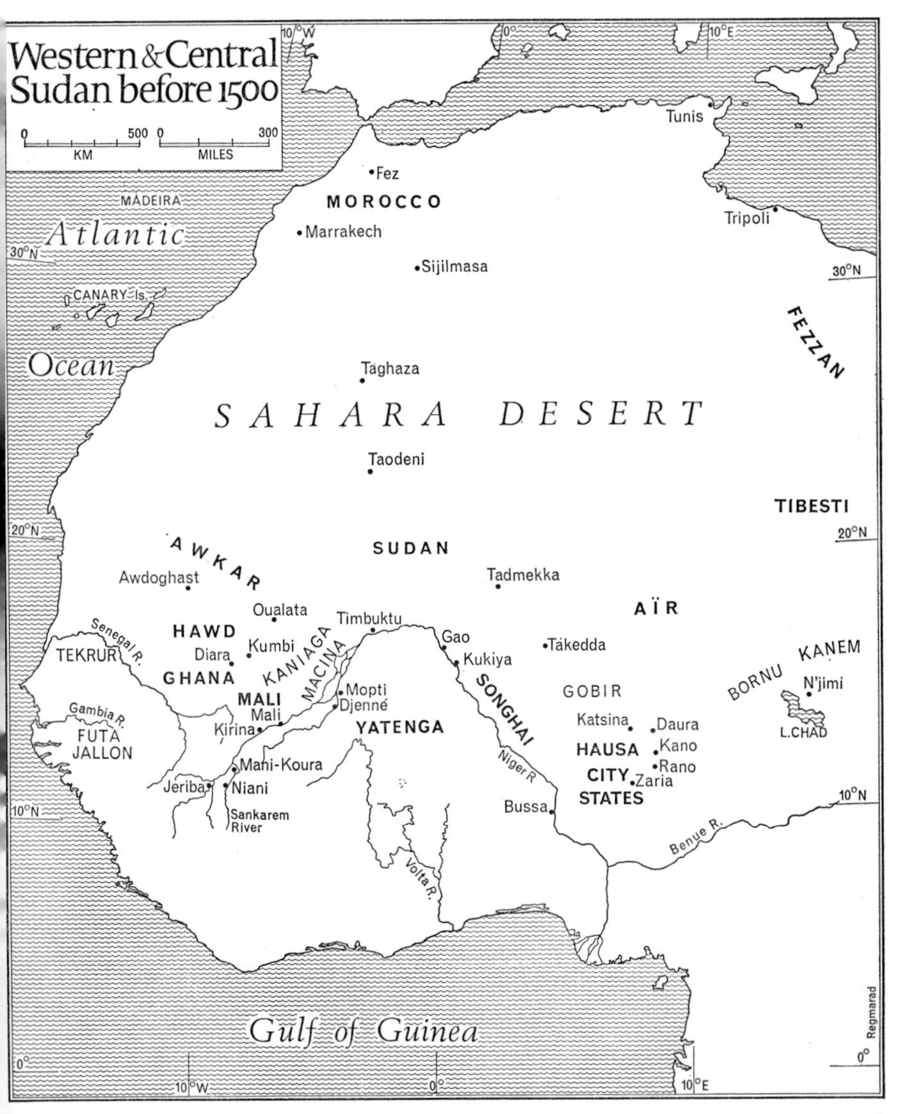

6. Western and Central Sudan before 1500

7. Kingdoms of the Western and Central Sudan and States of the Western Forest 1500–1800

6. Bornu conquest and empire

YVES URVOY *Histoire de l'Empire du Bornu* Larousse, Paris 1949; pages 61–6, 87–92 (In translation)

Fourteenth to Fifteenth Centuries

The gradual inflow of Kanembu settlers to the West of Lake Chad starting in the twelfth century, but more particularly the effective political conquest in the fourteenth century and the establishment of the dynasty and its followers, radically changed the distribution of peoples in Bornu. The wholesale introduction of a large core of Kanembus backed up by the dynasty, introduced to this area the phenomenon of assimilation that had progressed so far on the East of the Lake. The new people thus formed were called the Kanuri, who are now pre-eminently the Bornu people—thus, in effect an offshoot of the Kanembu people and likewise of diverse origin. The ethnic history of the following centuries—up to the nineteenth century—is composed of the gradual assimilation of tribes that had already settled there, and of the addition of new elements, especially nomads. Its pattern is simple: extension, particularly by contagion, by a gradual spreading out towards the south at the expense of the pure Negroes; and enrichment through the north and east with elements of more or less long-established white origin.

Let us consider briefly the main outlines of these movements in the fourteenth and fifteenth centuries, when the basic ethnic characteristics of the country were fixed.

The greater part of the Sos were submerged and absorbed by the Kanembus-Kanuris. In two regions they resisted absorption better, whilst being more or less subject to political domination. In the south-east, round the marshy lands of Yedseram, they survived almost up to the present. In the north-west, there was the same survival in the regions of the middle Yo. Since then, some of these bands have merged with the Kanuri people, some have been absorbed by the Beddes who arrived in the seventeenth century, and some have joined their cousins who had emigrated—the Mangas.

For in the wars of conquest in the fourteenth century, one group did not accept Kanembu rule and moved away to regions where they could keep their independence. In this way there appeared a series of new peoples who were offshoots of the Sos.

The *Dagras* left Bornu about the fifteenth century and took refuge in the hills of North Munio (now Guré).

The *Mangas* form the largest group. They occupy South Munio and the lands north of the Yo near the river.

Further away still, the Sos who had been driven back, infiltrated amongst the Hausa tribes that lived to the west of the meridian of Guidimuni, and they settled the lands that form the present French circumscription of Zinder. The basic element of the population was Hausa, related in the north-west to Daura people and in the south-west to Kano people, whose scars they still bear; Sos infiltrations, few in the south, were considerable in the north. This wave, increased later by Kanuri additions which it is now difficult to distinguish clearly, reached the region of Korgom between Zinder and Tessaua.

The little *Sosebaki* states of *Dungass*, *Oacha*, *Mirria* and *Illela* come from this Sos and Kanuri thrust towards the west. They were probably founded about the thirteenth century by a Bornu prince.

Machena likewise probably goes back to a So who came from the middle Yo in the fifteenth century, after the founding of Gasreggomo.

These frontier lands of mixed population come at this time into the Bornu sphere of influence. In spite of the basic Hausa element of the population and the widespread use of the Hausa language, from the fifteenth century onwards they form part, more or less loosely, of the empire, and this remained so until the disturbances of the nineteenth century.

The Sos have for a long time been merged with the later additions of various bands and fugitives coming from the Manga lands and from the various tribes subject to Bornu. These form a population that speaks Kanuri and is called by the Hausas Beriberis.

It is certain that a large number of Sos took refuge on the islands in Lake Chad, and there joined congeneric peoples who had fled centuries earlier from the eastern shore; and that by fusion with the Kotokos—of whom there were also large numbers on the Lake—they formed the mixed people of the Boudumas which appears about this time and whose numbers are swollen from the fifteenth century onwards by Kanembus in flight from the Bulalas.

Amongst the autochthonous peoples of Southern Bornu, the situation is much the same as in the thirteenth century.

To the west, *Chira*, *Techena* and *Auoyo* were completely formed by about 1500. They constituted three clearly characterized tribes and spoke a language that is their own. Chira, the most important, dominated Gombe and Bautchi, and was adjoining Kwararafa on the south and on the west reached Dutchin-Layawa between Gaya and Kano.

They came under Bornu suzerainty in the sixteenth century.

Now let us consider the immigrants. They included Negro Kanembu farmers and tribes of white origin which remained nomadic and had more or less kept the purity of their blood and their own character.

All more or less merged over the centuries to form the new Kanuri people. Some groups, however, keep their name and certain traditions; the Magumis have produced the royal family of the Sefs, which is perhaps the reason for their survival, bound up with social pride.

The *Ngalma-Dukkus* descend from a younger branch of the royal family from the beginning of the dynasty and are scattered.

To be added to these are Tubu offshoots that came at different times to settle in Bornu, either of their own accord or because they were forced. The *Tomagueras*, fragments of that great Teda tribe which is also found in Tibesti, in Kauar, etc., are completely Kanembu-ized. They can be found scattered everywhere, living with the Magumis; a noble tribe like the latter, they provided in particular the vassal dynasties in Mandara and Munio.

The *Turas*, Tedas of Tibesti, used to live at one time in Kauar. They are now scattered like the Magumis, but are less numerous.

Cut off from the main body of Tubus and having lived for a long time in farming lands, these groups have almost entirely abandoned their old way of life and have become real Kanuris; they keep only the memory of their origin and the feeling of forming a special nobility.

Finally, some small Arab groups that may have accompanied the dynasty to Bornu and who jealously preserve their light skin free from any mixture—the *Djoamas* and the *Aselas*—who seem to have kept themselves like this (supposing their claims to have settled there ten centuries before to be justified), provide us with a range of examples of the process of settlement, including cross-breeding and the assimilation of white nomads.

The Kanuri people, itself a mixture of various tribes, has in its turn put out a few branches that have acquired a particular character through historical circumstances, emigration and cross-breeding with neighbouring peoples: *Noguzoums* of Hadeidjia, *Guezawas*, *Bachars*, *Ngazzars*, *Leres*.

Finally, we must mention the appearance of a new element that is completely foreign to the Chad lands. Under Kachim Biri (1242–1262), the arrival in Kanem of two *Peul* sheiks from Mali is mentioned.

Later, the chronicle of Kano mentions the arrival in Kano between 1452 and 1463 of Peul scholars from Mali, bringing books of theology and grammar. (Before them, the men of learning had only the Koran, the hadith and lawbooks.) They go on to Bornu. These are the first allusions to this people who in the nineteenth century were to play a very important part in the history of Bornu and the whole of the central Sudan.

What was the political structure of these peoples at the end of the fifteenth century?

Whereas in the thirteenth century, Kanem and Mali formed both the only two important states and the two great centres of civilization in the Sudan, in the fifteenth century, upon the ruins and on the borders of these two empires, many new states flourished and Bornu merely occupied a position amongst states that were its equals.

To the east, Bornu's only neighbour was the *Bulala kingdom* which was still centred on the Fittri, forming the kingdom of *Gaoga*, still holding the greater part of Kanem and to the east ruling the pagan peoples who were to produce the Ouadai three centuries later.

To the south of the Lake lay the kingdom of *Baguirmi*, which had sprung up recently on the middle Chari.

To the south of Bornu was the group of pagan and

semi-anarchical tribes who occupied the mountainous countries from Mandara to Bautchi, and further on still, round the middle and lower Benoue, was *Kwararafa* (sometimes known as the land of the Jukuns), whose origin is obscure, but which was connected with a cycle of migrations from Egypt, perhaps about the sixth or seventh century. This was a warlike state that was to terrorize the central Sudan for several centuries.

To the west of Bornu lay the *Hausa kingdoms* that sprang up in the eleventh and twelfth centuries and which were then in full development: these were—*Daura*, small and peaceful; *Kano and Katsena*, two large trading cities; *Gangara*, which lost its principality in the sixteenth century and became absorbed by Katsena; *ZagZag* (or Zaria); *Gouber* (or Gober), hesitantly established to the North of Katsena; and a few lesser states between Bornu and Kano.

Still further to the west were the states of Hausa language, *Zamfara* and *Ader*, brought together at the beginning of the sixteenth century under the forceful hand of a soldier of fortune, Kanta, who set up at this time the kingdom of Kebbi at the western tip of the Hausa-speaking peoples.

Finally, to the west of Kebbi, extended the *Sonrai* empire or empire of Gao, which inherited all the northern part of old Mali and its prestige. It was in full expansion at the beginning of the sixteenth century, owing to a successful general, Mohammed Askia, the founder of the new dynasty. He ruled in particular Air, formerly under the protection of Mali and nominally governed by a Berber dynasty that had established itself thereabout a century before.

These, then, were the partners of Bornu in this new period of its history. About 1400, Makrizi, giving an account of the situation that existed a few decades previously, says that 'the king of Kanem is the greatest of the kings of the Sudan', and mentions as being grouped round him a cluster of vassal states, and even attributes to him the control of Zeila of Fezzan. After the disturbances about 1500, Leon the African—whom we shall come across again—points out that the kingdoms of the black lands, Mell (Mali), Tobut (Timbuctu), Gago (Gao), Guber, Agadez, Cano, Catsena (Katsena), Zegzeg, Zanfara, Guangara, Bornu, Goago (the Boulalas), etc., were then under the rule of three kings—the king of Tombout (Mohammed Askia, of Gao), who controlled the greater part, *the king of Bornu who was the weakest*, and the king of Gaoga. It is important to observe the hierarchy at this time. . . .

The Empire and its Vassals, from the Fifteenth Century to the Eighteenth Century

The conquests of Idriss Alama gave the empire the boundaries which it kept until the beginning of the nineteenth century. The following outline is concerned with the seventeenth and eighteenth centuries and describes the territorial position as far as it is possible to reconstruct it. At the same time this chapter will enable us to follow population movements since 1500.

The Kingdom

At the end of the eighteenth century, the kingdom was mainly composed of Kanuris, a people which is now much more homogeneous than it was in the fifteenth century after the conquest, although over the centuries there have been added to it several elements still in the process of assimilation. We have seen that Idriss Alama brought to Bornu and settled there farmers from Kanem, the people of the region of Kulu on the south-east corner of the lake near Bahr-el-Ghazal, and those of Ikima, Aghafi and Ago. Others followed him spontaneously, preferring the peaceful kingdom near the ruler to the borderland ravaged by wars and lack of stable authority. The Dietkos, for instance, appear to have come of their own accord about this time, and G'kenise Tubu tribes or offshoots which are now very Kanurized.

Two new and quite distinct ethnic groups date from this three-hundred-year period: Negroes who were driven back from Air by the attacks of the Tuaregs and who in the seventeenth and eighteenth centuries—at a date not known exactly and probably in small waves of migration spaced out over a fairly long period of time—went to settle in Damergon; then, infiltrating amongst the Mangas, they travelled west and occupied the banks of the Yo to the west of Gasreggomo. These are the *Beddes* who submitted to the rule of the Mais but who, being anarchical pagans, were difficult to control and took advantage of the Peul wars in the nineteenth century to make themselves virtually independent.

Other immigrants of a very different character, but who also were to play their part in the history of the nineteenth century, were the *Choa Arabs* who appear in Bornu in the seventeenth century, almost certainly brought there—at least the first of them—by Idriss Alama after his victories in Kanem. They came from the Nile basin and had begun moving westwards long before; they mixed easily with the Kanuris without, however, being completely submerged by them.

Finally, we must mention the small *Koyam* people, a religious clan. It was probably the remnant of a white nomadic tribe still unassimilated by the Kanembu people and tending to maraboutism.

We know practically nothing about the territorial divisions of the kingdom in this period; but it is certain that it was divided into provinces with governors chosen by Gasreggomo, and subdivided into districts with subordinate chiefs.

The majority of the unassimilated tribes retained their own indigenous chiefs, but were represented before the Mai either by a representative chosen by them, or—more often—by a court official who was also responsible for supervising them and for remitting to the sultan their taxes, part of which went to him.

We shall examine later the organization existing in the nineteenth century. It is probable that it retained the main features of the previous centuries.

The Vassal States

These were, from east to west:

Kanem, recaptured by Idriss Katagarmabe and then restored to order by Idriss Alama. Here the local Boulala dynasty still remained as a vassal of Bornu for some time after Idriss Alama. Then, at a date which cannot be given with any precision, it was driven back to the Fittri and replaced by a viceroy, a Khalifa (a word which became 'alfa' in the local pronunciation) called Dala Afunu, whose dynasty, weak and manoeuvring amongst the successive lords of Kanem, has lasted up to the present day in Mao.

The Alfa had to struggle ceaselessly against the vassal tribes: the Boulalas with their old dynasty which seems to have continued for a time in the south-east, the Toundjers and the

Tubus. He exercised a slightly tighter control over the Kanembus, especially near Mao. There was a constant unstable political situation in which disorders increased during the nineteenth century. Nevertheless, until about 1800, the Alfas seem both to have retained some authority but on the other hand to have accepted without difficulty the suzerainty of the Mais.

To the south of the lake, on the middle Chari, was *Baguirmi*. This country was not dependent on old Kanem, which was to find there at the most a slave-hunting ground. About the beginning of the sixteenth century, a new state was set up there, round a conquering group from the east. The dynasty was converted to Islam between 1620 and 1630, and between 1650 and 1675 the country came under the suzerainty of Bornu—a suzerainty that was more of an honorary nature and which did not prevent Baguirmi from having its own policy and making conquests.

On the islands in the Chad, the *Budumas* formed a group of tribes of varied origin which recognized one of their number, the Gourjias, as having a certain pre-eminence, but which were completely independent of the Mais. Not only were the efforts made to bring them under control in vain, but also they did not hesitate to plunder the Bornu villages on the shores. A similar situation arose in the nineteenth century, known to us in greater detail.

To the south of the lake and west of Baguirmi, in the plain of Logrone and the lower Chari, lived the *Korokos* (or Makaris). Those in the north at least, being placed in immediate contact with Bornu and situated on the way to Baguirmi, were certainly forced to become vassals, but it is only in the nineteenth century that we have any precise and detailed information.

To the west lies the bleak mountain-block of *Mandara* or *Mabina*, by this time an old victim of Bornu emperors' campaigns, and very probably an occasional and restless vassal. It had a small dynasty which was perhaps originally imposed by Bornu and which was of Tubu origin (Tomaguera, according to Nachtigal).

To the north-west of Mandara, the *Gamergus*, the remnant of an old tribe that had been master of all the district of Udje, still partly occupied this region. But defeated by Idriss Alama, subject to a kind of direct administration that was crushing and harsh and crippled by taxation, they had lost all political power and had much decreased in number.

To the south of these were the pagan *Marghis* in their hills; in the fifteenth and sixteenth centuries, without any struggle, they had become vassals of Bornu which influenced these anarchical tribes through its prestige alone. In the fifteenth century, a Kanuri came to settle amongst the Western Marghis and made himself their chief without resorting to force. His successors ended up by being practically independent of Bornu, but they made an annual journey to Gasreggomo as a token of vassality. About the same time the Eastern Marghis also became vassals. About 1580, a Mai, hearing of the wealth of this country, himself sent as chief a Kanuri called Zerma who was accepted by the natives.

To the west of the Marghis were the same pagan tribes as in the previous centuries, but they were being more or less encroached upon or even pushed back into the mountains by the invading Kanuris, and were in any case forced to become vassals.

In addition there had appeared:

The *Boles*, a small people formed at the beginning of the sixteenth century on the classic pattern: by the settling of bands coming from the east by way of the Fittri and Baguirmi, after they had wandered for some time in South Mandara and the middle Benue; and by the fusion of these more civilized conquerors—who still had some white blood—with the autochthonous people who lacked organization and were probably related to the Gamawas.

The *Teras* (with their *Hinna* and *Gwani* branches) are probably an offshoot of the Boles. Leaving the parent stock that lived near Fika, they made room for themselves in the present district of Tera to the south-west of the division of Gudjeba, by pushing back the autochthonous Kanakurus. The date of their conquest is not known, but it comes after the settling of the Boles and before the nineteenth century.

The *Keri-keris*, scattered over the common borderlands of Bornu, Kano and Bautchi, are a branch of the Gamawas that were separated from the main stem near Guddi (district of Fika) and who left for the north and the west. They speak Gamawa.

It is possible that the departure of the *Angass* from Bornu dates from this period. At present living in the South of Bautchi at the foot of the plateau, they seem to be the remnant of a people that was formed before the Kanuri conquest, around conquerors who had come from Kordofan and who were gradually driven back towards the south at the time of the Bornu occupation.

The mixed people of the *Baburs* was formed in the sixteenth century near Biu by the union of tribes of various origin, who had come from Bornu and Kanem under the command of a successful soldier of fortune claiming to be of Sefuira stock. At first vassals of Kwararafa, they came under the protectorate of Bornu, probably under Idriss Alama.

Then to the west is a cluster of little states: *Chira*, *Techena*, *Auyo*, *Hadeidjia*, *Gar-n-Gabbas*, *Gatarua*, *Kazore*, *Faga* and *Dawa*, the last six being very small principalities. Most were very old in origin. Gari-n-Gabbas is what used to be the Biram that is connected with the legend of Bayajidda, and is therefore one of the first—if not the first—settlement of Eastern conquerors, which were the seeds of the Hausa states. It is sometimes counted as one of the 'seven Hausas'. This title of honour is its only history.

We have seen the origins of Chira, Techena and Auyo. Chira became a vassal of Bornu in the sixteenth century, probably under Idriss Alama, and the other two did so probably in the same period. These two were dependent on the Galadima of N'Guru.

Hadeidjia was, until the nineteenth century, a principality of little importance.

To the west, *Goummel* was created in the middle of the eighteenth century by a small Manga group from Guidimouni.

The *Sosebaki States* developed at this time and enjoyed considerable prosperity.

At *Machena* there was a principality which was a vassal of Bornu and suzerain of the countries situated to the west of the Sosebakis.

To the east of these lay the expanse of *Manga* country which extended about as far as Mir, half-way between Gure and Lake Chad. We distinguish now between the dune-land or *Manga* proper, and *Munio*, a range of hills to the south of Gure, with a wide expanse of plain to the west. But Manga has never formed a political entity. The part nearest the Yo was directly subject to the more or less benevolent rule of Bornu; the north formed with Munio a small vassal kingdom. The latter country had at first an autochthonous dynasty—that of the Gamagamas—which was supplanted at a date which is not known exactly (about the seventeenth century) by a dynasty that descended from a prince of Mandara of Tomaguera origin, sent by Gasreggomo to defend its vassal Munio against the raids of the Immakitane Tuaregs.

To the north of Munio, *Kutuss* and *Alakoss* had formed since about the sixteenth century a small principality which was peopled by Dagras and was semi-anarchical. The small local dynasty established at Kelle is known only in the nineteenth century. It was vaguely subordinated to the dynasty of Munio, but the real masters of the country were Tuaregs who originally came from Air and whose most important tribe was the tribe of the *Immikitanes* or Amakitanes. Driven out of Air by a forceful sultan in the fifteenth century, it seized Alakoss and Kutuss; being involved in Bornu affairs in this period, it seems to have been for a time the ally of Ali Dhajidenni, and eventually resumed a nomadic life between Kutuss and Air, whilst tending more and more to settle in the south. Resuming their raids on the Peuls of Bornu at the close of the sixteenth century, they were pursued by Idriss Alama and recognized allegiance to him. Their centre was Kelle, as it had been for the *Dagras*. These had a double tribute to pay—to Bornu and to the Amakitanes. As for the neighbouring countries, Damagaram and Manga, the Tuaregs plundered them heavily whenever they could.

Another tribe, the *Iskaskazanes*, a fraction of the great confederation of the Kel-oui, lived to the west of the Amakitanes. Their chief's centre was Garazu in Alakoss. But they did not arrive there from Tegama until the end of the eighteenth century.

From the middle of the seventeenth century, the Tuaregs resumed their plunderings on the northern borders of Bornu. In 1667, they even beseiged Ngazargamu without success. In the eighteenth century, without clashing with Bornu troops, they harassed Munia and Manga.

To the north of Damagaram and to the north-west of Alakoss

was a country called *Damergu*, inhabited for the most part by Kanuri-speaking people who had fled from the Dagras and the Mangas, etc., and who lived under the protection of Turaeg tribes—especially those of the Kel-oui confederation—and who had no political relations with Bornu.

Finally, on the far west of the Bornu lands there lived in what is now the region of Zinder a mixture of Hausa and So fugitives, Mangas, Kanuris, etc.; this was a small border area which for a long time was of no interest and had no history, which had been loosely controlled by Bornu since the sixteenth century, but which was made up of a host of small villages—probably vassals of Machena. Here there came into being in the eighteenth century a small state, *Damagaram*, which was to have a brilliant career in the nineteenth century.

To the north-west of this region and to the south-west of Damergu, there had lived for centuries a small Hausa people which in the Middle Ages had been driven back from Air and then from the steppes by the Tuaregs. In Idriss Alama's time they were vassals of Bornu. Their chief bore the title 'Zanua' and was dependent on Machena. In the seventeenth century he was forced to cease owing allegiance to Bornu and to promise it to Karsena instead.

All these protectorates in the west made up '*Galadi*' and were dependent on the Galadima established in N'Guru.

To the north of the Yo and Lake Chad, Bornu had in theory retained its suzerainty over the *Agram* and *Kauar* and over the *Tubus* who roamed the steppes lying to the south. In fact, the only people to recognize the Mais—and this merely in theory—were the small Kanuri (or Manga) groups still living in some villages in Kauar and Agram. But the Tubus were the real masters, from the seventeenth century they regarded themselves as independent of Bornu and in the last reigns they did not hesitate to plunder Kanem and the countries of the Yo. Like the Tuaregs, Bornu was forced on to the defensive on the edges of the farmlands, in Kanem, on the shore of Lake Chad and on the lower Yo. In the nineteenth century the position was to become worse and the nomads were to make extensive encroachments on the farming lands.

At the beginning of the nineteenth century Bornu, now well on the wane, received a heavy blow. The Peuls, large numbers of whom had settled centuries ago between the Niger and the Chari, rose in rebellion everywhere, with the excuse of waging a holy war, and in ten years managed to make themselves masters of the whole of the Central Sudan. Bornu, only a hair's breadth from collapse, was saved by the intervention of a notable of Kanem, Sheikh Lamine, who eventually took away all effective power from the old dynasty. His son destroyed it completely and officially established his own, that of the Kanemis, which reigned until our arrival and still exists today. Bornu, revived by Sheikh Lamine, managed to recover almost all its former power during the first half of the century, but declined again more and more rapidly in the second half. A fresh attack by an adventurer, Rabah, who had come from the Nile with an army of hardened men, finished it off. When the French arrived at Lake Chad, Bornu was nothing more than a ten-year-old memory, whilst Rabah's rule was still only that of a conqueror who had hardly settled down. It is the French and the English who saved what could be saved of the old empire of the Beni-Sefs.

Translated by Mrs C. P. Bagley

7. Songhay

JEAN ROUCH *Contribution à l'histoire des Songhay* Institut Français d'Afrique Nègre, Dakar 1953; pages 179–86, 213–21 (In translation)

. . . During the whole of the beginning of the fifteenth century, Songhay thus increased its power at the expense of the dying Mali. Souleyman Dandi went and took possession of the town of Mema in the north-east of Masina and, according to Kati, he struck a fatal blow at Mali, pillaged its territory and destroyed its power. Songhay was ripe for the great adventure of Sonni Ali.

Sonni Ali, the Witch-doctor-Conqueror (1464–1492)

The son of Souleyman Dandi, Sonni Ali, better known by the name of *Ali Ber*, 'Ali the great', and, in Songhay, by the simple name of 'the *Si*', was in fact the real founder of the Songhay empire. During the thirty years of his reign, he conquered the vast territory which his successors, the Askias, were to organize and administer for another century. This chief, despite his notorious impiety, has left so much to be remembered by that the pious chroniclers of Timbuctoo, while insulting him, described his conquests in detail and with pride.

Sonni Ali had a privileged youth; from his mother and father he acquired different but complementary powers.

His mother originated from the country of Tarou (Sokoto). This is an infidel nation, which worships wooden and stone idols. Should some good or evil happen, it is the idols which have been favourable or unfavourable. War is not made unless they have given their judgement. The false gods, to serve them and worship them, have priests directed by diviners and witch doctors who also give consultations. Sonni Ali spent all his youth among these men and his mind received the imprint of their idolatry and of their customs. (El Moucheli)

The art of magic, as noted elsewhere, is received with the mother's milk. Thus from his first suckling Sonni Ali received his first powers. Through his paternal heredity he had the requirements: through his father he was the heir of those 'witch doctor kings' of Kuka, descendants of the 'dragon killer'. His youth was spent in contact with those wise men from the country of Tarou, keepers of the arts of black magic, and he was in contact also with the sorceresses of Kuka, whose art was a complex mixture of Negro, Christian, Lybian and oriental occultism. Finally, as is still the custom followed by his descendants, his father Souleyman Dandi initiated him. And the traditions of these same descendants imply that he mysteriously received the master-word (gyindize dyine, 'first formula') which made divinities of every kind his submissive servants. Thus when Sonni Ali took over the power in Songhay he was the most powerful magician the Sudan had ever known.

We shall indicate later the power of the present-day descendants of Sonni Ali, but the extraordinary prestige which these witch doctors have retained (despite the catastrophes and the fall of their nation), not only in Songhay, but also among the neighbouring peoples, gives an idea of what must have been the power of Sonni Ali. The chroniclers of Timbuctoo, despite their hatred for 'the cursed one', could not keep from praising his extraordinary successes. Sadi is the most discreet: 'This tyrant master, this celebrated scoundrel . . . was a man gifted with great strength and with powerful energy.' Kati writes with his habitual fire: 'The tyrant, the profligate, the accursed one, the oppressor, the *Chi Ali*, last king of his dynasty . . . was always victorious and pillaged all the countries on which he had set his heart. When he was present, none of his armies was routed: always victor, never vanquished.' And this last phrase could be the motto of Sonni Ali: 'Always victor, never vanquished'. Few conquerors or war leaders have left so much to be remembered by. It is the achievement of a man endowed with supernatural powers.

The twenty-seven years' reign of Sonni Ali were twenty-seven years of conquests;[1] 'the scoundrel was always on an

[1] Summary of the conquests of Sonni Ali. He began by extending his residences. To Kuka, he added residences at Gao, then as the conquests advanced, at Kabera and at Quara to the north of lake Debo. But he did not stay in these residences as he was always on expedition.
1464–1465. He settled at Dire from which point he attacked the Mosi following them as far as Bambara, helped by the people of Timbuctoo who had just been attacked by the Mosi. It was perhaps at this time that he laid siege to Djenné.
1465–1467. He attacked the Dogon of the cliff region and decimated the Peul tribes of the Bandiagara region.
1467–1468. He attacked the inhabitants of Hombori.
1468–1469. On 30 January 1468 he entered Timbuctoo, which had been under Tuareg domination since 1433. The Tuareg chief Akil had fled to Oualata. Sonni Ali massacred or persecuted the inhabitants of Timbuctoo until 1470. After it was taken, Sonni set out on an expedition against the Mosi of Yatenga.
1469–1470. He sent an expedition against Tosko and attacked the Tuareg to the north of Timbuctoo.
1470–1471. He set out for Dendi, at Lollo (near Illo), there raised (from among the Bariba) an army which he sent on expedition against the capital of the Mosi, which he destroyed. He equipped an army and sent it, under the command of the *hi koy* (flotilla leader), against the Mosi. He sent another army, commanded by the *dendi fari* (chief of Dendi), against the Peuls of Nurma.

The army reformed at Djenné which he attacked after a siege which lasted seven years, seven months, seven days. The town was blockaded by the infantry men at low tide and by four hundred canoes at high tide. He entered Djenné.

expedition'. The outstanding events of these conquests are the taking of Timbuctoo from the Tuareg and the struggle against them (1468–1469), the campaign against the Bariba of Borgu (1470), the capture of Djenné and of all the lake region (1470–1476), the continual struggles against the Mosi and the Gourmanthé (1469, 1470, 1477, 1483), the campaigns against the cliff people of Bandiagara and of Hombori (Dagon and Koromba) (1465, 1466, 1476, 1484), the campaigns against the Peuls of Gurma (1465, 1470, 1488, 1492). These campaigns extended the Songhay considerably; the nucleus of Kuka-Gao now controlled a vast territory which covered approximately the whole of the northern Sudan. Delafosse says that the army of Sonni Ali was taken from the whole population which was continually being called to arms. No doubt this was so at first but very quickly the conquests of Sonni Ali brought him soldiers in sufficient numbers. It is difficult for us to envisage African-type wars, where the prisoners look upon themselves as the captives of their conqueror, do not dream of escaping and are quite ready to fight in the army which has defeated them. This, however, is what emerges from all these tales. Thus the campaigns in Dendi and the campaigns against the cliff peoples or the Tuareg had no other goal than to provide the Songhay with soldiers. Both had indeed a reputation for bravery and among the Songhay they still speak of the great

1471–1472. He brought his Peul prisoners back to Gao.
1472–1476. He pacified the lake region, founded there the province and the government of Dirma, stayed at Lake Dé and attacked Honbon.
1477–1480. He pursued the Mosi who had been making their way towards Oualata. He caught up with them and took their goods and their captives. He came back to Gao, but the Mosi resumed their project and went to Oualata,which they pillaged.
1480–1483. He went to Ras el Ma at the end of Lake Faguibini. He tried to reach Oualata, more than four hundred kilometres away, by water, clearing away the sand banks. He was interrupted in this undertaking by the flight of the Mosi. He set out quickly in pursuit of them, caught and routed them.
1484. Returning from the expedition he attacked the Dogon of the cliff region.
1486–1488. He persecuted the Moslems of the Gao region.
1488–1492. He led new attacks against Gourme, the Peuls and the Tuareg. On 6 November, on his return from an expedition to Gurma, he died in a mysterious manner 'drowned in the Koni'.

deeds of the *Tondi kado*, the 'strangers from the mountains', who fought as foot-soldiers in the Songhay army.[1]

The foot-soldiers were surrounded by horsemen, especially young men of distinction, from among whom Sonni Ali chose his officers. Delafosse, impressed by the chroniclers, implies that it was above all a lieutenant of the Sonni, the future Mohammed Askia, who led Songhay to its victorious conquests. It has already been said that Sonni Ali took a full part in these conquests. If his officers helped him it was nevertheless on him alone that the initiative and the glory rested. Besides, the bravest of his officers seems to have been the *Dendi Fari* Afoumba, governor of the down-stream provinces from Kuka to the Borgu. Then came the *Fondi farma* Mohammed (the future Askia), governor of the cliffs and mountains of Hambori, his brother the *Kourmina Tari* (or Kanfari), Omar Kombyango, governor of the province situated up-stream from Timbuctoo, the *Kotelo Farma*, the *Faren* Aboubakar and Ousman, the Askia[2] Baghna, the *Timbuctoo Koy* Mohammed Nadi, chief of Timbuctoo,[3] and Boukar and Yate, *hi koy*, flotilla leaders.

The Songhay flotilla played a decisive role in these conquests, of which the Niger was the main artery. The *hi koy*, the flotilla leader, was probably a Sorko and the whole fleet of canoes was composed of Sorko. These, as already stated, had colonized the river, showing the possibilities for extension. Sonni Ali, no doubt, understood the advantage in allying himself with these bold navigators, firmly established in the middle of the territories to be conquered.[4] The alliance between this magician

[1] The Songhai still make a distinction between these *tondi kado* and the *kado Si* black strangers. These latter, also captive during the campaigns, were assigned to work in the field. These were, to my mind, "voltaics", especially Koromban, reputed for their agrarian skills.

[2] Sadi points out that the use of this title of Askia from the time of Sonni Ali 'is a very strange feat'.

[3] Mohammed Nadi was a Berber; he was chief of Timbuctoo from 1433 to 1467. He was allied with Sonni Ali from the time the latter took over the power. At his death in 1467, his son Akil turned against Sonni Ali, and this was the reason for the capture of Timbuctoo.

[4] The traditions of Sorko collected by Dupuis Yacouba relate a very curious episode on this subject, 'Farang and the king Si'. The king Si (Sonni Ali) wanted to get hold of the marvellous guitar of Farang. He did not succeed. Farang pursued Si, who 'fled among the Christians', and Farang said to him 'Go, fool! You will never come back any more to enlarge the

and these masters of the water is difficult to understand, but it is certain that the Sorko collaborated with Sonni Ali in such a way that the latter used his fleet in conditions that seem hard to credit. He used it to oversee the territory, then to lay siege to Djenné (blockaded by four hundred canoes) and to Anganda in the lake region (blockaded by two hundred canoes), but especially in the attack on Oualata. The Mosi being at Oualata, Sonni Ali decided to attack them by water, setting out from Rad El Ma on Lake Faguibini, more than four hundred kilometres away from Oualata. As no waterway united these points, Sonni Ali decided to dig a canal. This operation, which appears 'fantastic' (Delafosse), was not in fact so fanciful. It was a question of clearing away some sand banks so that the Niger could run once more in one of its old courses. Sonni Ali was interrupted in these works by the flight of the Mosi (whom he caught with his horsemen), but the *sin fansi*, 'Si's canal', still exists near Ras el Ma.

The methods of war used by the armies of Sonni Ali are unknown. The traditions of his descendants say that he made his soldiers and his horses take *korte* (magic charms) by means of which they could fly in the sky, make themselves invisible or change into serpents. He himself, as a result of a mysterious alliance with the vultures, changed into a vulture and transformed his wonder horse, *Zinzinbadio*, into a vulture. It is thus that he is represented on the little silver ring of one of his descendants. And the mottoes of these descendants are still the mottoes of *Si*':

> *Si* flies in the night
> *Si* flies at first cock-crow
> *Si* takes all the souls
> *Si* kills the man between the hair and the head
> *Si* kills the man between the shoe and the foot
> *Si* kills the man between the jacket and the neck
> (Mottoes of the *Sohantye* of Wanzerba)

The enemies of Sonni Ali were especially the Peuls, the

number of the Songhoyhye' (the word songoytye today denoting the descendants of Sonni Ali). Is this a question of a kind of habitual joke between Senekou people, dating from an ancient kinship between the Sorko of Kuka and the Za allied with them?

Tuareg and the Mosi. His hatred for the Peuls made Kati say:

He had no enemy that he hated as fiercely as the Peuls. He could not see a Peul without killing him, whatever he might be, wise or ignorant, man or woman. He accepted no Peul wise man, neither in the political administration nor in the magistracy.

Sonni Ali thus gave proof of a certain political sense lacking in his successors. They had distrusted these infiltrators whose insidious threat to subjugate the African peoples this brilliant man had understood. His aversion for the Tuareg can thus be considered as an almost prophetic measure of defence.

The conquered territory extended on the river 'from Mali as far as Lollo', exactly 'from Kanta to Sibiridugu, which form the boundaries between our states and those of Mali'—that is to say, from Kebbi (the boundary between Burgu and the still very anarchic Hausa States) to the region of Segou (the Mali boundary). The north of Gurma, including the cliffs of Bandiagara and Hombori, to the present-day Goruol, formed the southern boundary of these states with the Mosi, the Koromba and the Gourmantche. To the east the Aur boundaries were undefined. To the north of the bend the Tuareg wandering on the banks of the Niger were subjects of the Songhay. In the west the Songhay extended as far as the semi-desert zone of ancient Ghana.[1] All Songhay was divided into provinces placed under the government of the officers of the Sonni. This territory had a clear advantage over the empires which had preceded it, the natural unity of the Niger 'knitting' together the different provinces and permitting rapid and effective liaison. Probably, but for the Moroccan attack, this empire would have succeeded in holding the leadership in the Sudan for several more centuries.

The picture left us by Delafosse of Songhay at the time of Sonni Ali, 'a population continually in arms, not being able to attend to the work of the fields', seems to me to be ill-founded. The creation of provincial governors, which this author (Delafosse) attributes to Mohammed Askia, was the work of Sonni Ali. Furthermore, I believe that his canal-digging

[1] The Tarrikh el Fettach gives a list of the different regions making up Songhay. Eru, Dendi, Koulane, Kerli Hausa and Gurma, the territories of Kuka and Gao, Aterem and the whole lake region.

activities allow us to attribute to him an important part in the hydraulic works, dams, feeder canals and cisterns, traces of which Mourgues has found in the interior of Gurma. All this region would correspond to eastern Kurmina, inhabited by skilful stock breeders and cultivators, including some Koromba or other 'voltaic' people displaced by force as the need arose. Songhay was as prosperous in the time of Sonni Ali as in the time of the Askia, its tireless chief keeping his eye on everything, not only on conquest but also on administration. His subjects respected, obeyed and at the same time feared him. As for his soldiers, they worshipped him. Sadi, despite his bias, writes: 'The people of his time and his soldiers had given him the name of *Dali*, and each time he called upon someone that person would reply, "Dali . . .".' It is not permitted to give such a title to anyone, because this word means 'the most high' and ought to be reserved for the master of omnipotence, the most mighty God. This man had such prestige that he was almost deified during his lifetime, being recognized as an equal of the ruler of the world.

The religious position of this enigmatic personage is also remarkable. He was one of the few great chiefs of the Sudan to oppose Islam. On this subject the chronicles are verbose: 'He persecuted the learned and the pious people by attacking their lives, their honour and their reputation.' He massacred the scholars of Timbuctoo from 1468 to 1470 to such an extent that there was no one left able to read Arabic. He took thirty virgin daughters of these scholars as his concubines, but then had them killed. He gave Muslims as captives to other Muslims. He had the children of the scholars crushed in mortars, and the stomachs of their pregnant wives opened. He killed people 'without the least necessity'. This cruelty made him equally famous far from his country, and a commentator on the Moslem traditions of El djelal, Es Soyouti, writes, 'We have learned that there has appeared in the land of Tekrur, under the name of Sonni Ali, a person who makes men perish and ransacks the land.' No doubt these testimonies have been exaggerated by the pious chroniclers to suit themselves, but this pitiless cruelty towards Islam seems to be in character with Sonni Ali, who once again correctly considered Islam a great threat to the African world.

Sonni Ali, however, was himself a Muslim. According to custom, he had had to take the oath of conformity to the faith at the moment of his investiture (Songhay was well worth a 'salaam'). He was of the intolerant Kharedjite sect but he hurried over his religious duties none the less, continually postponing his prayers. His private life was so dissolute that one questioned whether he was a true Muslim. He did, however, esteem learning and learned men. He always had the deepest respect for the learned El Mamoun, whom he called 'my father': 'Without the learned men', he said, 'there would be in this world neither amusement nor pleasure.' This attitude seemed so irrational to Delafosse that he concludes from it that Sonni Ali was lacking in consistency. But if one looks on Sonni Ali as a witch doctor, his behaviour becomes clearer. El Moucheli traces without any ambiguity in this respect the religious evolution of Sonni Ali:

At first he fasted during the month of Ramadan and made sacrifices and other offerings in the mosques. Then he came back to the idols and to the soothsayers, seeking help in magical practices, honouring with sacrifices and offerings the trees and sacred stones, addressing prayers and vows to them, and asking them for the realization of his desires. He consulted the soothsayers and the witch doctors in all his cares.

If Sadi or Kati did not point out these magical practices, it is, in my opinion, because they had not completely disappeared under the Askias. It took a stranger to describe them with this exactitude; to present to us Sonni Ali as a veritable *korte Konia*, 'master in charms', making sacrifices to the trees and to the sacred stones (the *tôru* of the present-day witch doctors), and asking soothsayers to tell him what to do. Also, the witch doctor, although he is hostile to Islam, is quite prepared to make use of it. Sonni Ali, who massacred the scholars of Timbuctoo because their growing influence seemed dangerous to him, thought highly of their learning; he eliminated enemies and kept only those who could teach him something. His curiosity led him especially towards oriental occultism, which clung parasitically even to the most orthodox beliefs, and it was no doubt Sonni Ali who introduced effectively into the beliefs and rites of the Songhay those elements of Arab esoterism which still mark them so profoundly.

This extraordinary person died in circumstances full of mystery. On his return from a campaign to Gurma he was said to have been drowned 'in a torrent-like river called Koni', which Delafosse supposes to have been swollen by the rains. In November, however, all the small temporary tributaries of the Niger have long been dry. His soldiers embalmed his body and buried him, but no one could say where his tomb was. I like to think that Sonni Ali died like a true witch doctor, his body disappearing into the bush but his soul, thanks to the attention of his sons, remaining present, nourished by them and then by their descendants, always continuing to guide their hard labours.

Such was Sonni Ali. His disturbing and terrible personality dominates the history of the Songhay, for whom he is the great and cruel hero. The twenty-seven years of the reign of the *Si*, conqueror, engineer, organizer, master-magician, represent the brief peak of Songhay civilization. He succeeded in ridding his country of foreign influences (Mali and Islam) by foreseeing the threat of the Peuls, the Tuareg and the Muslim scholars, relying only on himself and on his faithful followers, building a purely African state, conceived by a Negro (for his Berber origins were very remote) for other Negroes. It is hardly astonishing that Muslim tradition has dragged him in the mud, or that chroniclers have represented him nevertheless as the leading Songhay chief, or magical tradition as the leading magician, or mythology as a god, *za beri wandu*, the great dangerous Za, the father of the spirit of the water. . . .

The Moroccan Conquest: Seventeenth Century

The fall of Songhay had been predicted for a long time. The Sheikh Abderrahman Es-Soyouti had announced to Mohammed Askia in the course of a pilgrimage to Mecca: 'You will have numerous sons, about a hundred, who will follow your precepts during your reign, but who, after you, will change their behaviour entirely . . . so that your kingdom will be overthrown.'

For a long time the Sultan of Morocco had coveted the rich empire of Gao, which he thought was a land of gold. When the rivalry of the pretenders to Gao had sufficiently weakened Songhay, the Sultan decided to attack it. The slight motive for this campaign was the possession of the salt-mines of Taghaza.[1] When, after several refusals to hand over these salt-mines, the Sultan Moulay Ahmed received from Issihak II 'javelins and iron shackles', he replied to this insult with war.

In November 1590, 3,000 armed men, both horsemen and foot-soldiers, accompanied by twice the number of followers of all kinds, tradesmen of different sorts, doctors . . . 'set out under the command of the Spanish renegade, the pasha Jouder', a man who 'was of small stature and had blue eyes'.

1. *The Collapse of Songhay (1591)*

The course followed by this handful of men, mainly formed of renegades and Andalusians, is known. Jouder arrived at the Niger after a five-month voyage on 30 March 1591. The Songhay, warned of the departure of the Moroccan column, had been unable to take any defensive measures: 'each time that any sensible advice was given, they hastened to reject it.' The downfall of Songhay had been decided by God, foreseen since the time of Mohammed Askia, and it was useless to fill in the wells, poison them or to retreat to the Gurma bank of the Niger.

On 12 April 1591, however, the Songhay army (of 30,000 to 40,000 men) hastily gathered together and went to meet the Moroccans at Tondibi. The magicians warned the Songhay that the Moroccans had new arms, so a herd of cows was made to charge in front. The 3,000 soldiers of Jouder indeed had guns; they opened fire and the cows turned on the great Songhay army of about 40,000 men. The Moroccan

[1] I have already said that in 1561 the Sultan of Morocco had had Taghaza and the Tuareg salt caravaners attacked. In 1578 the Sultan had demanded the surrender of the mines from Askia Daoud.

In 1584 a Moroccan embassy had gone to Gao for the purpose of spying on the Songhay army. This same year an army of 20,000 men had tried to cross the Sahara but had been almost completely annihilated by the hardships of the journey and by thirst. In 1585 the Moroccans attacked Taghaza again and occupied it for some time, when the Berber mines were opening up, some distance away, the new salt-mine of Taodini. Finally, in 1585, a Berber interned by the Askia at Taghaza fled to Marrakish and described to the Sultan of Morocco the bad political state of the Songhay. It was at this time that Moulay Ismail sent an ultimatum to Askia Issihak.

horsemen charged the Songhay wings, and the battle was engaged.

At this moment there intervened a shady character, whom Kati calls 'the *askya alpha* Boukar Lamber'. This was the Muslim priest, the *alfa*, who was assigned to the very person of the *Askia*[1]. The *askia alfa* Boukar Lambar leapt down from his horse and, seizing the Askia's bridle, said to him, 'Fear God, Askia.' 'One would think', the king replied to him, 'that you wish to give us the order for flight and retreat. God forbid! I am not one of those who turn their back! If there are any who want to save their lives let them flee!' Ould Bana was holding the prince by his stirrup, for the latter had his sabre and his shield and wanted to go off into the midst of his troops, around whom the Moroccan cavalry was executing a turning movement with the object of encircling them. However, the *askia alfa* said again,

> Fear God, do not go to meet death, do not cause your brothers to die and do not make all the Songhay perish at once and in the same place! God will call you to account for the lives of all those who perish here today, for it is you who will be the cause of their death if you do not make them flee. We shall not give you the order to flee but we can ask you to move your men today out of the range of fire. Then we shall reflect on what we must do, and tomorrow we shall return to the battle resolute and decided, if it pleases God. But fear God!

The *Askia* and his courageous men did not listen to him, rushing upon the enemy and attacking them in hand-to-hand fighting, but the *askia alfa* did not stop insisting at the prince's side and he finally overcame his resistance. Then, holding in his hand the reins of the *Askia*'s horse, he dragged him along and made him take flight. This was the signal for the general rout. Only ninety Songhay foot-soldiers stood firm. These the Moroccans killed to a man. The Moroccans praised God and did not pursue the defeated Songhay.

The *askia alfa*, as can be seen, was to a great extent responsible for the rout of the Songhay. He acted like a traitor instead of 'making courage' like the griots; that day he made 'fear'. It matters little whether he had been bribed by the Moroccans or

[1] Called 'the secretary'.

whether he was convinced that the Moroccans were the immutable arm of God; at the decisive moment of the battle when nothing was yet lost, this sinister priest prevented the combatants from fighting. Thus Islam led Songhay to defeat and shame.

It was an almost intact army that returned to Gao, 'as though none had found death in their ranks'. The Askia gave the order to the people of Gao and to the people of Timbuctoo to cross the Niger, which was done in indescribable disorder. The Askia wanted to set out for Dendi, but his close friends opposed this. He crossed the Niger near Ansongo, and settled at Bara. From there he sent peace proposals to the pasha Jouder, asking him to withdraw from Songhay in return for 1,000 pieces of gold and 1,000 slaves.

Jouder entered Gao, which was empty, and found the town in a wretched condition. He sent a message to the Sultan of Morocco to acquaint him with the peace proposals of the Askia and to describe to him the destitution of the land. Then he went to Timbuctoo, where he received a relatively warm welcome from certain Muslims who had stayed in the town and who looked favourably on Moroccan Muslims. Jouder, however, constructed a fort and awaited events. He received there the reply from the Sultan in the form of a dismissal (the Sultan was furious because of the small profit from this costly expedition) and an order to hand over command to the pasha Mahmoud who, at the head of 80 soldiers, had arrived at Timbuctoo on 17 August 1591.

Mahmoud immediately had canoes made from the doors of the houses of the town. Then he set forth in pursuit of the Askia. The battle took place on 14 October 1591 at Bamba. This was another complete rout for the Songhay. Askia Issihak fled to Dendi, having the retreat covered by some of his brothers, of whom some became traitors and joined the Moroccans. Jouder stopped at Gao and Mahmoud continued the pursuit as far as Tentyi, near Kuka.

Askia Issihak sent against him the *hi koy* Laha Sorkia at the head of his 1,200 choice horsemen. But rivalry between the *hi koy* and the *Balama* caused the failure of the expedition. The soldiers then proclaimed the Balama Mohammed Gao as Askia. Issihak, thus deposed, set out for Gurma, not without having handed over the regalia,[1] but he was massacred by the king of the Gourmantche.

The new Askia, Mohammed Gao, sent to the pasha Mahmoud messengers bearing peace proposals and supplies to assist the Moroccans to combat the famine! Then he sent the *askia alfa* Boukar and the *hi koy* Laha to the pasha, where they were well received. On their return, the *alfa* urged the Askia to go himself to visit the pasha (who, according to Kati, had bribed him), but the *hi koy* was of a different opinion. '. . . Now, for myself, I think only ill of him [the pasha] . . . if you reject my advice and if you go there, for God's sake, you will never come back . . .' At this vital moment the enmity between the marabout traitor and the Sorko who was determined to fight is striking. As we shall see, until the final catastrophe, the Askia was to be torn between these two counsellors. But the God of Islam had decided on the downfall of Songhay, and his priest was to triumph over the wisdom of the Sorko who, right to the end, tried to save Songhay. The Askia, therefore, followed the opinion of the *alfa* and set out for the camp of the pasha (where his brother Souleyman had already gone). Shortsightedly, he set off surrounded by all his dignitaries. On the way, the *hi koy* tried to stop him, proposing to go there himself and begging the Askia not to involve all the high-ranking Songhay men in their adventure. But the *alfa*, when consulted, replied, 'All this chattering is not befitting to royal dignity.' The Askia, attended by all his nobles, was approaching the pasha's camp when forty distinguished Moroccans came to meet him. The *hi koy* immediately suggested massacring them: 'Let us kill all these dignitaries and the Moroccan army will no longer have any leader.' The Askia, impressed by this firmness, was getting ready to follow his advice, when the *alfa* intervened again, assuring him that no danger awaited the Askia among the Moroccans. The Askia accepted these assurances and saluted the Moroccan dignitaries, who surrounded the Songhay. The *Kanfari*, won over by the arguments of the *hi koy*, also proposed to the Askia to kill the Moroccans and to attack their camp; the pasha's army, taking the Songhay for their own dignitaries, would thus be taken by surprise and could be wiped out: 'In this way we could have a

[1] He kept with him the Islamic insignia of Mohammed Askia, the ring, the turban and the sabre.

hand-to-hand battle with them. If we die it will be on the backs of our own horses and that will be better than throwing ourselves into their hands and falling into a trap from which we shall not be able to escape.' But the Askia, on the advice of his *alfa*, refused to use this trick and went into the Moroccan camp.

The pasha received the Songhay for a meal of welcome, then, after having consulted his men, he called the Askia and had him tied up with his turban.[1] Then he had the prop pulled out of the tent where the Songhay were. Some succeeded in fleeing. The Pasha ordered his soldiers (in Spanish, says Kati, '*Kor li Kabissa*', which shows that Spanish was the language used by these Moroccans and renegades) to cut off the heads of any who might resist. The 83 dignitaries, among them the *hi koy* and the *Kanfari*, were bound with chains. With the exception of the *askia alfa* Boukar, who was left free, and who went and completed his holy career at Timbuctoo, all the prisoners were sent to Gao until the sultan should decide their fate. One last time, in the canoe which carried them towards Gao, the *hi koy* and other Songhay suggested to the Askia to flee, and one last time the Askia rejected this proposition. At Gao they were all imprisoned and the Sultan of Morocco, having sent the order to put them to death, caused the walls of their prison to fall upon them. The *hi koy* Laha was given special treatment; he was killed, then put on a cross in a square in Gao.

Such is the last episode of the victory of the Moroccans over the Songhay. In less than a year, practically without a fight, divine vengeance was accomplished. To the last moment, the Muslim high priest of the Askia contributed with all his might to the irremediable fulfilment of this vengeance. To the last moment too, the Sorko, the flotilla leader, tried to combat this stupid capitulation, and no doubt many dignitaries, following his example and that of the *Kanfari*, less blinded by Islam, were ready to follow him. It is not impossible that if the Songhay had put into action one of the ruses proposed by the *hi koy*, they might have succeeded in wiping out this handful of Moroccans and Spaniards, and at least have avoided their ignominious death. But the Askia foolishly followed the advice of his

[1] There is cruel irony in this gesture: the Songhay chief was bound precisely with the great turban, 'the bonnet', which was an insignia of the leadership.

priest. He went of his own free will and dragged his dignitaries with him to death. Historians have never made clear this heavy responsibility of Islam in the collapse of Songhay, whose true martyr was not the Askia (who payed for his stupidity with death), but the *hi koy* Laha, killed and crucified at Gao. Thus Songhay, born from colonies of Sorko fishermen, came to an end with the final execution of the leader of the Sorko fishermen.

2. *Songhay Cut in Two*

The Open Struggle of the Dendi against the Moroccans (1591–1599)

The Askia's brother, Souleyman, who had gone over to the Moroccans was, before this episode, named as Askia by the pasha Mahmoud. However, the Songhay who had remained in the Dendi chose as Askia, Nuhu, one of the brothers of Mahammed Gao (and of Souleyman), who had been interned in Dendi by Askia Issihak and therefore not been captured in the Moroccan ambush. Songhay was cut in two. In the north a pasha was established at Timbuctoo and the Songhay, mere collaborators, were placed under the command of a puppet Askia nominated by the Moroccans. In the south, in Dendi, there was Songhay 'resistance' under the command of an Askia freely chosen by them. This division corresponded, moreover, to a religious division; the Songhay of Timbuctoo were occupied but faithful to Islam; the free Songhay of Dendi were returning little by little to the ancient beliefs (the chroniclers were soon to call the people of Dendi 'the pagans').

The subsequent struggles between the Moroccans and the Songhay of Dendi are abundantly described in the chronicles and Delafosse gives an excellent account of them.[1]

[1] Recapitulatory table of the open struggle of the Songhay and the Moroccans:

1591. Crossing of the Sahara by the troop of Jouder, then of Mahmoud. Battles of Tondi-bi and of Bamba. Deposition of Askia Issihak.

1591. Askia Mohammed Gao. Ambush of Kuka.

1591–1599. Askia Nuhu (Askia Souleyman 'collaborator').

End of 1591. Defeat of Uame. Installation of the Moroccans at Kulen. Attack on Timbuctoo by the Tuareg. Installation of the Moroccans at Timbuctoo and Djenné.

1592–1593. Fruitless struggles of pasha Mahmoud against Nuhu.

Despite the defeats of Tondibi, Bamba, and the ambush of Kuka, Askia Nuhu had indeed succeeded in gathering together a considerable number of Songhay; all the Songhay of the north who had been able to flee had sought refuge in Dendi: 'The Askia had with him a considerable crowd of people from Songhay, adults, children and slaves of both sexes, who had emigrated with him and who were composed of inhabitants of Gao and of the surrounding areas of that town.' In Dendi, these Songhay had found the descendants of Sonni who had been established for a century in Anzuru and in Gorud, and also some newly arrived Zarma groups. The *Sohantye* welcomed the descendants of the old usurper and, forgetting the old quarrels, they helped them with all their skill. They prepared the most powerful war charms, and to hear the present-day traditions of Wanxerbe one would think that it was due particularly to these magic arts that the people of Dendi were able to resist the Moroccans.

For, during the seven or eight years of struggle, the Songhay of Dendi, behind Askia Nuhu, resisted the Moroccans victoriously. Nuhu 'was one of the most cunning of the sons of Askia Daud' and during his whole reign he did not enjoy one single month of rest, occupied as he was with making war and fighting. To be sure, most of his battles were lost by him, but none was decisive and he ended by getting the better of the Moroccans through wearing them down. The pasha Mahmoud began by pursuing the people of Dendi as far as the border of Kibbi at Uame, where he inflicted a serious defeat on them which greatly shook the cohesion of Songhay but did not

Loss of all the Moroccan cavalry. Installation of Jouder at Gao. Creation of the post of Bamba. Mahmoud goes to combat the Tuareg at Gao, he terrorizes the inhabitants of Timbuctoo, has the scholars deported to Morocco.

1594. Evacuation by the Moroccans of the fortress of Kulen. Nuhu installs himself at Hombori. Mahmoud is killed at Hombori.

1595. The pasha Mansour replaces Mahmoud. Mansour inflicts a defeat on Nuhu near Hombori.

1596. Campaign of Mansur against Nuhu in Dendi. Death of Mansur (poisoned by Jouder?).

1597. Mohammed Taba, Mansur's replacement, dies (poisoned).

1598. Jouder, who has resumed command, struggles against Masina.

1599. Askia Nuhu is replaced by his brother Musta. Jouder returns to Morocco having been replaced by Ammar.

destroy it. Without doubt the battle of Uame resulted in strengthening the fighting spirit of Nuhu's people. The Moroccans left an outpost on the river, the fortress of Koulen. Two hundred Moroccan fusiliers took up position there.[1] Nuhu's tactics changed; he understood that large-scale engagements would be fatal for him, so he went over to a war of harassing, and 'despite the small number of his followers, Askia Nuhu achieved results which Askia Ishaq would not have achieved with more considerable forces.' Thus, at the battle of Birnai, the pasha Mahmoud lost eighty of his best footsoldiers. This war of ambushes and also the very taxing climate of Dendi caused the Moroccans terrible losses. All the Moroccan cavalry perished, and the pasha Mahmoud had to ask for help from the Sultan who sent him six army corps as reinforcements. Nevertheless, at the end of two years of this war, the pasha Mahmoud gave up Dendi, and the following year he was obliged to evacuate Kulen by canoe, so effective was the blockade (1594).

Nuhu, now freed in Dendi, went further north and settled at Hombori. Mahmoud came and attacked him there. Having learnt that the Sultan of Morocco had decided to dismiss him, he attacked with mad recklessness the positions of Nuhu and was killed with a poisoned arrow (1594). His successor, however, inflicted a severe defeat on Nuhu, who had to surrender numerous prisoners to the Moroccans. Nuhu doubled back to Dendi, then set out again towards Hombori, where he held his own against the small-scale attacks of the Moroccans until he was deposed (1599). It was at this same period that Jouder was recalled to Morocco. The disappearance of these two combatants put an end to the period of continual wars, Dendi remaining practically intact but without hope of liberating the rest of Songhay.

The brutal fall of Songhay, however, had been accompanied by external troubles and the former vassals took advantage of the situation to regain their liberty or even to attack their old

[1] I have already said that no decisive reason explains the fixing of Koulen at Sabongari, in the 'W'. One does not easily understand why the Moroccans should have chosen this position on the Niger, one of the most unfavourable from all points of view: insanitariness, thick bush allowing surprise attacks, situation in the midst of an almost deserted bush. The islands upstream or downstream from this area were much more favourable.

masters. The Peuls of the Masena ravaged Ras El Ma; the Tuareg pillaged Bara and Dirma; the Bambara sacked Djenné and seized free women; and furthermore, in 1591, the Tuareg attacked the Moroccans of Timbuctoo and set fire to the town, since they were unable to force them out of their fort. In the south, the position seems to have been quite different. The Hausa states encouraged the Songhay of Dendi to resist the Moroccans and the Kebbi gave them effective aid.

The Moroccans, therefore, had to face two fronts, the resisters of Dendi and the external enemies. The pasha Mahmoud spent his time attacking Nuhu and defending Timbuctoo and its surroundings. He set up posts at Gao (under the command of Jouder, more or less superseded), at Bamba and at Djenné. At Timbuctoo, the pious inhabitants had not been slow in collaborating with such well-behaved occupiers: 'Bonds of comradeship and sincere friendship were established between the two groups who visited each other's homes reciprocally.' Traffic on the river had resumed and the life of the marabouts and merchants seemed to continue normally (the Moroccans had even given them an Askia with an army of a hundred men at his disposal). But in the autumn of 1593, the pasha Mahmoud, furious at his set-backs in Dendi, gathered together all the scholars of Timbuctoo in the courtyard of the mosque of Sankorai, had a large number of them massacred and deported the others to Morocco. Thus Muslim Songhay itself was crumbling:

> The lowest caste of the population became the highest, and the highest caste became the lowest; the meanest rabble had precedence over the nobility. Religious objects were sold for the goods of this world, and faith was exchanged for error. The rules of justice were suppressed, tradition became a dead-letter, new doctrines came to light and at this period there was no longer anyone in the town who kept the law or walked in the path of the fear of God . . .

Thus Timbuctoo which 'had not its like among the towns of the country of the Africans', which possessed more than a hundred and fifty Koran schools, which was called 'the city of God', which was also a commercial city of the first importance (there were reckoned to be twenty-six master tailors there, each employing sixty apprentices), was ruined by the Moroccan conquest which many of its inhabitants had once desired.

Yet in the midst of these troubles the position of the Moroccans was not strong. Counting all the troops sent to the Sudan by the Sultan one finds about 11,000 men.[1] These men could hold only the immediate approaches to the four Moroccan posts. Moreover, if at the beginning the fever of conquest had roused the enthusiasm of the soldiers, very soon the rivalries between the officers, the rigours of a climate which sapped the strength of these hardened adventurers, and, above all, the disillusionment at having conquered not a kingdom of gold but a vast, wild country of dust and sun, had singularly embittered them. The Songhay were treated, after their resounding defeats, as people to be despised. Before long, however, as their stay began to drag out, the Moroccans were forced to reckon with the Africans, even if only with their women. The 'collaboration' could have been fruitful. To be sure, Songhay would have remained the vassal of Morocco, but with such support it would have kept its superior position over the other African states. But it would have required less greediness on the part of the distant Sultan who was only concerned to see the benefits of his costly expeditions returning to him, as well as a greater genius for colonization on the part of the Moroccan captains, and also perhaps a less corrupt native element.

The Songhay of the north seem to have collaborated with the conquerers in the most stupid manner, at least during the early years. The appointed Askia had only a ridiculous army at his disposal and almost non-existent power. His followers swelled their numbers somewhat from the captures made from the Askia Dendi, which allowed him in 1598 to furnish for the Moroccan expeditions against Masina the contribution of the 'most valiant men of Songhay'.

The Songhay of Dendi were very different. Adversity had forged a nationalism among these militant exiles. Settled on the borders of Kebbi, they had received from their old enemy the warmest welcome and, no doubt, effective assistance. To thank the people of Kebbi for their help, Nuhu sent them the finest trophy of his struggles against the Moroccans, the head of the pasha Mahmoud, which was displayed on the market

[1] The crossing of the Sahara had not always been without loss. Thus when the pasha Mansur came to the Sudan, he led an army of 1,000 soldiers, renegades and Andalusians of whom half were lost en route.

place at Likki. To the north, the boundary of Dendi was approximately on the Ansongo parallel, and this line, which cut Songhay in two, is still maintained in certain forms to this day. The capital of Dendi was Loulami,[1] but it was only a base since the people of Dendi were continually on expeditions. This group, which was still very cohesive and which had considerable military value, ought to have gradually conquered the rest of Songhay. But after some years of active resistance, weariness took hold of the people of Dendi who no longer wanted to follow Nuhu. 'As Nuhu had been away from his family and his own people so far and so long, the Songhay, wearied at his continued absence, deposed him and named in his place his brother, Askia El Mostafa. . . .' After seven years of heroic struggles, fraternal rivalries were revived and Nuhu, the hero of Dendi resistance, was sacrificed to palace quarrels (1599).

The Moroccan troops were weakened by similar rivalries. The pashas who replaced Mahmoud died one after the other, poisoned, it is said, by Jouder. When the latter was alone, he once more took up the command of the Moroccan army, organizing the expedition against Masina. But Jouder had ceased to please, and he was recalled to Morocco on 25 March 1599.

Thus, at the end of seven or eight years of struggle, the two most fearsome combatants disappeared, the conqueror Jouder and the Askia Nuhu. Jouder had certainly desired to carve out for himself an empire in the northern Sudan (as Voullet and Chanoine did later), and this thirst for grandiose adventure explains perhaps the prestige of this Spanish renegade, not only over his own men, but also over the Songhay themselves who still remember him. His disappearance from the Sudan marks the end of the glorious phase of Moroccan conquest. After him the Moroccan dynasty was shaken and its decadence steadily increased. The adversary of the Dendi, Askia Nuhu, ousted from power, would have been the only leader capable of reconquering the Songhay. But the people, after the whiplash of defeat, had once more returned to their pleasures and their

[1] Delafosse situates Loulami round about Say. Local traditions have not retained any mention of it. It is quite tempting to equate Loulami and Al Silami, the capital of Kanta of Kebbi. It would then be in Kebbi that Dendi had had its base.

quarrels. With the deposition of Nuhu, the glorious phase of Dendi resistance came to an end. Henceforth, the Moroccans abandoned all claim to Dendi, and reciprocally, the Songhay of Dendi gave up all claim to the north of their territory. The borders between Ansongo and Hombori were now drawn definitively. The Songhay of the north and the Songhay of the south were to have, apart from commercial contracts, only a common language (with noticeable dialectical differences) and the same memories of a glorious epoch.[1]

3. *Pagan Dynasty of the Za of Kuka. Migration of the Sorko*

Apart from this story, the chroniclers of Timbuctoo do not tell us very much about Songhai at this period. Za Al Ayamen, taking over the leadership by a lightning blow, succeeded no doubt in reuniting around himself groups which until then had remained independent. The name of Za (or Dija) became the title of the new dynasty. There were fifteen Zas who succeeded each other in Kuka and died there without having embraced the Muslim religion. The list of names handed down to us by the chroniclers seems composed of Songhay names (rather than Berber ones as Delafosse says). The small number of immigrants must have favoured their intermingling with the local Africans; thus Za Al Ayamen was said to have married a Kuka woman, Oueïza Kuka, according to the anonymous author addition to the *Tarikh el Fettach*. And these people who had originally been Christians had seen fit to abandon their first religion.

What did the Sorko do during this time? Delafosse, interpreting the 'legends of Farang' collected by Dupuis-Yacouba, and basing his argument on the hypothesis of a very lively opposition between the Sorko and the Za of Kuka, supposes that the Sorko, defeated at Kuka, returned up the Niger and founded the town of Gao 'where a fisherman, called Farang-Ber (Farang the great), created a kind of independent kingdom.[1] The traditions of the present-day Sorko go back indeed to Gao, but there is no reference to any struggles with the Za of Kuka. It is possible that Delafosse had information which he does not quote, but I believe rather that he has interpreted the stories transcribed by Dupuis-Yacouba in the 'Songs of Farang', and

[1] It is at this time, 1599, that one of the chronicles, the *Tarikh el Fettach*, ends.

in particular the one which relates the struggle of Farang and of Si 'who governed half the earth'. Delafosse has made Si the Za of Kuka. In actual fact, Si represents the following generation of the Songhay, the Si or Sonni of Gao.

Be that as it may, it is possible that the Sorko, accustomed to independence, sought to remove themselves from the growing authority of the Za of Kuka, or, more simply perhaps, continued their migrations upstream. Was the leader of these Sorko the 'fisher king' as some would have him, or was he a subject more independent than the others, as the chroniclers of Timbuctoo describe him? I prefer to believe that he held a position quite similar to that of certain present-day Sorko, a man free to travel the river that was his domain, barely submitting himself to the local resident authorities, despised and feared at the same time.

One can retain the pattern of Sorko migration as given by Delafosse. 'Around 690' they came and settled in the region of Gao which they founded. With each fishing expedition, like their descendants the Sorkawa of our day, they proceeded farther and farther upstream. They reached Bamba, where, according to local tradition, Feran Maka Bate established himself and made his base. The numerous hippopotami of the Bamba Sorko basin, the favourite meat of the fishermen, had attracted them there. A small fraction led by the Sorko Fono (who was married to Feran's sister) continued on upstream as far as Gouras, on the shores of Lake Dibo where, because the Bozo fishermen from upstream did not allow them freedom of movement, they settled. Fono called in his brother-in-law Feran to help combat these Bozo and the river dwelling Soninke. The Sorko were victorious and moved down farther south to Djenné. Some mixed with the Bozo and formed the most northerly group of the Bozo fishermen, the Sorgo or Sorko. However Fono and Feran contested the leadership; Fono was defeated by Feran who changed him into a monkey. Then Feran visited all the lake region, established 'the village of Feran' *farankoyra*, which the Peuls have made into Sarafere, fished even in Lake Faguibini leaving fishing encampments throughout the area. Then he returned to Bamba-Sorko, where he died, and where his grave is still to be found (information from the Sorko of Gourao, Dyedes, Kermachaive).

Arab chroniclers, with their often disdainful silence on all pagan traditions, do not speak of these Sorko voyages, but, on the occasion of the founding of the town of Tindirma, they state that this site was occupied by a Sorko (Tensii, married to Marma), from the region of Gao.

Despite this absence of a landmark in time one may suppose that this migration of the Sorko extended over several generations ascribed as is usual in tradition to one single hero, Feran Maka Bate, between the seventh and eleventh centuries. The regions through which they passed were certainly not uninhabited, settled farmers and no doubt also occasional fishermen (*do*) lived on the banks; some remained autonomous, others were assimilated.[1]

Thus the beginning of the domination by the Za of Kuka was marked by the formation of a small homogenous Songhay nucleus concentrated around the capital, and by the spread along the river of the Sorko fisher group. The future Songhay was thus being prepared, those whose descendants were to be great warriors gathered themselves around the chief and the little island of Kuka became an unusual capital, where the arts of magic were practised even more than the arts of war, where African and Oriental skills confronted each other; sometimes a passing fisherman would mention the name of the village which the Sorko had reached that year. For upstream on the river, a handful of men armed with sharp harpoons, eating fish or hippopotamus flesh, travelling in fragile canoes made from hollow trunks or woven plants, founded towns and established distant colonies, an advance guard of the conquests to come.

4. *The Zas of Gao* (*Eleventh to Fourteenth Centuries*)

While this embryo of the Songhay was being formed, northern Sudan had already seen the formation of an important empire. Probably, towards the beginning of the fourth century, Cyrenaian Semites had founded the empire of Ghana. From the eighth to the eleventh century, they had been succeeded by the Soninke, and it was with these that the Sorko fishermen clashed near the Debo.

[1] The Gow hunters engaged in a similar migration which led them to Bara. They helped the Sorko in their struggle against the Bozo and subsequently intermingled with these Bozo, who were themselves hunters.

But in the eleventh century an important element was introduced into the Sudan: Islam. Until then the Berbers from the north, like the Zas of Gao, were Christians. But suddenly, following the pilgrimage to Mecca of Tarsina, chief of the Zenaga, the first holy war began. It started the Almoravid conquests.

The Appearance of Islam

Tarsina's son-in-law continued the holy war. In 1035 he brought back from Mecca the scholar Abdullah, who undertook the conversion of the Berbers. In view of the small success of his enterprise he withdrew to Senegal, to the Tukulor territory, and established himself in a hermitage (*ribath*). It is known that his disciples became numerous, they were called the hermits (*el mrabethin*), from which come the terms '*Almoravids*' and '*marabouts*'. In 1042 Abdullah set out at the head of 2,000 hermits and, sword in hand, began the conversion of the western Sahara. He proceeded to Morocco, conquered Spain and died in 1058. His successor Abu Bekr won, in 1076, a complete victory over Ghana, forcibly converting the inhabitants. At his death (1087) the Almoravid conquest was coming to an end in the Sudan; Ghana, exhausted, was falling into the hands of the Soso but Islam had penetrated black Africa, leaving an indelible trace.

To be sure Kuka was far from Ghana, but from this period marabout proselytizers travelled all through the Sudan. A new factor was to bring about a relatively rapid conversion to Islam of the Songhay: the commercial development of Gao.

Gao, founded by the Sorko and then abandoned by them in favour of Boumba, had become the most practical convenient rallying point for the caravan parties from Tunisia, Tripoli or Egypt, via Tadimekkit and Tikadda. Moslems had come and established themselves there in quite large numbers. And to facilitate trade with Songhay these traders of Gao are said to have asked the Zas to come and settle in Gao. Za Kosoy was the first to settle there, and in 1010, according to Sadi, he was converted to Islam. For this reason he was given the name *moslemdam*, 'he who has embraced Islam voluntarily'.[1]

[1] Translation given by Sadi. I prefer to translate *dam* 'placed', from den or dan, which would give 'placed in Islam' which seems to me, moreover, to suit better the character of this conversion.

This conversion, brought about by itinerant merchants, for primarily commercial interests, could not have been very sincere. The Za no doubt saw nothing more in it than a simple formality, without suspecting that he was thus setting Songhay and the whole of the northern Sudan on a path which was to lead them to destruction. Around Za Kosay, only a few dignitaries must have followed their chief. The conversion, at first, did not change anything with regard to their customs, no Islamic name was given to the seventeen successors of Za Kosoy, whose names have been preserved for us by the chroniclers.

Moreover, if the Za came and settled at Gao, they none the less retained Kika as a 'traditional' capital. The investiture was received there, perhaps because the religious or magic ceremonies which accompanied this assumption of power could proceed far from the gaze of the pious men of Gao.

For the Songhay of this period, through Arab authors, we have the first information to come from outside. Ibn Haukal (tenth century) mentions Gao, El Bekri (1068) speaks about it at greater length, El Bekri never went to the Sudan, but he had good informants, Jewish or Berber merchants. He tells us that Gao (which he called Kaou Kaou 'because their drums made the sound of this word very distinctly') is made up of two towns, 'one is the residence of the king, the other inhabited by the Moslems. Their king is called Kanda'.[1] This shows that the Za, although converted to Islam, lived in the midst of the mass of the Songhay who 'just like the Africans adore idols'. El Bekri then describes the ritual of the king's meal: 'When the king is seated, the drum is beaten and the negresses begin dancing letting their thick hair swing down; no one transacts any business in the town until the king has finished his meal; then the leftovers are thrown into the Nil (Niger) and those present utter cries and exclamations, which announce to the people that the king has finished eating.' This ceremonial meal is similar to that of a king who 'although professing Islamism', and receiving the enthroning in the form of a seal, a koran and a sword, has remained faithful to his ancient beliefs.

Edrissi, writing in 1154, is less clear than El Bekri, but he

[1] This is the title of the old fisher chiefs, no doubt taken up again in the mottoes of the Za (as it will be taken up again by the Chief of the Kibbi).

describes cougha (which to my mind is more likely Kuka than Gao), unexpectedly as a capital of magic:

It is a well populated town, not surrounded with walls, where one finds the products of the arts and the trades necessary to its inhabitants. The women of this town indulge in the practice of magic and it is said that they are very skilful and renowned in this art with the result that one speaks of cougha magic . . .

Thus, in the middle of the twelfth century, the Songhay women had kept their old skills. No doubt they played in the state a role as influential, although secret, as that held today by the old woman Digyel Kasani, patroness of the harvests of the region of Hombori. And it is from these women, their teaching and their initiation, that Sonni Ali, the *Si*, was to obtain the greater part of his irresistible power.

The Songhay Vassal of Mali (*End of the Thirteenth Century–End of the Fourteenth Century*)

It was under the rule of Za Assibai ('the ignorant') that Songhay came under the yoke of Mali.[1]

The Ghana empire ruined by the Almoravids had given way to a Soso state, led by the legendary chief Sumanguru. The Soso tribe occupied approximately the Segou Sassin. Upstream, on the Niger, the Mandings country was also beginning to organize itself; the 'Mali' vied with the Soso. The Mali chief, Sundiata Keita, succeeded, by magical devices, in conquering Sumanguru. He annexed the Soso territory and took Ghana which he destroyed (1240). Mali then extended all along the western basin of the Niger.

Sundiata's successor, Uali, made the first pilgrimage to Mecca about 1260. According to Monteil it was this pilgrimage which afforded the Mali the opportunity to make Songhay its vassal. And, indeed, it is tempting to consider the religious pretext. Islam, in whose interest it was to favour trade with Mali which possessed the gold mines of Tamélé and of Siguiri, used the prestige of the new El Hadj to ask the Za of Gao to submit

[1] It remained in effective subjection during the reign of the last four Za. The duration of these reigns and their exact dates are open to question, either 1260–1275 (Monteil) or 1325–1375 (Delafosse).

to his spiritual authority, thus gaining access to the gold route. At first it was doubtless a question of the free circulation of merchants, through Songhay. It was at this period that traders, the apostles of Mandingo, with Islam began to cross the bend of the Niger in order to penetrate to the still very anarchic tribes of the Hausa.

It was at this moment too that the land west of the bend assumed great importance. The Berbers who frequented this region traded mainly at Firekka, but certain of them had started making their way west to the place called Timbuctoo, where they set down their wares. The development of Mali brought with it the development of this port, the nearest to the western basin, and Timbuctoo became a commercial town of the first importance. A staging post was set up at Djenné: Timbuctoo was in short the outer harbour of Djenné. The transport monopoly no doubt belonged to the Sorko groups of the lake area, and Mali subjugated them.[1]

The duration of the subjugation of Songhay to Mali is not known precisely. Whereas Barth and Delafosse believed that it had lasted from 1325 to 1335 (from Za Assibai to Za Bada), Monteil, basing his argument on documents which neither Barth nor Delafosse knew, deduces that this subjugation took place in two stages: from 1260 (*Mansa* Uali makes Za Assibai his vassal) to 1275 (Ali Kolen flees from the court of *Mansa* Maghan), then from 1290 (reign of *Mansa* Sakura and of Sonni) to 1400 (sack of Mali by Sonni ma Dau). I think that in fact this domination by Mali during the period from the end of the thirteenth to the end of the fourteenth century was essentially fluctuating. Mali was usually the dominant Sudanese state. The subjugation was effective when the *Mansa* had sufficient authority; at other times it was very slack, even non-existent.[2]

It seems necessary here to mention Mali in the fourteenth

[1] From this period dates no doubt the partial servility of the Sorko fishermen or at least a part of this group, for there is a great difference, still very noticeable today, between the rising servility of the boatmen of the west and the pride of the fishermen of the east.

[2] We should note that the domination of Timbuctoo, which was independent of Goa, was no doubt more efficacious. On the other hand the exploitation of the copper mines of Tekadda in the reign of Agades by Mali could very well be carried on without any Songhay intermediary.

century, dominated by the figure of *Mansa* Musa or Kanban Musa (1312–1337). He was one of the greatest zealots of Islam in black Africa; his pilgrimage to Mecca, from 1324–1325, had a considerable repercussion on the Sudan; this was the start of a new era, marked by the economic and social influence of Egypt on the western Sudan. Until then, Al Maqqazi implies, western Sudan was mainly dependant upon Morocco, upon Ifriquia and through them upon the Mediterranean countries. Henceforth the imports from Egypt took on an importance which Ibn Batouta and Ibn Khaldoun both stress: the Mali capital became moreover the metropolis of the west; Oualata 'was no longer anything more than a temporary warehouse . . .' (Monteil). From this period, no doubt, dates the prestige of Mali throughout the Sudan, a prestige which was still to be maintained for a long time despite the vicissitudes of this empire. To this very prestige was due that of Songhay, placed now on a privileged axis on the commercial route from Egypt to the Sudan.

This commercial evolution was bound up with a religious evolution. Musa attempted what the Almoravids had failed to do, namely the systematic conversion to Islam of the whole of the Sudan by means of the sherifs who had come from Arabia, the introduction of Muslim law and customs, and even the introduction of oriental architecture (works of the Andalusian architect Es Sahili). If the chroniclers represent Musa as a very pious Muslim, certain Mande traditions liken him to Makkanta Ayigi the magician who brought back from Mecca the most powerful idols in the Sudan. And here, for the first time, Mecca appears in the double and unusual aspect of a capital of Islam and a capital of magic. I shall speak about this again in the course of this study, but let us note, for the moment, that it is undoubtedly Kankan Musa and his heterogeneous entourage of distinguished persons, courtesans, servants and griots who were the first to introduce into the Sudan the occult beliefs and practices which have always encumbered Islam. When Musa later sincerely tried to diffuse Islam as widely as possible, he spread, unwittingly, oriental magic among Africans greedy for the miraculous. And this magic spread more widely and more deeply than the religion.

Following the death of Musa, Mali prospered for a few years. However, in 1337, the Mosi began to be restless in the centre of the bend of the Niger and made raids on Timbuctoo. Calm was re-established and, in 1352, when Ibn Batouta made his celebrated voyage to the Sudan, he could move about in complete safety in Mali. Having visited Mali (where he notes that Islam is nothing but a façade covering a pagan foundation) he returned via Timbuctoo where he embarked by river for Gao. The Songhay which he describes to us are prosperous, Gao is 'one of the most beautiful of African cities, one of the richest in provisions. One finds there much rice, milk, fowl and fish', and his account seems to imply that Songhay was in effect dependent to a certain extent on Mali.

From 1360 Mali prestige decreased. The *Mansa* no longer held the whole of the territory under their authority; slave-leaders took the title of *Mansa*. In 1400 the Mosi laid waste the commercial centres of the region of Debo. The Songhay, led by Sonni Ma Daou, took possession of the town of Mali and sacked it. In 1431 the Tuareg took Timbuctoo. Mali now existed only in fragments, Songhay was ready to take first place in the Sudan.

The Songhay of the Sonni (Fourteenth–Fifteenth Centuries)

1. *Liberation from Mali*

The first liberation of Songhay is described for us by the *Tarikhs*. The *Mansa* of Mali had the habit of taking children from the chiefs' families and of keeping them at his court as hostages or as ordinary courtiers. Thus the two sons of Za Assibai, Ali Kolen and Souleyman Nari, were employed in Mali as leaders of military expeditions.[1] Ali Kolen, each time he led an expedition, left secret caches of arms along the Gao route; and one day this man 'of well-known bravery, very energetic and very courageous' fled from Mali with his brother; thanks to the cache of arms, he was able to rid himself of his pursuers.

Ali Kolen, having thus returned to Gao, deposed Za Bada and assumed the leadership of the Songhay, with the title of *Sonni* or *Si*. This title probably meant, *koy benindi*, that is 'the one replacing the chief'.

[1] There is a contradiction between the *Tarikhs* and the anonymous addition to the *Fettach*, which says that, 'Ali Kolen was born in Mali and had grown up in the service of the king of Mali'.

In fact, as Delafosse remarks, this was not a new dynasty, but simply a change of title of the descendants of the Berber Zao.

The new dynasty was moreover incapable of maintaining total independence, Gao being too much threatened by Mali, so the Sonni went and established themselves anew at Kuka. During the whole of the fourteenth century, Songhay, though it is described as being particularly prosperous by visiting strangers, remained very small in area, limited to the region of Kuka, and to the immediate neighbourhood of the river, the surrounding bush being always occupied by 'voltaic peoples'.

The first seventeen Sonni, whose names are a curious mixture of Muslim first names and 'pagan' family names, did not leave any important traces in the chronicles. Songhay traditions represent them as '*korte koni*', that is to say witch doctors (perhaps the first were initiated by the companions of Kankan Musa).

Thus driven back upon itself and cut across by external influences, Songhay fortified itself and when it judged its powerful neighbour Mali to be sufficiently weakened, it advanced to the attack.

It was Sonni Ma Dau (or Ma Dogo, that is to say 'Mohhammed the giant') who *c.* 1400 attacked Mali and sacked the town of Mali. He carried off riches which were a precious aid to Songhay finances and thus helped to assure the first richness of this state. But, more important, he liberated twenty-four tribes enslaved by Mali and who, according to Sadi, had 'become vassals of the Mali Koy, at the period when the ancestors of the latter had increased their power and after having themselves held the first Mali Koys under their authority'. This explains the unusual state of servility of certain groups of Sorko fishermen which we have already mentioned. The Sorko groups who had been the first to reach the Djenné region, having conquered the Bozo and the Soninke, were the masters of this area of the river and perhaps even further upstream, keeping the Mali chiefs under their protection. When Mali became more powerful it, in its turn, subjugated these Sorko fishermen and the other groups who had joined them. After more than a century of captivity, when the Songhay delivered them, they once more became part of Songhay, but some remained the property of the chiefs and others were set free.

Translated by Marilyn Beattie

HAET

8. Precursors of Samori

YVES PERSON *Cahiers D'Etudes Africaines* Vol. 4, No. 1, 1963; pages 127–33, 134–9, 139–50 (In translation)

1. *Origin and Diffusion of the Ture 'Dyamu'*[1]

The Ture[2] are normally considered on the Upper Niger to belong to the Manika-Mori. They form a clan of average size which is characterized by its extreme dispersion into countless little groups of descendants in the vast zone which extends from Lower Senegal to the Middle Niger and from the Sahel to the forest. Here and there Ture are to be found in large groups, but these are exceptional cases due to recent events, such as the political upheavals they have caused in the region of Odienne (Ivory Coast).

Dispersion is the rule. This is not surprising when you consider their essentially 'dyoula' characteristic, that is to say the characteristic of being traders and marabouts.

Up until the nineteenth century they do not appear to have had any political role of importance. It is true that it is often written that Ture was the 'dyamu' of the Askia dynasty in Gao, but this is due to a false interpretation made by Delafosse, whom everybody has since copied.[3]

[1] This refers to the clan name.—Ed.

[2] If we adopted Murdock's vocabulary (*Africa*, p. 32) we would have to say 'sib' or 'phratrie', as the name of clan is reserved for a mixed related group living in a defined spot or district. This revolution in vocabulary runs the risk of being a source of confusion and I shall continue to use the word clan in the sense used by Delafosse (*Haut-Senegal-Niger*, III, pp. 98–109) as do all French African scholars. The best of the most recent analyses of the West African clan in relation to lineage are to be found in, Denise Pauline, *Les gens du riz*, Paris, 1964, pp. 72–97 (Kissi) and G. Dieterlen, *Essais sur la religion bambara*, Paris, 1950, pp. 73–85.

[3] A Ture, the Almamy Sire-Hasan, was however in charge of Futa-Toro at the beginning of the nineteenth century, after the Islamic revolution in Abd el Kader; cf. Delafosse and Gaden, *Chronique du Fouta Senegalais*, Paris, 1913, p. 102.

For the origins of the Askia Mohammed, Tarikh-es-Soudan only says that he is called 'Et-Turi, or according to other authors Es-Selenki'. Delafosse interpreted this text by saying that the Askia was a 'Soninke named

We shall see later that there are also Ture who form a caste society.

The Distribution of the Ture

Before looking for the origin of this 'dyamu', it seems necessary to give a precise account of its present geographical distribution. On going from the west, it becomes obvious that Ture is a fairly frequent name amongst the Tukulor, where it is borne by families who are fundamentally marabouts. It is still more widespread amongst the Sarakole, but unevenly: very frequent amongst those in Upper Senegal (Bakel-Guidimaka-Kayes), it is much less so in the Sahel. Almost unknown amongst the Nior peoples, it is only to be found again in the Nara region (Bakunu –Wagadu, Murdya).

The highest density of Ture is to be found on the Middle Niger, between Timbuktu and Bamako, amongst the Marka-Soninke who have been completely assimilated to the Malinka-Bambara. They are numerous in the historic townships of Dya and Djenné. With the river, favourable to traders, forming an axis, the Ture have swarmed somewhat irregularly towards the south, along the routes of Mande penetration towards the forest and the sea. They have settled here and there in Bambara country towards Bugomi and in big groups in the old dyoula centres of Bobo-Diulasso, Bunduku, Kong and Boron. A large

Mohammed, from the group formed by the Silla and son of Abubakar Ture'. This can hardly be possible as Ture and Silla are two noble Soninke clans (Wago) which have nothing in common. The Silla, unlike the Ture, do not descend from Dinga the mythical ancestor of the Soninke. Before his arrival, the Silla are supposed to have been ironsmiths amongst the Dyinu (administrative governments), but there is nothing to prove that they included the Ture.

When Delafosse was writing his *Haut-Senegal-Niger* that has been followed ever since, he did not have at his disposal the Tarikh-el-Fettach, the translation of which he published with Houdas (Leroux, 1913). This text settles the question once and for all. It tells us that the father of the Askia Mohammed 'had as his nickname Arloum and belonged to the Silla clan which, it is said, came originally from the Toro'. The Askia were thus not Ture but Silla who came from Futa-Toro. The mother of the Askia was, it is true, Songhai (a daughter of the chief of Koura, an island that Delafosse situates upstream from Timbuktu).

This document has been known for a long time and Rouch used it correctly (*Contribution à l'histoire des Songhay*, IFAN, Dakar, 1953).

number of animistic clans, such as the Fondyo,[1] tend to become assimilated with them as a result of local alliances. Although their concentration around Odienne is of recent date, they took part in the formation of the old Muslim centre of Kankan, from where they swarmed out along two axes: towards the Kola areas, and in the Kuranko and Konyan.[2]

We began in Tukulor country, outside Mande territory. To be complete, we should also cross the boundaries to the south, for Ture are to be found amongst the Kissi, the Senufo, the Dagomba and also in the east in Bariba country as well as amongst the Songhai and the Jerma.[3] In these peripheral areas they are, however, not very numerous, and are often descended from immigrant families who have finished up by becoming assimilated to their new milieu. And yet this is not always the case and we often find autochthons who have adopted Ture as the equivalent of their national 'dyamu', through a desire to compensate for a feeling of ethnic inferiority. This is a common practice in all the countries of West Sudan.[4]

[1] The Fondyo are to be found in the region of Odienne (Kabasarana, Ivory Coast). The Samake who are particularly numerous around Buguni and in the Eastern Konyan (Guinea) also have the elephant as 'tanna'. This results in there being a tendency for them to identify themselves with the Ture.

[2] Especially around Forecaria in the Susu country. On the other hand, there are few of them amongst the Kuranko; they are limited to the Muslim nucleus of the Niumamandu (Kissidugu, Guinea Republic).

[3] Note is to be made, in Senufo country, of the large nucleus of Kolya (near Boundyali, Ivory Coast), which came in the eighteenth century from Djenné and is mostly assimilated to the milieu. Elsewhere, amongst the Senufo and the Kissi, it is above all a question of an equivalent 'dyamu'.

Amongst the Dagomba and the Bariba, the Ture are normally of Songhai or Jerma origin. Lombard points out that they possess in Bariba country the small chiefdoms of Wawa (Nigeria) and Tunru (Dahomey); cf. Lombard, 'Les Baribas du Nord Dahomey', *BIFAN*, 1957.

There remains the whole of the Songhai-Jerma country where the Ture are numerous. According to Rouch, this name is applied fundamentally to 'Muslims and Arma descendants of the Moroccans', therefore to elements which have come from the river. They were to play a significant role in the expansion of the Jerma across the bend of the Niger in the second half of the nineteenth century. One of them, Mori Ture, was to start off the 'Holy War' in the Taguana and the Djimini and then to found the important centre of Marabadyasa (Ivory Coast, Bouake circle); cf. Rouch, *Les Songhay*, Paris, 1952, and 'Migrations en Ghana', *J.S.A.*, XXVI, 1956.

[4] As an example, Ture is considered amongst the Kissi as being the equivalent of the 'dyamu' Tolno and, amongst the Senufo, of Tuo.

The Ture and Ghana

Since the Upper Senegal and the Upper Niger form the boundaries of this peripheral distribution, a classical diffusionist might be tempted to place the origin of the name in the intermediate region, the Soninke country of the Sahel, although the name is relatively rare there. In fact, this is indeed the case: like the majority of the typically dyoula 'dyamu', Ture is of Soninke origin. In their language the word means 'elephant'. In fact the elephant in certain regions is the taboo (tanna) of the Ture; although it is more rarely so than the python, which dominates all the upper part of the river as far as the Konyan.[1]

In the Wagadou legend, the Ture form one of the authentic Soninke clans and descend from the mythical ancestor Dinga. From his last wife, Singo-Gille-Bune-Kibo, Dinga is said to have had five sons who were the ancestors of a part of the Douaich and the Masna (the Soninke Azer in Mauretania) as well as of the clan Kumma. One of them, Mamadi or Mandya Ture, is the father of the last 'maga' of the Wagadu, Ture Khankhedyaba.[2] This Mandya is considered to be the ancester of all the Ture, including casts such as the Dyongo (cobblers) and the Dyaresi (ironsmiths). After the fall of Ghana, the two sons of Khankhedyaba are said to have separated. Dindin Ali went towards the west and is supposed to be the origin of the Ture in the Bondu and Tukulor country, and Silmanganda, who went towards the east, is supposed to be the founder of the Ture of the Mande, including the Samori.

These legends agree with what we are able to reconstruct of the past elsewhere. However little we may know about the

[1] The python is Samori's 'tanna'. Marty noticed, unlike Arcin following Binger, that the 'tanna' keeps its importance in areas which have been converted to Islam. Delafosse's observation (op. cit., III, p. 109) seems to be very localized.

The second characteristic of the 'dyamu', the 'senakuya', the joking relationship, a cathartic affinity, to use Griaule's terminology, is extremely particularized.

[2] He is also called Mandya Lagare Ture. He is the only 'maga' of this name, the others are Sise, as at a later date were the Sovereigns (Tunka) of Ghana. It must be remembered that the Tunkara (or Samura, Dukure, Dyarisa) are not, as it is so often written, connected with the clan of the 'Tunka' ('Emperor' of Ghana) but with that of the 'kusa', or captive chiefs.

history of Ghana,[1] it is certain that this Soninke state[2] was born from trans-Saharan trade, especially the gold trade. An indication of this is the predominance of the 'dyamu' of Soninke origin amongst the Dyoula. It shows their essential role in the organization of long-distance trade within a world of which the structure was, up to then, closed local collectivities such as are to be found right up to this century amongst the last of the Paleonegritics. During the period that Ghana was a strong force and after its fall, the network of organized trade moved gradually towards the south and east. The old word 'wangara' is still used by the Hausa to refer to Mande society. It is normal that the agents of this revolution decided to follow, from their country of origin, the gold routes: towards the Upper Senegal, in the direction of the Bambuk, towards the Upper Niger, and in the direction of the Boure. These are precisely the zones where the Ture are distributed.

The Ture and Marka

The Ture of the Niger, who alone retain our interest, probably reached the river over a large area well before the fall of the Empire (eleventh century).[3]

According to Monteil, the nobles (Wago) lived in the area of Lake Debo while different clans, such as the Kummo and the Sako, settled upstream, near Ségou, around the old centre of Sama that Sansanding was to replace much later.

But it is in the centre, at the southern limit of the Masina which is subject to flooding, that they concentrated, creating the old centres of Nono and Dya, whence was to emerge later Djenné. The region was probably populated by the Bozo, and

[1] The best account is still by Mauny, 'Etat actuel de la Question de Ghana', *BIFAN*, 1951, pp. 463–75, brought up to date in his thesis 'Tableau Geographique de l'Ouest Africain au Moyen Age', *MIFAN*, No. 61, Dakar 1961.

[2] I keep the name of Soninke for the Sarakole as this is in fact the one they use themselves. Delafosse explains it by 'Soni' (dispersion) and in this case it should not be earlier than the Middle Ages (*La langue mandingue*, t. 2, Paris, 1955). Care must be taken not to confuse this word with the word soninke (from so-sacrifice, soninke-sacrificer) which is used on the Upper Niger, without any ethnic sense, to make the distinction between the animistic Malinke and the Muslims. Soninke is then the synonym of 'sorogi' or 'totigi' that are to be found in the Ivory Coast.

[3] For the moment I respect Delafosse's dating.

further to the south by the Bwa (Bobo-Oule). It became a focal point where the old routes of the Sahelm, the one from Ghana and one from Timbuktu, extended by river navigation, were to meet. This characteristic of being a crossroads of communications was to be strengthened from the fourteenth century onwards by the opening up of the bend of the Niger, in the direction of the Mossi and the new gold areas in the Volta basin.

In this way various Soninke clans, amongst them the Mana, the Sise and the Ture, from which the Diabu would have separated at a later date, formed the nucleus of the Nono. These, in symbiosis with the Bozo fisherfolk, form until now the basis of the population in the South Masina. It is arbitrary to make a distinction between them and the Marka.[1] This term, used by the Bambara, and with some variants (Maraba, Marba) by the non-Mande peoples of the bend of the Niger to mean the Soninke in general, has assumed very different meanings. Sometimes it ends up by covering the whole of the commercial peoples of northern origin, including the Hausa and even by being exclusively used for the latter (Middle Ivory Coast, Republic of Ghana), sometimes it is restricted to the region of the South Masina and to its neighbouring settlements, such as the Dafinin in Upper Volta.

In fact, the only criterion which enables a distinction to be made for the Marka is that they tend to be more urbanized and more mobile and hence more Islamized than the Nono. They are characterized by an exceptionally large number of 'dyamu' which denotes their composite origin. They come from countless stocks of all origins brought together by their commercial activities in this old meeting point of the South Masina.

Their chief centres are, of course, Dya, which seems to date from before the eleventh century, and Djenné, which only seems to have crystallized in the fourteenth century, when the

[1] There is a good study of the Nono in Monteil, *Djenné*, Paris, 1932. Maraba like Marka comes from the Mande root 'mara' (an expanse without a river, a Sahel). Maraba 'Great Sahel' refers to the country to the east of the bend of the Niger and finally assumes the meaning of 'Hausa'. 'Mariba' is then in opposition to 'Mara' which still applies to the Western Sahel (the old country of Ghana) and which gives 'Mara-ka', by adding the ethnic suffix -ka. The two terms 'Maraba' and 'Marka', originally very distinct, tend to be frequently confused in use (cf. Delafosse, *La langue mandingue*).

routes in the bend of the Niger were opened.[1] But naturally, the Marka or Nono have swarmed all along the river, from Timbuktu to the Mande. They are to be found especially in the lake area, round Nyafunke (Nunu, Sumpi) and to the east of Lake Debo, in the Korombana of which the chief town, Korientze, is an old Marka centre. On the actual shore of the lake, the village of Dyindyo, eight kilometres to the north-west of Gurao, numbers amongst its Marka some Ture, from amongst whom came the ancestors of Samori.

Thus by indulging in their mission of spreading trade, the Soninke-Marka became radically changed. First of all, they lost the use of their language in favour of a Malinke-Bambara dialect which, after various transformations, was to give rise to the Dafin of Upper Volta and to the Dyoula of the bend of the Niger.[2] This linguistic revolution undoubtedly took place in the twelfth and thirteenth centuries as a result of the military hegemony of the Malinke, which coincided with the decline of the old routes from the Sahel towards Ghana in favour of the Timbuktu route and, as a result, led to the complete predominance of the fluvial axis. In any case, when from the fourteenth century onwards the Dyoula, for the most part from South Masina originally, left the familiar banks of their river to penetrate towards the forest, they no longer spoke Soninke.

Islam and Trade

Elsewhere, they had become Muslims. Tradition places round about 1300 the conversion of the chief of Djenné, but the

[1] Mauny (1961), it seems to me, gives too early a date to the opening of the routes in the bend of the Niger. There can be little doubt that this fact is linked, if not with the foundation, at least with the urbanization of Djenné.

[2] It is worthy of note that the Soninke, in spite of the pride they attach to their origin, have shown signs for a long time of a weak linguistic identity. In any case Lavergne de Tressan mistakenly puts the South Massina and the Dafin country in the domain of the Soninke language. Reading Monteil (1932) should have been sufficient to prevent him from doing so.

To the North of Lake Debo, the same thing applies. But this time, the little Nono islands that we mentioned near Nyafounke have abandoned their language in favour of Songhai and no longer Malinke. This goes back to the sixteenth and seventeenth centuries, during the hegemony of Gao and the Timbuktu pashalik. It is at that time that the town of Djenné itself partially adopted the Songhai language. Dyindo is at the limit of the zones of expansion of the two languages.

process linking Islam with trade is certainly much older. This religion, the prophet of which was a caravaneer from the Quraysh tribe, readily adjusts to an atmosphere of city trading. Since the commercial life of the Soninke of Ghana had been formed by contact with the trans-Saharan trade, it is certain that the autochthonous traders were converted to Islam long before the political class. They must have felt from the beginning the incompatibility of their ancestral religions, connected with a restricted area, with a life made up of moving from one place to another. The process which today tends towards the general Islamization of the masses uplifted from the roots they have formed over the last thousand years, certainly began, on a smaller scale, within these early communities of traders. Although it is impossible to give a date to the stages, the revolution seems to have been complete by the thirteenth century and it was through the traders 'wangara', that is to say the Mande, that Islam was to make its first appearance in Hausa country towards the year 1350.

It was of course with these neighbours converted to Islam that the Berber caravaneers and the Maghreb traders intermarried, if they settled in the area. These influxes of northern blood seem to have been small in number but constant, especially along the edge of the Sahel and on the commercial axis of the river. Racially, these white elements have been completely absorbed, as is shown by the well-known example of the Arma. On the other hand, they account for the traditions of eastern origin which are to be found so frequently amongst the Marka and the Dyoula. They must not be taken literally, but neither can they be totally rejected.

Once Islam was firmly implanted, religious life very quickly tended to become separate from commercial life and to the traders of northern origin was added an increasing flow of holy people and of doubtful shereefs who were also absorbed into the mass of African people and, helped by the snobbery of the people, spread the oriental traditions.

It seems established that the Ture were one of the Soninke elements which were among the earliest and most strongly converted to Islam. With their relations, the Diabu, they made Dya, long before Djenné, one of the most active centres of Islamic influence in Black Africa.

Maghreb Influences

The marabout characteristic of the Ture explains the frequent occurrence in this clan of traditions of white origin which seem to contradict our account of its Soninke origins.

The oldest written mention of the name Ture comes from Ibn Battuta who, when passing through Dya in 1353, makes reference to the presence of wangara (Mande) traders alongside white Muslims of the Ibadite rite who were called 'Saganogo' and of orthodox Malekites called 'Touri'. The fact that these people had adopted African 'dyamu' leads me to follow Marty's interpretation, which considers them to be not Magrebins but descendants of white traders who had settled and married in the area.

Amongst the Hausa, who mark the eastern boundary of our enquiry, 'ture' is no longer a 'dyamu' but a word 'bature' (pl. 'turawa') which is used to refer to everybody of white stock, Arabs as well as English. Since this word is not explained by a Hausa root, Barth, who says that it is of recent introduction, wanted to link it up with the Peul word 'tura' to pray.[1] In fact, the Peul verb 'turade' does not mean exactly 'to pray' but to bend right forward. I think that this word does not come from the Peul but from the Soninke 'dyamu', and if it is of recent introduction, this took place at a time when on the Upper Niger the name of Ture was often held by families which had a little white blood.[2]

[1] Barth, *Travels* (London, 1858), t. I, p. 471. It should be pointed out while on this subject that Ture is the name of one of the 'pagan' paleonegritic tribes pushed back on to the Butchi plateau. It has about 16,000 members. It is apparently a purely onomastic coincidence.

[2] Ibn Battuta testifies in the sixteenth century to this tendency to christen Ture the peoples of white origin and the first Muslim groups (Mande as it happens) which appeared in Hausa country at about this time. It thus seems hardly possible to trace the adoption of this word further back. I tend to place it in the sixteenth century at the time when the Askia did their utmost to subject the Hausa to their suzerainty, or even in the seventeenth century when the assimilation process of the Maghreb elements on the Upper Niger was at its peak.

As for the neighbouring populations who use the root 'tur' to describe the white people (Nupe, Kapa, Ebe, Kambali, Nuru, Moni), they have probably borrowed it from the Hausa. The Kanuri, who are by far the most important, should be added to this list.

Indeed, Rouch affirms that in Songhay country, the 'dyamu' Ture, which is not in any case widespread, is borne by the 'muslims or the descendants of the Arma'.

It does not seem unlikely that from 1591 to 1670, as long as the Moroccan pashalik of Timbuktu retained some links with the Morocco of the Saadians, an exceptional influx of peoples from the Maghreb took place, especially on the fluvial axis and upstream as far as Djenné. Apart from the military and administrative element, we know that this migration included a large number of religious elements from South Morocco, amongst whom some claimed they were shereefs. Some of the families which descend from these immigrants and women of the area seem to have adopted the 'dyamu' of Ture. Apart from the Arma in the region of Timbuktu, we find them all along the river upstream and although the area has not been the subject of a systematic study, it is possible to follow the history of some families.

Thus at Djenné, two Ture families, which provide the chiefs of the Sankore and Farmentalla districts, are said to be the descendants of Arma who were stationed in the town at the time of the pashalik.

Further to the south, at Bamako, the first French reports describe as 'Moors' the powerful Ture families of the town. It seems beyond dispute that these two families, who described themselves as 'Twati' and 'Darawe' respectively, had as ancestors people who came from the south of Morocco, probably in the sixteenth century. The fact remains that they had already been firmly planted in Djenné for a long time when, towards the end of the eighteenth century, they joined with the Nyare of Bakoma and helped to make that town into an important commercial centre.

In conclusion, it must be borne in mind that a 'Mande' clan includes a host of branches of local families who only have in common a name ('dyamu'), and not always a taboo ('tanna'). They do not have to be related, all the more so since some are in castes and others not. In the last analysis all is reduced to a

In conclusion, it should not be forgotten that some people have sometimes explained 'tur' by the name of the town of Tyr which would have been generalized to describe all the Syrians (cf. M. D. W. Jeffreys, 'How ancient is West African Maize?' *Africa*, Vol. XXXIII, No. 2, April 1963).

vague feeling of solidarity, which is nevertheless very useful for traders obliged to be always on the move and in need of friends almost everywhere. The 'dyamu' is not transferred by hereditary principle alone: the captives willingly adopt that of their master and unattached strangers that of their host in order to mark their desire to be accepted. We have seen that the Soninke legend places alongside the Ture, as children of the same mother, the Masna or Soninke-Azer of the Awkar[1] and a part of the Dwaich. Although the latter were unquestionably Soninke, assimilated by the Moors from the twelfth century onwards, it can be deduced that the Ture have long been considered as being in especially close relationship with elements of the white race, hence with trade and with Islam. Now, it is manifestly impossible to become integrated into the Mande society without adopting a 'dyamu', which is correctly speaking an 'honorable name' with all the socio-religious consequences that it implies (tanna, senanku, etc.). Forced to choose a name, the half-caste children of these Maghreb peoples must have often chosen in favour of Ture and, class-consciousness playing its part, the authentic Ture certainly seized this opportunity of adopting the tradition of eastern origins. It is of course impossible to distinguish the cases where this tradition may have an element of truth.[2]

2. *From the Middle to the Upper Niger*

The paternal ancestors of Samori were part of the Diula current which, leaving the Marka home of the Masina, went up the river and its tributaries as far as the edges of the forest and finally reached the sea in the eighteenth century, between the Rio Pongo and Sierra Leone.

[1] Here again snobbery plays a role, bringing into action the equivalencies of name and leading to assimilation. It is to these Masna that the Chronicle of Oualata and Nema (Marty, *Revue des Etudes Islamiques*, 1927, III and IV) allude on the subject of the wars between the Bambara of Segu and Kaarta. It is through a mistranslation that Tauxier finds the confirmation of his theory on the origin of the Bambara kings in whom he wrongly sees the Peul of the Masina; cf. Tauxier, *Histoire des Bambara*, Paris, 1942, pp. 112 et seq.

[2] It is, however, possible in some families whose origins can be traced back to the seventeenth or eighteenth century. Even in this case, the proportion of Maghreb blood is now negligible, since the ancestor came alone.

By leaving Masina for the mysterious territories of the south, Marka became Diula. The origin of this name is not known and the etymology proposed by Delafosse is hardly satisfactory. It will be sufficient to stress that it is not regarded as a proper noun but as a common one.[1]

Diula-ke-bara and diugo-ke-bara are indifferently used in the sense of trader and it is not proven, as Delafosse would have it, that they are derived from an ethnic name. On the contrary, it appears that the ethnic sense is recent and secondary. In fact, the Diula are considered as a nation only in the areas of the bend of the Niger to be found mainly to the east of Bagoe and the Bandama, where they have developed a special Mande dialect, of which the type is the language of Kong. In this area, the Diula form enclosed nuclei within the peoples of the Volta. This enables them to resist the environment in which they find themselves.[2]

To the west, on the other hand, Islam and trade remained linked, but the name 'diula' has no ethnic meaning and does not appear ever to have had any. It is purely a professional name. The Muslim traders are one professional group among many others, within an animistic but Mande population from whom no cultural boundary separates them. The Diula, on the same footing as the smiths or the weavers, accompanied the Sugu,[3] animistic Mande warriors, at the time of the vast

[1] Gyu (dyu) 'foundation, founder', 'diula', 'those of the foundation', for they claim to descend from the most eminent noble families of the former Sudanese kingdoms (Delafosse, 1955, op. cit.). In the mind of those using the language the word is regarded as an exact synonym of 'diugo', 'trader'. If we reject this idea, the radical 'dya' can have a pejorative sense 'beneath, inferior'. One can also think of 'dyo', 'law or trial', which would not be surprising as it is about traders. I believe, however, instead of looking for difficulties where there are none, it suffices to refer to 'dyo', 'to take place regularly, to frequent' (a market), 'logo dyola', 'he who frequents the markets'' (logo). (Cf. *Dictionnaire Bambar-Français* by Mgr. Morin, Les presses missionnaires, 1955.)

[2] This originality is purely cultural. On the plane of physical anthropology, the Diula appear on the contrary to be completely assimilated to the milieu of the Volta; cf. Paels, 'Raciologie comparative des populations de l'Afrique Occidentale', *Bulletins et Memoires de la Société D'Anthropologie de Paris*, t. IV, 10 série, p. 259.

[3] Soogyi, sorogyi, sononi, 'he who follows the ceremonies of the Sono', therefore an animistic. Delafosse, op. cit., 1955. The etymology relating the

movements towards the south which, from the sixteenth to the eighteenth century, accompanied the dislocation of the Empire of Mali.

The Ture on the Middle Niger

The migration of the Ture upstream along the Niger enables us to follow this movement and to a certain extent to know their aims. The oral traditions I was able to collect at Siguir, Kankan, Kissidugu, Beyla and Odienne all tell the same story. They enable us to link up the genealogy of Samori and the Ture of Kabasarana (Odienne). The last six generations before Samori and Vakaba are presented with enough accuracy and agreement for us to consider them as being historical. This takes us back to the end of the seventeenth century. Beyond that we enter the realm of myth.

The first ancestor, Magandyu, would be placed at the end of the fifteenth century, if we count thirty years per generation. We are told that he came from the Yemen and his children settled down successively at Timbuktu, Djenné, then at Sidikilia, according to one version; at Guindio, or Gurao, Dya, or Djenné, then at Sidikila according to others. In fact there is no contradiction; Dya and Djenné are the twin towns of the South Masina, both of them have a large number of Ture and they are socially and intellectually similar. If one leaves from the lakes to go up the upper river one has to stop off in Dya or Djenné. Guindio is manifestly the place of origin of the families of Samori and of Vakaba. Ture are still to be found there.

As for the Yemenite origin, it could obviously account for a Maghreb ancestor come by way of Timbuktu. I doubt this, however, for the reconstructed genealogy, which does not appear completely fictitious, takes us back to the fifteenth century, that is to say more than a hundred years before the creation of the pashalik of Timbuktu and the establishment of a relatively high number of white people on the Niger. The mention of Timbuktu probably refers to the whole region,

word to the 'sunna' (Bernus, 'Kong', *Etudes Eburneennes*, t. VIII, Abidjan, 1960) is a fine example of Islamizing snobbery. Soogyi and totigi (from 'to'—custom) are synonyms in the Upper Ivory Coast. They are in opposition to 'silama' (muslim). On the Upper Niger the corresponding expressions are 'Soninke' and 'Maninkamori'.

including the area of the lakes. It would simply be the substitution of the name of a famous town for the obscure village of Guindio. Moreover Magandyu and his children have purely Mande names. We may ask whether Magandyu is not simply a deformation of 'Mandya', the mythical ancestor of the Ture of the Wagadu.[1]

It remains an established fact that a branch of Ture, probably of pure Soninke origin, has lived for a long time on the east bank of Lake Debo, which marks the mid-way point on the Timbuktu–Djenné route. Towards the end of the sixteenth century, it decided to move upstream and after a period at Djenné, came on to found Sidikila in Mande country.

The Sidiki Ture and Gold Digging

Sidikila, which in 1958 had 1,287 inhabitants, is a large village on the left bank of the Sankarani, on the frontier of the Republic of Mali and the Republic of Guinea, in the ex-canton of Dyumawanya. The founder who gave it its name, Sidike Ture, seems to be the first historical character of the clan. Reckoning thirty years per generation his date of birth can be put about 1590 and the founding of the village in the first half of the seventeenth century. Sidikila is about fifteen kilometres from Niani, which is the supposed site of the ancient capital of Mali. However, when the Ture arrived, it seems that the area, ravaged by the Fulani invasions of the sixteenth century, was sparsely inhabited. It was in the process of being colonized by descendants of the Keita tribe whose chief Masagbere had founded Kamaro about the beginning of the century. The Ture, being traders and marabouts, held no political command. A Keita branch, headed by Nandubane, the son of Masagbere, came to carry out this task.

[1] Ma is in fact only a contraction of maga, a variant of the old Soninke title that we have met before and which remains in Susu in the form maga; maga-dya thus means 'the long lord' (dya) whereas maga-dyu is 'the bad lord' (wicked).

The other names of the genealogy need little commentary. 'Fabu', 'the father who grows' (who is spreading out), is a normal equivalent of brema. (Ibrahim is contracted to brema when another noun is prefixed to it.) Silimaga—silama—maga—'the muslim Chief'. Feremanano—fere is the name given to children who are born howling (fere—howl); manano stands for 'man of the "brush"' (mana—wild vegetation).

Sidiki seems to have been an outstanding man. He is still remembered not only among his descendants but in all Mande territory, right up to Bamako. One may wonder how this Diula reached such prosperity in a country which is semi-arid and ruinous. The tradition has it that he dug for gold. The Mali-Guinea frontier zone near Kouremale, to the north of the Niger (and that between Niger and Sankarani), is in fact a traditional gold-digging area scarcely less important than the Bure area. In 1957 the nearest diggings being worked were near Koniakokoun, thirty kilometres north of Sidikila. According to Kela tradition Sidiki went still further afield. Thus, with the agreement of the Keita, he is said to have started the diggings at Kofoulate on the north bank, about forty kilometres west of Kaaba (Kangaba).

If we admit Sidiki's interest in gold digging it is logical that this trader of the Masina should have gone off to the sources of the gold supply to organize the production which had been jeopardized by the invasions of the sixteenth century.

The two most famous lines of the Ture, the Vakaba of Odienne branch and the Samori branch, claim to be descended directly from Sidiki by genealogies which seem accurate and trustworthy. It is clear that a rich and powerful man like Sidiki must have had a large family, and that his dependents would not have hesitated to adopt his dyamu. We cannot be sure therefore about the direct line of descent from Sidiki to Samori or Vakaba. But the sociological line of descent, which is the only one that need concern us, is beyond doubt.

There are three fundamental clans in Sidikila. The third is represented by the line which is more recent and descends from Foundo Dumbuya (Kuruma).

Right up to today the marabouts of the village are Ture, more or less direct descendants of Sidiki. Since the village has become totally Islamized—this happened in 1940—they provide the Iman, the chief, of course, being a Kete.

The Ture on the Upper Niger

Leaving the Vakaba line, which was to remain fixed at Sidikila until the middle of the eighteenth century, we turn next to the fortunes of the Ture on the Upper Niger.

If one accepts the genealogies, it was in the second half of the seventeenth century that various lines of the Ture joined the Kaba, the founders of Kankan, in this town and in several villages in the Bate area. Some of them say they came directly from Djenné, others say from Sidikila. They fell into the habit of referring to themselves by the name of Situru, which may be considered as being synonymous with Ture.

The spread of this clan is thus linked with the development of Kankan, the metropolis of the Maninka-Mori. This development in turn is bound up with a massive population movement of the Malinke towards the south, following on the disasters of the fifteenth and sixteenth centuries, which took two main directions. First, it sought out forests, on the edges of which kola trees were to be found producing kola, and to a lesser extent the gold-diggings of the Toma country. Then, especially from the seventeenth and eighteenth centuries onwards, it sought to open up routes towards the European trading posts of the coast, reversing the thousand-year-old flow of trans-Saharan trade.

Both of these movements began from Kankan. The second came into its own during the eighteenth century when Islam was victorious in the Fouta-Djalon. Among the Maninka-Mori, who from then on spread along the southern rivers, are many Ture from the Bate area. Some of them settled among the Susu and adopted their language. Then, however, they began to Islamize the country, particularly in the Mellacoree (the circle of Forecaria in the Republic of Guinea). At the beginning of the nineteenth century, Buari Fode Ture felt himself strong enough to start a minor holy war, inaugurating the line of the Almami of Morea.

Towards the forests one finds the Maninka-Mori in two regions: in the Kouranko country, where they run the kola markets of Kisi; and in Konyan, from where they go to trade with the Toma, Guerze and Dan. The Ture seem to have preferred the routes to the coast, and are not strongly represented in this area. In Nyumamandu they occupy a part of the village of Lero. In north Konyan some Ture lines are dispersed among villages of Kamara animists, with whom they are closely intermingled. This is the environment which was to produce Samori.

The Ture in Konyan

These Ture of Nyumamandu and Konyan all say they come from Binko. This little village of 173 inhabitants stands on territory which belongs not to the Kaba of Bate but to the Konde of Sakara Gberedugu. Sociologically it is a satellite of the old Muslim city at the junction of the route which goes towards the sea via Farana and Falaba and the route to Kisi country.

Binko, even today, is inhabited almost entirely by Ture. It is true that they are divided among several branches, and that the branch of the founder does not come from Sidikila. The village indeed is said to be very old, dating from before the foundation of Kankan. It would go back, therefore, at least to the sixteenth century. According to the tradition of the Konde, Faramani, after founding Sakara, went east to visit his brother Mansa-Brema, the ancestor of the Kone of Konyan. When he arrived at the site of what is now Binko, he met the great marabout Kyeni Ture who had come directly from Djenné. They formed an alliance, the Ture becoming the Muslims of the Konde.

If one accepts the genealogies, it was in the course of the seventeenth century that Amadu, the 'son' of Sidiki, left the valley of the Sankarani and came to join the Ture who had been long established at Binko. It is he who is always claimed as their ancestor by Samori. Still reckoning thirty years per generation, his children Binko-Mori and Oumiri-Ba would have been born at Binko about 1650.

Now we find ourselves on firmer ground. The last ancestors of Samori have clear characteristics which enable us to identify them as individuals. For, according to tradition, they settled in a particularly localized area. Fabon, the son of Binko-Mori, established himself in Konyan.

Among the Suga who occupied this vast zone when the power of the Mali Empire was declining, a first wave, including the Koni and the Konate, settled fairly quickly between the Niger and the Dyon. A second wave, in which the Kamara were dominant, can, by cross references with European data, be dated with some accuracy from the sixteenth and seventeenth centuries. It first went in the direction of the Mau in the present-day Ivory Coast, then flowed back towards the west, driving back the Koni in various places, and made Konyan its chosen land. Among their numerous lines, the Fandiarasi were centred on the upper Dyon, while the Fe semenesi, after occupying the Milo valley, went in the direction of the sea, penetrated deeply among the Toma on the Atlantic slopes, from Makona to Diani (Saint-Paul). The chiefs of the Konianke who had resided at Dumbadu from the eighteenth century are Fe semenesi. They had set up, a kilometre away from their village, the great market of Lofero, which was in the nineteenth century one of the principal centres for buying kola and also slaves.

After bold raids which took them right to the sea in the seventeenth century, all these people had settled down and become broken up into small dyamana, solidly established in their territories and very closed societies. Their animism had lost many of the old Sudanese structures, but had developed new forms, by borrowing from their new neighbours, the Senufa, Toma or Kisi. The Muslim groups which had followed the migration had become settled in their functions as marabouts and traders. They lived apart, concentrated in large villages at the edge of the kola zone, particularly in Konyan, the high broad plateau which surrounds Beyla and Musadugu. Following the 'customs of Musadugu' they were the Silama (Muslims) of the Kamara, who owed the kola protection.

The Stabilization of the Ancestors of Samori

It was in this complex and already rigorously fixed group of peoples that Fabu Ture was to come and settle in the early years of the eighteenth century. We are told that he left Binko, accompanied by his captive Kama, laden with a bundle of Arab manuscripts. He established himself on the northern limit of Konyan, in Blamana, on the high plateau which stretches between the mountains of Simandu and the upper stretches of the Dion. He married the grand-daughter of Sirikiyo Kone, the chief of Kofilakoro, and lived with his father-in-law.

Two of his sons, Makesa and Yaba, remained at Kofilakoro, where their descendants live to this day. The third, Valfere, quarrelled with his family, following a misalliance, and went to live twenty kilometres further on, in Bambadugu. He settled with the Kamara of Manyanbaladugu. His descendants remained in this place for more than a century, until Samori, of whom Vafere is the great-great-grandfather.

Four generations lived in the same village. This is a far cry from Diula mobility. The genealogies which we possess bring out one essential fact: Ture marry exclusively from among the animists who received them. At least all the marriages mentioned by tradition are of this type. Fabu set the example by marrying the daughter of Sirikiyo. It is true that we do not know whom Vafere married, but there is no reason to believe that she was an outsider. Subsequently all the known marriages were with Kamara. Karfa married a woman from some distance away, Sa Kamara of Dumbadu, the daughter of a Konyanko chief. Their son Samorigbe found his bride nearer at hand: he married Dianka, the daughter of Fadima-Kisya, the chief of Lenko. The child to whom she gave birth between 1800 and 1810, Lafiya Ture, is well known. The five women whom he married came from villages situated less than thirty kilometres from his home. Among them we find the daughter of a minor village chief, Masorona Kamara of Fandugu, who became the mother of Samori.

We therefore accept the evidence. These Ture not only settled in this area: they were genetically assimilated. Not far off, towards Odienne, and in Konyan, round Beyla, we find Muslim lines evolving differently. The reason was that the Ture of Sameitigila, like the Dore or the Kuruma of Musadugu, if they took root in animist country, did not spread themselves among the native villages. They remained grouped in big Muslim villages, and in the great majority of cases were endogamous. But the ancestors of Samori, isolated individuals or small families scattered among the animist mass, were too few in number to remain independent. They could only become accepted by inter-marriage with their pagan neighbours, and this was what they did. With each generation the stream of Maninka-Mori blood grew thinner, and when Samori was born the process was more or less complete. The heredity of our hero came from the Kamera, to a lesser extent from the Konate and the Koni, but much less from the Ture.

Their assimilation into the milieu went forward at the same speed on the spiritual plane as on the sociological. Fabu was probably a healing marabout. It is probable also that the knowledge of writing disappeared in his time, although his descendants did not necessarily adopt immediately the habits of settled farmers. Karfa married Sa Kamara, whose native village Dumbadu was less than two kilometres from Lofero, the biggest kola market in the region, and one may suppose that he had gone there to trade. His son Samorigbe occasionally traded among the diula. This is confirmed by the tradition which tells us that Lafiya was born at Konokoro in the Worodugu, where her parents happened to be travelling. As for Samori's father we are told that in his youth he went to buy kola in the forest: it was in this way that he formed a friendship with Konyamorif ig Sware, the famous marabout of Nyonsomoridugu. It is true that later the tradition represents him as positively settled down and very much against the first signs of trouble-making by his son.

This progressive tendency to settle confirms the evidence yielded by the marriages that were made in this ever decreasing area. Once settled the Ture seem to have prospered. Their fortune was based chiefly on cattle, the most common form of wealth in black Africa. In Konyan, whose high plateaux free from the tsetse fly are favourable to stock-breeding, the farmers always had many cattle, and the strong wave of Fulani immigration at the end of the eighteenth century considerably increased this livestock. It is significant that several times the tradition stresses Lafiya's wealth in cattle. Settled at Manyaubaladugu, with his great herds and five wives, all of whom had their dowry before the age of thirty, he was certainly a rich and influential person. His maternal relatives, the Kamara, had someone to reckon with.

Translated by Dr Keith Cameron and Dr S. I. Lockerbie

9. The Question of Ghana

R. A. MAUNY *Africa* Vol. 24, 1954 Oxford University Press for International African Institute; pages 201–5, 207–12

. . . The first unequivocal mention of Western Sudan dates from Arab times and is to be found in Ibn Abd Al Hakam (A.D. 803–70), who speaks of an expedition made *c.* A.D. 734 in

Southern Morocco (Sus) and Sudan: 'Ubaïd Allah gave to Habib ben Ubaïda the command of an expedition in Sûs and Sûdân; that chief had an immense success and seized a considerable amount of gold. . . .' Less than twenty years later the son of the same Habib, Abd-er-Rahman ibn Habib, organized the caravan route between Southern Morocco and Aoudaghost by digging new wells.[1]

Ibn Al Hakam does not speak of Ghana, although in his time (before A.D. 870) it was already known. The first to mention it is the astronomer Al Fazari who, writing shortly before A.D. 800, enumerates several African countries and refers to 'the territory of Ghana, the land of gold'; then comes Al Khwarizmi, the geographer (before A.D. 833), who places Ghana on his map which is, in fact, merely a copy of Ptolemy's.

Yakoubi (A.D. 872) mentions 'the king of Ghana, a great king; in his territory are gold-mines and he has under his domination a great number of kingdoms'.

A century later, Ibn Hawqal (*c.* 977), who had visited Aoudaghost, says that 'the kings of this town have relations with the king of Ghana, who is the richest on the earth because of his gold'. Then comes El Bekri (1067), our best source of information for the medieval Western Sudan, whose *Description de l'Afrique Septentrionale* is well known. It is advisable to give extracts from his account of Ghana since the text is not easily accessible. He wrote:

Ghana is the title of the kings of that people; the name of the country is Aoukar. . . .[2] Ghana consists of two towns situated in a plain. The one inhabited by Muslims is very big and includes 12 mosques. . . . In the neighbouring country are wells giving water for the inhabitants and near which vegetables are cultivated. The town the king lives in is six miles away and is called *El Ghaba*, which means 'the forest'. The territory between the two towns is covered with

[1] El Bekri, 1913, pp. 296–8. The *Kitab al Istibar* (*c.* A.D. 1192), adapted from El Bekri, speaks of this same road and says that it went from Draa river to Ghana. A prehistoric road used by carts followed roughly the same itinerary.

[2] Aoukar is a sandy region of South Mauritania, roughly in the polygon El Kheddia-Tichit-Ualata-Nema-Timbedra. Kumbi Saleh is just south of it, in a region of fixed sand dunes. It is difficult to distinguish between Aukar, Hodh, and Uagadu.

dwellings. The houses are built of stone and wood. The king's palace is composed of a castle and round roofed huts, the whole being surrounded by an enclosure similar to a wall. In the king's town, not far from the royal court, is a mosque where the Muslims coming to fulfil missions to the prince come to pray. . . . The king's town is surrounded by huts, woods and groves in which live the priests of the nation who look after the religion. They have placed there their idols and the graves of their kings. Men are put in charge of these woods to prevent anyone coming in or seeing what is going on inside. There are also the king's prisons; when a man is enclosed therein he is never heard of again.

The king's interpreters, the controller of his treasury, and the majority of his vizirs are chosen from among the Muslims. The only persons who are allowed to wear tailored clothes are the king and his heir-presumptive, that is to say, the son of his sister; persons following the prince's religion wear cotton, silk or brocade cloth, according to their means. All men shave their beards, and women their heads. The king is adorned, as the women are, with collars and bracelets; as a head-dress they wear several gilded bonnets, surrounded by very fine cotton cloths. When he gives audience to his people, to listen to their complaints and set them to rights, he [the king] sits in a pavilion around which stand his horses caparisoned in cloth of gold; behind him stand ten pages holding shields and gold-mounted swords; on his right are the sons of the princes of his empire, splendidly clad and with gold plaited into their hair. The governor of the town sits on the ground before the king surrounded by the vizirs, also sitting on the ground. The entrance to the pavilion is guarded by thoroughbred dogs which almost never leave the place where the king is; they have gold and silver collars with bells of the same metals. The beginning of the royal session is announced by the noise made by a kind of drum which they name *deba*, made of a long hollow log.

The people gather at the sound of this instrument. When the co-religionists of the king come before him they kneel and throw dust on their heads; such is their manner of saluting the king. The Muslims show their respect by clapping their hands.

The religion of these negroes is paganism and the worship of idols. At the death of the king, they build a large dome of wood which they place on the spot chosen for the grave; then they put the corpse on a bed with a few carpets and cushions and place it within the dome; they put near the dead man his ornaments, weapons, and the dishes and cups which he had used for his food and drink, and they shut up with him several of his cooks and drink-makers. The edifice is then covered with mats and cloths and all the crowd throw earth on the grave till it forms a large mound. They sacrifice victims to their dead and bring them inebriating drinks. . . .

All the gold nuggets found in the mines belong to the king; but he leaves to his people the gold dust, with which everybody is familiar; without that precaution gold would become so plentiful that it would have practically no value. . . . It is said that the king has in his palace an ingot of gold as big as an enormous stone. . . .

The king of Ghana can raise 200,000 warriors, 40,000 of them being armed with bows and arrows. The horses in that country are very small.

In 446 (A.D. 1054–5) Ibn Yacin [the Almoravid][1] marched on Aoudaghost, a rich country whose metropolis is very large and has several bazaars, a great number of date-palms, and henna-trees as big as olive-trees. It was the residence of a black king who bore the title of Ghana before the Arab entered the town of this name. . . . Aoudaghost is two months' journey from Sidjilmessa and a fortnight from Ghana.

These are the principal passages from El Bekri concerning the famous city. Later information is scanty and of smaller value. Idrisi's work (1154) is only a compilation and is full of errors; for example, he describes Ghana as being on the Niger river. But he gives an interesting reference to the kings of his time: 'Its king [of Ghana], according to what is said, is descended from Salih, son of Abdallah, son of Hasan, son of Ali, son of Abou Talib.' An echo of Idrisi is to be found in Ibn Khaldun (before A.D. 1400) who writes about the Ghana kings: 'It is said that there was in Ghana an empire whose kings belonged to the family of Ali and formed a dynasty of the descendants of Saleh. According to Idrisi, Saleh was the son of Abd Allah. . . . That dynasty no longer exists today and Ghana belongs to the sultan of Melli.'[2]

It is worth noting that Ibn Battuta (1353–4), the only Arab author after Ibn Hawqal who had travelled in Western Sudan, does not even mention Ghana: it appears to have been already destroyed by then. But we have, in modern times, two impor-

[1] The Almoravids were Berbers from Mauritania who conquered Morocco during the eleventh century.

[2] Ali ben Abou Talib was the fourth Caliph (died in A.D. 661); his wife Fatima was Mohammed's daughter and Hasan, one of their sons, was the ancestor of the Idrisid Moroccan dynasty. Abdallah, son of Al Hasan, was the father of Idris I of Fes.

tant local texts, both written in Timbuctoo by negro scholars, which give us most valuable information on Ghana: the *Tarikh el Fettach* (written in Arabic between 1519 and 1665 by Mahmoud Kâti and one of his grandsons) and the *Tarikh es Sudan* (written before 1655 by Es Sa'di), both translated and published in French.

The first says:

The Malli [Mandingo] empire was really only created after the fall of the Kayamaga dynasty, whose power extended over all the western country without any exception. Before that time the chief of Malli was only one of the Kayamaga's vassals, one of his officials and ministers. *Kayamaga*, in Ouakore language, means 'king of the gold', *kaïhou* meaning gold and *maga* king.

The Kayamaga were indeed powerful princes. A responsible person told me that he knew from a lawyer, *cadi* of Mâssina, the *alfa* Ida El-Massini, that the Kayamaga were among the most ancient kings, for twenty of them are said to have reigned before the coming of Allah's messenger [A.D. 622]. The name of their capital was Koumbi, and that Koumbi was a big town. Their dynasty came to an end during the first century of the Hegira.

The same text says:

People do not agree as to the tribe to which these princes belonged. Were they, as some claim, Ouakore or, as others say, Ouangara?[1] That is unlikely and probably inaccurate. According to other sources, they might have been Sanhadja,[2] which seems to me more likely, for they are named in their genealogies by the term *Asko'o-Soûba* which is equivalent to Ham as a surname in Sudanese usage.[3] What is certain is that they were not negroes. God knows it better than anyone; for these events are very old and took place in countries far from ours; therefore it is not possible nowadays for historians without fear of contradiction to agree on this subject, for they have no ancient chronicle upon which they can rely.

[1] The Ouakore are the Soninke or Sarakole people still surviving in the Western Sudan, chiefly around Nioro. The author of the *Tarikh el Fettach* belonged to that ethnic group. The Ouangara in this text means the Mandingo.

[2] The Arabic form of the great Berber tribe of Zanaga.

[3] The meaning of Asko'o-Soûba and Ham is uncertain. But in his paper Delafosse suggests a possible meaning: *hasko* in Fulani means genealogy, and *souba* in Mandingo, caster of spells.

According to the second work, the *Tarikh es Sudan*,

> Malli is the name of a very big country lying at the extreme occident, towards the Ocean. Qaïamagha was the first prince to reign in that region. His capital was Ghana, a big town in Baghena country.[1]
>
> We are told that this kingdom existed before the Hegira, that twenty-two princes reigned before that time and twenty-two after. That makes forty-four kings. They were of white race, but we do not know their origin. As for their subjects, they were Ua-Kori. When that dynasty disappeared, it was replaced by that of Malli whose princes were of black race.

Such are the important texts dealing with Ghana. We can now consider the problems which arise concerning the origins of the old empire and its kings and concerning its capital and its history.

The Problem of the Origins of Ghana and its Kings

We have seen that very little is said about this by the Arab authors. Delafosse, followed by others, has put forward a theory of the Jewish and Syrian origin of Ghana,[2] but we are not obliged to agree with this view.

The suggestion that the Ghana princes were not negroes, but were probably Sanhadja Berbers, was put forward in the *Tarikh el Fettach* in the sixteenth century. But this opinion is qualified by so many doubts ('People do not agree as to the tribe to which these princes belonged . . . they might have been Sanhadja . . . God knows it better than anyone . . . it is not possible nowadays for historians without fear of contradiction to agree on this subject . . .') that we cannot regard the text as a reliable basis for believing the first Ghana kings to have been of white race. It has to be remembered also that Mahmoud Kâti was of Soninke race, and may well, for this reason, have tried to attribute to his race's dynasty a white origin.

Among the earlier references, Yakoubi, in A.D. 872, places the Ghana people among the negroes and Maçoudi (*c.* A.D. 944)

[1] Baghena (in Mandingo) and Uagadu (in Sarakole) have the same meaning: the land of flocks (or herds). Uagadu is the modern name for the country where Koumbi Saleh lies.

[2] In his 1924 paper, Delafosse maintains that he still thinks the founders of the state of Ghana were Semites.

does the same. Ibn Hawqal (*c.* 977), who had crossed the Sahara to Aoudaghost and therefore knew what he was talking about, also places Ghana in the land of the negroes, and so does Al Birouni (*c.* 1036). El Bekri, speaking of the people of Ghana, says: '. . . the religion of these negroes is paganism'.

Idrisi (1154) states that Ghana, now Muslim in religion, is the greatest town of the land of the negroes, but relates, as we have seen, that the kings are said to be descended from Salih ben Abdallah, a descendant of the Prophet (see p. 112 above). Since, a century before, El Bekri had recorded that the kings were negroes, we must take it as probable that after the Berber Almoravids took Ghana in 1077, the pagan dynasty was replaced by a Muslim one, which perhaps had, as Idrisi claims, Cherifian and therefore white blood in its veins. This tradition of a Cherifian, probably white, dynasty could explain why, several centuries later, the *Tarikhs* speak of non-negro kings of Ghana.

At present, therefore, nothing certain is known of the origin of Ghana—a state first mentioned only at the end of the eighth century—or of its founding dynasty, but that it was regarded by the earliest authors as a black kingdom, of Soninke or Sarakole race. . . .[1]

The History of Ghana

All that can be said of the history of Ghana before the coming of the Arabs in the eighth century must, in the present state of our knowledge of West Africa, be merely speculation. We know from El Bekri that Ghana was attacked by the Umayyads (that is to say, from the West Maghreb) between A.D. 734 and 750, and that the descendants of the soldiers then sent against it continued to live in the Black kingdom. It was known before 800 as a big country, Al Fazari even giving its size: 1,000 *farsakh* by 80, nearly equal to that of the Idrisid Moroccan state. All the later authors insist on the great power of its kings. Yakoubi (872) says 'the king of Ghana is a great king. In his territory are gold-mines and he has under his domination a great number of kingdoms.'

By the ninth century a new power had arisen: the Sanhadja

[1] Nevertheless, the word Sarakole may come from *sara kollé* or *sere khoullé*, meaning white man. The Sarakole language belongs to the Mande group.

Berbers, recently converted to Islam, with Aoudaghost as their capital. El Bekri says[1] 'Between 961 and 971 A.D. [but most probably before 920] Aoudaghost had as king a Sanhadja [Berber] named Tin Yeroutan, son of Ouichenou, son of Nizar. More than twenty negro kings recognized him as sovereign and paid him tribute. His empire extended over an inhabited country two months' journey in length and breadth. He could mount 100,000 [warriors] on fine camels. . . .' The text goes on to say that he made an expedition against the negro king of Augham[2] on the invitation of the king of Macin (probably Macina). The fact that the king of Aoudaghost had negro kings under his domination and that he was obliged to cross the territory of the Ghana empire to reach Augham points to a temporary decay of the Ghana empire, unless, as the texts of *Roudh el Kartas* and Ibn Khaldoun suggest, El Bekri was mistaken.

Aoudaghost, in Ibn Hawqal's times (before 977), still seems to have been separate from Ghana and at peace with its kings. Ghana probably took advantage of the 120 years of anarchy among the Sanhadja Berbers (*c.* A.D. 920–1040?) to seize Aoudaghost, which, according to El Bekri, still in 1054–5 recognized the authority of the king of Ghana; it was sacked for that reason by the Almoravids. We must place the apogee of the Ghana Sarakole empire between 920 and 1050, according to dates suggested by the *Roudh el Kartas*.

The rise of the Almoravid power after 1048–9 led to the ruin

[1] Ibn Khaldoun also mentions these Aoudaghost Berber kings. His version is different from El Bekri's. According to him, Tiloutan died in A.D. 836–7; his successor Ilettan in 900; Temin, son and successor of Ilettan, in 918, when he was killed by the Sanhadja. The *Roudh el Kartas* (A.D. 1326) gives different information again: Tiloutan died in 836–7, aged 80. His nephew El Ethir ben Bithin ben Tiloutan was king after him and died in 851–2, aged 65; then the son of the latter, Temin ben el Ethir, reigned till 918–19, when he was dethroned by the Sanhadja sheikhs. The nation remained in a state of anarchy for 120 years, after which they recognized as king Abou Mohammed ben Tilat, known by the name of Tarsina el Lemtouni.

[2] Augham is mentioned elsewhere by El Bekri as lying to the east of Ghana. It probably corresponds to the ancient ruined city of Arham, mentioned in all Sudanese traditions as one of the oldest towns of the country. Arham is on the Niger river, some forty miles south-west of Timbuctoo.

of Ghana. In 1054–5 Ibn Yacin took Aoudaghost while, on the eastern border of the empire, King Tarem of Anbara resisted the rulers of Ghana, although the latter were still very powerful. In 1076–7, according to Al Zouhri (1150), the people of Ghana 'became good Muslims under the influence of the Lemtouna'. Knowing what happened in Aoudaghost, we can imagine the fate reserved for the enemy capital by the Almoravids of Abou Bekr.[1]

Ibn Khaldoun is probably nearer the truth when he says: '. . . [the Almoravids] spread their domination over the negroes [of Ghana], devastated their territory and plundered their property. Having submitted them to poll-tax, they imposed on them a tribute and compelled a great number of them to become Muslims. The authority of the kings of Ghana being destroyed, their neighbours, the Sosso,[2] took their country and reduced its inhabitants to slavery.' We can be sure, however, that a fraction of the pagan inhabitants and some survivors of the ruling family fled to the south, to more remote provinces of the empire (Sosso, Kingui, Galam, Kaniaga, etc.) and to the Niger in the region of Dia and Djenné.[3] Small groups of Sarakole scattered at the end of the thirteenth century over wide areas in the Sudan. This movement of population continued from the fourteenth to the nineteenth centuries; their language was almost completely lost.

It is possible that a new ruling dynasty, certainly of Muslim religion, but perhaps connected by marriage with the former Sarakole pagan princesses, was founded in Koumbi. But one thing is certain: 1076, far from being the end of Koumbi Saleh, was the beginning of a second period of prosperity under Muslim rule, during which the commercial activity of the town rose to a high level. The finely built stone houses, the huge Muslim cemeteries, etc. revealed by recent excavations must date from that period, which lasted for more than a century, until the king

[1] According to the local legend, Bouhahim, companion of Abou Bekr, is said to be buried in Soubi or Sohobi cemetery, a mile south of Koumbi, where his grave is still to be seen today.

[2] Delafosse stresses that one must say king of Sosso, not of the Sosso or Sousou. He dates this Sosso expedition in 1203, using a source unknown to me.

[3] The Marka-Sarakole of Dia are descended from the former inhabitants of the Ghana country.

of Sosso, as Ibn Khaldoun mentions, took the country and reduced its inhabitants to slavery. This Sosso expedition against Ghana is dated 1203 by Barth and Delafosse on the basis of local traditions. According to other local Mandingo traditions collected by Delafosse, the king of Mali, Soundiata, took Ghana in 1240 and destroyed the entire town, or, more exactly, what remained of it after the disastrous Sosso expedition of 1203. The commercial functions of Ghana then passed to Ualata (founded *c.* 1224) and Djenné to the south (founded *c.* 1250).

Ghana is referred to several times in later centuries by Arab geographers who recall its prosperity, but it was only in 1914, as we have already said, that the ruins of the town were found by Bonnel de Mezières.

Conclusion

The repute of the Ghana empire in the Middle Ages was remarkable. It was, for the Arab writers especially, the legendary country whence came a great part of the gold circulating in the Muslim world. Today, knowing the mines of the Transvaal, California, Alaska, Siberia, and Australia, with their high annual output, we forget that, in antiquity and during the Middle Ages, what we should now consider as very poor mines were then held to be first rate. The Western Sudan was, from the eighth century until the discovery of America, the chief supplier of gold for the western world; the trade, commercialized first by Ghana, came under that name to the Mediterranean and enhanced the prestige of the kings who owned such a source of wealth.

Yet we know little of the pre-Islamic Ghana civilization. El Bekri is practically the only author who mentions it, and the excavations of Koumbi Saleh from 1914 to 1951 have not yielded indisputable remains of it: all that has been found so far must be regarded as Islamic. On the other hand it is likely that the numerous mounds of Macina, Killi, etc. to the west of Timbuctoo belong to that civilization. Some have been excavated in those regions and give us an idea of the high level of culture which was already flourishing in the bend of the Niger before Islam destroyed it.

Much of that culture certainly still survives in West Sudan, chiefly in pagan districts. The kings of Ghana have been imitated by a host of later and lesser sovereigns and, apart from the Islamic elements, we have an echo of the description of *tounka*,[1] Menin's court, by El Bekri in Ibn Battuta's picture of the court of the king of Mali in 1353. Nor is that so different from the modern court of the king of Mossi in Ouagadougou. We can be sure, too, that the famous Ghana model was copied even farther west and south, and that, for instance, we shall identify numerous borrowings from it even as far as the Bight of Guinea, in all countries linked with the West African medieval gold traffic (Gold Coast *inter alia*). The pages written by El Bekri could be applied even today with little change to more than one West African state.

What then of the contemporary belief of some Gold Coast scholars that the Akan are descended from the ancient Ghana kingdom?

The first author to speak of a possible link between Ghana and the Akan was, I think, the Rev. W. T. Balmer, who wrote: 'It is very probable that the Fanti, Ashanti, Ahanta and Akan people in general formed originally part of this ancient Negro Kingdom [Ghana], dwelling in districts more or less remote from the central city of Government, Walata. One sign of this is the similarity between the name "Ghana" and "Akan". . . . Moreover, there still exists, among the coast people, a tradition of a powerful and influential city called Walata. . . .'

Mr W. E. F. Ward has indicated how we should regard such an hypothesis of the relationship between Akan and Ghana, giving arguments coming from the Gold Coast itself, and also what may be regarded as the more probable origin of the Akan peoples. I may add, against the arguments of Mr Balmer concerning the region north of the Gold Coast, that no tradition suggestions that the territories subject to the kings of Ghana extended south of the River Bani; that it is impossible to say that the Akan are related to the Sarakole,[2] who are the real inhabitants of Ghana country; that Ghana was the name of the kings, and not of a people, and therefore it seems most improbable that an ethnic stock took as its name a word meaning

[1] *Tounka* still means in modern Sarakole 'political chief' and in Mandingo 'superior sovereign'. The first Mossi capital was named Tenkodogo.

[2] Even if, as is very possible and even probable, a few Sarakole merchants went as far as the Gold Coast for their trade and settled there.

'king' in a country lying 8° north of it; that Walata was never the capital of the Ghana empire, but, on the contrary, was founded when that state was destroyed; and that it is very natural that the coast people remember Walata as a powerful and influential city, for the Gold Coast was in direct relation with it, by the old caravan trade-route from what is now Ashanti to the northern markets (Kong, Djenné, Timbuctoo, etc.), from the thirteenth century to 1900 when Walata was powerful and influential.

Mrs Meyerowitz has claimed that in the *Tarikh es Sudan* '44 kings reigned before the kingdom was conquered, about A.D. 790 by a black people, who had come from Dia or Gyana, situated on the Niger Bend'. The actual text referring to these 44 kings is as I have translated it (see p. 114 above), and is quite different. It says that 22 princes reigned before the Hegira (viz. A.D. 622) and 22 after. There is no mention, even approximate, of A.D. 790. As for the conquest by a black people coming 'from Dia or Gyana' let me recall what precisely the *Tarikh* says: '[The dynasty of Ghana] was replaced by that of Malli whose princes were of black race.' The people of Mali were Mandingo, and we know from several sources that their conquest of Ghana dates from the thirteenth century and not the eighth.

What of the 'Dia-Lemta, Guan and Gara' whom she supposes to be the conquerors of Ghana in A.D. 790? Dia is the name of an ancient town that really existed near the Niger, but it has nothing to do with the dynasty of the Dia of Koukiya. The Lemta are a well-known group of Berbers. The Wangara are nothing else but Mandingo in Sudanese texts. As for Guan, no people of that name has been shown to have existed. The word seems to have been formed by breaking down Wangara (Guangara) to suggest Akan.

The same author continues:

In 1009–10, according to the *Tarikh-es-Sudan*, the Dia kingdom, or Gyana, was destroyed by the Azawad. . . . The people, as in Ghana, had to become Muslims and the king, possibly a son of the last king by a Songhay mother, moved from Gunghia, Guan-gya or Guan-Dia, the capital, to Gao on the Niger. Thousands of refugees fled south and founded new states. One of them was in Mossi and stretched down to the Northern Territories of the Gold Coast. When this was destroyed by peoples from the eastern border, again thousands of refugees fled south, and beyond the Black Volta river they founded the Bono Kingdom in 1300. These are known today as the Brong people, a branch of the Akan. To them also belong the Fante, the Eguafo people and the Afutu, who founded at the same time their states along the coast of the Gold Coast . . . [and] Kumbu, whose capital [was] Kong.

But the fact the *Tarikh es Sudan*, speaking of the origin of Songhay princes (named Zâ *alias* Dia), says: 'Zâ-Kosoï . . . became a convert to Islam. On this occasion he was called *Moslem-dam*, an expression meaning in the local language "he who willingly embraces Islam without being forced to do so". That event happened in A.H. 400 [A.D. 1009–10].' There is no mention, as we can see, of the destruction by the Azawad or any other people of the kingdom of Dia 'or Gyana' or of refugees to the south. On the contrary, the *Tarikh* speaks of voluntary conversion and gives the names of 16 more Dia after that date. Let us recall also that the Songhay capital is really Koukiya and not 'Guan-gya or Guan-Dia'.

As for the alleged similarity between Kumbu and Koumbi, Shamaa near Elmina and 'Châmâ,[1] as the country round Walata was called', this is mere playing on words, such as may be applied to all languages in the world, when one does not know the difficult rules that must be followed in toponymy. I place the comparison suggested between Akan, Ghana, and Akkad in the same category.

Thus I do not consider these assertions of a connexion between the Akan and Ghana as being worthy of serious consideration: every nation looks for noble ancestors (Yoruba look towards Egypt, all Muslims want to be of Arab blood, as sixteenth-century Frenchmen wanted to be of Trojan descent. Salomon Reinach, who was a Jew, called this state of mind the 'oriental mirage'. Examples of it exist by the score in Europe).

One important point is, however, in my opinion, worth consideration: the Akan tradition of ancient relations with Dia. It may not be the dynasty of the Songhay named Dia but the city of Dia (Macina) said by Delafosse 'to have the reputation of being one of the most ancient in the Sudan and whence came

[1] In reality, Sama, mentioned by El Bekri, 4 days' journey from Ghana.

the oldest Soninke migrations'. The famous city of Djenné, commercial emporium of the products of the south (gold, slaves, kola-nuts, etc.) and of the north (salt, cloth, etc.) is said to have been founded by people of Dia. The name of Djenné itself would mean 'little Dia'. It is in this direction that one must look for possible connexions between the empire of Ghana and the Gold Coast. The 'Diula', itinerant traders known all over West Africa, who are often of Sarakole stock, certainly came in contact with what is now the Gold Coast, through the gold-trade, in very early times.

The real origins of the Akan are unknown; most probably they are descended from some obscure peoples of prehistory, and there are only very slender possibilities of an important link between their ancestors and the people ruled by the Ghana kings, the Sarakole. We may admit the probability that Sarakole traders were to be found at an early date in every West African gold-mining country, and the Gold Coast is one of these. . . .

10. Baguirmi and Kanem

JACQUES LE CORNEC *Histoire Politique du Tchad* Pichon and Durant-Auzias, Paris 1963; pages 18–21, 25–7, 29–34 (In translation)

The Countries which have Monarchies: Baguirmi and Kanem

Among the monarchic sultanates which made up the 'Black Empires of Chad', Wadai, Bornu, Kanem and Baguirmi, it is the last which can best serve as a model.

1. *Baguirmi*

The area of the state of Baguirmi, before the 'colonial' expansion, corresponds to what is now the sub-prefecture of Massenya, its ancient capital. At its greatest extent it extended from Fort Lamy in the west to Lai on the right bank of the Logone, in the south up to the Sara-Mbayes of the Upper Logone (Doba) and the Sara-Kabas of Upper-Shari (Kyabé), in the east as far as

Melfi, and to the north as far as Bokoro, but this included a periphery of vassal march-lands, and one must also add that Baguirmese expeditions regularly went beyond this boundary in collecting slaves and pillaging.

Baguirmi can thus be thought of as being made up of three concentric circles round Massenya, these circles marking the gradual decline of its political influences and authority. They are:

1. A central organized nucleus, the state or Sultanate of Baguirmi proper.
2. A ring of small feudal chiefdoms, march-lands of animist populations, which were vassals of Baguirmi: the Buas in Korbol, the Nielims and Miltus in Bousso, the Somrais and Gabris in Lai between the two rivers. Taking their example from the Mundangs' borrowings from the Peul and Bornuan political vocabulary, the leaders of these tribes called themselves in Baguirmese terminology 'Alifas' or representatives of the Sultan.
3. An outer zone comprising the other empires to the north, in turn allies or enemies of Baguirmi, and nominal or real suzerains of it: Wadai and Bornu; and the 'barbarian lands' to the south, the Sara countries, which were its store-house of captives and its great hunting ground for slaves.

Whether it was supplying its own needs, or those of the Sultanates of the north, which it provided with slaves, particularly through its annual tribute in kind, Baguirmi was the linch-pin of the internal slave trade in Central Africa. In 1900 the annual quota of slaves handed over to Baguirmi by the tribes under its control was nearly 1,000.[1]

In Baguirmi there are good written sources; they are not local sources, but rather, on the one hand, a collection of oral traditions gathered together by the German explorer Nachtigal, who lived in the country in 1873[2] and whose work remains the

[1] G. Bruel: 200 slaves by Laï, 100 by the Nielims, Tumaks, Somrais, Ndams, Goulayes, 50 by the smaller tribes. The author reports also that all the grand dignitaries had fiefs where they could collect captives and that selling individual slaves was general.

[2] After H. Barth (1852) who left the first account *Travels and Discoveries in Northern and Central Africa* (1860), t. III and Vögel (1854): all three also visited a part of Mayo-Kebbi.

basis of our historical knowledge, and, on the other, monographs like those of the administrator Devallée.

History of Baguirmi. Nachtigal has drawn up a chronological list of the twenty sultans of Baguirmi, from the founder of the Empire, about 1522, to the reigning sultan of 1872. The present sultan, who is now only a cantonal chief, is the twenty-fifth sovereign.

It was at the beginning of the sixteenth century that a group of emigrants coming from the east settled in what was to be Baguirmi, at that time inhabited by the original black tribes, the Massas and others, and by Arab and Fulani immigrants. Islamized Africans like to claim that they are of Arabian descent, and so the Baguirmese claim that they came from the Yemen[1] led by twelve chiefs, one of whom, Birni-Bessé (1522–1536), conquered the Fulani, the Massas and the Arabs in succession, founded Massenya, and supposedly became the first 'sultan'.

His principal successors were:

Malo, the Third (1548–1568), who conquered the land of Moito (Bokoro).

Abdullah, the Fourth (1568–1598), was the first usurper. His long and brilliant reign is thought to mark the real foundation of the Baguirmese state. He was publicly and solemnly proclaimed Sultan, and he decreed, in addition, that any person who did not give him his title would be punished by death. He extended his kingdom by conquering villages and tribes[2] along the Shari for a distance of four hundred kilometres, by vanquishing the Bulalas, the sultanate of Lake Fittri, the neighbouring Sokoros, as well as the little sultans of the Lower-Logone who paid him tribute. Within his own boundaries he organized his kingdom by adopting Islam, making it the official religion and propagating it, by building a palace, creating a Court and numerous dignitaries, by organizing justice and the administration.

Burkomanda I, the Seventh (1635–1665), a great conqueror, was the Baguirmese Alexander. He undertook a victorious expedition, which lasted three years, on an east-north-west

[1] The Kanembu make the same claim. Birni-Bessé is supposed to be connected with the Koreish of Mecca.

[2] Upstream from Bousso; the Sarwas, Miltus, Nielims and Ndams.

circuit: Khenga, Kanem, Borku, Kaouar,[1] back to Lake Chad and over the river Shari into Kotoko[2] country, then into Mandara and Fulani country, over the Logone into Massa country and back to Baguirmi.

Hadji, the Fifteenth (1751–1758), restarted either himself or through his patias (lieutenants) the military expeditions to the north (Fittri, Kanem and Borku) and to the south (Saruas, Miltus, Boas, Somrais). The custom of having eunuchs dates from his reign, as does the custom by which the sultan who assumed power put out the eyes of all princes who could be possible claimants to the throne. In the meantime Baguirmi had had to submit to Bornu.

Abd er Rhamane Gaurang I, the Sixteenth (1785–1808), made an incestuous marriage. He married his sister despite the opposition of the Ulemas (doctors of Muslim law) and this was the pretext invoked by Saboun, the sultan of Wadai, to intervene in the name of Islam, besieging, capturing and sacking Massenya, and massacring the royal family almost in its entirety. From his reign dates the beginning of Baguirmese decadence.

Burkomanda II, the Eighteenth (1807–1846), defeated by his patia Aruéli, the greatest of Baguirmese military chiefs, called for help from the Sultan of Bornu, then from the Sultan of Wadai, who re-established him on his throne in return for the payment of regular tribute. He and his successors continued the tradition of expeditions into 'Kirdi' country.[3]

Mohamed Abu Sekin, the Twentieth (1858–1877), threw off the suzerainty of Wadai[4] on which Ali, the Sultan, came to lay siege to and retake Massenya.

Abd er Rhamane Gaurang II, the Twenty-First (1883–1918), suffered the invasion of Baguirmi by Rabah in 1892. A relief column from Wadai was defeated by Rabah, who besieged, took and sacked Massenya. But soon afterwards Gaurang re-entered his capital, while Rabah was busy fighting Bornu. It

[1] Saharan region of Bilma (on the caravan trail Tripoli to Chad).

[2] The Kotokos, descendants of the original inhabitants, the Sos or Saos, were a fishing people on the banks of the Shari.

[3] Pagans of the south, especially in the territories of the Massas, Gabris, Miltus, Somrais, Ndams, Kumras and Tumaks. But the Alifa of Korbol (Boas) was already trying to gain his independence.

[4] Even though, raised in captivity in Wadai, he was actually put on his throne by a Wadai expedition into Baguirmi.

was at this time that the French reached the valley of the Chad, and Gaurang took advantage of their coming to save his throne from Rabah. He met Emile Gentil at the end of 1897 and signed with France a treaty of protectorate. Following raids by Rabah's troops Massenya was burnt down and evacuated, and Guarang sought refuge in Kuno, in the extreme south of the country. He was to fight alongside the French later, with his troops, in the battles of Nielim, Kuno and Kosseri against Rabah. . . .

The organization of the State comprised the organization of the palace, administration and justice.

In a monarchical regime the role of the court or the palace, an organized body of friends of the royal household and the principal dignitaries of the State (often but not always the same), is an important one; and the hierarchy and protocol were strictly laid down. The most important dignitaries were sixteen men and four women, of whom eight were appointed within the 'tata' or palace, and eight outside it.

The dignitaries outside the palace were the 'Mbarma', the first war lord, who ranked immediately after the Sultan; he was generally a free man and of aristrocratic origin; the 'Patia', the second war lord, was generally a captive; the 'Kirema' was the Sultan's favourite; the 'Ngacmane' was the leader of the eunuchs, and also a war lord and Sultan's messenger. Then came four counsellors, with their respective titles.

The dignitaries of the palace were the 'Coumson', who was the first wife of the Sultan, removable and interchangeable, a free woman or a captive; then came the other wives, the 'Tchiroma', the eldest son of the Sultan and crown prince, then three 'Ngars', that is, in their order, the second, third and fourth sons of the Sultan.

The seventeenth and eighteenth dignitaries were the 'Tchikotma', the eldest sisters of the Sultan, head of all the women of Baguirmi with their own feminine court.

Round each of these principal dignitaries there was a group of a certain number of secondary dignitaries each with his title: relatives, representatives, wives and eunuchs.[1]

[1] The principal eunuch, the 'Katurli', is 'a sort of administrative delegate entrusted with the supervision of the distant provinces and especially with carrying out for the Sultan raids to take captives'.

There were also two grand dignitaries with territorial functions: the 'Alifa Moito', who enjoyed certain privileges in the Moito region, and the 'Alifa Ba', the master of the river, i.e. of the Shari. There was said to be about seventy-nine dignitaries in all.

All these titles were bestowed by the Sultan: they were venal but precarious privileges; they could be bought but could be taken away at any time.

Administration was carried out by the headmen of villages and tribes, and feudal dignitaries. More precisely there were as many administrative hierarchies as there were ethnic groups: Baguirmese, Arabs, Foultse, Saras.

The Baguirmese hierarchy was made up of, at the lowest level, the village headmen or 'boulamas', some of whom were sometimes more important than others.[1] These boulamas were put forward by the village people, and named (and dismissed) by the Sultan on payment of dues called 'Lag el Kadmoul' or turban dues. Above them there were feudal dignitaries, the alifas (e.g. Alifa Ba, one Alifa of Moito Milton and Karbol), who were the governors of distant provinces. They did not reside at Massenya, and were veritable viceroys enjoying absolute power in their territory, directly subordinate only to the Sultan to whom they paid tribute periodically. But still other numerous dignitaries had authority over a village or several villages, and even whole areas, making up something like feudal domains.

The Arab hierarchy was made up of heads of families or heads of 'cachimbets'[2] and headmen of villages or tribes called 'cheiks': between the two ranks there were sometimes others called 'lauanes'. All were appointed by a degemina (or assembly) and assisted in their functions by it.

The Fulani hierarchy had headmen of villages or 'diauru' and headmen of groups or 'ardo'. The principal headmen, who did not exist in Baguirmi, were called 'lamidos'.

In animist Sara country there were heads of families,

[1] They were called 'Ngars' or 'Mlsangs'. Mlsang Dolo the Grand Sultan was the Sultan of Baguirmi. In the little sultanates on the banks of the Shari which were attached to Baguirmi, the headmen kept the title Mlsang Mafaling and Mlsang Bousse.

[2] Groups of tents, nomad villages.

headmen of villages and tribes appointed according to different customs, and those headmen of tribes vassalized by the Sultan of Baguirmi became Alifas.

It can be seen that if one leaves aside the Arabs and Fulani groups which were 'self-administering' the Baguirmese administrative organization was very largely feudal in origin, with lords' domains, and hierarchies of suzerains and vassals.

In Baguirmi country, justice was administered by 'cadis', but even there, there was no strict separation between the administrative and judicial authorities, and all the headmen, to some extent, settled the 'palavers' subject to their authority. In animist country, justice was exercised by the headmen, or arbitrators, in those cases where the people did not settle it by dealings among themselves or by taking the law into their own hands.

The State needed considerable revenue for the upkeep of the Sultan, the Court and the Army, and to meet the expenses of foreign relations, such as the annual tribute to Wadai, and the traditional presents sent to the authorities of Mecca via pilgrims.[1] Their principal sources of income were slave-trading, the tax levied on villages in cash,[2] or in kind,[3] the sale of honours and positions, the revenue of war, pillage and the courts, and the religious taxes 'zakra' and 'fotra'.

2. *Kanem*

The history of Kanem is tied up with that of Bornu of which it was the parent state, and then simply a province. The principal source is the *History of Bornu* by Urvoy.

About 700 white conquerors coming from the east established themselves in Kanem. The Dugawa dynasty, the pagan branch of the Sefawa dynasty (the people of Sef or Beni-Sef), arising from the conversion of Numé (1085–1090) to Islam, was to last until 1846.

The territorial expansion of Kanem began with Dunama the

[1] 'Baguirmi' is said to derive from 'baguer mia', the hundred oxen taken to Mecca.

[2] Notably in Austrian thalers, stamped with the head of Maria Theresa, still found today.

[3] Cattle, boubous (clothes), straw mats, millet, hides, pottery, gabaks (lengths of cotton), ivory, produce of hunting, fishing, etc.

First (1090–1150) and the eleventh and twelfth centuries saw the intermarriage of the populations, the development of Islam, the conquering of Kauav and the Zaghaugs.

At the end of the thirteenth century Kanem, weakened by civil wars, was invaded by the Bulalas and the Sefawa dynasty fled to Bornu with the faithful tribes: the original Kanembu nucleus then became the Kanuri or Bornuan people.

The sixteenth and seventeenth centuries saw the development of the new empire of Bornu. Idriss Katakarmatse (1507–1529) reconquered Kanem which, with the Bulala dynasty, became a Bornuan protectorate; and Idriss Alooma (1580–1617) unified Bornu by attaching Kanem to it. Bornu was then at the peak of its power and able to impose its protectorate on Baguirmi.

In the eighteenth century the seeds of Bornuan decadence were sown; in the nineteenth century Bornu was attacked by the Peuls and the reigning Sultan called to his aid his vassal Kanemi who regained the upper hand, set up in his own capital, and took the title of 'Shehu'. His successor[1] put himself in the place of the Setawas and the Sultan was killed by Rabih in 1893.

After the successes of the Peuls, Baguirmi and Kanem escaped from the control of Bornu. Against Baguirmi, who threw off its suzeranity,[2] Bornu called in Wadai whose sultan pillaged Massenya for his own gain. Kanem, engulfed in dynastic disputes, divided between the supporters of Bornu, Wadai and the Ouled-Slimane Arabs, finally remained under the suzerainty of Wadai.

The State and the sovereignty were organized in Kanem in the same way as in Baguirmi.

The Kanem of the eleventh and twelfth centuries had, alongside the Sultan, the grand council of the twelve principal officers of the Empire, a curious type of strong feudal organization coming straight from the nomad origins of Kanem; but as a monarchy evolved, it organized provincial administration in such a way as to make their titles purely honorary—increasingly territorial authority was handed over to members

[1] 'Umar Sheha, who received Barth in 1851.

[2] 'Baguirmi will from now and for most of the century be pulled this way and that between its two masters, generally paying tribute to both and serving as their battle field'. Y. Urvoy, op. cit., p. 105.

of the Sultan's entourage who were of more humble estate.

The Court, with its strict protocol, included, grouped round the 'Mai', the emperor appointed by the reigning prince from among his children or brothers, the Queen Mother or 'Maguira', the first wife or 'Cumsa', the counsellors or 'Koganas', the princes of the royal family or 'Mainas', and the Muslim scholars and jurists or 'Mallams'. The grand officers and functionaries, who were theoretically dismissable, were appointed by the Sultan from among the Mainas and Koganas: they were, in order of precedence, the head of the army or 'Kaigamma', two territorial governors, the Yerima and the 'Galadima', the crown prince, 'Tchiroma', and so forth.

The geo-political structure was the same as in Baguirmi, i.e. at the centre round the dynasty, the Kanembu people and a ring of vassal tribes, these latter being continually absorbed by the 'nucleus' at the centre, and new elements being added from outside. The basic unit was the tribe, primitive Kanem being no more than an aggregate of white and black tribes (the conquering tribes and the conquered). Later, after the process of assimilation it became customary to distinguish between the direct subjects of the Sultan, the Kanembus, and the vassal communities represented at the Mai's Court, the first being taxed individually, the second paying their tribute as a lump sum.

The principal vassal state of the Bornu empire from the fifteenth to the eighteenth centuries was Kanem, first a Bornuan protectorate with its Bulala dynasty, then a decentralized province ruled over by a viceroy or 'Khalifa' (which became Alifa) whose precarious dynasty has lasted right up to today at Mao. In the nineteenth century Kanem fell under the tutelage of Wadai.

In the nineteenth century the movement of centralization was completed, the grand titles had lost all their substance, and the feudal system had given way to a civil service. In fact, effective power belonged to the Koganas who, with the Mainas, formed the council of the King, the last remains of the 'old aristocratic constitution of the country'.

The administrative hierarchy in the country ruled directly was the following: the 'Mharmas' were village headmen, the 'Lauanes' heads of groups or factions, the 'Ayias' heads of districts, and the 'Mainas' governors of large towns and provinces.

The Lauanas and Ayias, appointed by the central authority, had in the villages local agents or political commissaires called 'Bulamas'. . . .

The Colonial Period (1900–1946)

The beginning of the twentieth century coincided with the establishment of French domination in Chad, and the different countries that it now comprises were to be under a colonial regime for the first half of the century, until 1946.

The main stages in the history of the colonization are well known: on 29 February 1892 Casimir Maistre signed a protectorate treaty with Mlsang Dallem, chief of Galcis of Lai; in 1897 (October) Emile Gentil signed another with Abdessamane Gausang II, Sultan of Baguirmi; in 1899 the Bretonnet mission was massacred by the war-parties of the conqueror Rabih at Niellim-Togbao, but the second mission repulsed them at Kuno (1899). Furthermore Lieutenant Joalland Meynier signed with the Alifa Djerab of Kanem another protectorate treaty (1899). The three forces, Joalland Meynier coming from F.E.A., Foureau-Lamy from Algiers, and Gentil from the Congo, met up at Kousseri where Rabih's army was defeated and he himself killed, along with Major Lamy on 22 April 1900. A 'military territory of the countries and protectorates of Chad' was set up by the decrees of 5 and 8 September 1900.

French colonization brought about directly and indirectly a profound upheaval of long-established structures: local societies were projected from a limited and static society into one which was socially dynamic and geographically undefined.

As long as the colonial regime lasted the local groups had no political life of their own: all politics were of the administrative and 'superimposed' kind—that is, the administration's policies were what passed for politics in general, since no other was allowed, and were the corollary of a general policy emanating from Paris: political life was thus at one and the same time imported or external in its motives and aims, and superimposed on traditional local customs.

In other words all problems were on a purely technical level —that of administrative and methodological organization.

As far as the chiefdoms were concerned the two essential aims of administrative policy were:

1. The setting up of a general administrative superstructure imposing on numerous heterogeneous local societies a network of uniform administrative districts.

2. The creation of an administrative sub-structure by adapting and generalizing the chiefdoms.

This effort of organization was undertaken simultaneously and in parallel order in all countries.

The Administrative Superstructure

When the French took over, all the countries making up Chad were reorganized in administrative districts by an administration first military then civil. Not only this reorganization but also the political consequences of it are important.

The Military Administration

As the successor of the Commissariat of the Government in the Shari (Decree of 26 September 1897) the military territory of the countries and protectorates of Chad was brought under the control of the General Commissariat of the Government of the French Congo. This was created in 1891, and replaced in 1910 (Decree of 15 January 1910) by the General Government of F.E.A. and by the Government of Ubangi-Shari-Chad, made up at the time of two parts, Ubangi-Shari, a civil territory, and Chad, a military territory which was being extended towards the north (B.E.T.) and the east (Wadai).

Placed successively under the authority of a Commissaire of the Government, of a permanent delegate of the General Commissaire, and of the Lieutenant-Governor of Ubangi-Shari-Chad, the military territory had in its early days a flexibly changing organization according to the fluctuating fortunes of colonization and the different paths it followed. But if it was flexible where it chose to take root, the military administration, aiming at pacification, was naturally blunt in its methods. It destroyed in its operations if not the political structures at least the old relationships and substituted new ones. Thus the military administration was the first organization of these new relationships, and the administrative organization was in effect a hierarchy of military posts.

At the apex was the territory with its new capital Fort-Lamy, built near Kousseri; the middle echelons were the regions impressive in outline and immense in extent; at the base and within the districts, there were sub-divisions, and over and above that small military posts. In other words the typical administrative chain of command was: at territory level, a major, at region or district level, a captain or lieutenant, at sub-division level, a lieutenant or warrant officer, at special postal agency[1] level, a sergeant.

The climax of the conquest dates from the military period. Forts marked the stages of the advance into the interior, starting from Ubangi, each bearing the name of a soldier or explorer: Fort de Possel, Fort Crampel (both in Ubangi-Shari), Fort Aschambault (in Tounia Kankao), Durand Autier (in Kyatzé), Fort Bretonnet (in Bousso), Fort de Cointet (in Mandjaffa), Fort Laimy, Fort Millot (in Ngouri), Fort Pradio (in Bir Atali), and also Behagle (in Lai), Maistreville (in Kélo) and Largeau (in Faya). Most of these names have fallen out of use, but Aschambault, Laimy and Largeau seem to have been definitely established.[2]

Finally, having been ceded to Cameroon in 1911 (in exchange for [French] freedom of action in Morocco), all the countries of the left bank of the Logone and the Mayo–Kebbi rivers and the military posts of Bindu and Lere were placed under German control until they were re-conquered in 1914. . . .

Translated by Dr S. I. Lockerbie

11. Nigeria 1600–1800: a summary

THOMAS HODGKIN *Nigerian Perspectives* Oxford University Press 1960; pages 23–34

Fifteenth Century

In the fifteenth century three developments stand out: the rise of the Hausa States, at a time when Kanem-Bornu was passing

[1] A centre for tax collection.

[2] The title of 'commandant', which the natives give to the person in charge of the districts, whether he be a lieutenant, sub-prefect or administrator, also dates from the military period.

through a period of relative weakness; the expansion of the kingdoms of Oyo and Benin; and the arrival of the Portuguese.

In the continual competition for power which took place among the Hausa States, Zaria for a time achieved predominance, under the semi-legendary Queen Amina, who, according to *The Kano Chronicle*, 'conquered all the towns as far as Kwararafa and Nupe'. But Kano, where iron helmets and coats of mail were introduced by the Sarki (King) Kanajeji in about A.D. 1400, strengthened its position in the course of the century, and Muḥammad Rimfa (?1463–99) is remembered in history as the greatest of the pre-Fulani Kano kings. It is probably to his reign that Leo Africanus refers when he says that the King of Kano 'was in times past of great puissance, and had mighty troops of horsemen at his command'. The twelve reforms which *The Kano Chronicle* attributes to Rimfa seem mainly to have been directed towards strengthening the internal structure of the State and intensifying its Islamic character: for example, the extension of the city walls, the construction of the market, the appointment of eunuchs to offices of state, the introduction of *kulle* (purdah), and the public celebration of the *'Īd al-kabīr*, the major Muslim festival. There is other evidence of the further Islamization of Kano at about this time: the arrival of Fulani from the west, bringing with them works of theology and grammar, to supplement the Qur'ān and the *Ḥadīth*; and the visits of travelling Muslim scholars from the University of Timbuktu. From the end of the fifteenth century onwards, 'the influence of Timbuktu . . . in the full tide of its intellectual activity . . . spread slowly through the west and central Sudan . . .'. One interesting aspect of this closer relationship between Kano and the intellectual centres of the Muslim world was the friendship between Muḥammad Rimfa and Shiekh Muḥammad al-Maghili of Tlemcen. Al-Maghili, a major figure in the history of the western Sudan at the turn of the fifteenth century, and a powerful influence on the thinking of 'Uthmān dan Fodio and the Fulani leaders three centuries later, seems to have functioned for a time in Kano as an *éminence grise*, advising the king on statecraft, and addressing to him the treatise on *The Obligations of Princes*—which combines insistence on the strict application of the *Shari'a* with an awareness of the problems facing a centralizing and reforming Muslim ruler.

Two states to the south of the Hausa system which by this time had begun to play a part in recorded history were Nupe and Kororafa (the Jukun Kingdom)—the one lying north of the Niger, above the confluence with the Benue, the other based upon the valley of the Benue. Both were ruled by pagan dynasties of divine kings. There are grounds for believing that a Nupe state existed—with its centre farther north, in the region of modern Kontagora—at a much earlier period; but that it was refounded in the fifteenth century, and that it is to this refounding that the story of Tsoede, the 'mythical charter' of modern Nupe, relates. The early history of Kororafa is also obscure. The state is first referred to in *The Kano Chronicle* in the reign of Yaji, in the late fourteenth century, who is said to have made war against Kororafa and to have died there. During the fifteenth century Kororafa had not yet been welded into the powerful system which, later, was able to threaten or overrun the Hausa States, and appears as tributary either to Zaria or to Kano.

During the fifteenth century both Oyo and Benin appear to have been passing through a period of military expansion. By the time the first Portuguese arrived in Benin the Alafin of Oyo was already regarded as the ruler of a powerful empire, 'the lord of many peoples'. Possibly Shango, the deified Alafin, the inventor and strategist who perished by his own *hubris*, can be associated with this phase of Oyo history. Ewuare the Great, historically a more definite and datable figure, achieved a similar reputation as a subtle prince, 'a great magician, physician, traveller, and warrior', in the early period of Benin's expansion among the Ibo peoples west of the Niger. While the maximum extension of the Benin Empire, eastward as far as Bonny and westward to Lagos, belongs to the sixteenth century, when Benin had begun to exploit the advantages derived from its European trade, particularly the use of fire-arms, the Benin tradition, which makes the first phase of expansion pre-date the arrival of the Portuguese, can be accepted as correct.

For present purposes we must reject the Europe-centred approach implied in talking about 'the discovery' of West Africa, or Nigeria, or Benin. From the African standpoint, it was not the Portuguese who first 'discovered' Benin, but Benin which first 'discovered' the Portuguese—according to tradition, in the reign of Ewuare the Great. About the actual date of his first encounter there has been some controversy. Professor Blake accepts in substance Antonio Galvão's account—that Ruy de Sequeira reached Benin in 1472, more than a decade before the first contact to which de Pina and de Barros refer, when João Affonso d'Aveiro presented his credentials at the court of Benin, some time between 1483 and 1486. By the end of the century, as Pacheco Pereira makes clear, the peoples of the Niger Delta had also 'discovered' the Portuguese; diplomatic relations had been established between the kings of Benin and Portugal; the Portuguese had built their factory at Gwatto, as a base from which to develop trading and missionary activities; and slaves—sold at twelve to fifteen brass bracelets in Benin and eight to ten copper bracelets in the Delta—had already become the staple export, with pepper, ivory, palm-oil, leopard-skins, etc., as subsidiaries.

Sixteenth Century

The sixteenth century is relatively rich in material, at least as regards Bornu, the Hausa States, and Benin. Essentially this was the period of the renaissance of Bornu, and the organization of the second Kanem-Bornu Empire; of the increased military pressure and cultural influence of the Gao Empire, under the Askia dynasty, upon Hausaland; and, in the south, of the extension of the imperial frontiers and authority of Benin—which, while maintaining close commercial relations with Portugal, made its first contacts also with other European nations, in particular the English and the Dutch.

Leo Africanus, writing near the beginning of the century, speaks of Bornu as third in order of importance among the major states of the Sudan—coming after Gao and Gaoga. He stresses the importance to Bornu of the trans-Saharan trade—especially the export of slaves and the import of horses; the part played in the trade by visiting North African merchants; the wealth of the royal house; and the strength of the royal army, which made possible these annual slave-raiding expeditions. His statement that the people of Bornu were pagans might seem to conflict with the fact that Islamization had been going forward there for more than four centuries. But it may well be true, if applied to the mass of Bornu subjects, rather than to the dynasty and court officials. Throughout the history of the Sudan the spread of Islam appears to have followed a definite rhythm—periods of intensive Islamization alternating with periods of the resurgence of animism. As late as the beginning of the nineteenth century Sultan Muḥammad Bello claimed that the majority of Bornu people were *kuffār*, pagans. But the end of the sixteenth century coincided with a new phase of religious reform and political reconstruction, under the leadership of the greatest of the Bornu Mais, Idris Alooma, who recovered the lost provinces of Kanem, and extended the frontiers farther eastwards, probably as far as Darfur. Aḥmad Ibn Fartua, Idris Alooma's chief Imam and chronicler, who accompanied him on his campaigns, is especially valuable as a contemporary historian, because—though his main theme is battles and victories—he has also taken the trouble to record some of the reforms and technical developments of his time: the new emphasis upon the *Sharī'a*, and the transfer of judicial authority from tribal chiefs to *qāḍīs*; the introduction of Turkish muskets and the raising of a local corps of musketeers—a major factor assisting Idris Alooma's policy of imperial expansion; the adoption of new methods of military transport; the construction of red-brick mosques. And even Ibn Fartua's somewhat repetitive descriptions of successive campaigns give a marvellous picture of late sixteenth-century Bornu society in one of its main aspects—the life and activities of its feudal army.

From their first appearance in history the Hausa States were subject to constant pressure from more powerful states on both sides: to the east, Kanem-Bornu; to the west, Mali, and later Gao (often itself referred to by the Hausa chroniclers simply as 'Mali', in the sense of 'the Western Empire'). By the year 1500 Gao, under Askia the Great, was dominant throughout the western Sudan; and the states of Kano, Katsina, and Zaria became for a time formally subject to the Gao Empire, paying tribute to the Askias, and compelled to accept a resident agent of the imperial power. However, Gao's suzerainty was not maintained throughout the century. Katsina recovered its independence at any rate by 1554, the date of the heroic resistance of the Gao cavalry at the battle of Karfata, described in the *Ta'rīkh as-Sūdān*. Moreover, the new state of Kebbi—founded, according to tradition, in 1516 by Kanta, a dissident general and provincial governor under Askia the Great—became in the course of the century a major power, functioning as a kind of buffer between Gao and Bornu. Gao's impact upon the Hausa States at this period was in any case not merely political and military: fertilized by visiting scholars from the University of Timbuktu, Katsina in particular began to develop as a secondary centre of learning.

In the sixteenth century Benin achieved something like the same kind of predominance in the south as Bornu in the north. But, whereas in the case of Bornu the principal non-African power with which diplomatic relations were maintained, and from which muskets and missionaries could be secured, was the Ottoman Empire, in Benin's case it was Portugal. (It might even be worth speculating, if the main focus of technical and industrial development over the next four centuries had been Turkey and the Middle East, rather than western Europe, how this would have affected the course of Nigerian history.) Accounts of the exchange of ambassadors between the courts of Benin and Portugal occur both in the Portuguese historians and in Benin tradition. Indeed, the latter supplements the former in an interesting way—giving the name of the first Benin ambassador to Portugal, Ohen-Okun of Gwatto, the nature of the royal presents, and the location of the first Christian churches. From Duarte Pires's letter to King Manuel it seems that a semi-permanent Portuguese mission was established at Benin. This letter is described by Professor Black as 'the only known contemporary account of direct negotiations between the King of Benin and the Portuguese living in his country. It should, however, be regarded as an illustration of what was constantly happening rather than as a story complete in itself.'

Although, from a political and commercial standpoint, Portuguese influence in Benin had begun to decline by the middle of the century, its culture remained a force. Portuguese missionaries seem to have enjoyed a large measure of freedom of worship and propaganda in Benin itself—the Catholic religion being regarded as an addition, rather than an alternative, to the state religion. Richard Eden, in his account of Windham's voyage in 1553—which contains the first description of an actual interview with the King of Benin—states that 'he himselfe could speake the Portugall tongue, which he had learned of a child'; and similar references to the use of Portuguese at the court of Benin recur in the literature of the next two centuries. At the human level there is evidence of friendly relations between Obas and individual Europeans: as in the case of Affonso d'Aveiro, who died in Benin, and 'was buried with great lamentations by the Oba [Esigie] and the Christians at Benin City'; or James Welsh, who presented a telescope to the Oba Ehangbuda, and described the people of Benin as 'very gentle and loving'.

Seventeenth Century

There is a strange shortage of material on which to base an understanding of the seventeenth century. One significant change, however, was the shift in the direction of the trans-Saharan trade, after the defeat of Askia Ishaq II by Moroccan forces at the battle of Tondibi, in 1591, and the consequent break-up of the Gao Empire. Tondibi, where mainly Spanish renegado troops under Judar Pasha demonstrated the superiority which fire-arms and the solution of the problems of trans-Saharan transport gave them, certainly deserves to be counted among the decisive battles in West African history.

This collapse of the western Empire brought with it unprecedented prosperity [for Katsina]. The anarchy prevailing in the Niger bend diverted to Katsina, now the commercial centre of the Hausa States, the caravans which had formerly followed the route from Gao to Egypt. The seventeenth and eighteenth centuries marked the height of its power. But, having once become rich and powerful . . . Katsina was involved in frequent conflicts with its neighbours—Kano, Kebbi . . . and perhaps above all Kororafa. . . .

Relations between Kano and Katsina, from the fifteenth century to the nineteenth, took the form of a continuing struggle for control of the central Sudanese end of the trans-Saharan trade, in which—as in the struggles between medieval Genoa and Venice—each in turn achieved a temporary supremacy. By the seventeenth century Kano was in a position of relative weakness—exposed to attack from Bornu in the east and Kebbi in the west, as well as involved in intermittent conflicts with Katsina. In the latter half of the century the Kororafa (Jukun) wars were renewed, leading to the destruction and occupation of the city of Kano. Katsina, on the other hand, though also exposed to periodic Kororafa invasions, was more successful in maintaining its independence; and in 1650, after inflicting a defeat on Kano, made an alliance, countersigned by three of the '*ulāma*', against the common, pagan enemy. Nominally, as Barth points out, Katsina remained tributary to Bornu throughout the period, but this seems to have involved little more than a formal recognition of overlordship such as in Europe a sovereign Christian king might give his emperor. In Bornu itself the extensive empire which Mai Idris Alooma had constructed remained intact, at least until the middle of the century, when it began to weaken under the combined attacks of northern Tuareg and southern Kororafa. Mai 'Ali's victory over both forces, celebrated in Dan Marina's poem, seems only to have checked a gradual process of decline. Internally, as the 'Song to the Kaigama' makes clear, the Bornu State had achieved greater centralization through the system whereby slaves—instead of princes of the royal house as in earlier times—were appointed to the chief offices of state.

In the south the two major powers—Oyo and Benin—maintained their ascendancy: they were, at this period, subject to no serious external threats, and—partly perhaps on account of their common acceptance of the religious supremacy of Ife—there appear to have been no continuing conflicts between them. The view that the Oyo Empire had already begun to decline by 1700 seems to lack any basis of fact. According to Oyo tradition, by the late seventeenth century the imperial frontiers extended to the Niger in the north and east, and included Dahomey in the west. Internally the power of the Alafin was severely limited by the Basorun and the Council of State, who made full use of the traditional procedure of 'rejection', described by Johnson. But this does not appear to have involved any weakening of the authority which the Alafin's government exercised over the Oyo dominions.

In Benin the highly complex political system, which the Dutch observers describe—with its various 'Estates', or associations of title-holders, pivoting upon a sacred monarchy and a palace bureaucracy—remained efficient, and well adapted to carry out the various public functions required of it—land distribution, the control of local administration, war, foreign trade, taxation, state ceremonial, and the like. It is only in

Van Nyendael, writing at the end of the century, that there is evidence of decline. By 1700 Benin had become involved in civil war and the city was partly depopulated—primarily as a consequence of the state's effort to satisfy the expanding European demand for slaves:

> The profits from the trade with Europeans gave the rulers and merchants of Benin an incentive and also, in the form of fire-arms, the means, to extend their rule so that they could secure from their own territory the exports most in demand. Armies were continually sent out to capture slaves and to subjugate the small tribes of the Niger delta. . . . By the end of the seventeenth century . . . the continual warfare was destroying the prosperity and even the structure of the State. . . .

This weakening of the power and coherence of Benin was, however, an intermittent process. 'Between periods of dissension the kingdom seems to have shown remarkable powers of recovery. . . . The history of Benin is one of alternating periods of territorial expansion and contraction in accordance with the degree . . . of authority at the centre.' During the greater part of the seventeenth century the process of expansion was still continuing.

Farther south Warri, the kingdom of the Itsekiri—founded, according to tradition, by Ginuwa, the son of an Oba of Benin who had to flee from the city in the mid-fifteenth century—had by the seventeenth century achieved a measure of independence from Benin. As Dapper puts it, 'The King of Ouwerre is the ally and in some manner the vassal of the King of Benin, but in other respects is entirely absolute in his dominions'. Warri is interesting partly because Portuguese-Catholic culture sank deeper roots there than in Benin, or anywhere on this coast, involving for a time the conversion of the dynasty. This is reflected in the story of Antonio Domingo, Olu in the 1640s, whose father 'went to Portugal to be educated and returned with a Portuguese lady of high birth as his wife'; and in the rational bargain struck a generation later between Church and State, whereby the then reigning Olu agreed to practise monogamy on condition that the Capuchin Vice-Superior provided him with a white wife.

This was also the period of the rise of the Delta States—Brass, Bonny, and Old Calabar—the product of migrations: initially, in the case of Brass and Bonny, of Ijaw, coming possibly from Benin; later of Ibo from the hinterland. 'By the end of the sixteenth century the process of forming the city-states may be said to have been complete. From the seventeenth century on the Delta became the most important slave mart in West Africa.' James Barbot gives a lively account of the procedures of negotiation and trade between the Pepple dynasty and European merchants, as they operated at the end of the century.

Eighteenth Century

There is a tendency to regard the eighteenth century as a period of decline, or at least of a weakening of established political systems, which eased the way for the empire-building movements at the beginning and end of the succeeding century, Fulani and British. There are obvious dangers in this method of interpreting history backwards: reality was certainly much more complicated. Unfortunately there is a lack of contemporary historians for this period who can tell us how the situation appeared to them; and little of the contemporary material that has survived is as yet accessible.

In the north, it is true, the power of Bornu was much reduced.

All the princes of this epoch stayed quietly in their capital, N'gazargamu, or their favourite residence, Gambaru. And all of them died in their capital—a bad sign. They lived on the memories of ancient glories, blinded by the flattery of courtiers, absorbed in state ceremonial and the infinite quarrels of Kaigamas, Mestremas, Chiromas, Galadimas, of generals without armies and governors without provinces. Meanwhile the nomads [the Tuareg] harassed the north of the Empire, and vassal tribes stealthily freed themselves from their old bonds of subjection.

M. Urvoy's reconstruction may seem highly coloured. But he may be right in arguing that the frequent references in the state chronicles through the century to Mais who were 'pious', 'friends of science and religion', 'well-disposed towards the '*ulamā*'', indicate a period of relatively ineffective rulers, in which power tended to pass into the hands of the Mallams. . . .

IV. EARLY PEOPLES IN NORTH AFRICA

12. Berbers and Negroes of the Sudan fringe

GEORGE MURDOCK *Africa, its Peoples and their Culture History* McGraw-Hill 1959; pages 111, 133–41

Berbers

Since late Paleolithic times the Mediterranean littoral of North Africa has been inhabited by people of Caucasoid race. Sometime after 4000 B.C., following a transitional Mesolithic period called Capsian, they acquired cultivated plants and domesticated animals from Egypt and entered a Neolithic phase. In the second millennium B.C. they received metals from the same source. When the Phoenicians and Greeks, and later the Romans, colonized the North African coast, they found the region occupied by a people of comparatively homogeneous culture known collectively as the Berbers. These had occupied a few marginal oases but in general had penetrated only slightly into the Sahara Desert. In the west, however, they extended somewhat farther south and had even settled the Canary Islands.

In physical type the Berbers resemble the Mediterranean sub-race of southern Europe, although they appreciably exceed the latter in average stature and show a somewhat higher incidence of blondness in beard, hair, and eyes. Their languages, which are so closely related as to be almost mutually intelligible, constitute the distinct Berber sub-family of the Hamitic linguistic stock.

Though they had withstood earlier foreign invasions with considerable success, the Berbers were shattered by the Arab conquests of the seventh century and particularly by the mass Bedouin immigrations beginning in the eleventh century. Some fled or were driven into the desert, where they in turn displaced or subjugated the indigenous Negroes. Others submitted, becoming Arabized in language and to some extent racially mixed. All, without exception, embraced Islam. Nearly thirteen centuries of acculturation have brought about such a degree of fusion and assimilation that North Africa today must be classed as an integral part of the great Middle Eastern culture area. Berber speech survives only in mountain fastnesses and other relatively protected pockets in the original homeland and in areas of dispersion in the desert.

Although some groups who have adopted the Arabic language are still basically Berber in culture and some Berber speakers are strongly Arabized, it is nevertheless generally true that the tribes who have retained their original language have also preserved more of their ancient customs. We shall therefore adopt a strictly linguistic classification in segregating the Berbers from the Arabs in North Africa. The peoples who still speak Berber, at least in part, fall into the following twenty-nine groups. . . .

Negroes of the Sudan Fringe

The early agricultural civilization which arose around the headwaters of the Niger River and gradually diffused eastward across the entire breadth of the Sudan to the Nile Valley also spread northward to the edge of the Sahara as far as geographical conditions permitted. As we have seen, however, it did not penetrate the desert, where the Negro inhabitants continued to live a nomadic life of hunting and gathering until their Caucasoid neighbours to the north had received from south-west Asia the Neolithic crops and techniques that could be adapted to oasis conditions. It was not, of course, until much later that the Berbers occupied portions of the Sahara. But they, and presumably the Egyptians even earlier, did establish trade relations across the desert with the Sudan, thus stimulating the adoption of agriculture by the Saharan Negroes.

As this trade developed, its impact was naturally felt first and strongest by the Negro peoples inhabiting the northern fringe of the Sudan. It was they who enjoyed the resulting economic prosperity, who benefited by the new products of Mediterranean origin, and who were in a position to enrich their cultures by borrowing adaptive elements from those with whom they traded. In consequence, they must then have achieved the cultural leadership in the Sudan which they seem to have held ever since. During the historical period most of them have accepted Islam and much of its associated culture, so that they must be regarded today as constituting the African frontier of the Moslem world and of the great Middle Eastern culture area. Elements of Arabic origin now obtrude so prominently, indeed, that it is no easy problem to isolate the features of culture borrowed during earlier periods.

The most intensive impact must naturally always have been felt in the immediate vicinity of the Sudanic termini of the four major trans-Saharan caravan routes. At precisely these points, from the dawn of recorded history to modern times, there have existed strong native states with relatively complex cultures and comparatively elaborate political systems, whose antecedents doubtless go far back into the prehistoric past. The spheres of influence of these states enable us to divide the Sudan fringe into a number of distinct provinces. At the termini of the easternmost trail, the Selima, leading from Egypt, lie the states and provinces of Darfur and Wadai. Farther west, the Bilma Trail links Libya with the states and provinces of Bagirmi and Bornu. The Gadames Trail from ancient Carthage and modern Tunisia terminates at the major cities of the Hausa states and province. From Morocco the Taodeni Trail leads to the middle and upper Niger. The states of the latter, notably Ghana and its successors, have already been described, together with the cultures of their surviving populations. The alternative terminus on the middle Niger, with Timbuktu as the principal mercantile centre, is occupied by the Songhai nation and province. The several provinces in order from east to west, with the peoples who compose them, are briefly characterized below.

(a) *Darfur Province*

Exclusive of Arabic and other intrusive peoples described elsewhere, all the constituent groups of this province speak languages of the Dagu branch of the Eastern Sudanic subfamily, with the single exception of the Fur, who constitute the sole members of the independent Furian stock. The province has a total population of about 750,000, but no reliable breakdown by tribes is available. Although Darfur was doubtless the first province to experience contact with ancient Egypt, via either the Selima Trail or the Nile Valley, its actual historical record does not begin until the fourteenth or fifteenth century.

1. Dagu (Dadio, Dago, Daju, Tagu), with the kindred Bego (Baygo, Beigo).
2. Fur (For, Forawa), embracing the Dalinga, Forenga, Kamminga, Karakarit, Kungara, and Temurka. They are the dominant people of the province politically and probably also numerically.
3. Kimr (Ermbeli, Guemra, Guimr). They are the inhabitants of Dar Kimr.
4. Sila (Sula). They are a branch of the Dagu, from whom they split off several centuries ago to settle in Dar Sila. An offshoot of the Sila, the Shatt (Dagu), later migrated to Kordofan and settled in the western Nuba Hills, where about 2,000 still survive.
5. Tama, with the kindred Erenga (Djebel, Iringa) and Sungor (Soungor). They are a branch of the Sila who settled Dar Tama, whence they displaced the Kimir.

(b) *Wadai Province*

Except for two groups, the Merarit and Mubi, all the indigenous tribes of this province speak languages of the independent Maban stock. They have a total population of nearly a million. The historical record begins at the same late date as does that for Darfur.

6. Maba (Wadaians), embracing the Bandula (Banadoula, Madala), Fala (Bakka), Ganyanga, Kashmere (Kachmere), Kadjanga (Abu Derreg), Karanga (Malanga), Kelinguen (Kelingane), Kodvi (Kudu), Madaba, Marfa, Matlambe, and Moyo. They number nearly 300,000 and dominate Wadai politically.
7. Masalit (Massalat).
8. Merarit (Mararet), with the kindred Ali, Chale, Kubu (Koubou), and Oro. These tribes constitute the distinct Merarit branch of the Eastern sub-family of the Sudanic linguistic stock.
9. Mimi (Mima, Moutoutou).
10. Mubi (Moubi), with the kindred Karbo (Korbo, Kourbo). These people speak languages of the Chadic sub-family of the Hamitic stock and are doubtless intrusive from the west.
11. Runga (Rounga). They are the inhabitants of Dar Rounga.

(c) *Bagirmi Province*

Since the beginning of dependable history in the early sixteenth century, political hegemony in this province has rested with peoples of the Central Sudanic linguistic sub-family, but they are probably intrusive into the area from the south. The Bua group of Eastern Nigritic speech presumably represents an even later arrival from the south-west. The original inhabitants appear to have belonged to the Chadic sub-family of the Hamitic linguistic stock, which is still numerically strong. Cultural and demographic data are nearly as scanty as for Wadai, but a total population of 150,000 was reported in 1925. Islam has not as yet penetrated the entire province.

12. Bagirmi, with the Busso. The Central Sudanic Bagirmi, who dominate the province politically, were reported to number 31,000 in 1925.
13. Bua, with the Koke (Khoke), Nielim (Njillem, Nyelem), and Tunia (Tounia). This Eastern Nigritic group, reported in 1925 to number about 7,000, is still mainly pagan.
14. Fanyan (Fagnia, Fanian, Nuba). This tribe, reported to number 1,200 in 1925, is only partially Islamized. The linguistic affiliation of this group, though not specifically reported, is probably Chadic.
15. Gaberi (Gabri, Ngabre), with the Chiri (Chere, Shere, Tshire), Dormo, Lele, and Nangire (Nancere). This Chadic group is pagan in religion.
16. Kenga (Kenya, Khenga), with the Babalia, Diongor, Masmadje, and Saba. This Central Sudanic group, numbering about 3,000 in 1925, is still pagan.
17. Kun (Kuang, Kung). The linguistic affiliation of this pagan group is not reported but is presumably Chadic.
18. Lisi, embracing the Bulala (Boulala, Maga), Kuka (Kouka), Midogo (Medogo, Mudogo), and Semen (Abu Semen). These peoples, who are also found in Kanem, are Central Sudanic in speech, indifferent Moslems in religion, and considerably mixed with Caucasoid elements.
19. Musgu (Mousgou, Musgum, Musuk). This Chadic tribe, numbering about 35,000, is only slightly Islamized.
20. Sokoro (Bedanga), with the Barein (Barain) and Yalna.

This Chadic group, still pagan in religion, was reported to number about 13,000 in 1925.

21. Somrai, with the Deressia, Kabalai, Mesme, Miltu (Miltou), Modgel, Ndam, Sarwa (Sarua), and Tumak (Toummak, Tummok). This Chadic group is still pagan.

(d) *Bornu Province*

The indigenous population of this province, as of Bagirmi, appears to have been Chadic in language but not specifically Hausa. They have long been politically dominated, however, by peoples of the Kanuric linguistic stock akin to the Saharan Negroes who control the Bilma Trail and who very probably penetrated the region from the north with the aid of superior socio-cultural techniques acquired from the North African Berbers in the caravan trade. They enter history in the eighth century with the establishment of the Sef dynasty, which held power, first in Kanem and later in Bornu, until 1846—perhaps the longest dynastic reign on record anywhere in the world.

22. Auyokawa, with the Shirawa and Teshenawa. This Chadic people, now largely acculturated to the Hausa, number about 50,000. They were Islamized in the seventeenth century.
23. Bede (Bedde). This Chadic group, numbering about 50,000, is still largely pagan.
24. Beriberi, with the Dogara (Dagra). This Kanuric people, numbering about 110,000, are strongly acculturated to the Hausa, whose language some of them have adopted.
25. Bolewa (Bole, Borlawa, Fika). This Chadic group, with a semi-independent kingdom, has a population of about 35,000.
26. Buduma (Boudouma, Jedina, Yedina), with the Kuri (Kouri). These Chadic people, who number about 20,000, inhabit about seventy islands in Lake Chad, where they subsist primarily by fishing and animal husbandry with only auxiliary agriculture.
27. Kanembu (Hamedj), embracing the Bade, Baribu, Chiroa (Tschiroa), Dalatoa, Danoa (Danawa, Haddad), Diabu, Galabu, Gudjiru, Kaburi, Kadjidi, Kankena, Kanka (Konku), Maguemi, Ngejim (Ngischem), and Sugurti

(Tsugurti). This Kanuric nation, numbering about 75,000, was Islamized in the late eleventh century.

28. Kanuri (Beriberi, Kanoury), with the Magumi (Magomi). This Kanuric nation, numbering nearly a million, has been politically dominant since 1380, when the ruling dynasty moved from Kanem to Bornu.
29. Karekare (Kerekere), with the kindred Ngamo (Gamawa). This Chadic group, still largely pagan, numbers about 55,000.
30. Kotoko (Logone, Makari), with the kindred Ngala. These Chadic people probably number in excess of 100,000.
31. Koyam (Kai, Kojam). This Kanuric tribe numbers about 15,000.
32. Mandara (Ndara, Wandala), with the Gamergu and Maya. This Chadic group numbers about 80,000, mainly Moslems.
33. Manga (Mangawa). This Kanuric nation numbers about 100,000.
34. Mober (Mobber). This Chadic tribe has a population of about 25,000.
35. Ngizim (Ngezzim). This Chadic tribe, numbering about 25,000, is only partially Islamized.
36. Tera (Kemaltu, Terawa), with the kindred Hina (Hinna) and Jera (Jara, Jerra). This Chadic group, numbering about 40,000, is incompletely Islamized.

(e) *Hausa Province*

All the peoples of this province speak languages of the Hausa branch of the Chadic sub-family of the Hamitic stock. At least some of them appear to have come from the north, where they once occupied the central portion of the Sahara, whence they were driven by the Berbers under Arab pressure. That Chadic peoples have long inhabited the Sudan, however, is indicated by the presence of other branches of the sub-family, not only in the Bornu and Bagirmi provinces, but also in the Nigerian plateau area. Though never politically unified until their conquest by the Fulani in the nineteenth century, the Hausa peoples, probably as a result of long experience in the trans-Saharan caravan trade, have achieved a degree of cultural unity comparable to that of the great nations of Europe in modern times and are perhaps the only nation of Negro Africa where this can definitely be said to have happened prior to European colonial occupation. They are likewise literate. Long ago they adopted the Arabic alphabet for writing their own language and have since produced an extensive literature, especially of a historical character. The famous Kano Chronicle, for example, gives us unusual historical depth for this part of the Sudan, although the events recorded before the fourteenth century deal mainly with wars among the various Hausa states.

37. Adarawa (Aderaoua), with the Azna (Anna, Arna, Asna, Azena), Gubei, and Tulumi (Touloumey). They number about 250,000 and are incompletely Islamized.
38. Hausa (Haoussa), embracing the indigenous inhabitants of the former states of Daura (the Daurawa), Gobir, Kano (the Kanawa), Katsena (the Katsenawa), Kebbi (the Kebbawa), Zamfara, and Zaria (the Zazzagawa). With their pagan kinsmen, the Maguzawa, they number about 5 million.
39. Kurfei (Kourfey, Soudie). They number about 40,000 and are largely pagan.
40. Maguzawa (Pagan Hausa). These people are pagan in religion but otherwise indistinguishable from the Hausa proper. Since they are geographically interspersed with the latter, the mapping of their territory is arbitrary.
41. Mauri (Maouri). This pagan tribe numbers about 75,000.
42. Tazarawa, with the Tegamawa and substantial remnants of the Hausa of Daura and Gobir now residing in French territory. They number about 600,000, of whom approximately a third are still pagan.

(f) *Songhai Province*

West of the Hausa, along the Niger River where its great bend touches the edge of the Sahara Desert, reside the peoples who constitute the sole representatives of the independent Songhaic linguistic stock. They appear to have come from the western part of the Hausa country, whence they ascended the Niger to their present location. They enter history about A.D. 700.

43. Dendi. These people, who number about 40,000, occupied

their present territory by conquest from the Mande-speaking Tienga about 150 years ago.

44. Songhai (Songhoi, Sonhray). This nation, numbering about 330,000, has usually exercised political domination in the province.
45. Zerma (Djerma, Dyerma, Zaberma). These people number about 250,000.

Since actual recorded history begins earlier in the western than in the eastern provinces of the Sudan fringe, we may present our historical summary in reverse geographical order. When the Songhai first appeared in history, they were ruled by a dynasty of pagan Lemta Berbers who had been driven from Tripolitania in the first Arab conquest. From their capital at Kukia on the Niger below Gao they gradually extended their sway up the river and, in 1009, removed their administrative centre to Gao. The conversion of the people to Islam began at about this time. In 1325 the Malinke of Mali captured Timbuktu and Gao and dominated the middle Niger until 1433, when they lost Timbuktu to the Tuareg. In 1465 a Songhai prince of Gao, named Sonni Ali, drove the Tuareg from Timbuktu and, in 1473, occupied Djenné. After his death one of his principal lieutenants, a Soninke named Askia, overthrew Sonni Ali's son and founded a new dynasty in 1493. Askia tried unsuccessfully to reduce the Mossi state, but he wrested large territories from Mali and, in 1512, launched a series of attacks against the Hausa states, conquering Gobir, Zamfara, Katsena, Zaria, and Kano in rapid succession. In 1515 he turned against the Tuareg, occupied Agades, expelled the bulk of the local population, and established there a Songhai colony, of which remnants survive to the present day. Under Askia the Songhai enjoyed enormous prosperity, a university was established at Timbuktu, and the fame of the kingdom was spread throughout the Moslem world by a pilgrimage which the ruler made to Mecca with a large force of retainers and a huge gift in gold for charitable foundations in the holy city.

The wealth of the Songhai state aroused the cupidity of the Sultan of Morocco, Ahmed el Mansur, who seized the rich salt mines of Terhaza in the Sahara in 1585 and, in 1591, dispatched an army equipped with firearms which took Gao by surprise.

Within a year his forces had also occupied and sacked Timbuktu and Djenné. The Moroccans withdrew their military forces in 1618 and left the administration in the hands of a pasha. After 1660 the pashas of Timbuktu achieved independence, but the Moroccan regime of pillage and extortion had so disrupted the economy of the region that the trans-Saharan trade shifted to more easterly routes and prosperity vanished. After 1780 the Tuareg achieved political dominance on the middle Niger and held it, except for a brief period of Bambara rule around 1800, until the French occupation in 1893.

The Hausa peoples received their first knowledge of Islam from the west in the fourteenth century, when the Malinke kingdom of Mali, then at its apogee, dispatched merchants and emissaries to their country. The conversion of King Yaji of Kano (1349–1385) initiated the penetration of this new religion, which has proceeded at fluctuating rates ever since and is today nearly complete. After their conquest by King Askia of Songhai, the Hausa gradually recovered their independence. With the Moroccan conquest of Gao and Timbuktu in 1591 they entered on a period of great economic prosperity. Under the disturbed conditions prevailing on the middle Niger the bulk of the trans-Saharan caravan trade, which had heretofore followed the Taodeni Trail to Timbuktu, shifted to the Gadames Trail, whose termini, Kano and Katsena, now became the great mercantile metropoles of the Sudan. A new threat soon appeared from the south with the rising power of the Jukun state of Kororofa, which repeatedly invaded the Hausa country and exacted tribute from Kano and some of its neighbours throughout most of the seventeenth century. The pastoral Fulani, who had begun to infiltrate the region in the fifteenth century, had become a significant element in the population by the eighteenth century, but the story of the holy war waged by Osman dan Fodio and of his conquest of the Hausa states (1804–1809) must be reserved until a later chapter.

Islam penetrated the Bornu province in the latter part of the eleventh century. During the early thirteenth century, political and military expansion carried the borders of the state of Kanem to Fezzan in the north, Wadai in the east, and the Niger River in the west. In 1380, however, the Bulala tribe of Lisi from Bagirmi occupied Kanem, and the ruler fled to the west of Lake Chad, where he founded the state of Bornu, the centre of political power in the province ever since. King Idris Alowa (1571–1603) of Bornu, obtaining firearms from the Turks of Tunisia, embarked on an ambitious career of conquest. He subjugated the Asben Tuareg of Air, the Hausa state of Kano, and the Kotoko, Mandara, Margi, Musgu, and Ngizim tribes to the south and, in the seventeenth century, also reduced Bagirmi to tributary status. During the latter part of the eighteenth century the Fulani began to infiltrate the country, but an attempt by the followers of Osman dan Fodio to conquer Bornu was repulsed in 1809. Kanem, however, suffered invasions by the Bagirmi and the Soliman Arabs, and Bornu, weakened by these struggles, was conquered by Wadai in 1846, bringing to a close the long reign of the Sef dynasty. In 1894, Rabih, an Arabized Negro slave raider and adventurer from Sennar on the Nile, after a career of depredation and conquest in the central Sudan, reduced Bornu and established there the capital of a completely exploitative state. He was defeated and slain by the French in 1898, and shortly thereafter his country was parcelled among the British, French, and Germans.

Although Islam was introduced into the Bagirmi province around 1600, its spread there has been relatively limited. Throughout much of their history, the dominant Bagirmi have fought and frequently subjugated the Lisi, Kotoko, Mandara, Sokoro, and Somrai. Wedged in, however, between the stronger states of Bornu on the west and Wadai on the east, the Bagirmi have usually been tributary to one or the other and at best have been able only to harrass them by an occasional attack without the prospect of conquest. Tribes of Baggara, or Cattle Arabs, began to infiltrate the province from the east during the seventeenth century, and the Fulani from the west somewhat later. In the early nineteenth century the Soliman Arabs from Tripolitania ravaged Bagirmi, which survived only with help from Wadai. Rabih conquered the province in 1892 and, from his subsequent capital in Bornu, subjected it to nearly a decade of systematic plunder.

The Arabic-speaking Tungur arrived in Darfur in the fourteenth or fifteenth century and later spread to Wadai. Because of their language the Tungur have usually been assumed to be Arabs, but they do not regard themselves as such, and the assumption is further contradicted by indications that they did not accept Islam until the seventeenth century, the period of the conversion of the other peoples of Darfur and Wadai. The fact that they still use the sign of the cross suggests that they may formerly have been Christians, and there are other intimations that they were originally Arabized Berbers or Nubians who reached the Sudan from, or by way of, the Christian kingdom of Dongola in Nubia. They intermarried with the Dagu, who had previously been politically dominant in Darfur, and succeeded them in power. Soon afterward they extended their sway to Wadai. Race mixture and acculturation continued, and after 1600 dynasties of native origin replaced them in both states. Since then the Fur have been the dominant group in Darfur and the Maba in Wadai. The two states, traditional rivals, have waged war intermittently throughout their history. Darfur, the stronger until the seventeenth century, also had political ambitions in the east and even conquered Kordofan and temporarily reduced the Fung kingdom of Sennar. Wadai dominated Bagirmi and frequently warred with Bornu. Both yielded considerable territory to the Baggara, or Cattle Arabs, in the expansion of the latter into the central Sudan, and Darfur succumbed to the Egyptians in 1875 and to the Mahdists in 1883 before the establishment of British rule. . . .

13. Roman times

JANE NICKERSON *Short History of North Africa* Devin-Adair, New York 1963; pages 3–5, 15–20, 21–4, 25–9

Remote Antiquity

North Africa has been called Africa Minor, which is a good name, for it implies that separation from the rest of the Continent which is its essential characteristic. The long strip of territory bounded on the north by the Mediterranean is cut off from the south and east by a barrier even more impenetrable than the sea, the Sahara. It is inhabited by a race of people—the Berbers—wholly different from the populations to the south of the desert. Unfortunately in modern parlance the term 'Arab' has come to be almost universally applied to them, a mistake which leads to misunderstanding, for they are not of the same race as the Arabs of Arabia, anthropologically speaking.

The name Libya was given to the easternmost part of the North African coast by the Greeks. The name Africa came into general use through the Romans, and applied to territory which corresponds roughly to present-day Tunisia. The Arabs coming in from the east called the North African coast the Maghreb (the West) and Morocco the Maghreb-el-Aksa—(the Far West). During the Middle Ages the term 'Barbary States' came to be applied to all North Africa, deriving from the Latin word 'barbarus' which means barbarian. This term has now fallen into disuse, but the Arab name 'Maghreb' is often employed, and usefully—for it implies the essential unity of all the North African coast west of Egypt.

Barbary, from the beginnings of recorded time, has been invaded, and ruled, by invaders; but these have always come either from the north or the east, never from the south. And though in the very distant past there has been some Egyptian influence, its effect was transitory and unimportant. North Africa is separated from the Valley of the Nile by the great eastern desert and Egypt forms no part of North Africa nor, consequently, of this book. Its unique and immensely ancient civilization is a different chapter of history.

This tract of country, North Africa, stretching from the eastern Egyptian desert to the Atlantic, now divided into the four provinces of Morocco, Algeria, Tunisia and Libya, has only recently been 'on the map'. The Roman Empire occupied both shores of the Mediterranean, but its successors were not strong enough to do so and North Africa after the Roman dominion ended had a wholly different destiny from that of the other provinces of the Empire. By the end of the Dark Ages all connection between Europe and Barbary was gone, to be renewed only in our own times. It is a most extraordinary historical truth that as late as the middle of the eighteenth century Europeans knew far more about the geography of distant North America and India than they did about the southern shores of the Mediterranean.

Now, to attempt a sketch of the past, however brief, it is essential to begin somewhere. Yet the present is joined continuously to the past, and becomes the future; today is influenced by yesterday and will condition tomorrow. Habits of mind, traditions and memories persist through the greatest apparent changes, and any history which does not try to show continuity is incomplete. Still there are great turning points of which one can say, if not that the world began anew, at any rate that it changed direction. The turning point at which the detailed account of North Africa must begin is the end of the Third Punic War, for its history falls inevitably into four periods:

1. The pre-Roman, up to the year 146 B.C., when Carthage was finally taken and destroyed.
2. The period of the Roman-Byzantine domination, interrupted in the year A.D. 430 by the curious episode of the Vandal invasion and ending with the first Muslim invasions in the middle of the seventh century.
3. The transition to the third period dates from A.D. 642, when the invading armies from Arabia crossed what is now the Egyptian frontier and entered Cyrenaica. Then began a movement which, though not without initial setbacks, continued steadily until A.D. 708, when all North Africa (with the exception of one garrison holding out in Ceuta) was in Muslim hands and so remained until the beginning of the last century. For a thousand years North Africa was cut off from Europe—a world apart, alien, Mohammedan, unknown. There were many attempts to break the wall; the Knights of Malta, Portugal, Spain, France and Great Britain all at different times either established a temporary foothold on the North African shore or imposed treaties upon the Barbary States. But practically speaking, the latter maintained complete independence of all European domination and influence until the nineteenth century.
4. The fourth, or modern period dates from 1830, when the French Army landed at Algiers.

Africa Romana

The original Roman colony, which was to have so great a sequel, comprised only a small portion of north-eastern Tunisia, from a point on the Mediterranean coast a little west of Carthage down to the Gulf of Gabes. By senatorial decree it was immediately annexed as a Roman province after the fall of Carthage, and became the starting point for the great expansion which was to follow.

It is important to realize that the Romans destroyed Carthage partly because it was a dangerous rival and partly from an instinctive antagonism, a loathing for the foreign, oriental thing which threatened to become powerful and influential. Thus they established themselves in Africa lest, Phoenix-like, the Punic empire should rise again from its own ashes, or some other power allied with it become a menace to Roman interests. The subsequent expansion of the original Roman colony was a purely empiric thing, following the needs of the moment. Nor was North Africa ever required by Rome as an outlet for a surplus population—the prime cause of modern colonial development. At the height of Roman power in North Africa the population of Italy was actually declining and there was never any large number of Italian colonists.

The Romans carried the war into Africa because Carthage had become a dangerous rival: they stayed primarily to make money. Their North African possessions were a paying proposition. But to make North Africa pay, the Romans were obliged to Romanize. The native Berber population was of a far lower standard of cultivation and civilization than their own; the soil was there, but they did not know or did not care how to make the most of it. To quote Charles-André Julien (*Histoire de l'Afrique du Nord*), when one speaks of the Roman colonization of North Africa, it must be understood that Rome pacified and organized Barbary, but that the natives did all the manual labour.

How was it done? And, the results being what they were, why did it fail, after so many centuries of success, and leave hardly a trace behind?

The transformation was achieved by extremely modern methods, and it failed in the end for reasons which compel a contemporary comparison. The Romans provided the cadres, and used the native population to do the work. There were frequent rebellions in the early days of their occupation, and a continual threat of raiding and invasion from the unpacified and largely unknown territory to the south. But from the fall of Carthage for five hundred years there was no serious menace to their ever-growing and increasing power. That menace when it came was of foreign origin—though it could probably have been met had it not received local support.

There were originally a certain number of immigrant Italian colonists settled on the land by the State, but these never provided more than a fraction of the labour required, which was always native. The country was divided into provinces and the whole structure of government was, of course, founded upon the army, the Third Augustan Legion of about five thousand men, plus organized native auxiliaries recruited locally. The regular army originally came from Europe and was of European stock, but as time went on it was recruited more and more from local material. Soldiers' sons born on African soil of African mothers took their fathers' places in the ranks, and by the second century of our era the Army of Africa was wholly African-born. It formed an invaluable colonial school. By the time of the Emperor Augustus the twenty years' service period was instituted, the troops automatically acquiring Roman citizenship, and after the better part of a lifetime spent in the ranks, whether native or foreign, they had learned Roman methods and science and had no thought of leaving the country. On retirement they were given grants of land, very often near their barracks, and could be counted upon for invaluable loyalty and support in case of barbarian incursions, and still more as forming an element in society of purely Roman sympathies. Modern European armies do not attempt to mix native and white troops in the same corps; but the Third Augustan Legion did not recognize racial differences, and became latterly entirely composed of Roman citizens who had acquired much Roman science and at all events a veneer of Roman culture, but were of African race.

The Romans gradually extended their territory to include the whole fertile coastal plain from the gulf of Sirte to the Atlantic coast. It was bounded by the Limes, a fortified frontier line to keep out barbarian invasion comparable to the Roman wall on the Scottish border. Owing to its much greater length it was built on a far less elaborate scale; consisting of a deep trench with fortified posts at intervals. Beyond the Limes the Romans allied themselves with the native chieftains in the territory which they did not directly control, gave them titles of command and presents to ensure their loyalty. Apart from intermittent raids there was no serious peril from the south until the middle of the fourth century.

The Roman frontier finally included all the best agricultural land. Starting in Libya only a few miles from the coast it enclosed all the fertile part of southern Tunisia and Algeria, following along the northern foothills of the high tableland which separates the sea plains from the desert to the south, but never including that plateau, which remained in native hands. Morocco also fell under Roman rule but was never so thoroughly colonized as the other provinces. The boundaries of effective Roman control in the Maghreb-el-Aksa are not yet certainly defined, but it has been established that the Romans knew and used the pass through the mountains by Taza and Oudjda to go from the plain of Oran westward, and their control of the Atlantic seaboard extended down to Sale. It would probably be accurate enough to include all modern Morocco north of a line drawn from Rabat across to Fez and so north-eastward to Taza. There was little penetration south of that.

Quite recently excavations have revealed interesting vestiges of the Roman tunny fishing establishment on the west (Atlantic) coast of the Tangier peninsula at Cape Spartel, close down at the water's edge—with walls, and pillars and brine tanks for salting the fish and temple all complete. And it is remarkable to note that although the Portuguese fishing fleet still comes every year to trawl off the coast, the local Muslim population has neither part nor lot in this enterprise, not being of a sea-faring race.

Even at the height of her power, Rome never extended her territory farther than the fertile land to the northern (Mediterranean) side of the chain of mountains which starts with the Atlas in Morocco, extends through Algeria and Tunisia and starts again east of the gulf of Gabes in Tripolitania; and even in that territory, islands of second-rate land were left in native hands. Beyond the Limes there were observation posts only, notably that at Cydamus (the modern Ghadames), an oasis on the present Libyan-Algerian frontier.

Roman Africa, bounded by the Limes and protected by the

Third Legion and its auxiliaries, was organized into four provinces which formed part of no pre-conceived plan but simply grew up according to the exigencies of the moment: Africa Proconsularis, the nucleus of the original colony (part of Tunisia including the coastal region of Tripolitania to the east), Numidia (what is today the eastern part of Algeria) and the two Mauritanias—Mauritania Caesariensis, the governor of which resided at Cherchel, an important port on the coast a little west of Algiers; and Mauritania Tingitana, which took its name from Tangier where the governor resided, and included the northern portion of Morocco.

In this territory the population remained mostly Berber, apart from the Roman magistrates, landed proprietors, merchants in the ports and principal towns and the descendants of the original troops who had served with the army in Africa.

The glory of the Carthaginian fleet was gone. The Romans maintained only sufficient naval strength to patrol the coasts and ensure the safety of the grain transports carrying wheat and oil from Africa which came to play so important a part in the life of the metropolis.

The colony was run for profit, and that profit was derived almost exclusively from agriculture. Its whole prosperity—the great increase in population, roads, towns and centres of culture and learning which grew up—were all paid for ultimately by the native Berber labourer who tilled the soil. In the earlier part of the period wheat growing was particularly encouraged and the planting of vines even forbidden lest they should encroach upon the grain lands. Later on, olive oil became also an extremely important product and was exported to Europe in vast quantities. Many hundreds of amphorae (jugs) have been discovered in Italy and elsewhere which bear the mark of African manufacture. But Algerian and Tunisian olive oil was not considered to be of the best quality and in Italy was used rather for lighting and cosmetic purposes than for cooking.

Wood was also exported in large quantities to Italy, it is believed largely for heating the public baths which were such a feature of Roman life and must have consumed an enormous quantity of fuel. Other exports were marble, elephant ivory, horses and fruits—African figs being especially appreciated by Roman gourmets. But corn, wine and oil were the main products which made the country so valuable a possession; and it was due to the Roman genius for engineering and political organization that production increased so vastly. The Berbers could and did learn to become Roman citizens of equal culture with their rulers, but it was Rome herself which supplied the genius for cooperation and the driving power which got the work done. . . .

But though Africa Romana was an agricultural society depending for its wealth upon the land, Roman civilization was essentially an urban thing. Civic life centred in the towns which grew up with all the characteristic Roman features of forum, basilica, temple and baths and were richly ornamented with statues, triumphal arches, marble columns, altars and inscriptions. A glance at the map will show how many of these towns remain: from Volubilis in Morocco to Cyrenaica their stones still stand as witness to that amazing period when there was one culture, one official language, one law, one literature and one style of architecture from the Atlantic to the Nile Valley and from the Mediterranean to the Scottish border.

In Phoenician times the great merchants of Carthage possessed large estates cultivated for them by slaves or landless Berber labourers attached to the soil. But their territory was comparatively small and not designed to supply the needs of a large European export trade; the rest of North Africa remained in the hands of its original inhabitants. When the Roman government succeeded, it annexed large areas as State property and made grants of land to its citizens and the ex-soldiers of its army; and it taxed the peasant cultivators in the territory under its control. As that area expanded and the productivity of the soil was largely increased by Roman methods two important tendencies appeared, destined to have a profound influence upon the economic character of the whole country.

First, the Romans gradually pushed out the native population from the ownership of all the best land. The Berber peasants who had cultivated their little patches to provide food for themselves and their families or pasture their flocks found themselves expropriated, with a choice of either leaving Roman territory altogether and taking refuge in the far less fertile mountainous country to the south of the Limes, or remaining on the soil of their birth to work for their masters as wage labourers. Secondly, as in all countries where there is a very large export trade in agricultural produce, the ownership of the land under cultivation tended progressively to become concentrated in a few hands. The small farms and peasant proprietors were gradually eaten up by the large domains, either State owned and administered by overseers or the property of great landlords, in many cases absentees who spent only a small part of the year in their country villas. And all land was taxed, the State receiving its income in kind, the wheat being stored in huge central depots from which the military garrisons and civil magistrates drew their rations, and the surplus exported to Rome to provide the emperors with the means to supply *panem et circenses* to the turbulent Roman populace, in default of which they were under the continual menace of revolt. The African annona—the tax in kind—became an absolute essential to the City of Rome, which without it would have been menaced with starvation, and the safe arrival of the grain ships in Ostia was a constant preoccupation of the emperors, who always feared that a recalcitrant provincial governor would hold up the fleet and thus involve him in conflict with the Roman populace—as indeed happened more than once.

The large demand for wild beasts to figure in the circus and gladiatorial combats was supplied chiefly from North Africa; leopards, lions, boars, hyenas, bears, ostriches and antelopes as well as elephants being sent regularly to Rome for the entertainment of the Colosseum. Of all this wild life there are today few survivors save the wild boar and a very few leopards. The explanation is as simple as the reason for the disappearance of the American bison; wild animals are gradually exterminated as the human population increases. We know that the population of North Africa increased enormously during the period of Roman prosperity; and the number of animals exported speaks for itself. In the reign of Augustus no less than 3,500 wild beasts from Africa were put to death for the delectation of the Roman populace in the course of one single series of celebrations lasting twenty-six days. At that rate it is hardly wonderful that there were no survivors.

Two animals, the Carthaginian elephant and the camel, played a major part in North African history and may count almost as historical personages of the first rank. In very early times, as has already been noted, elephants were indigenous to the country. The Carthaginians caught and tamed them in their own territory, while one of the diversions of the early Roman invaders was elephant hunting. But as man encroached upon the vast tracts of virgin land essential to elephant life they gradually died out. It is obviously impossible to give an exact date but certainly by the end of the third century they had disappeared; partly because the Romans made no use of them in war and consequently had no motive for preserving them, while their ivory was a valuable article of export and they were mercilessly hunted.

After the disappearance of the native North African elephants, of prime importance in the Carthaginian period, they were succeeded in the later Roman period by a domestic animal of far greater significance—the single-humped Arabian camel or dromedary. The origin of this strange creature is unknown, as far back as the record goes it only appears in history as a domesticated beast, though the Bactrian camel with two humps is known to have existed in a wild state in Central Asia. Camels were introduced into North Africa from Egypt. The exact date is not known, but they were certainly numerous in Tripolitania by the middle of the fourth century A.D., and their appearance proved to be the turning point in the history of the desert. They were imported to facilitate the already established commerce with black Africa which at that time reached to the frontier of the Roman zone of occupation. But their range and ability to live and work in the great desert opened up that vast area into which Rome had never penetrated, and made it possible for a nomadic population which has lasted up to the present day to escape from Roman domination, and eventually attack the Roman settlements. Professor Gautier goes so far as to say that the history of the Sahara might well be divided into pre-cameline and post-cameline periods. . . .

Roman rule raised North Africa to a hitherto unknown height of prosperity and culture, but it created also a vast landless proletariat to whom that rule brought no benefit, and who therefore had little incentive for loyalty to their masters.

By the end of the first century of our era the head of the Roman Empire—the Emperor—depended not only for support but also for nomination to office upon the main instrument of government, the army. The Emperor ruled by consent of the Legions, who chose their own man in the provinces, and his recognition in Rome was in reality little more than a sort of registration of an accomplished fact. But the Legions, widely separated over the whole Mediterranean world and recruited locally from all the different nationalities, were not always of one mind. There were rival claimants supported by opposing factions, and when these disputes had been decided, the Emperor, as the nominee of the soldiery, was obliged to give more and more attention to provincial government and to treat the Senate with increasing contempt.

It is a measure of the high importance of the African provinces and the intellectual equality between the Romanized upper classes and European-born citizens that one of the best and most successful of these latter soldier–emperors was of African birth, a loyal son of his native land, who by the accident of his accession to the highest position in the State did much to further the interests of Africa Romana.

Septimius Severus was born at Leptis Magna in Tripolitania in the year A.D. 146 of the Romanized ruling class. He received a good education in his native province and adopted an official career as civil magistrate and military commander which took him to Rome. Eventually, after the murder of Marcus Aurelius' worthless son, Commodus, he won the support of the provincial Legions and made good his claim to the imperial throne. It was a claim which had no shadow of justification save the right of the strongest. He became Emperor by virtue of a military pronunciamento, but thanks to exceptional ability he was able to maintain his candidature against all rivals, and his reign (A.D. 193–211) marks the summit of Africa's importance under Roman rule. His unusually forceful personality has left many memorials, including numerous portraits. The triumphal arch commemorating one of his eastern campaigns still stands in Rome, and recent Italian excavations have revealed the magnificent monuments with which he endowed his native city of Leptis.

Septimius Severus retained the imprint of his African birth and education all his life. It is known that he was bilingual, as were all his compatriots (like a modern Welshman whose culture is wholly English, yet who speaks Welsh at home). He learnt Punic at his mother's knee, and to the end of his life spoke Latin with a provincial accent, though his whole education and culture were Roman. After his accession to the imperial honours a sister from Africa came to visit him, who was hastily sent home because she made herself ridiculous at Court by her lack of command of the language. Her brother, of more adaptable material, was an enthusiastic student of Roman literature as well as a successful military commander. Some of the habits acquired in his youth stayed with him and it is recorded that he never lost his taste for African cooking; and fruits and vegetables grown in North Africa were specially brought to Rome for his table.

For the first and last time African interests were of paramount importance to the head of the Government; but it must be borne in mind that it was not the lot of the oppressed Berber peasant which interested the Emperor, but the Romanized upper class in the towns where he had himself lived as a boy. He knew instinctively that his power and their prosperity were equally bound up with the strength of the army, and his policy was aimed at ensuring its loyalty to his house. He enormously increased the material gains and honorary distinctions of the service, to such an extent that he was even charged with corrupting the troops. But none the less, on balance, he left the army of the empire more efficient than when it had first carried him to power. It was increased in strength by three Legions, while the Pretorian Guard was reformed and made into a more effective force. Its ranks were now filled by promotion from all the Legions in service, instead of its recruitment being limited to Italy and one or two of the neighbouring provinces. Indeed the whole administration acquired more and more of a military character, many retired military officers being appointed to posts formerly filled by civilians of equestrian rank.

African interests, in the Roman sense of the word, were furthered in every possible way; and it seems certain that Septimius Severus realized the enormous value of camel-breeding and we know that the number of camels in Africa, hitherto small, increased very considerably during his reign. His knowledge of local conditions was no doubt, in this as in many other cases, an invaluable asset to his compatriots at the time.

Yet in the long run his policies contributed to changes which were to prove fatal to Roman rule.

To increase the sphere of Roman influence and add to the Roman area of cultivation the indigenous Berber population was pushed out and driven further south, while the Limes was advanced to its furthest extent. This policy, coupled with the introduction of camel transport, wrought a revolution in the Sahara, hitherto occupied by the negroid population whose remote ancestors left the remarkable wall paintings in the Hoggar Mountains. Camels carried the Berbers who had been expelled from their lands in the fertile coastal belt deep into the desert, from which they drove out the negroid inhabitants. Nobody knows exactly how this revolution took place; it may have been the work of generations, it may have been accomplished in a relatively short time. At all events, where formerly the Roman coastal provinces had to deal with easily controlled negro populations to the south, these now disappeared, pushed down towards the river Niger by the Berber invaders mounted on camels who established themselves outside the Limes. Exiled by the advance of Roman agriculture, they were unwilling to submit to Roman discipline. Turbulent, and always ready to raid the Roman lands and rebel against Roman jurisdiction whenever an opportunity offered, they proved far more dangerous than the former inhabitants of the Sahara.

The African Emperor's amazing career terminated in Great Britain. Faithful to his lifelong preoccupation with military matters, Septimius Severus spent the last three years of his reign reorganizing and strengthening this northern frontier of the Empire. He was accompanied by his son Caracalla, who succeeded him. It is said that he stayed in one of the most distant and barbarous of the provinces partly because he wanted to keep that son away from the deleterious and corrupting influence of the Court. He died at York in February 211, and there are vague traditions that his end was in some way hastened by Caracalla. At all events the climate of Yorkshire in February cannot have contributed to the recovery of this son of the south, at sixty-five years of age, after an exceptionally strenuous life. It would be interesting to know how long the news of his demise took to reach Leptis Magna, his home-town, which he had embellished with monuments and public buildings of the utmost magnificence and where his popularity was enormous. It is a far cry from the hot sea-plain of Tripolitania, its olive groves and fig trees which the emperor so much loved, and the blue waters of the Mediterranean, to the short pale light and great wood fires of a Yorkshire winter. . . .

V. THE ARAB CONQUESTS

14. Arab invasions and trans-Saharan trade

LLOYD BRIGGS *Tribes of the Sahara* Harvard University Press 1960; pages 40–50

. . . Over the more than twenty centuries that have passed since the first flickering rays of the light of history began to dissipate the shadows of prehistoric times, the peoples of the Sahara have been in practically constant touch commercially with southern Europe and the East, both Near and Far; and yet this very important fact has been overlooked by nearly everyone. Even though the commercial relations were usually indirect, because of intervening middlemen, they resulted in a steadily increasing flow of foreign trade goods and ideas into and across the desert, and so must have exerted a continuous and increasingly profound influence on Saharan ways of life. And, in addition to the kind of influence produced by trade, special political situations gave rise every now and then to cultural relations which, although less close in general and less far-reaching geographically in most cases, must have left some mark on the Saharan tribes, especially those of the northern desert. For example, the Roman administration in the north maintained a chain of outposts along the northern boundary of the Sahara, in direct contact with the nomad tribal territories immediately to the south. The settlement of Ghirza (a hundred and seventy-five miles south-east of Tripoli), made up of a group of large fortified farms and two elaborate cemeteries, with imposing monuments, may be taken as indicating the general nature of such installations from the third to the sixth centuries. The farm owners of Ghirza were retired veterans of the Roman army, Europeans at first and later Berbers, who acted both as vanguards of Roman civilization and as militia to keep desert raiders at a distance. Most of their farm labourers, however, must have been recruited locally, and so must have been active in spreading Roman culture. One or two Roman military expeditions are known to have crossed the Sahara to the Sudan about two thousand years ago, but unfortunately almost no information has survived concerning what they saw or what they did along the way, nor do they seem to have left behind them any lasting traces of their passage.

Unfortunately, too, the extent of Roman trans-Saharan trade and its importance for the tribes inhabiting the interior remain unknown. Negro slaves, gold, and ivory were probably brought up across the western desert, but it seems likely that these operations were almost entirely in the hands of native nomads. Nevertheless the impact of Roman material culture made itself felt to some degree far to the south; for the rich grave furniture from the 'Tomb of Tin Hinan', at Abalessa, included at least three impressions of coins of Constantine the Great as well as jewellery and other objects of eastern Roman style which date probably from between the fourth and sixth centuries. Surprising as it may seem, Roman coins were still in circulation less than sixty years ago in some of the commercial centres of the northern central desert. Indeed the common North African word for small change, *floos*, is merely a corruption of the Latin *follis*.

The Arab invasions of the seventh and eleventh centuries must have displaced many tribes and even whole confederations of pre-Islamic Saharan nomads, and at the same time overrun and engulfed to some extent the sedentary communities of negroid agriculturists, Jewish artisans, and Berber refugees in and around many oases and trading centres of the northern desert. As early as the second quarter of the eighth century Arab expeditions from Morocco were already marching southward to seek gold in 'the land of the Negroes'. In the tenth and eleventh centuries, the nomadic Berber peoples of the western half of the Sahara seem to have expanded with a suddenness and force that carried them northward through Morocco and into Spain, as the Almoravids, and southward, under the name of Zaghawa, into the Sudan. The fact that the word Almoravid is a Spanish corruption of the Arabic *mrabteen*, meaning holy men of Islam, suggests that it was the massive shock of Arab invasion and the resulting turmoil of conflicting cultures which set off this explosion. But in spite of such dramatic shiftings of populations, the Saharan peoples in general seem to have been but little affected in their ways of life except by the gradual and usually very superficial spread of Arabic language and Moslem religious doctrine.

During the Middle Ages as a whole, trans-Saharan trade seems to have become increasingly lively. Sugar, cloth, brass-ware, coral, books, horses, and many other things were shipped southward in exchange not only for slaves and gold dust, but also ivory and ostrich feathers, 'Morocco' leather, civet, and even occasional live civet cats. The channels of this trade passed through the various Saharan oases and commercial centres, and these in turn exported their own local products such as dates, ostrich feathers, and a few manufactured articles of gold. Indeed, as early as the eleventh century merchants from Barbary and the Mzab were frequenting the slave market of Kumbi, the capital of the original Ghana, which lay between the Niger and the headwaters of the Senegal.

Striking evidence of the ease with which merchants moved in all directions at this time is to be found in the diary of a famous Moroccan traveller, Abou Abdallah Mohammed ibn Battuta, of Tangier, who set out in 1352 to visit the Sudan. Before venturing into the desert wilderness, he stopped off for a few days at a town on the north-western edge of the Sahara, where he stayed with a learned man whose travelling merchant brother he had known some years before in China, possibly at Foochow on the coast opposite Formosa. Continuing southward he then crossed the western desert to Teghaza, which he found to be 'an unattractive village, with the curious feature that its houses and mosques are built of blocks of salt, roofed with camel skins,' and he added, 'There are no trees there, nothing but sand. We passed ten days of discomfort there, because the water is brackish and the place is plagued with flies.' From Teghaza, Ibn Battuta went on to Timbuctoo and Gao, through country which was then all under Tuareg control. In 1353 he left Gao with a caravan that included a singularly disagreeable commercial traveller from Barbary, several merchants recently arrived from Ghadamès, and six hundred Negro slave women. The exact route followed has been much disputed, but it seems to have led south-eastward and then eastward along the northern border of Nigeria to a place called Tagadda (the modern Tegguidda, or Tedjidda, a hundred miles north-west of Agadès), and from there northward through the Air to In Azaoua (three hundred odd miles north of Agadès). Here the trail divided, one branch leading eastward into Egypt and the other northward through the Ahaggar, and then north-westward through the Mouydir and Tidikelt to Bouda (twelve miles west of Adrar) in the Touat, and finally to Morocco.

The first European who is known to have crossed the Sahara in post-Roman times was a Frenchman from Toulouse, named Anselm d'Isalguiers (or Ysalguiers), who left home in 1402 and travelled to the Niger Bend by unknown means. There he married a Songhai princess of Gao, and returned northward with her right across the desert, accompanied by their infant daughter and six Negro slaves. In 1413 the whole party at last reached Toulouse, where one of the slaves, a eunuch named Aben Ali according to the story, established himself in medical practice using West African 'witch doctor' methods. A few years later when the French Dauphin, Charles, who was destined to be crowned as Charles VII by Joan of Arc, fell seriously ill while visiting Toulouse, the doctor-slave cured him and was richly rewarded in consequence.

In 1447 a Genoese travelling merchant, named Antonio Malfante, sent home a report from the Touat stating that he had landed at a seaport on the coast of western Algeria, and had gone on from there southward across the desert with a grain caravan as far as Tamentit. He reported that the population of the Touat was largely negroid, but that trade was mainly in the hands of the Jews while nomadic Tuareg tribes controlled the open country. Dates were the staple food, meat of any kind was a great luxury, and grain had to be brought in by caravan. Copper was imported from Alexandria to be traded to the south for salt and Sudanese gold. There was also an active local trade in camels and cattle; but since the cattle seem not to have been eaten ordinarily, presumably they were kept for milk. The merchants of Tamentit must have constituted a highly privileged class, for the normal profit margin in transactions of all kinds was at least a hundred per cent. Malfante wrote that he was the first Christian ever seen in the Touat; but where he went from there or what finally became of him remains a mystery.

During the first half of the fifteenth century the Portuguese, under the leadership of Prince Henry the Navigator, established a series of commercial outposts in what is now the Spanish Sahara, and began to extend their trading operations southward along the coast beyond. By 1448 they had built up a flourishing slave trade all along the Atlantic coast of West Africa, from Rio de Oro to the mouth of the Senegal River. About this time they also established regular commercial relations with the western desert trading centre of Ouadane, where the Tuareg supplied them with slaves in exchange for horses, silk, and 'other merchandise'. Weapons doubtless figured prominently among the 'other merchandise', for many Tuareg swords that are preserved in collections, as well as a few still in use among the modern Tuareg, bear the marks of sixteenth- and seventeenth-century German bladesmiths of Solingen and Passau, as well as those of the royal swordsmiths of Spain which were so freely copied in both Germany and northern Italy, and even in the Sudan.[1] Apparently the Tuareg still trade for European sword blades now and then, for in 1955 I saw one, bearing a late nineteenth-century dated mark of the Spanish Royal Arsenal of Toledo, in the workshop of the smiths at Tamanrasset in the Ahaggar. Cheap copies, often with forged European marks, have long been made and still are made occasionally by Saharan and particularly Sudanese smiths, both for the Tuareg and for the tourist trade.

Foreigners other than the Portuguese were also active during the fifteenth century in developing commercial relations with the peoples of the south-western Sahara and the western Sudan. A commercial agent of the great Florentine merchant house of the Portinari, a man named Benedetto Dei, is the first European known to have reached Timbuctoo, where he arrived in 1470 and set up shop as a dealer in cloth imported from Lombardy. And at that time there was already a system of regular and direct caravan connections between Timbuctoo and Fez in Morocco, Tunis, and even Cairo. El Hassan ibn Mohammed (better known as 'Leo Africanus'),[2] wrote in the early

[1] A Tuareg sword in my own collection bears on its blade the inscription: VIVA EL REY DE PORTUGAL. Sir James G. Mann, Keeper of the Armouries of Her Majesty's Tower of London, agrees with me that the style of the lettering and the form and quality of the blade alike suggest that it was made at Solingen in the seventeenth century.

[2] Leo Africanus was an Arab, originally named El Hassan ibn Mohammed el Wezzan (but also known as 'El Fasi', meaning 'the man from Fez'), who was born at Granada about 1490, and a few years later accompanied his parents into exile in Morocco. When about twenty-five years old he was

sixteenth century that commercial agents from Algiers and Bougie, on the Mediterranean coast, were in the habit of meeting and trading in the Mzab with merchants from Timbuctoo.

Intellectual exchange across the desert naturally increased along with the development of commercial intercourse. From the early Middle Ages onward, travelling Moslem scholars of the north kept their Saharan colleagues in touch fairly regularly with the rest of the Moslem world and even with countries far beyond its boundaries. Men like El Bekri, Ibn Battuta, Ibn Khaldoun, and many others, wandered about freely for years over tremendous distances. The surprising ease with which they travelled was made possible by the fact that they could read and write, whereas most of the populations that they visited could not. Because the Koran is written in Arabic, pious Moslems look on Arabic writing as more or less sacred, while some of them go so far as to think it a grievous sin to tear up or even crumple up a piece of paper which has been written upon —in Arabic of course. This reverence for writing is automatically extended to the writer, so that even a mediocre Arabic scholar is looked on as a holy man of sorts. Every door is open to him, and there is a place for him at every table and in every caravan. In addition, scholars who achieved even minor reputations were usually adopted by patrons, just as European scholars were in the days of Rome's greatness and in the Middle Ages and the Renaissance; such patrons often paid for travel in the interests of pure scholarship as well as for the gathering of political and commercial intelligence. Another factor which facilitated travel in those days, and which has generally escaped notice, is the degree to which banking facilities were developed throughout the Moslem world. Ibn Battuta, for example, was able, in the middle of the fourteenth century, to have a sum of money sent all the way from India to Meknès in Morocco.

While Barbary continued to influence the Sahara intellectually more and more, from at least as early as the twelfth century onward, European commercial influence also became

captured at sea by a Christian pirate from Sicily, Pietro Bovadiglia, who gave him as a present to Pope Leo X, a son of Lorenzo the Magnificent. Two years later the Pope freed him, converted him to Christianity, baptized him Giovanni Leone (the Pope's own name), and put him on a pension because of his remarkable knowledge of African geography.

increasingly important during the fifteenth and sixteenth centuries. During the closing years of the sixteenth century, however, the economic situation began to change again, chiefly because of two new factors which came into being at that time. In the first place, the discovery of the Americas, whose undreamed-of riches apparently were available within easy reach of even the humblest adventurer, quickly turned the attention of European speculators away from the comparatively negligible profits of Saharan trade. For the same reason, trans-Saharan trade with the Sudan fell off sharply, as Sudanese gold quickly lost much of its previously almost unique charm, and as slave traders discovered that it was often more profitable to deliver their merchandise to New World buyers on the Guinea Coast than it had been to ship it northward into and across the desert. And, in the second place, while all this was going on, Morocco entered a period of rapid economic growth.

Under the Moroccan Sultan Moulay Ahmed el Mansour, the pressure generated by new-found prosperity led in turn to the organizing of a series of expeditions designed first to capture the commerce and particularly the salt trade of the south-western Sahara, and then to establish Moroccan control over the great commercial centres of the Niger Bend. In 1590 a huge army was assembled under the command of Judar Pasha, a blue-eyed Spanish eunuch[1] from Andalusia, who had been captured in infancy and brought up in the royal palace at Marrakech. Judar's forces, made up mostly of Moslems but including also a few Christian renegades, are said to have numbered two thousand cavalry, a camel corps of a thousand mounted men, two thousand infantry, six hundred engineers, and a baggage train of a thousand horses and eight thousand camels. Artillery support was included in the shape of six large

[1] In our natural horror at the medieval Moslem custom of making eunuchs of exceptionally promising slave boys we should not forget that the same practice was long tolerated in Europe. Bovill has pointed out that 'During the Middle Ages large establishments, mostly under the direction of Jews, were maintained in France, notably at Verdun, for the supply of eunuchs to Muslim Spain,' and he adds that 'The *Soprani* of the Sistine Chapel, "the musical glory and moral shame" of the papal choir, were not abolished until late in the nineteenth century, but the gelding of boys continued in Italy for some time after that.'

cannon and 'various smaller pieces' which, together with the ammunition for them, had been obtained from England in exchange for sugar and saltpetre. The gunners were mostly British sailors. Water for the expedition was carried on camel-back in bullock skins.

Judar crossed the Sahara, losing perhaps as much as two thirds of his army along the way, and finally reached the Niger on 28 February 1591. After destroying a Sudanese army, which greatly outnumbered his own forces, he entered Gao unopposed and found there, among many other odds and ends, some Portuguese cannon, a crucifix, and a statue of the Virgin. He then turned west to Timbuctoo, where again his entry was unopposed.

As a result of Judar's victorious campaign, trade between the western Sudan and Barbary remained under effective Moroccan control until 1610, when the last of the Moroccan military governors was driven out by a revolt of his own officers. The bulk of the Moroccan troops, however, stayed on in the Sudan after this uprising, and proceeded to elect their own local pashas in an attempt to establish themselves as independent rulers of the area. But soon they became more and more mixed with the local population, and thereby lost not only their tight military organization but also the prestige of glamour and fear of the unknown that had clothed the original Moroccan conquerors from across the desert. Out of this new hybrid population there arose a distinct ethnic group, the Arma, who survive to this day.

The western Sudan and the adjoining regions of the south-western desert were characterized during most of the seventeenth century by a varying state of political chaos, with the Arma, based on Djenné, Timbuctoo, and Gao, exercising a fluctuating and more or less limited control over these commercial centres and the waterways connecting them, and paying tribute now to the Sultan of Morocco, now to the pagan Negro king of the Bambara. But, in spite of this confused state of affairs, trans-Saharan trade between Barbary and the western Sudan flourished unabated, and many merchant houses of Barbary, and Italy as well, continued to maintain resident representatives in Timbuctoo and Gao.

Almost no definite information has survived concerning the

relations between the eastern half of the Sahara and the outside world during the thousand years or so that follow the abandonment of the last Roman establishments along the coast of Cyrenaica and Tripolitania, the modern Kingdom of Libya. And yet this very lack of information suggests that the situation there must have been quite different from that which characterized the western desert during the same period. Indeed, it seems that after the final collapse of Roman power in Africa, the eastern desert was cut off almost entirely from outside influence and trade, excepting on the small and strictly limited scale made possible by more or less regular caravan connections with northern Egypt. Although there is no way of knowing how long this state of affairs lasted, it seems likely that more generalized inter-regional and inter-continental commerce did not begin to assume significant proportions until the seventeenth or early eighteenth century, and that it continued to expand slowly after that.

The trans-Saharan trade of the eastern desert, as it was during the first quarter of the nineteenth century, has been described in some detail by an early British explorer, Captain George Lyon of the Royal Navy. He tells us that the assortment of goods passing southward through the Fezzan, from Tripoli, Cyrenaica, and Egypt to the central Sudan, included cloth, rugs, and garments, sheet tin and tin-plated copper vessels, iron and steel tools, needles, swords, and firearms, gunpowder and shot, green leather, and horses. There were many luxury articles too, such as silks, silver and gold thread, embroidered cloth, gold and silver jewellery and cheap trinkets, glass arm bracelets from Venice, beads of china and glass, mirrors, sugar, and perfumes of various kinds, sacred books, and even 'handsome girls from Abyssinia, educated in Mecca or Egypt'. Northward across the Fezzan there moved slaves ('chiefly female') and ivory, gold, and cotton cloth and garments, leather goods of various kinds including ostrich skins with the feathers still in place, mortars and bowls of wood, civet, pepper, honey, kola nuts, and even live parrots. Lion skins had once been imported, but they were no longer to be had in 1820, 'owing', says Lyon, 'to the Sultan of Bornou buying them all up for his negresses to sleep on, to prevent their bearing children, as he has already a large family. It is implicitly believed,' the author added, 'that a woman who sleeps on a lion's skin never can become pregnant.' Towards the end of August 1819, Lyon saw a mixed caravan of Arabs and Teda, northward bound from the Sudan, arrive at Mourzouk with '1,400 slaves of both sexes and of all ages, the greater part being females'. This seems to have been a perfectly ordinary occurrence. Local exports from the Fezzan itself are said to have been mainly dates, soda (natron), and hairy sheep.

However great the volume and the value of Saharan commerce may have been at various times in different parts of the desert, commercial activity on an important scale was always at the mercy of those warlike tribes through whose territories the main trade routes passed. Although it is not known just when the various nomad confederations of the Sahara first established systematic control over its three main channels of north-south caravan traffic, it is clear that by the sixteenth century the Ajjer[1] Tuareg controlled the eastern route through the Fezzan from Ghat northward, while the Tuareg of the Air controlled its southern extension. The central route, from the neighbourhood of In Salah southward, was in the hands of the Ahaggar Tuareg confederation, while its northern part was under Arab control. The western route too seems to have been under Tuareg control at times, although to exactly what extent it is difficult to say. Eventually it fell into the hands of the Tadjakant and finally the Moors, but for a long time thereafter it still remained more or less subject to Tuareg raids designed to force payment of tribute or to obtain plunder when payment was not forthcoming. And the Niger Bend country, the southern terminus of the great western trans-Saharan caravans, suffered so regularly from raids of the south-western Tuareg, who were being driven farther and farther southward by the expansion of their Arab nomad neighbours, that it was under almost constant Tuareg domination for all practical purposes from the early seventeenth century until the early twentieth.

During the seventeenth and eighteenth centuries life in the Sahara seems to have flowed along monotonously and with very little change, aside from the local territorial reshufflings and minor shifts of power which always go on unendingly between nomadic tribes. . . .

[1] Pronounced Azguer or Azjer, according to the district.

15. The Fāṭimid and Abbayid dynasties

BERNARD LEWIS *The Arabs in History* Hutchinson University Library 1950; pages 111–14, 155–9, 160

. . . The first three Fāṭimid Caliphs reigned only in North Africa, where they encountered a number of difficulties. The establishment of a state and a dynasty involved different requirements from those of a revolutionary opposition sect. At the very beginning intransigents were not wanting who accused the new Caliphs of watering down and betraying the tenets of Ismā'īlism. At a later date the Fāṭimids were to come into conflict with the Carmathians of Baḥrain for much the same reasons. The expansion of the new dynasty eastwards was accomplished after three unsuccessful attempts by Mu'izz, the fourth Caliph, who conquered Egypt in 969. The conquest had been long prepared by secret emissaries and propagandists, who had undermined the resistance of the Egyptians. The conquest of Egypt was followed almost immediately by a clash with the Carmathians, who, for the moment, constituted a real danger to the new regime. Later they seemed to have returned to their Fāṭimid allegiance.

Mu'izz was well served by two remarkable men. One was his general Jawhar, a Mamlūk of European origin who was the real conqueror of Egypt. It was he who built the new city of Cairo as the Fāṭimid capital, and the great mosque of Al-Azhar as the centre of their faith. Converted to orthodoxy centuries later, the Azhar Mosque has remained to the present day one of the main centres of Islamic thought and religious life. The other great servant of Mu'izz was Ya'qūb ibn Killis, an Islamised Jew of Baghdadi origin who had joined Mu'izz in Tunisia and helped him before, during and after the conquest. Ya'qūb ibn Killis was a financial genius, who organised the taxation and civil service system which lasted almost throughout the period of Fāṭimid rule.

The Fāṭimids rapidly extended their sway into Palestine, Syria and Arabia, and for a while greatly surpassed the power and influence of the orthodox Caliphs in Baghdad. The peak of the Fāṭimid period in Egypt was the reign of the Caliph Mustanṣir (1036–1094), under whom the Fāṭimid Empire included the whole of North Africa, Sicily, Egypt, Syria and western Arabia. In 1056–57 a pro-Fāṭimid general succeeded in seizing even Baghdad itself and in proclaiming the sovereignty of the Fāṭimid Caliph from the pulpits of the 'Abbāsid capital. He was driven out in the following year, however, and thereafter the power of the Fāṭimids declined. The breakdown was first noticeable in the civil administration, and led to the rise of a series of military autocrats who exercised their authority in Cairo just as their counterparts had already been doing in Baghdad for some time. Deprived of their immense powers, and reduced to the status of helpless puppets of the Amīrs, the Caliphs gradually lost the support of the sectaries and their regime was finally abolished by Saladin, who restored Egypt to orthodoxy.

The regime of the Fāṭimids in Egypt at its height differs in a number of respects from those that had preceded it. At the top was the infallible Imām, an absolute monarch, ruling by hereditary right transmitted by the divine will through a divinely ordained family. His government was centralised and hierarchic and was divided into three branches: religious, military and bureaucratic. The last two were in the charge of the Wazīr, a civilian, under the Caliph. The religious branch consisted of a hierarchy of missionaries in several grades under a missionary-in-chief, who was an extremely influential political personage. This department was responsible for the higher schools of learning and for the propagandist organisation of the Ismā'īlī sect and seems to have played a role not unlike that of the Party in modern one-party dictatorships. The propagandist branch directed a vast army of agents throughout the eastern provinces still under the nominal control of the 'Abbāsid Caliph in Baghdad. The effectiveness of this propaganda can be seen in a number of ways. From Iraq to the borders of India repeated outbreaks attested to the activity of the Ismā'īlī agents, while the intellectual life of the whole of Islam testifies in a number of ways to the seductive appeal of the Ismā'īlī allegiance for the radical intelligentsia. The poets Mutanabbī (*d.* 965) and Abu'l-'Alā al-Ma'arrī (*d.* 1057), two of the greatest in Arabic literature, were both strongly influenced by Ismā'īlī ideas. In Iraq an encyclopaedist movement was organised by a group known as 'The Sincere Brethren of Baṣra'. These published a series of fifty-one epistles covering all branches of knowledge known at that time, and with a strong Ismā'īlī bias. The Epistles of the Sincere Brethren were read from India to Spain and exercised a vast influence on later writers. Their spread was helped by the organisation of semi-secret study groups under the direction of members of the Brotherhood.

The Fāṭimid period was also an epoch of great commercial and industrial efflorescence. Except for a few periods of famine due to the misbehaviour of the Nile or of military cliques the era was one of great prosperity. From the first, Fāṭimid governments realised the importance of trade both for the prosperity of their Empire and for the extension of its influence. Ya'qūb ibn Killis initiated a commercial drive which later rulers followed. The pre-Fāṭimid trade of Egypt had been meagre and limited. The Fāṭimids developed plantations and industries in Egypt and began an important export trade of Egyptian products. In addition they developed a wide net of commercial relations, especially with Europe and with India. In the West they established close relations, dating back to their early Tunisian days, with the Italian city republics, more particularly with Amalfi, Pisa and Venice. A great volume of seaborne trade passed between Egypt and the West, and Egyptian ships and merchants sailed as far as Spain. The two main harbours under Fāṭimid rule were Alexandria and Syrian Tripoli, both markets of world-wide importance. The Fāṭimid fleets controlled the eastern Mediterranean.

In the East the Fāṭimids developed important contacts with India, gradually extending their sovereignty southward over both shores of the Red Sea. They succeeded in shifting the Indian trade of the Middle East from the Persian Gulf to the Red Sea and especially to the great Fāṭimid port of 'Aidhāb on the Sudanese coast. They traded too with Byzantium and with the Muslim States, though these were of less importance. Wherever the Egyptian merchant went, the Ismā'īlī missionary was not far behind, and soon we find the same ferment of ideas among the Muslims both of Spain and of India.

With the decline of the Fāṭimid Caliphate at home, the links between the dynasty and the sect grew weaker and were eventually broken. The Fāṭimid Caliphate lingered on for a while as a puppet dynasty in Egypt and was eventually abolished, but in the eastern lands of the Caliphate, now under the rule of the Turkish Seljuqs, the revolutionary organisation took on a new lease of life. . . .

In the middle of the thirteenth century the power of the Turkish Mamlūks in Cairo was supreme and a new regime emerged, the Mamlūk Sultanate, which ruled Egypt and Syria until 1517. In 1260, after a period of confusion following the death of the last Ayyūbid, a Qipchaq Turk called Baibars became Sultan. His career in many ways forms an interesting parallel with that of Saladin. He united Muslim Syria and Egypt into a single state, this time more permanently. He defeated the external enemies of that state, repulsing Mongol invaders from the east and crushing all but the last remnants of the Crusaders in Syria. An idea of genius was to invite a member of the 'Abbāsid family to establish himself in Cairo with the title of Caliph. The line of 'Abbāsid Caliphs in Cairo were mere court functionaries of the Mamlūk Sultāns. The Egyptian historian Maqrīzī (*d.* 1442) remarks:

> The Turkish Mamlūks installed as Caliph a man to whom they gave the name and titles of Caliph. He had no authority and no right to express his opinion. He passed his time with the commanders, the great officers, the officials and the judges, visiting them to thank them for the dinners and parties to which they had invited him.

The Cairo Caliphs represent the final stage in the decay of the Caliphate.

The Mamlūk system of Baibars and his successors was feudal and was an adaptation of the Seljuq feudalism brought into Syria and Egypt by the Ayyūbids. An officer or amīr received a grant of land in lieu of pay and on condition of maintaining a certain number of Mamlūk soldiers, varying between five and a hundred according to his rank. He normally devoted two-thirds of his revenues to their upkeep. The grants were not hereditary though there were many attempts to make them so. The system was based on the permanent eviction of the Arabized descendants of the Mamlūk officers by newly imported Mamlūks, thus preventing, perhaps deliberately, the formation of a hereditary landed aristocracy. A Mamlūk officer received his grant for life or less. He did not normally reside on his estates, but in Cairo or in the chief town of the district where his fief lay.

He was interested in revenue rather than possession. The system therefore developed no *châteaux* or manors or strong local authorities of the Western type. There was no subinfeudation, and even the division of land in Egypt into fiefs was not permanent, being subject to a periodic territorial refount.

The Mamlūks themselves were bought slaves, trained and educated in Egypt. At first they were mainly Qipchaq Turks from the northern shores of the Black Sea; later they included Mongol deserters and men of other races, chiefly Circassians, with occasional Greeks, Kurds and even some Europeans. But Turkish or Circassian remained the language of the dominant class, many of whom, including some Sultans, could hardly speak Arabic. The Mamlūk state as developed by Baibars and his successors was based on a highly elaborate dual administration, civil and military, both sides controlled by Mamlūk officers with civilian staffs. Until 1383 the Mamlūk Sultans followed one another in more or less hereditary succession. Thereafter the Sultanate was held by the strongest commander. On the death of a Sultan his son succeeded as formal head during an interregnum while the real succession was decided.

In the first period the Mamlūks were threatened by Christian and Mongol enemies, and their supreme achievement is their defence of the Islamic civilisation of the Near East against these enemies. During the fifteenth century a new power arose—the Ottoman Empire, rising like a phoenix from the ruins of the Seljuq Sultanate of Anatolia. Relations between the two states were at first friendly, but conflicts arose when the Ottomans, safely established in Europe, turned their attention to Asia.

The trade with Europe, and particularly the trade between Europe and the Further East via the Near East, was of vital importance to Egypt, both for the trade itself and for the customs revenues derived from it. During periods of strength Mamlūk governments protected and encouraged this trade, which brought Egypt great prosperity and a new flowering of arts and letters. But the Mongol threat, warded off by Baibars, was not yet averted. In 1400–1401 the Turco-Mongol forces of Tīmūr (Tamerlane) ravaged Syria and sacked Damascus. Plague, locusts and the depredations of the unleashed Bedouin completed the work of the departed Mongols, and the Mamlūk

Sultanate suffered a blow to its economic and military strength from which it never recovered.

The crises of the fifteenth century brought new fiscal policies aimed at extracting the maximum profit from the transit trade. After first encouraging Indian and even Chinese merchants to bring their wares to ports under Egyptian control, Sultan Barsbay (1422–1438) had the idea that it might be even better to seize the trade than to tax it. He began by making sugar a royal monopoly, and followed it with pepper and other commodities. These policies, maintained by his successors, led to rising prices, foreign reprisals, and ultimately to general economic collapse, in which the government could survive only by currency depreciation and by drastic and violent taxation.

The historians of the period paint a vivid picture of the increasing corruption and inefficiency of the regime in its last days. One historian, speaking of the Wazīrs, remarks:

> They were cruel rascals, inventors of a thousand injustices, arrogant and presumptuous. They were famous neither for their knowledge nor for their religious spirit. They were the scourges of their age, always with a causeless insult ready in their mouths. Their existence, passed exclusively in oppressing the people of their time, was a disgrace to humanity.

When Sultan Barsbay convened the four chief Qāḍīs of Cairo and asked them to authorise new taxes over and above those laid down by the Holy Law, one of them was reputed to have replied: 'How can we authorise the taking of money from the Muslims when a wife of the Sultan wore on the day of her son's circumcision a dress worth 30,000 dinars; and that is only one dress and only one wife.'

In 1498 came the crowning catastrophe. On 17 May of that year the Portuguese navigator Vasco da Gama landed in India, having come by sea round the Cape of Good Hope. In August 1499 he returned to Lisbon with a cargo of spices. He had opened a new route from Europe to the Further East, cheaper and safer than the old one. Other expeditions followed rapidly. The Portuguese established bases in India, and developed direct trade, dealing a mortal blow to the Egyptian route and cutting off the very lifeblood of the Mamlūk state. The Mamlūks, recognising the immediate consequences of these events, and urged to action by their Venetian fellow-sufferers from this diversion, tried by diplomacy and then by war to avert the Portuguese menace. Their efforts were fruitless. The Portuguese fleets, built to face the Atlantic gales, were superior in structure, armament and navigational skill to those of the Muslims. Soon they were able to defeat the Egyptian squadrons, systematically destroy Arab merchant shipping in the Indian Ocean, and penetrate even to the Persian Gulf and the Red Sea. In the sixteenth century, after the Ottoman conquest and the growth of European commercial enterprise, the Levant trade revived to some extent, but remained of secondary importance. The Arab Near East had been outflanked. Not until the nineteenth century did the main routes of world trade return to it.

During the long period that we have been considering three significant changes merge. The first of these is the transformation of the Islamic Near East from a commercial monetary economy to one which, despite an extensive and important foreign and transit trade, was internally a feudal economy, based on subsistence agriculture. The second is the end of the political independence of the sedentary Arabs and Arabic-speaking people and their replacement by the Turks. In the vast but thinly peopled deserts the Arab tribes retained the independence they had recovered during the decay of the 'Abbāsids, defying repeated attempts to impose control over them and often eroding the frontiers of the cultivated land in their long struggle with the Turks. In a few mountain outposts, too, men who spoke Arabic retained their independence. But everywhere else, in the cities and in the cultivated valleys and plains of Iraq, Syria and Egypt, for a thousand years people of Arabic speech were no longer to rule themselves. So deep-rooted was the feeling that only the Turks were equipped by nature to govern that in the fourteenth century we find a Mamlūk secretary of Syrian birth addressing the Arabs in Turkish through an interpreter rather than in his mother-tongue, for fear lest he should lose face by speaking the despised language of the subject people. As late as the beginning of the nineteenth century Napoleon, when he invaded Egypt, tried unsuccessfully to appoint Arabic-speaking Egyptians to positions of authority and was forced to resort to Turks who alone could command obedience.

The third change is this shifting of the centre of gravity of the

Arabic-speaking world from Iraq to Egypt. The disorganisation and weakness of Iraq and its remoteness from the Mediterranean, across which both the traders and the enemies of the later period were to come, ruled that country out as a possible base. The only alternative was Egypt, the other trade-route, and the irrigated valley of a single river, which by its very nature demanded a single centralised government—the only powerful centralised state in the Arab Near East.

With the power of the Arabs went the glory. The Persian and Turkish-speaking rulers who inherited the thrones of the Arabs patronised poets who could praise them in their own languages, according to their own tastes and traditions. First the Persians then the Turks developed independent Muslim culture languages of their own, and, with the political leadership, assumed the cultural leadership of Islam. Under Seljuq and Mongol rule the Islamic arts entered new periods of efflorescence. Both Persian and Turkish literatures, while strongly coloured by the Arab-Islamic tradition, branched out on independent and significant lines. After Seljuq times the literary use of Arabic was confined to the Arabic-speaking countries, except for a limited output of theological and scientific works. The movement of the centre of gravity of the Arab world westwards gave greater importance to Syria, and still more to Egypt, which now became the main centres of Arabic culture. . . .

In 1517 the weakened and decaying Mamlūk Empire crumbled before the Ottoman assault and for four hundred years Syria and Egypt formed part of the Ottoman Empire. Soon the Barbary States as far as the frontiers of Morocco accepted Ottoman suzerainty, and with the final Ottoman conquest of Iraq from Persia in 1639, almost the whole Arabic-speaking world was under Ottoman rule. . . .

VI. EARLY PEOPLES OF EAST AFRICA

16. Historical geography of Uganda

MERRICK POSNANSKY *East African Geographical Review* April 1963; pages 9–17

Using the traditions it has proved possible to draw four maps of Uganda to show the changing political geography at different times. It is clearly impossible to give these maps absolute dates and the boundaries are variable as the different traditions often contradict each other on the territorial extent of the kingdoms.

The first map (Figure 8), that of the Bacwezi under their first ruler Ndahura, is difficult to draw. The traditions all agree that the Bacwezi were a marvellous folk who preceded the present dynasties in the major kingdoms of Uganda, Rwanda and the Bukoba district of Tanganyika. Unfortunately the Bacwezi are a somewhat legendary people. It would appear that they existed perhaps some twenty to twenty-five generations ago, possibly some time in the fifteenth century, but details of their existence are shrouded in so much myth that some authorities reject them. The traditions relate that they built spectacular earthworks like those of Bigo, with its 6½ miles of trenches, Munsa and Kibengo. Certainly from the archaeological evidence we can speak of a Bigo culture typified by a distinctive pottery and by its earthworks. When we come to look at the scatter of Bigo culture pottery, however, we find that it is confined almost entirely to Bunyoro, Mubende district, Ankole, Eastern Toro and Mawogola county of Buganda.

It is impossible to plot the edges of the distribution of the Bigo culture since some regions have witnessed very little archaeological investigation, but the absence of pottery in the relatively well-prospected areas of Buganda would suggest its absence from the greater part of the two Mengo districts. It is also significant that it is in Buganda and in Kigezi (including Buhororo) that the well-developed Bacwezi cult of the other areas is weak. The uniformity of many of the Bacwezi traditions is suggestive of a need by the later kingdoms to create for themselves a recognizable and respectable identity. When we look carefully at the traditions, though the territorial claims of the

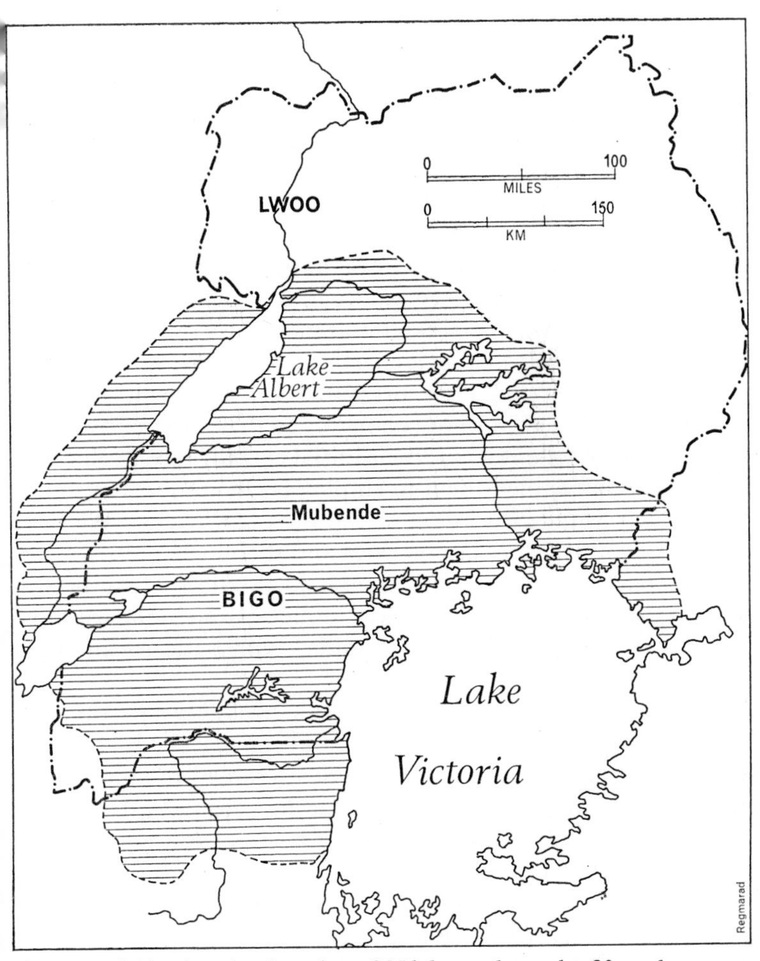

8. Bacwezi kingdom in the reign of Ndahura about the fifteenth century (based on traditions)

Bacwezi, or their kingdom successors, were large, their main activities were restricted much more to those areas suggested by the distribution pattern of the Bigo culture.

The traditions suggest a pastoral aristocracy centred on Bwera (the present Mawogola), where Wamara had his capital at Ntusi, and in Mubende. The sites, like the huge earthworks (which are only interpretable as royal villages and the camps of regional 'consuls' surrounded by elaborate cattle enclosures), support this suggestion as does the distribution of the Bigo culture in the short grass region of the central spine of Western Uganda. It is probable that at this time much of Buganda was unsuitable for pastoralism on account of its woodland and elephant grass cover. The archaeological picture from the stone age suggests that this damper country of the savanna forest mosaic with an annual rainfall of over 30 inches saw the first iron age settlement, which was perhaps also synonymous with the Bantu language speakers and with cultivation.

The Bacwezi sway persisted for at most three generations and again the archaeological evidence from sites such as Bigo is not at variance with the story presented by the traditions. The Bacwezi owed their power presumably to their greater mobility, clan or family cohesion and their initial control of a surplus food supply which enabled them to employ large numbers in public works such as the Ntusi dam or the Bigo earthworks. We have to envisage that before the Bacwezi and their even more legendary parent dynasty the Abatembuzi, Western Uganda was occupied by Bantu agriculturalists, millet-eating in the west and probably banana-eating in Buganda, with little social unity beyond their families and clans.

The Bacwezi 'disappeared', though probably not literally, and their power, limited by their numbers, was dissipated over too large a domain whilst their subjects gained in cohesion. It is possible that their end was connected with the Lwoo folk movements from the north. It has, of course, been suggested by Crazzolara that the Bacwezi may have been the first advance movement of the Lwoo themselves who eventually became cut off and isolated in a predominately hostile Bantu and Bahima world. The Lwoo movement was however directly responsible for the Bito dynasties of Buganda and Bunyoro.

The Lwoo movements mark a significant break in Uganda's history. The dynasties (Hinda) which were developed in Ankole, Karagwe, Rwanda and the small principalities like Kiziba were closely linked to the past and retained their royal village pattern on a model close to that of Bigo. But Bunyoro-Kitara was the principal heir to the Bacwezi domains although its dynasty represented a greater discontinuity from its predecessors than was the case with the Hinda dynasties.

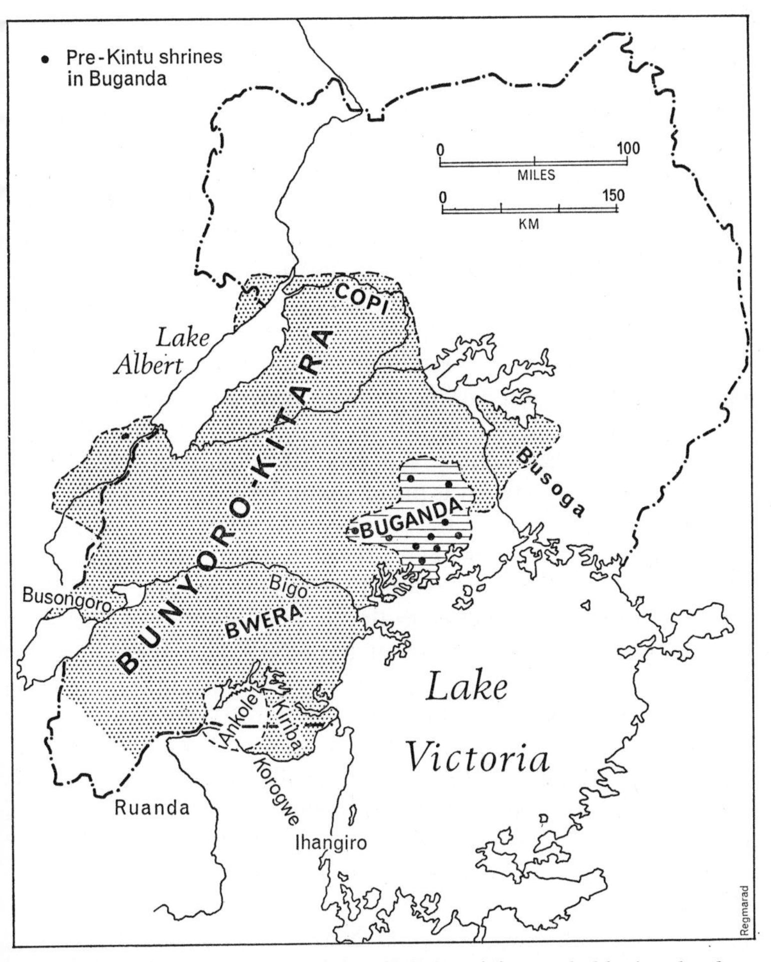

9. Uganda kingdoms at the time of their origin, probably in the late fifteenth century

The second map (Figure 9) attempts to represent the situation around the beginning of the present kingdoms, perhaps at the turn of the fifteenth century. The present-day linguistic map gives a rather similar picture of Uganda controlled chiefly by Bunyoro-Kitara (Figure 12). Except for Buganda and southern Bugaso all the other languages like Lusesse, Luvuma, Runyankore, Luhaya (in Karagwe), Lutoro, etc., have a much greater affinity to Lunyoro than does Luganda. At this time Buganda was small. Five clans claim to be pre-Kintu, the first *Kabaka* in the dynastic list of *Kabakas*, whilst fourteen clans claim to have come with Kintu. At the time of Kintu three *ssazas* existed (Figure 13): Busiro, Kyadondo and Mawokota. At the time of Kimera, the first *Kabaka* in the continuous dynastic sequence and the second after Kintu, there were *ssazas* also in the southern Ssingo, Bulemezi and Busuju. A further seven clans accompanied Kimera. Thus at the beginning of the continuous Buganda dynasty twenty-six of the thirty to forty clans and five or six of the *ssazas* were in existence. The river and swamp Mayanja was for a time a boundary, whilst the Katonga was not crossed until the nineteenth century. Mawokota seems to have been very much a frontier district and the term *Kaima* for the *Ssaza* chief of that county suggests a foreigner or herdsman. Part of eastern Kyagwe was probably under Buganda suzerainty though it would appear to have been forested. The shrines of the *Kabakas* credited to have preceded Kintu fall within this nuclear area and it is probable that in this original Buganda, where neither the Bacwezi traditions were strong nor the Bigo culture existed, small groups of Bantu-speakers were already living, perhaps with the banana as a staple food, and these had been drawn together by the arrival of the Bito dynasty.

The traditions suggest that at this time the small *Omukamas* like Bwera, Buzimba, Buhweju, Busongora and Kiziba and possibly even Buddu existed within the large Bunyoro-Kitara, each with a tenuous link with the preceding Bacwezi and often with their own royal drums. Their existence would mean that Bunyoro-Kitara was weak administratively with little centralism. Ankole (or more correctly Nkore or Kaaro-Karungi), it would seem, was restricted to the hilly fastnesses of Isingiro and was rather more independent from Bunyoro. Busoga existed outside the bounds of Bunyoro as a cluster of disunited petty principalities.

Bunyoro, like its predecessor, was a pastoral state depending for its very existence on the control of the grazing lands of the central spine of Western Uganda in Bulemezi, Ssingo, Buwekula, Mawogola and Kabula of the present Buganda; Kyaka and Mwenge in what is now eastern Toro and Nyabushozi, Mitoma and northern Isingiro of modern Ankole. This area clearly comes out as fairly dry and mainly wooded or grass savanna, or what used to be termed short grassland to differentiate it from the elephant grassland of the forest-savanna mosaic. At the beginning of the history of the kingdoms, therefore, we are presented with a territorially strong but administratively weak Bunyoro dependent on the control of extensive grazing land and having within its boundaries several semi-independent chieftainships or principalities; a small but centralized Buganda dependent mainly on agriculture, but with pastoral activities probably on its frontiers and situated in the region with the best agricultural potential; and a small Ankole owing its existence largely to its geographical isolation in Isingiro.

The third map (Figure 10) represents the situation around the turn of the seventeenth century about the time of Ntare IV in Ankole, Cwamali in Bunyoro and Tebandeka or Ndaula in Buganda. Buganda, which had been almost completely overrun by Bunyoro some five generations earlier, had now established its southern boundary on the Katonga and its eastern boundary on the Nile, whilst the Sesse islands which had previously had their own rulers had been brought under Buganda rule. In the south, Mpororo had mushroomed into being the third largest territorial unit. Mpororo lasted for only two generations and after the death of Kahaya (the contemporary of Ntare IV) was principally divided between Ankole and Rwanda, although for over a century Igara retained a separate existence. Bunyoro's territorial extent was thus severely reduced though she was still by far the strongest state. The chief difference from the situation some two centuries before was that the rising powers of Buganda and Ankole were beginning to balance Bunyoro between them. Both were developing from tiny into large states and Buganda in particular was becoming highly centralized with an efficient local government. Both had a unity arising from adversity and though Bunyoro had nearly crushed both she had extended herself in the process. Both were in a position to encroach on the rich pastoral lands of Bunyoro on which Bunyoro depended. Buganda in addition had a far better agricultural/pastoral balance—there was not the same vulnerability as that suffered by Bunyoro whose economy must have been very dependent on pastoral activities and whose better land was limited and exposed. The cattle of Bunyoro could be seized but in retaliation

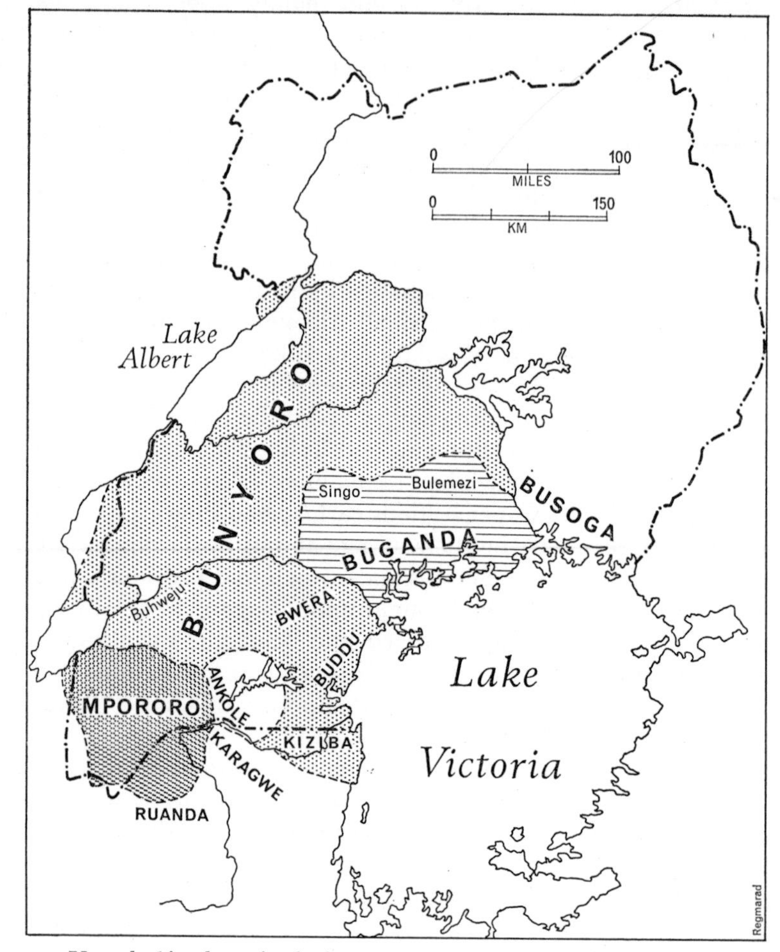

10. Uganda kingdoms in the late seventeenth and early eighteenth century

Bunyoro could do little but destroy the crops in Buganda's less populous marginal agricultural lands. During this period the Buganda capital and the tombs were centralized in the nuclear core of Buganda in and around Busiro and Kyaddondo. On the other hand, although the royal tombs of Bunyoro were mainly located in Mubende district or in north Ssingo, the *Omukamas* in their life-times were very peripatetic, moving from Toro to north of the Kafu and raiding into Ankole, Rwanda and Busoga.

The fourth map (Figure 11) shows the situation by the first quarter of the nineteenth century. The century that had elapsed was probably the most crucial in the history of the kingdoms. Buganda had pushed its northern boundary into southern Bugerere and expanded its territory in both Ssingo and Bulemezi and under Kamanya, the father of Suna II, Buwekula had been taken from Bunyoro. In the last quarter of the eighteenth

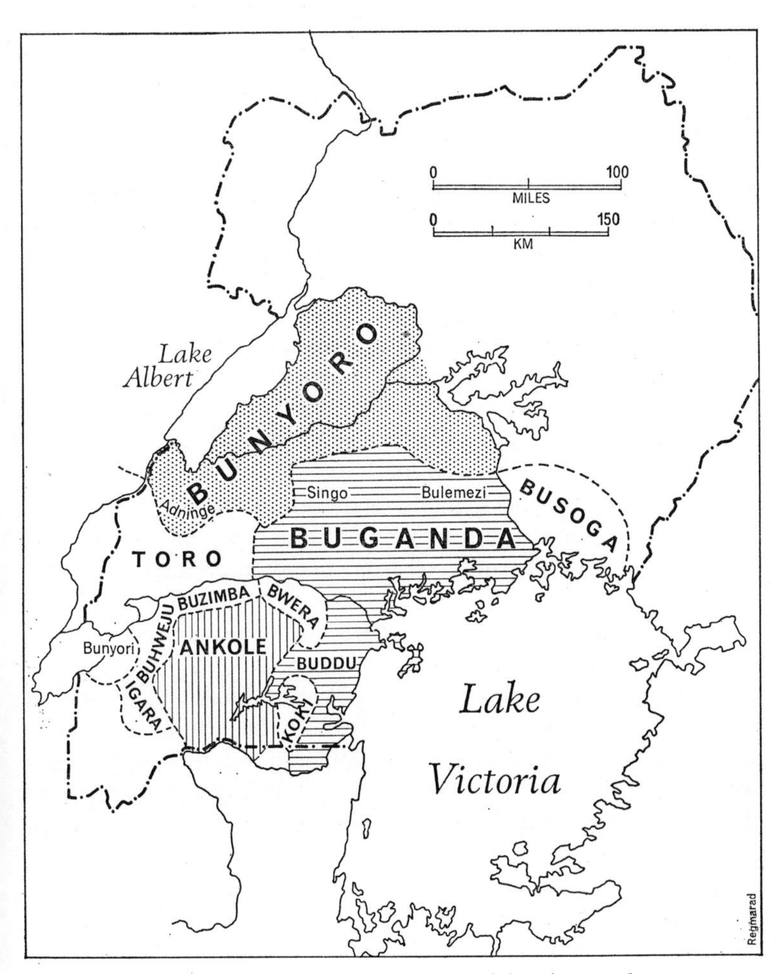

11. Uganda kingdoms in the first quarter of the nineteenth century

century *Kabaka* Junju had taken Buddu, whilst the kingdom of Koki, disappointed by the treatment they had received as a vassal state of Bunyoro, came under Buganda suzerainty. Bunyoro had undergone an unfortunate period. Duhaga I, who began as a successful *omukama*, lost both Buddu and Koki to Junju and died on the field of battle against Buganda; his son Kyebambe III, dabbling in Buganda succession disputes, lost Buwekula to Kabaka Kamanya. His son Kabayo split Toro from Bunyoro, whilst Ankole seized the moment of Bunyoro's weakness to annex Kabula. The eclipse of Bunyoro allowed Ankole and the smaller states on her boundaries to expand considerably. Most unfortunately for Bunyoro this final eclipse coincided with the development of the Arab trade.

The Arabs had settled in the Tabora region by 1820 and sometime before 1832 they were already trading in Koki. Trade, which had mainly been in Wanyamwezi hands before this and had resulted in coastal imports coming into Buganda by *Kabaka* Kyabagu's reign, was only becoming well organized in the 1830s and 1840s. Buganda, by its newly gained control of the corridor from the present Bukoba district, which was mainly part of Karagwe kingdom in the nineteenth century, was in a position to exploit this contact with the outside world. By the middle of the century the canoe trade from Buganda as well as the overland route were well established, with ivory as the chief export and cotton piece goods as the main import. After 1850 the quest for ivory from the north led to a development of slave trading and Bunyoro suffered from her own contacts with the outside world.

Thus the early nineteenth century saw Buganda in the ascendent. Mawanda in the eighteenth century had attempted to gain control of Busoga, but by Kamanya's and Suna's reign much of south Busoga appears to have been tributary to Buganda. Buganda by her conquest of Buwekula had almost separated the western grazing lands of Mwenge and Buyaga from those of north Bulemezi, Buruli and northern Bugerere. Constantly in the nineteenth century Buganda was able to raid the eastern grazing lands with impunity until in the last quarter of the nineteenth century Kabarega's aggressiveness, coming too late, restored the balance slightly. Neither Ankole, with its buffer zone of small states around it, themselves the result of Bunyoro's weakness and the earlier disintegration of Mpororo, nor Buganda, was as vulnerable as Bunyoro. It is also probable that the continued agricultural development of Buganda had led to population increases which would inevitably have resulted in a desire for territorial expansion, particularly as the population increase had been accompanied by a strengthening of the centralized power of the state under the Kabakas succeeding Semakokiro. The question of personalities cannot be overlooked. Bunyoro, until Kabarega in the nineteenth century, had no rulers who were so evidently capable as Semakokiro, Suna and Mutesa. Both Kamurasi and Kabarega, however, were aware of the need to reconquer the valuable 'marches' of Bulemzi, Ssingo, Buwekula and Toro, as can be seen by Kamurasi's choice of capitals in Buruli and Kabarega's in southern Bunyoro and northern Toro.

It is often difficult to realize fully the nature of the pastoral societies of the nineteenth century. The early 1890s which saw the political, social and economic intervention of Europe were disastrous years for the pastoral kingdoms: first came jiggers which constituted a maiming scourge until the nature of the sores was realized; later came rinderpest (1892), and finally smallpox. The rinderpest outbreak crippled the purely pastoral societies. Karagwe, which underwent the added affliction of succession disputes, never recovered, though Ankole, through the resourcefulness of an able *Enganzi*, Nuwa Mbaguta, managed to expand its boundaries at the expense of the small *omukamas* and to vary its economy. Much of the land wrenched by Ankole and Buganda from Bunyoro throughout the centuries was once useful grazing country; thus in the time of the early explorers it was fairly open grassland with only a few trees, mainly *Ficus* and *Euphorbia*. The domestic animal depopulation allowed secondary regeneration of bush scrub with varieties like *Acacia hostii* and the movement into the grazing areas of game from the drier marginal lands. The game prospered and provided excellent hosts for the tsetse fly, which expanded into Uganda at the time of the first German-British war and which has led subsequently to a further relative depopulation in the disputed areas.

The traditional ceremonies of Bunyoro reveal a kingdom where pastoralism was held in the highest respect even though

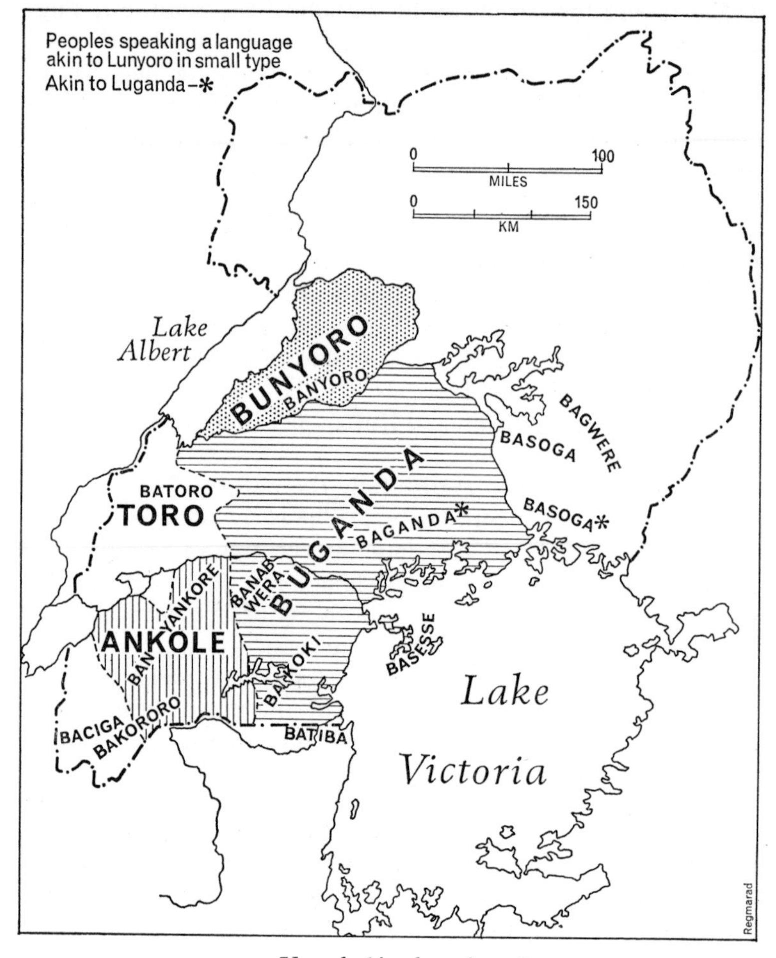

12. Uganda kingdoms in 1962

there was not a Bahima ruling dynasty. In Buganda cattle were neither as suited to the natural vegetation nor important socially. The cattle keepers were often foreigners, and the archaeological remains give evidence of people becoming more settled: pottery becomes more elaborate (including, for example, huge immobile beer jars).

The map of the present-day kingdoms (Figure 12) reflects the final changes which took place in the 1890s. The British government operating from a Buganda base confirmed the expansion of Ankole, revived a Toro which Kabarega had regained for Bunyoro, and expanded Buganda's boundaries to include all of Buruli, Bugerere, Bulemezi, Ssingo, Buyaga and Bugangazzi. It has often been wondered what the result would have been had the Europeans made Bunyoro their base and not Buganda. The result might have been a larger, more important Bunyoro but sooner or later the logistics of communications would have weighed against the route from the north, and in fact it was the territorial losses of Bunyoro before the advent of the Europeans which were crucial. The areas lost since the middle of the century were neither very populous (perhaps not more than 100,000 people in terms of present population) nor, since the cattle depopulation of the late nineteenth century, so economically

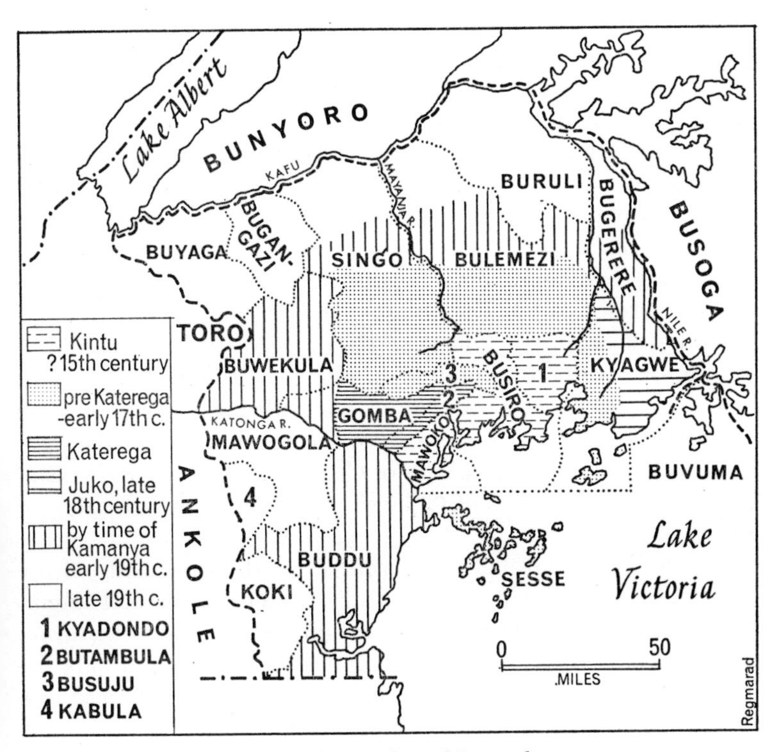

13. The expansion of Buganda

valuable as the earlier losses of Buddu, western Toro, Buwekula and south Bugerere.

In time, by giving closer attention to a comparative study of the traditions, particularly of the smaller principalities, it should prove possible to construct more detailed historical maps of Uganda. . . .

17. The Land of Zanj

GERVASE MATHEW *The Dawn of African History* (edited by Roland Oliver) Oxford University Press 1961; pages 50–2

. . . Our knowledge of this period in East Africa is increasing steadily through archaeology. Most of the medieval towns along the African coasts seem to have come into existence about the twelfth century and to have reached the climax of their prosperity about the year 1500.

Small trading towns, probably mainly built of wood, turned into great merchant cities, with their own characteristic architecture and with contacts throughout the Middle and Far East. In the ruined palace city of Songo Mnara on a coral island off Tanganyika, each pointed arch with its thin stone edging is reset within a rectangle of cut stone, and fluted demi-domes rest on fluted pilasters. There is an intricate system of sanitation, with stone piping. Everywhere there is an evident delight in geometrical precision. I found scattered among the ruins, broken glazed pottery from the Persian area, stoneware from Burma and Siam, pieces of Cornelian, and amber, crystal and topaz and a mass of Chinese porcelain from late Sung to early Ming.

There was a parallel development on the other side of the Indian Ocean. The fifteenth century cities of Kilwa in Tanganyika and Malacca in Malaya had similar functions as Muslim trading centres—it is significant that I have found not only the same types of porcelain at both, but in similar proportions. Even their organization was similar; much of the power lay with an hereditary 'Mayor of the Palace'; the Amir at Kilwa, the Bendahara at Malacca. The lost original of the *Kilwa Chronicle* seems to have resembled the early sixteenth-century *Chronicle of Malacca*.

Then suddenly the whole of that Indian Ocean world was transformed by the coming of the Portuguese. In November 1497 Vasco da Gama rounded the Cape of Good Hope and then sailed up the east coast on his way to India. Eight years later the Portuguese sacked Kilwa and Mombasa. For more than a hundred years they treated the Indian Ocean as if it were a Portuguese lake.

There are surprisingly few traces of this Portuguese period in East Africa north of Mozambique—a few fortifications in the coastal towns, some loan words in Swahili and perhaps an occasional custom like the bull-fights on Pemba Island, north of Zanzibar.

The Portuguese Empire could survive only as long as it held control of the sea routes. This was lost early in the seventeenth century.

The most flourishing of the Portuguese settlements in East Africa were destroyed in a revolt. Swahili states were able to come into being and to maintain a precarious independence.

This period in the history of the East African coast lasted from about 1637 to about 1810. All down the shores of what had been the Land of Zanj, there were small towns, oligarchic in social structure, trading in ivory and in slaves and using a currency of beads and rolls of cloth. All were consciously Muslim, all Swahili-speaking. The sites of this period are linked by the same type of house and mosque and fortification and pillar tomb and by the use of great quantities of Chinese blue and white porcelain. In the early nineteenth century their trade was sapped by the development of New Zanzibar under Arab rulers from the Persian Gulf. Now all are decayed and many of them deserted.

We can reconstruct much of the life in such towns from Swahili poems. It seems clear that though dependent for their wealth on Indian Ocean trade they still remained integrally African. Pate was perhaps the wealthiest among them—it became a proverb that the nobles there climbed by silver ladders into ivory beds, but we have a description of the rich men of Pate arching their long necks and swinging their many-jointed arms as the common people gazed at them, an African not an Arab ideal of deportment. There is much to remind us of West Africa. It seems clear that in each little state the Great Drum or the Ivory Horn were something more than ritual objects, in some fashion they enshrined not only the strength but the spirit of the people. Women were their guardians—they are perhaps the 'Queens' referred to in contemporary European accounts. Even the 'Decorated Ones', the courtesans, possessed a definite status. Witch doctors were potent and the religion of the coast though nominally Islamic was impregnated by the dread of spirits and of vampires.

If this was true of the seventeenth and eighteenth centuries it may well have been true in medieval East Africa. When the greatest of all travellers, Ibn Battuta, reached Tanganyika in the fourteenth century he describes Kilwa as a beautiful and well-constructed city, but he also noted that its inhabitants were jet black and had incised their faces apparently for ornament. His detailed description of one of the Somali States suggests a Negro State like those that he had visited along the southern borders of the Sahara. No one can question the constant presence of Arab, Indian and Persian merchants in the medieval ports. We still possess the long genealogies by which the early sixteenth-century rulers of Kilwa claimed descent from Persian kings. But some at least of the cities discovered by the Portuguese may have been African kingships which had become Muslim and had slowly acquired the techniques and organizations of Islamic States.

Certainly to all medieval geographers the Land of Zanj is a land of Negroes. It is impossible to tell how long a form of Bantu had been the language of the coast, but it underlies all variants of Swahili and back in the tenth century an Arab traveller had referred by a Bantu title to an emerald-crowned king of Zanj.

But two things, at any rate, seem clear. The first is that the history of the East African coast only becomes intelligible when it is studied as a part of the history of the Indian Ocean. The influences that stimulated its cultures, like the wealth on which its towns were founded, came primarily from Eastern trade. But the second is, that it has always remained a part of Africa.

The Dawn came from the East, but it was an African Dawn.

18. Early days in Tanganyika

MARGARET BATES *African One-Party States* (edited by G. Carter) Cornell University Press 1963; pages 396–9

. . . About the history of this country and its inhabitants there is an incomplete picture, and much of the available information is only educated guessing. Less historical work has been done in the eastern part of Africa than in the west. Geological and archaeological research has in recent years uncovered much evidence of the Stone Age cultures of eastern Africa in early periods, and following Dr Louis Leakey's discovery of *Homo zinjanthropos* in Olduvai Gorge it now seems possible that Tanganyika may be man's aboriginal home. Knowledge of Tanganyikan history does not automatically improve, however, in approaching the present. It is difficult to speak with any certainty of events or personalities in the interior of the country before 1800.

What is known about the coastal regions is somewhat more certain. The Greeks had some knowledge of eastern Africa, which they called Azania, and contacts existed across the Indian Ocean with Arabia, Persia, India, and possibly China. By the twelfth century, a series of city-states had been established along the coast from Mozambique north to Somalia; in Tanganyika there were a number of settlements of which Kilwa, Mafia, and Pangani were probably the best known. These were independent Arab principalities, with a Muslim society and architecture, and were based on some trade with the immediate interior, though Arab influence did not at this time penetrate very far inland. The major cities had independent political authorities and their own coinage, and an Arabic history of Kilwa survives. The first European to arrive, the Portuguese Pedro Cabral in 1500, found that the city-states frequently warred among themselves, and the Portuguese soon were able to conquer the coastal cities. Their dominance lasted for over a century, though the extent of their control fluctuated even on the coast, and there is no evidence in Tanganyika that they ever went inland at all. In the seventeenth century the coastal populations gradually reasserted themselves and managed to oust the Portuguese, but their earlier prosperity and influence were not entirely revived.

In the interior, a number of tribes existed. The word tribe is not a very precise one, and its connotations are constantly changing; here it is used to designate a group with some similarities of material culture, language, and spiritual belief. In Tanganyika, at least, the term does not always imply ethnic similarity, for modern tribes have frequently been formed by groups of varying ethnic and geographic origins; nor does it necessarily imply a single political allegiance. It is known that during the last four to five hundred years tribal structure has changed in Tanganyika along with the economy, social structure, and physical habitat, though only recently has it become possible to speak at all intelligently of what changes have occurred. Certainly the traditional Western picture of a static African society is practically pure myth.

The interior of Tanganyika in the early nineteenth century probably contained three major ethnic groups. The largest of these was the Bantu, which is really a grouping by linguistic affiliation of many separate tribes. Culturally they tended to be cultivators or mixed farmers, living in relatively small areas with unoccupied bushland separating the tribes. New tribes, in fact, seem to have been formed when one or two families opened up a new section of land; other settlers might arrive, and eventually a separate social and political entity was created. The rate at which these disparate elements coalesced varied considerably; among the Chagga of Mount Kilimanjaro, for instance, it is sometimes still possible, after at least four hundred years, to trace the origins of individual families and clans.

A second group, arriving possibly as late as the eighteenth century, were Nilotic-Cushitic peoples from the north, pastoral nomads who were taller and lighter-skinned and possessed more aquiline features than most of the Bantu. Their progress south was not always peaceful, and Bantu resistance confined them to the northern areas of modern Tanganyika. About the third group very little is known, but they speak click languages and may be related to the Bushmen of South Africa. This group is small, being represented today by only one or two tribes.

In none of these tribes (with minor exceptions) was there a strong, centralized political authority. Groups of families and clans might reside together, but authority tended to be familial and was exercised either by a senior male or by a group of elders acting together. Where a particular clan came to dominate an area, its head might be recognized as chief, or a man who had shown special ability as a leader in war or as a rain maker might gain power and transmit it to his descendants. In Tanganyika, however, this process of gradual coalescence had not often produced one central system, so that a number of chiefs might exist within the same tribe. This fragmentation is an important factor even today. As late as the 1950s the Sukuma, Tanganyika's largest tribe, which totals nearly 1,000,000 persons, had 57 chiefs, each technically independent of the others.

As available information becomes more extensive about the late eighteenth and early nineteenth centuries, these interior societies appear to have been in a disturbed state. Tribal migration occurred on a considerable scale; the Ngoni, an offshoot of the Zulu, travelled all the way north from Natal, while continual Masai pressure came south from Kenya. Among the Tanganyika tribes themselves a series of military leaders appeared, and in Karagwe, Usambara, and Unyamwezi local groups were reorganized into fighting units. At the same time, the ancient slave trade was intensified, to become perhaps the most disruptive element of all.

In 1840, the Sultan of Oman on the Persian Gulf, who had had long contacts with the East African coast, moved to Zanzibar; here, perhaps, the history of modern Tanganyika begins. The Sultan's agents soon controlled most of the Tanganyika coast and progressively exerted influence inland. Zanzibari traders penetrated farther and farther each year to obtain the two valuable commodities of slaves and ivory. They traded cotton cloth and cowrie shells and guns in exchange or, forming alliances with some African tribes, warred against others. The effects of the slave trade seem to have been felt most strongly in southern Tanganyika, on the routes to Lake Nyasa. Some of the northern tribes were strong enough to prevent slave raiding in their territories. Much of Tanganyika, however, was so thoroughly fought over and depopulated that by the 1870s the slave raiders had reached west of Tanganyika into the Congo.

European explorers and missionaries, arriving in the 1850s, therefore found anything but a placid and quiescent society.

Burton and Speke, travelling to Lake Tanganyika in 1858, and Livingstone a few years later commented extensively on the changing scene of their day: increasing trade and warfare, introduction of new goods and new ideas, and growing inter-tribal contact. . . .

VII. RACIAL MOVEMENTS IN THE SOUTH

19. Early migrations of the southern Bantu

I. SCHAPERA *Cambridge History of the British Empire* Vol. VIII Cambridge University Press 1963; pages 35–9

It was formerly believed that the earliest Bantu invaders reached southern Africa about the eleventh or twelfth centuries A.D., but recent archaeological investigations have shown that as far back as the eighth or ninth centuries A.D. there was established in Southern Rhodesia the highly developed culture associated with Zimbabwe and other stone ruins. Its builders, whose identities have given rise to much controversy, are now generally held to have been of Bantu origin, and the cumulative evidence suggests that they were the ancestors of the modern Shona peoples. The Zimbabwe culture attained its zenith during the tenth and eleventh centuries; then it gradually began to decline. Portuguese records of the early sixteenth century (which, incidentally, name many tribes still existing today) speak of the great Karanga kingdom of Monomotapa which centred internal dissension. After many vicissitudes, it was finally shattered about the end of the seventeenth century, when a new domination was established over the other Shona tribes by the Rozwi (a section of the Kalanga). For the next century and a half the Rozwi remained supreme, but their power collapsed with the arrival of Mzilikazi's Ndebele and other Nguni invaders from the south (*c.* 1825–40).

The Sotho peoples apparently came later than the Shona. The conventional view is that they entered South Africa, probably through the western portions of Southern Rhodesia, in three series of migrations. The first is represented today by the people collectively known as Kgalagadi, who settled in the eastern and more fertile parts of Bechuanaland, where they mixed freely with the Bushmen already there. Following them came the ancestors of the modern Rolong, who settled along the upper reaches of the Molopo River, whence they gradually spread south and west. They absorbed some of their Bushman and Kgalagadi predecessors, most of whom, however, retreated before them into the arid zones of the Kalahari Desert. The third and greatest migration brought the ancestors of all the other Sotho tribes. They settled as a united body in south-western Transvaal and then broke up rapidly into separate clusters, the most important of which were the Hurutshe, Kwena and Kgatla.

Even if the traditions are reasonably reliable, it is impossible to date the migrations that they record. All that can safely be said is that the Sotho were already in the eastern half of their present habitat by about A.D. 1600. During the next two centuries, each of the existing clusters became increasingly subdivided. It was a constantly recurring feature in Bantu history for part of a tribe, led by an ambitious or discontented relative of the ruling chief, to secede and become independent. The Rolong, for example, are the parent tribe of the modern Tlhaping, Kaa and many others; the Hurutshe, traditional leaders of the final migration from the north, broke up into the modern Hurutshe tribes (Manyana, Moilwa, etc.), Tharo, Khurutshe and others; the Kgatla, an early offshoot from the Hurutshe, broke up into modern Kgatla tribes (Mosetlha, Kgafela, etc.), Tlokwa and Pedi; while the Kwena, another early offshoot from the Hurutshe, broke up into the Fokeng, Mogopa, Phalane, etc. A section of the Mogopa subsequently seceded and moved westwards (*c.* 1720); these people, now known as the Kwena of Sechele, were the first important Tswana tribe to settle in the Bechuanaland Protectorate. The Ngwaketse and Ngwato broke away from them not long afterwards, and the Tawana then broke away from the Ngwato (*c.* 1790–1800).

The Venda, said to have come originally from the region of Nyasaland, settled for a long time among the Shona, to whom they owe certain features of language and culture. Then about three centuries ago, they continued their southward migration and finally became established in the Soutpansberg, which they found inhabited by Sotho peoples whom they brought under their rule.

The early traditions of the Nguni are much more confused. We know from written records that by the end of the sixteenth century they were already inhabiting the coastal regions of

Natal, but how long they had been there it is difficult to ascertain. Soga maintains that they are all derived from three parent stocks: Lala, Nguni and Mbo. The Lala (ancestors of the modern Bele, Hlubi, Zizi and, possibly, also Zulu and Thembu) belong originally to the Kalanga of Southern Rhodesia, but early broke away in large sections and, travelling south, were the first to enter Zululand and Natal. Next came the Nguni (ancestors of the modern Xhosa tribes and others), who are thought to have formed part of the Zimba hordes that during the sixteenth century devastated the country between the Zambesi River and Mombasa. The Mbo, remnants of tribes then living in the Lower Zambesi valley, fled before the Zimba, and some of them, cutting their way through the Tsonga and eastern Shona, ultimately crossed the Limpopo River and, pushing south, settled in Natal (*c.* 1620). Here they broke up again into their original elements (including, among others, the ancestors of the modern Mpondo, Mpondomisi, Bomvu, Bomvana, Xesibe and Swazi). The Xhosa and Themby subsequently pushed south-westwards, one after the other, conquering and partly mixing with the local Hottentots, until, towards the end of the eighteenth century, their vanguard first came into conflict with the advancing European settlers in the vicinity of the Great Fish River.

According to the views just summarized, the focus of Nguni development lay somewhere in Natal, whence the Cape tribes travelled farther south, whereas the Transvaal Ndebele and Swazi offshoots went north-west and north respectively. But, as van Warmela stresses, all the Nguni languages are distinguished from those of other southern Bantu by the presence of 'clicks', almost certainly derived from the Hottentots. This suggests not only that the Nguni must have developed their linguistic peculiarities farther to the south, where alone intensive contact with Hottentots was possible, but also that they got there much earlier than usually supposed since 'clicks' occur even in the language of those Ndebele who have been living in the Transvaal for at least three to four centuries.

Of the Tsonga little more can be said than that the tribes now composing this division entered Mozambique from different directions (north, west and south) and are therefore probably of mixed origins. They have been in the country for a very long time (Portuguese records of the mid-sixteenth century name several chiefs whose people still live round Delagoa Bay), but they were themselves preceded by other Bantu peoples represented today by the Chopi and by the Tsonga of Inhambane.

The western tribes, who like most of the others speak of having come from 'a land of great waters', seem to have advanced spasmodically to the south-west, until (according to Vedder early in the sixteenth century) they reached the Okovango River in the north-west of Bechuanaland Protectorate. The Ambo then gradually occupied their present territory of Ovamboland. The Herero migrated farther west to the Atlantic coastal region of the Kaokoveld immediately south of the Kunene River. Here they remained until about 1750. Then, in small groups, they began moving to the south-east and occupied the central districts of South-West Africa, conquering many of the local Bushmen and Bergdama, a negro people, living mainly on game and wild plants and speaking Hottentot, of whose early history hardly anything is known. In due course (*c.* 1830) they came into conflict with the Nama Hottentots to the south, with whom for the next sixty years they were often at war.

Despite the unreliability of the earlier traditions, it is at least certain that by the end of the eighteenth century most divisions of Bantu had already been living for some time in the regions where they are now found. The early years of the following century saw the creation in southern Africa of several strong native states, when many formerly independent tribes were amalgamated into single political entities. The process began at the end of the eighteenth century in Zululand, where there were then more than one hundred small separate tribes. Dingiswayo, chief of the Mthethwa, began gradually to conquer his neighbours and absorb them under his rule. Under his successor Shaka, originally chief of the Zulu tribe and a despot of outstanding ambition and military ability, the policy of conquest and amalgamation was carried to an extent hitherto unprecedented in Bantu history. By 1820, it has been estimated, Shaka had more than 100,000 warriors, and had added about 500,000 people to his rule, having deprived some three hundred tribes of their independence. His example was followed by several of his generals, who fled with their armies to found kingdoms of their own: Mzilikazi (Moselekatse), after terrorizing the central and western Transvaal (*c.* 1821–37), went on to conquer the Shona tribes of Southern Rhodesia, where he established the Ndebele ('Matebele') kingdom; Soshangane (Manukuza) conquered most of the Tsonga peoples of Portuguese East Africa and founded the Gasa ('Shangana') kingdom; and Zwangendaba, 'after an amazing march of some thousands of miles', set up the Ngoni kingdom in Nyasaland. In Basutoland a similar result was achieved more or less peacefully by Moshweshwe (Moshesh), who from the remnants of tribes scattered by the wars following in the wake of Shaka's raids built up what is now the 'Basuto nation'; Thulare and his son Sekwati welded various northern Sotho tribes into the strong Pedi monarchy, and Sebetwane, leading a horde of Sotho refugees from the south, established in far-off Barotseland the great Kololo kingdom of which David Livingstone wrote.

These wars and conquests led to a considerable disturbance of tribal conditions in southern Africa during the first half of the nineteenth century; indeed, the wholesale destruction of life and dispersal of people to which they gave rise undoubtedly facilitated the subsequent extension of European settlement over the country. Under the impact of Western civilization most of the new states were destroyed by the end of the century, but the 'kingdoms' of the southern Sotho, Swazi and Ngwato still survive as examples of the political development to which the Bantu could sometimes attain.

VIII. EARLY EUROPEAN ACTIVITY

20. Early Portuguese exploration in West Africa

J. H. PARRY *The Age of Reconnaissance* Weidenfeld & Nicolson 1963; pages 131–2, 133–8

The far-reaching plans and hopes attributed by the chroniclers to Prince Henry of Portugal have attracted more attention than his actual achievements. The exploration of the West African coast appears as a mere preliminary, a rehearsal for the opening of the India trade forty years after the Prince's death. Yet the two enterprises were separate and distinct. Guinea is not on the way to India; not, certainly, for a sailing ship. The Guinea trades had a value of their own, independent of the lure of India. The discovery of a coast where gold could be obtained from the same sources which supplied, by desert caravan, the cities of Morocco, was a geographical and commercial achievement of great significance in its own right.

The chroniclers, after the manner of their calling, concentrated their attention on voyages sponsored by the Prince and recorded the achievements of his captains: of Gil Eannes, who in 1434 first rounded Cape Bojador with its dangerous shoals stretching far out to sea; Nuno Tristão, who sighted Cape Branco in 1442, who two years later landed on Arguim island, within the curve of the cape, which was to become the first European slaving-station in Africa, and who in 1444 discovered the mouth of the Senegal; Dinis Dias who, also in 1444, reached Cape Verde with its high, rounded hill visible far to seaward, and explored Palmas island where the great slave barracoons of Gorée were later to be established; Nuno Tristão again, who explored the wide mouth of the Gambia where (probably) he was killed in 1446; Cadamosto, the Venetian, whose expedition in 1455 was probably the first to visit the Cape Verde Islands; Diogo Gomes, who disputed Cadamosto's claim and who certainly in the following year found the mouths of the Geba and the Casamance rivers; and Pedro da Sintra, who in about 1460 sighted the mountains of Sierra Leone and gave them their name because—it was said—of the thunderstorms that growled and roared, as they still do, about Mount Auriol. These, however, were only the most famous among many fishing, sealing and trading voyages of which no record now remains. The fisheries off the Mauretanian coast were valuable enough in themselves to have attracted Portuguese and Andalusian skippers. Prince Henry and his brother Prince Pedro, by placing gentlemen of their households in command of some of the ships and demanding from them longer voyages, more detailed reports, more captives to be converted or enslaved, and higher returns, gave energy and direction to a movement of maritime expansion which probably would have taken place in any event, but which might for many years have been confined to fishing and casual slaving. . . .

Prince Henry's death in 1460 removed an incentive to explore. The explorers had reached a difficult and dangerous stretch of coast, with no evident prospect of improvement; and some of them were alarmed by the probability that their friend the North Star, barely visible above the horizon at Sierra Leone, would disappear if they went further. The merchants were content to develop their modest but prospering trade at the mouths of the Senegal and the Gambia. The Crown, to which Prince Henry's African rights reverted, was willing enough to encourage discovery, but unwilling to incur expense, especially since Henry had left a load of debt. One voyage at this time may have been made on the direct order of the Crown: a second voyage, commanded by Pedro da Sintra, reached Cape Mensurado in 1462. But Afonso V was more interested in a straightforward crusade in Morocco, in particular in plans for seizing Arzila and Tangier and so securing control of the Straits, than in the exploration of Guinea. No official action was taken on Guinea until 1469, when Afonso agreed to lease the whole enterprise, excepting only Arguim and the Cape Verde Islands (where Portuguese residents had already settled) to a private individual. The lessee, Fernão Gomes, covenanted to pay an annual rent and to explore 100 leagues of coast annually during the five-year period of his lease. Little is known of Gomes as a person; but he was clearly a man of energy, a good organizer and a good judge of men, and his story is one of success. He carried out his obligations, and more; he made a fortune from his highly speculative investment; spent much of it serving his king in arms in Morocco; and was knighted for his pains.

In 1471 Gomes' captains reached Sama, near Cape Three Points, the first village of the Mina de Ouro, and in the next four years the coast was explored as far as Benin. Whether Gomes' people investigated the Cameroons coast is uncertain. The coastal current in the Bight of Biafra sets strongly from east to west and winds are notoriously unreliable; but certainly during this period Fernando Po discovered the fertile island which bears his name. Mount Cameroon is only ninety miles to the north, and clearly visible in good weather. Probably the discoverer followed the coast from there on his return passage, past the many mouths of the Niger delta. Finally, probably in 1474, Lopo Gonçalves and Rui de Sequeira discovered the southerly trend of the coast beyond Malimba, and followed it south to Cape López and then to Cape St Catherine, which is in 2°S. About that time, Gomes' lease expired. He did not seek to renew it, probably because of the increase in the cost and danger of the trade after the outbreak of war with Castile in 1475. During the years of his concession nearly two thousand miles of coastline had been roughly explored, the Guinea trade had assumed roughly the form which it was to retain for more than a century, and its commercial value had been clearly demonstrated. No doubt with that value in mind, the King, after the expiry of the lease, entrusted responsibility for the affairs of Guinea to his son, the future John II.

The immediate cause of the Succession War between Portugal and Castile was the determination of the Castilian nobility to exclude from the throne Juana, the daughter and heiress of Henry IV, and to install Isabella 'the Catholic' in her place. Juana was Afonso V's niece; he espoused her cause, married her, and laid claim through her to the throne of Castile. The sequel was nearly four years of bitter and destructive fighting, which quickly spread to Guinea and to the islands. The Portuguese Crown claimed a monopoly of the Guinea trade, on the grounds both of prior discovery, and of papal bulls of 1454 and 1456 granting to Prince Henry and the Order of Christ the sole right and duty of converting the natives of the region. Despite the claim and despite the bulls (the binding force of which was disputable), ships from the Andalusian ports were already trading in Upper Guinea before the war. The Andalusians had even hit on the ingenious idea of collecting sea-shells in their settlements in the Canaries and shipping them to the Coast, where they were used as coin. In 1475 Isabella issued a formal authorization to her subjects to engage in the African trade, and in 1476 and 1477 privateering fleets were fitted out in the Río Tinto to intercept Portuguese ships homeward bound from Mina. On the Portuguese side, an armed fleet under Fernão Gomes—as commanding officer, not as lessee—was sent out in 1477 to bring Guinea produce home, and made a successful passage out and back. The fighting throughout the war was extremely savage, prisoners usually being hanged or thrown over the side. The last big Spanish expedition of the war, consisting of thirty-five sail, went out in 1478; it was out-manoeuvred and out-fought, and many of the ships were taken by the Portuguese. In general, in sea and island fighting the Portuguese more than held their own everywhere except in the Canaries, where there were established Spanish settlements. Consequently, although at home the Portuguese were heavily defeated and withdrew all their claims in Castile, the Treaty of Alcaçovas, which ended the war in 1479, contained clauses dealing with oversea trade and settlement highly favourable to Portugal. Castile retained only the Canaries. The Castilians, according to Pulgar, were extremely reluctant to abandon their claim to trade with Mina; but many of their ships were still in African waters, and in danger of interception. Eventually, after very tenacious bargaining, Castile accepted the Portuguese monopoly of fishing, trade and navigation along the whole West African coast, and the Portuguese gave safe-conduct to Spanish ships returning from the coast at the end of the war. The Treaty of Alcaçovas was the first of a long series of European treaties regulating colonial spheres of influence, and in this respect was a signal diplomatic triumph for the Portuguese.

The treaty was followed in Portugal by a remarkable burst of enthusiasm for discovery and oversea trade, vigorously encouraged by John II, who succeeded his father in 1481. The new king immediately turned his attention to the problems of regulating and defending the Guinea trade. Spanish adherence to treaty obligations was not entirely to be trusted. Clandestine fishing continued off the Mauretanian coast. A proposed English expedition to Mina in 1481 was believed to have been instigated by the Duke of Medina Sidonia; and the treasonable correspondence of the Duke of Braganza, discovered in 1481, had included proposals for Spanish trade to Guinea. Legislation by itself could do little; though decrees were issued prohibiting the trade in shells from the Canaries and prescribing savage penalties for any foreigners caught in African waters. Serious attempts were made also, for the first time, to prevent the export of information about new discoveries. Probably they were not very effective. Genoese sailors went everywhere and peddled everyone's secrets; there were many Portuguese, from the Duke of Braganza downwards, whose national allegiance sat lightly upon them; and there was a regular trade in smuggled charts. The lack of documentary information about Portuguese voyages is probably due more to slovenly record-keeping and to the destroying hand of time than to a formal policy of secrecy. But these were relatively minor matters. Adequate defence was the most urgent need; and this was provided in 1482 by the construction of the factory-fort of São Jorge da Mina. This famous fortress—its successor still stands on the same site—was built by Diogo d'Azambuja, diplomat, engineer and soldier, of dressed stone shipped from Portugal, on a site acquired by negotiation with the local chiefs. It had a garrison of sixty soldiers—not always up to strength—and soon gathered round it a native village inhabited by labourers and fighting auxiliaries. Its provisioning was difficult: the water supply was poor, and food, other than local fish, and fruit and vegetables brought from the island of São Thomé, came out from Portugal; but interlopers kept away from it, and it served its purpose well for a hundred and fifty years.

The trade which Elmina Castle defended was chiefly in gold, slaves and pepper, with minor dealing in ivory, gum, wax, palm oil, occasional ostrich eggs and similar curiosities. The principal exports were cloth and hardware. The trade was carried on chiefly by firms and private individuals operating under licence from the legal monopolist, the Crown; and the Crown reserved the right of the sole purchase of some commodities on arrival in Portugal. Ivory was so reserved under the Gomes lease, but not subsequently. Dealing in pepper was always a royal monopoly in Portugal, and high-quality Benin pepper was an important source of revenue; but after the turn of the century its import was prohibited, in order to protect the price of Indian pepper imported by the Crown itself. Malagueta continued to be used as a cheap substitute. Slaves were valuable, though not very numerous; perhaps 500 a year at the end of the century. There was a 'country' trade on the Coast. The Portuguese factory at Gató on the Benin river exported slaves not only to Portugal, but also to Mina, where the local up-country traders needed carriers and would pay for them in gold. Gató was provisioned from São Thomé Island, which served as an *entrepôt* for the Gulf, as Santiago in the Cape Verde Islands did for Upper Guinea. Both exported food—rice, meat, sugar, and in the sixteenth-century maize—to places along the Coast. All in all, some twelve or fifteen Portuguese ships annually traded on the Coast at the end of the century, as Vasco da Gama, according to Barros, informed the ruler of Calicut. In the early decades of the sixteenth century the trade, especially the slave trade, steadily increased.

The discoveries of Lopo Gonçalves and Rui de Sequeira, by revealing the southerly trend of the Gaboon coast, disillusioned those who hoped for an easy passage to India. John II prudently developed the Guinea trade which he already possessed, while simultaneously but separately pursuing coastal exploration. He sent out a series of expeditions at Crown expense, in caravels equipped for discovery, not for trade, commanded by extremely capable professional navigators. Among their equipment they carried stone columns, which they were to erect at prominent points on newly discovered land; several of these *padrões* have been found, and brought back, two to the Lisbon Geographical Society, one to Germany, the most solid possible evidence of the achievements of the discoverers. In 1483 Diogo Cão set up his first *padrão* at São Antonio do Zaira at the mouth of the *rio poderoso*, the Congo; explored the river for some distance; and pushed on down the coast as far as Cape Santa María in 13°S, where he erected a second *padrão*. He returned to Portugal in 1484, bringing several Congolese natives with him to be instructed in the Christian faith and taught to wear clothes. Cão's reception was more than usually enthusiastic; his Congolese were fêted in Lisbon and taken into the King's household for education; and Cão was knighted. A curious story circulated both in Rome and in Lisbon in the following year, to the effect that the King of Portugal's men had actually reached the Indian Ocean and that the King had so informed the Pope. Immediately south of Cape Santa María is a large bay, the Lucira Grande; it is just possible—though, with so thorough an explorer, unlikely—that Cão took the Lucira Grande for the Indian Ocean, and so informed the King. If so, Cão's second voyage in 1485–7 was a severe disappointment: he sailed on south nearly to the Tropic of Capricorn and set up his last *padrão* on Cape Cross, in 22°S, just north of Walfish Bay. On the return passage he again entered the Congo, returned his Congolese passengers to their homes, was warmly welcomed by the local people, and took his ships up as far as the Yelala Falls, a most difficult and dangerous passage. Nothing is certainly known of his return or of his later life. Perhaps he was disgraced because of the King's disappointment, for John II had none of Prince Henry's patience; perhaps he died on the return voyage. He had explored 1,450 miles of unknown tropical coast, much of it against the Benguela current and the south-east trades.

The increasing length of the African voyages posed difficult problems in victualling the small caravels employed in the work. Wood and water could be taken in here and there on the coasts of Angola and South-West Africa, but no food was to be had there. Cão's successor, the equally capable and still more famous Bartolomeu Dias, took a store-ship in addition to his two caravels on the expedition which left Lisbon in 1487. He provisioned the caravels from the store-ship in Angra Pequeña, probably Luderitz Bay, and left the store-ship there with a small party on board, about Christmas. From there they beat against wind and current until, about Cape Voltas, with the south-east wind freshening against them, the caravels stood out from the coast to seek a better wind. They sailed south-west or sou'-sou'-west for many days until, about latitude 40°S, they at last picked up the prevailing westerly wind. They ran east for some days, hoping to regain the coast, until well east of the longitude of Cape Voltas, then stood to the north, and eventually fell in with the land about Mossel Bay. They had doubled the Cape without sighting it. They coasted on east and north-east past Algoa Bay and on as far as the Great Fish River. The current there sets to the south-west and the water is warm, corroborative evidence that the way to India lay open; but Dias' people, tired and anxious about their provisions, persuaded him to turn back. There was no mutiny; the habit of submitting major decisions to a general meeting was deeply ingrained in all seamen during the Age of Reconnaissance, and few commanders far from home ventured to override if they could not over-persuade. It was on the return passage that Dias sighted the great cape he had been seeking. He was a fortunate as well as a brave and skilful navigator; the southernmost point of Africa is not the Cape of Good Hope, but Cape Agulhas, further east. The Agulhas current sets strongly to the north-west, and a sailing ship rounding the Cape of Good Hope too closely ran the risk of being embayed in False Bay or running foul of Danger Point. Dias had discovered not only the way to India but one of the most important rules on how to get there under sail. At Angra Pequeña he found his store-ship, with only three of the ship-keepers still alive. He set up a *padrão* at the point now known as Point Dias, put in briefly at Elmina on his passage home, and finally reached Lisbon in December 1488. . . .

21. European beginnings on the West Coast

J. W. BLAKE *European Beginnings in West Africa* Imperial Studies Series, Vol. XIV, Longmans for Royal Commonwealth Society 1957; pages 7–14, 100–4

. . . It is not easy, so scanty are the records, to reconstruct West Africa as the Portuguese found it. They soon learned that, though the natives and the geographical environment varied very much, the same kinds of merchandise could be obtained along the entire coast from Senegal to Sierra Leone. Some of them settled in Santiago Island and traded along the mainland. They came, thus, to discern a unity in 'Guinea of Cape Verde' or, as we shall sometimes call it, Upper Guinea. Sailing forward, they first looked upon the land of Senegambia, bounded on the north by the river Senegal and on the south by the river Gambia. An Arab people, the dark Azenegues, inhabited the region north of the Senegal, but to the south was the first true negro kingdom where lived the Jalofos, whose black skin distinguished them sharply from the tawny Arabs of the Barbary Coast. The white discoverers learned, too, that away in the interior dwelt a mighty king named Mandimansa, who may have been the ruler of the empire of Mali. Many of the coast tribes were his subjects, but little was known about him. Occasionally the Portuguese attempted to get in touch with him, but no permanent contact was ever organised. The kingdom of Jalofo, however, was quite well known to the Portuguese. It does not seem to have been a political unit. There were a large number of small potentates, each the lord of a tribe, like the subjects of King Boudomel, and like the Barbacini and the Serreri, who were perpetually at war one with another. Nor were the Jalofos a very rich people. Yet they gave the Portuguese a fair welcome, so that treaties were made and a flourishing trade developed between blacks and whites.

The Mandiguas lived south of the Gambia, a powerful people and less easy to deal with because of native wars. They seem to have controlled the navigation of the upper reaches of the river Gambia where, at Setuku in the land of Cantor, they held a great fair once a year, and the smaller tribes, who lived in the river valleys further south, acknowledged their suzerainty. These subject tribes, the Beafares and the Guoguoliis, inhabited the land around the valley of the Rio Grande and as far south as the Cabo da Verga. The Portuguese found that they could trade with them as they did with the Naluns, the Teymenes, who resided beyond the Cabo da Verga, and the Bouloees of Sierra Leone.

All these tribes, from the Senegal southwards, were apparently confined to the coast. In the interior dwelt others about whom the Portuguese heard and wrote little. Pacheco and Alvise Cadamosto, the Venetian traveller who visited Guinea in 1455–7, collected a few scraps of information about Djenné, Mali and Timbuktu, and their records may be correlated with that of Leo Africanus. But they have handed down a meagre portion. Perhaps, by way of illustration, we may be permitted to quote from the *Esmeraldo de Situ Orbis*, compiled by Pacheco:

We know that the [Senegal] flows out of a mighty lake of the river Nile, thirty leagues long and ten wide . . . and at the head of the lake there is a kingdom which is called Tabucutu, which has a great city of the same name joined with the same lake. The city of Jany is that way, peopled by negroes, a city which is encircled by a wall of mud, and there are very rich stores of gold in it. Copper, tin, salt and red and blue cloths are very highly valued there, and all are sold by weight except the cloths. Furthermore, clove pepper, yellow pepper, fine silks and sugar are also valued highly, and the trade of that land is very great. . . .

It is plain that Pacheco, relying upon second-hand information, believed in the existence of a great interior lake from which flowed two mighty rivers, the Nile eastwards and the Senegal westwards. He and his contemporaries were even vaguer about the other inland kingdoms. The empires of Timbuktu, Djenné and Mali fascinated them because of the reports of their wealth, but the smaller kingdoms did not interest them much. It would seem that behind the Guoguoliis lived a tribe called the Jaalunguas and behind the Buoloees, the Souzos.

The Portuguese found a large number of petty negro kingdoms along the coast beyond Sierra Leone just as in Upper Guinea. But the regional names, which they applied, were derived from the names of the most plentiful articles of trade, gold, ivory, malagueta pepper and slaves.

The Malagueta coast acquired its name early. Eustache de la Fosse, a Fleming, refers to the 'Manigette Coast' which he had navigated in 1480; the *Journal* of Columbus mentions 'la costa de la manegueta' which the famous Genoese explorer visited; while the term 'Malagueta' is frequently used by Pacheco to describe the district where a species of pepper of the same name was gathered in abundance. All through the reign of King John III of Portugal, Portuguese and French writers continued to use the same word to designate the stretch of shore from Sierra Leone to Cape Palmas. In the middle of the sixteenth century, however, English corsairs began to refer to malagueta pepper as Guinea grains, and so the fashion arose of describing Malagueta as the Grain Coast. The Portuguese did not abandon their term, but most seventeenth-century writers generally used the later name. The native tribes of this region were, apparently, less approachable than those of Senegambia, for the Lusitanians never had any intercourse with them beyond the bare necessities of trade. The Bouloees, to whom Pacheco alludes, inhabited the coast as far east as the Cape of Saint Anna, but they were less civilised than their tribal relations of Sierra Leone. Probably these negroes were wilder because of the geographical fact that no good harbours, few rivers and a dangerous foreshore rendered impossible a very close contact between whites and blacks.

The modern Ivory Coast, running from Cape Palmas almost to Cape Threepoints, was as difficult to approach as Malagueta. Here the natives, like the Beiçudos, were treacherous and wild, yet they offered an abundance of elephants' tusks to the Portuguese traders. This commodity gave its name to the region, but not until the second half of the sixteenth century, when French interlopers began to refer to it as the Tooth Coast (*Coste des Dents*). It would seem, so far as records tell, that the Portuguese did not often distinguish between the modern Grain and Ivory Coasts. They generally used only one word, Malagueta, for both regions. This was not always the case, for Pacheco states categorically that the Malagueta coast ended at Cape Palmas. Still, during their frequent negotiations with foreign powers, the Portuguese always referred to Malagueta as though it included the Ivory Coast.

Ten years after discovering Sierra Leone, the Portuguese reached the Gold Coast. At first they called it 'the trade of gold' or 'the mine of gold', but later they generally spoke of 'the Mine' or 'Mina'. Mina included the whole region where gold could be bartered for in great quantities: it consisted of a littoral belt, about 160 miles in length, mainly on the east side of Cape Threepoints but extending as far west as Axem. Soon after its discovery, the white traders built on this gold-bearing coast a great castle which they called São Jorge da Mina, or 'Saint George of the Mine'. They had not, in fact, found a gold mine, though they had tried for half a century. The wish was father to the thought when they named the new land, but the much greater abundance of gold did suggest that they were very near to its ultimate source.

The Portuguese do not tell us much about the tribes whom they found living along this coast. However, a comparison of contemporary records with later descriptions of the Gold Coast suggests that, during the intervening period, the political situation did not change much. Duarte Pacheco Pereira, in his *Esmeraldo*, mentions four negro villages, which Jean Barbot long afterwards described: Samma, Great Fante, Little Fante and Little Sabou. Moreover, at least two of the tribes which dwelt behind the castle of São Jorge in the seventeenth century, the Fetu and the Comani, were living there in 1503. The first discoverers, like the white traders who came after them, noted the business acumen of the negroes, their treachery, their proneness to war and the fact that most of them lived by fishing off the coast in their *almadias*, or canoes. They also knew that the merchants, who sold the gold, brought it to the coast from the interior and sometimes found it difficult to persuade the coast tribes to give them through passage down to the shore. These examples indicate that conditions, like those existing when Barbot wrote, prevailed in the fifteenth century. He found a large number of small, warring tribes upon the Gold Coast at the end of the seventeenth century. We may conclude, then, that a similar situation obtained, when the Portuguese first visited Mina.

The Portuguese used no special term for the modern Slave Coast beyond Mina. It is true that one of the rivers of this part of Guinea was known as the Rio dos Escravos (River of the Slaves), and that, during the early sixteenth century, the Portuguese pursued a considerable traffic in slaves there. But, when speaking of this region, they were wont to refer to individual native kingdoms, like Benin, or to 'the five rivers beyond the castle of São Jorge da Mina'. They were familiar with the coastal navigation, but they knew practically nothing of the interior, not realising, for example, that the rivers which flowed into the Bight of Benin were distributaries of the Niger. Some of them visited the capital city of the kingdom of Benin. Thus, Pacheco records that he was in that city four times, and tells us of its port, Gató. He, like others, heard also of a mighty interior empire whose sovereign, the Ogané, wielded an extensive hegemony and furthermore, he supposed the Ogané might be Prester John. The coast tribes, all of whom the Portuguese called Jos, were semi-cannibals and always at war, especially those who lived in a big village at the mouth of the Rio Real—one of the 'five rivers'—and who possessed the largest *almadias*, some of which would hold as many as eighty warriors. The Jos negroes also inhabited the coast around the Bight of Biafra and were found as far south as Cape St. Catherine. With this region, however, the Portuguese had contact only as traders. There was commerce to be had at both Gabun and the Rio dos Camarões, but the Lusitanians, finding the negroes very treacherous, had ventured to neither place up to the time when Pacheco wrote his great book. Generally speaking, then, the whites were very ignorant of this last section of Guinea.

The unusual physical and climatic conditions of Guinea amazed the Portuguese as much as the habits, customs and tribal organization of the negroes and the commercial prospects of that coast. They found that certain geographical peculiarities of the country seriously restricted the nature of their activities. Firstly, white penetration into the interior was exceedingly difficult. A belt of dense tropical forest hindered land journeys up-country. This belt, which ran almost parallel to the coast, sometimes touching it, as at Benin, and sometimes stretching inland sixty miles and more, was terminated on its north and north-eastern side by a high plateau. The rivers were no easier to negotiate. Few of them, as the *Esmeraldo* shows, were navigable at the mouth, while further up-stream most were impassable by reason of swift currents and cataracts where they fell from the level of the interior plateau to that of the low-lying forest belt.

Secondly, experience taught the whites that they could trade only during the so-called Guinea season. Traffic in West Africa was practically confined to the northern winter because heavy tropical rains, a humid atmosphere and terrific heat, from May or June to September, made life, let alone the pursuit of trade, barely possible for white men during those months. Consequently, ships, which engaged in the traffic, made the out-journey generally between September and January, and the return journey before or in May. The Portuguese soon learned these vital facts, doubtless by dire experience. Their annual fleets to Malagueta and Mina, therefore, sailed regularly from Portugal in the autumn: indeed, as we shall see, their ships were later forbidden to go to Guinea or São Thomé except between August and March. Nor were their sixteenth-century rivals, French, English and Netherlanders, slow to discover the rules: their illegal voyages were made nearly always in the winter. The result was that the later struggles in Guinea between the Portuguese and the interlopers generally took place also in the winter. The northern summer was a time of little or no trade and of peace between the rival powers.

In the third place, the Portuguese had to contend with peculiar navigational difficulties both on the ocean voyage and on the Guinea Coast itself. A gentle current, flowing from southern Portugal to the Canary Islands and so to Cape Verde, together with the prevailing north-east trade winds, helped their caravels on the first part of the out-journey. Then, after taking in fresh water at the port of Beziguiche, just south of the Cape, they would push on to Sierra Leone and Malagueta, where they would meet the Guinea current. This current, which ran steadily eastwards, attaining its maximum velocity of three and a half miles an hour between Cape Palmas and Cape Threepoints, would serve to carry them forward to Mina. Thus, provided they experienced neither the tornadoes nor the calms, which are frequent in the doldrums, they might hope to reach the castle of São Jorge in less than two months. While in Guinea, great skill, exhausting toil and unceasing vigilance were required of them in avoiding numerous shallows and hidden rocks at river mouths, and in sheltering from sudden storms and variable daily winds. The most serious difficulty, however, lay in the homeward journey. If, as so often happened, they wished on the return voyage to trade on the Malagueta coast, they had to sail against the Guinea current. Moreover, the prevailing wind in Lower Guinea was south-westerly, except for a few weeks between December and February when the dry Harmattan blew off the land, and this south-west wind did not aid the returning caravels. The less difficult route from Mina to Portugal was to bear to the south until the Equator was reached and, there, to pick up the equatorial current which ran parallel but in the opposite direction to the Guinea current. In this way, by making a wide sweep, ships might more easily get back to Cape Verde, but, even so, the remaining part of the voyage to Portugal had to be made in face of adverse winds and currents. It follows, then, that it took much longer to come back from Guinea than to go there. Furthermore, as we have seen, ships were wont to return in the spring after trading during the winter. Accordingly, should they delay their departure from Guinea too long, as Captain Wyndham did in 1554, they might suffer untold harm. Their supplies of fresh water might give out and their biscuit might begin to perish. Moreover, the movement of the sun northwards after the end of March meant that they were more liable to be delayed still longer by the calms of the doldrums. Then it would often result that, for lack of proper food and by reason of the torrential monsoon rains of the summer months and the fierce heat of the sun's rays, many might succumb to fever and dysentery. Thus the rate of mortality on the return voyage was nearly always higher—sometimes far higher—than on the outward one.

In these circumstances, the achievement of the Portuguese was remarkable. . . .

The power of the Portuguese did not extend beyond the walls of São Jorge, and they soon discovered that only one fortress was of very little avail for protecting 2,000 miles of coast. Andrés Bernáldez, the Castilian chronicler, astutely pointed out this weakness as early as 1513, when he declared that the Portuguese were not lords of the land where the gold was collected, 'save only for their trade in a fortress, which they have recently erected'. A similar criticism was levelled against the Portuguese defences more than half a century later by Martin Frobisher, the famous English privateer. By that time, however, several more smaller forts had been built to remedy the defect.

The first of the minor forts was Axem, built originally in 1503 on a site to the west of Cape Threepoints. Both Pacheco and de Barros were familiar with it, and a document in the Portuguese Torre do Tombo contains a description of its foundation. It was attacked by negroes in 1515 and, therefore, was moved to a more strategic position. The Portuguese made some alterations in its structure in the middle of the century. In 1602 a Dutch writer described Axem as 'a little fortress . . . very ill defended'.

Two additional 'strong houses' were built on the Gold Coast: Samma and Accra. Unfortunately, we cannot be sure when these two lodges were first fortified.

Samma village lies just east of Cape Threepoints. Perhaps the Portuguese factory was built soon after 1471, when the Mine was discovered. Pacheco records briefly that Samma was the village where the first gold trade was made. De Barros confirms this, but in words that suggest he may have drawn his information from the same source as Pacheco or from the *Esmeraldo* itself. The apparent familiarity of both writers with the place-name, Samma, might be regarded as an indication that the native town included a Portuguese establishment. However, the earliest definite evidence of a fort at Samma may be found in Hakluyt's *Principal Navigations*: when John Lok sailed to Guinea, the inhabitants of Samma 'shot off their ordnance'; they had 'two or three pieces of ordnance and no more' (12 January 1555). These facts seem to prove that Samma was not fortified until the reign of King John III, when it was found necessary to strengthen the defences against French interlopers. There were only a few Portuguese stationed in the fort even at the end of the century. Pieter Marees describes Samma as a place 'where the Portuguese have another strong house, and because the region is very fertile, three or four Portuguese dwell there to collect the toll of the fish, and to buy several other food products on the coast, which they send daily to the castles of Axem and Mina'. Samma had evidently become an auxiliary to the other forts.

The last of the fortified stations on the Gold Coast was Accra. It has been found as difficult to date accurately the origin of Accra as of Samma. Jean Barbot, whose evidence on this point cannot be regarded as entirely reliable, states vaguely that 'some years after 1484 the King of Portugal formed a Guinea Company, with the sole privilege of trading there . . . which at first made a considerable profit, and caused fort St Anthony to be built at Axim, another small one at Accra, and a lodge at Sama'. His indiscriminate association of Samma and Accra suggests a contemporaneity of origin, which is not borne out by the facts. Neither Pacheco nor de Barros refers to Accra, though both mention Samma. This suggests a later origin for the former. Even Martin Frobisher, who was asked to declare what he knew of the Portuguese stations in Guinea in 1562, did not refer to Accra, though his demonstrable inaccuracy in other respects makes his statement untrustworthy. In fact, we have no unquestionable evidence of the existence of Accra until 1576, when the Portuguese were attempting, apparently, to extend its defences. Negroes attacked it and razed it to the ground in the same year.

It is probable that, in Portuguese eyes, their defences on the Gold Coast ranked first in importance. Nevertheless, some fortifications were erected in Senegambia, the Cape Verde Islands, Sierra Leone and the island of São Thomé. A native succession dispute was mainly responsible for a project to build a fort at the mouth of the Senegal. Twenty caravels sailed from Portugal for the Senegal, under the command of Pero Vaz da Cunha, to restore Prince Bemoij, who was the unsuccessful claimant, to build a fortress, and to open up the way to Timbuktu. João de Barros dated the enterprise in 1485–6, Ruy de Pina two years later; the former records that the fort was to be built on the banks of the Senegal, the latter that building was begun at its mouth. In the end, however, the whole scheme was abandoned, for Bemoij perished or was murdered, and Pero Vaz returned to Portugal. A start appears to have been made in the building operations, for Jean Barbot asserts that in his day at Byhurt, at the mouth of the Senegal, were 'still to be seen the ruins of a fort', which, he continues, was almost finished by the Portuguese in the reign of King John II. The projected fort at Byhurt is the only known instance of an attempt by the Portuguese to fortify Senegambia.

The Cape Verde archipelago was of greater strategic importance. Portuguese caravels, bound for Brazil, regularly called at Santiago Island. Portuguese fleets, which returned from São Thomé and the East Indies, also made for the islands. They stood, then, at the confluence of several of the chief highways of the sea. Moreover, interlopers, when they grasped the strategic significance of the archipelago, would hide in neighbouring creeks and inlets, ready to pounce upon fishing caravels and isolated trading caravels and carracks, should any be separated from the annual fleets. It is no wonder that fortifications were built in Santiago. Fort St Martha was erected on one side of the town of Ribeira Grande in the sixteenth century. Little is known about the details of this fort, but it would seem that few improvements were made until the third quarter of the century.

A fort was built in Sierra Leone in the reign of King John II, but this must have proved to be too expensive. After a few years the king ordered its abandonment. The Malagueta coast was never fortified, although at least two expeditions were sent from Portugal to establish forts in 1532 and 1540. We have seen that the slave and pepper trades of Benin were stabilised by the building of a factory in Gató village, which was kept up for fifty years after 1486. But there is no ground for supposing that Gató was ever fortified. More important was the island of São

Thomé, especially after the expansion of the slave trade with the new world, and, accordingly, more careful thought seems to have been devoted to the problem of its defence. Plans for a fortress were considered in 1493, when Alvaro de Caminha, the captain of the island, was appointed governor of 'the fortress which was to be built'. Materials for building were sent out and, by 1506, a small fort appears to have been built in the capital, Povoasan. Afterwards, however, the defence of the island was neglected, until a fearful raid by French interlopers in 1567 roused the inhabitants and the crown to a sense of their responsibilities. A handsome castle, named after the king, was then erected.

No other forts were built between 1454 and 1578 though, occasionally, various schemes seem to have been considered. Thus, for example, one for defending Malagueta was submitted by a contemporary in 1542. The chief obstacle to fortification was probably expense. This would explain why the only permanent forts on the mainland on Guinea were situated along the Mina coast, which was, relatively, the richest part of West Africa. On the other hand, the attempts to establish forts on the Senegal, in Sierra Leone and on the Malagueta coast, would suggest that the Portuguese attributed considerable importance to the rest of Guinea. . . .

22. South-east Africa in the early seventeenth century

E. AXELSON *The Portuguese in South-East Africa, 1600–1700* Witwatersrand University Press 1960; pages 2–14, 28–9

. . . The State of Portuguese India began (in theory) at the Cape of Good Hope, and extended to the Far East; it was administered by a Viceroy or Governor, with his seat in Goa, assisted by a *Conselho do Estado* with consultative functions.[1] It contained

[1] A royal letter of 1591 had ordered this to comprise all *fidalgos* in Goa and other persons of experience. The V. protested against the size of such a council and lack of secrecy, and in 1604 its membership was restricted. In 1605 it comprised the V. as president, the archbishop, the captain of Goa, the *Vedor da Fazenda*, and three others. (Panduronga Pissurlencar, *Assentos do Conselho do Estado da India*. Bastorá, 1953–7, I, pp. xx-xxi.)

12 cities and 23 fortress-towns for the control of trade; among the latter were three on the south-east coast of Africa.[1]

Officials in south-east Africa received their orders from Goa; and it was to Goa that they reported. The annual monsoons both facilitated and restricted such communication. The north-east monsoon begins on the northern coast of west India in mid November, becomes established on the south coast in December, and continues until March. The south-west monsoon begins on the south-east African coast in March; it is well developed by June, at its strongest in August, and continues until September or possibly October. Since communication was limited to brief periods each year, much depended on the local representatives of Portugal.

These were the captain of Moçambique and Sofala (which had been Portuguese since 1507 and 1505 respectively) and the captain of Mombasa (where a fortress had been founded in 1593). The King of Portugal granted the captaincies as favours to deserving noblemen, or the widows or daughters of deserving noblemen. There was invariably a long waiting list, and recipients had usually to wait many years, even decades sometimes, before they could profit from the award. Occasionally the grantee would occupy the captaincy himself. A daughter would receive it as a dowry, conditional on her marrying an approved suitor if she was still of marriageable age. Usually, however, whoever received the award sold the office to the highest bidder; sometimes the offices would even be put up to public auction in Goa. In theory the captain had to have certain qualities; but in practice it usually sufficed for him to know the Viceroy or Governor, or to make it worth the while of the Viceroy or Governor to know him. The captain paid the treasury an annual sum of money for his three-year lease, and he had certain financial obligations in his captaincy; but in return he received the monopoly of certain trading rights, and was free to extract as much money as he could from his captaincy.

[1] Apart from Sofala, Moçambique and Mombasa the main forts were at Masqat (on the Gulf of Oman); Hormuz; Diu and Damão (flanking the Gulf of Cambay); Goa; Onor, Barcelor, Mangalore, Cannanore, Cranganor, Cochin and Coulão (on the Malabar coast); Negapattinam and S. Tomé (on the Coromandel coast); Mannar, Colombo and Galle (in Ceylon); Malacca (in Malaya); and Ternate, Tidore, Solor and Ambon (in the Moluccas).

The captain of Moçambique and Sofala (the latter now only a minor adjunct) paid the treasury 40,000 *pardãos*[1] a year. This money was administered by the royal factor at Moçambique, who paid out of it the expenses of the fortress and the hospital, and of vessels bound for India that might be waiting for the next monsoon. The balance of the money, if any, was remitted to Goa. In return, the captain received the monopoly of trade in the area of Sofala and the Rivers of Cuama, as the lower Zambezi[2] was called.

The seat of the captaincy was at the seaward end of the long, low, narrow, coral island of Moçambique,[3] in the great four-bastioned fortress of S. Sebastião, begun in 1558 and then nearing completion, one of the strongest and most important in the whole of Portuguese India, and the essential base for Portuguese colonization in south-east Africa. The fortress had a garrison, by *regimento*, of only 100 soldiers, with a master-gunner and five bombardiers, but it contained what was thought to be adequate artillery. Its cistern contained 2,000 pipes of water, or some one-and-a-half million gallons. Outside the wall, on the seaward tip of the island, stood the chapel of Nossa Senhora do Baluarte, on the site of an early battery. . . .[4]

Between Moçambique and the Zambezi lay the Macua tribe. Towards the Zambezi were some small towns, the best known being Angoche, under Arab sheikhs, their inhabitants pitifully poor. Twice a year the captain sent a *pangãio* to those parts, to trade for ivory and amber, mats and straw hats, and large

[1] The lease of Moçambique was valued at 9,999 *milreis* (cfd with total receipts of 355,560 for the whole of Portuguese India) for some undisclosed year between 1598 and 1607; expenditure was 5,348 (out of a total of 235,677).

[2] This and most other topographical names of the area are variously spelt. The spelling followed here for names in Southern Rhodesia is that of the *World Aeronautical Chart Topographical Edition.* 1 : 1,000,000, Sheet 3176 (Pretoria, 1958); secondly, the *Geological Map of Southern Rhodesia.* 1 : 1,000,000 (Salisbury, 1946); lastly, sheets of the 1 : 250,000 survey (Salisbury, 1929–47). For names in Moçambique the maps followed are the *Provincia de Moçambique Esbóco Geológico*, 1 : 2,000,000, 1956, and sheets of the 1 : 250,000 survey (Lourenço Marques, 1938–50).

[3] 3,200 yards long, average width 350 yards (British Admiralty Chart No. 653, *Mozambique Harbour*).

[4] The chapel is probably the oldest roofed building extant in southern Africa.

numbers of slaves. Enslavement in south-east Africa, it should be mentioned, arose from selling by parents of their children in times of famine or other emergency; from kidnapping; from capture by chiefs for crimes; and from capture in war.

The northernmost mouth of the Zambezi was navigable only in winter. Two leagues from the bar was the town of Quelimane. Nearby was the Linde mouth, but the mouth mainly used, which was open all the year round, was the Luabo. Between the Luabo and the Cuama proper lay Luabo island where the captain of the Rivers used to stay when he supervised the unloading of the three or four *pangãios* which came every six months from Moçambique with trade goods. The vessels took away gold, in the form of dust, nuggets or sheets, ivory, hippopotamus teeth, honey and slaves.

The river came down in flood each year, especially in March and April, and inundated the banks, giving them amazing fertility, but adding greatly to the unhealthiness of the valley because of what the Portuguese considered to be its 'heavy airs'. One hundred and sixty miles up the river, on the right or Tonga bank, lay the town of Sena, the headquarters of the captain of the Rivers, who was appointed by the captain of Moçambique. A stone fort contained the factory and the church. The town had some 50 Portuguese residents, and 750 Christian natives and Indians, when João dos Santos, a Dominican friar who knew the region well,[1] visited it at the end of the sixteenth century. Around the town lay the lands of Chief Inhamroy. He was a vassal of Monomotapa, the Paramount Chief of most of the country south of the lower Zambezi.[2]

[1] Santos arrived at Moçambique from Portugal in 1586. He ministered in Sofala, Sena, Tete, Moçambique and the Querimba islands. He left south-east Africa for India in 1597 and sailed round the coast in 1600 on his return to Portugal. His book was printed in Évora in 1608, and published in 1609.

[2] In about 1420 a Chief Mutota moved northwards from Gunuvutwa, a country which lay to the south of the Umfuli river and stretched towards the sites of modern Bulawayo and Fort Victoria, a country which the Portuguese later called Butua. He conquered as far as the Zambezi, displacing Tonga and Tavara tribesmen who called him Mwene-mutapa, 'Master of the ravaged lands', which was adopted as a praise-name. Mutota Mwene-mutapa had his headquarters at a dry-stone kraal which he built on the slopes of Chitako hill, near the Utete river, at the foot of the escarpment north of Sipolilo. He governed until about 1445. The 'Empire' of Monomotapa began to disintegrate towards the end of the fifteenth century.

Twenty-five miles east of Sena lay the fertile hills of Murrambala, from which came most of the town's provisions. They were then known as the Shire hills, from the name of the river which issued into the Zambezi beneath them. Santos reported that the residents of Sena and natives navigated this river, but he did not refer to the Shire highlands or to Nyasa, which apparently had not yet been discovered.

Three hundred and twenty miles from the sea, also on the right bank of the Zambezi, lay the town of Tete. This had been in the hands of Chief Nhampanza until Monomotapa had conquered him and bestowed his lands on the Portuguese. The captain of Tete, appointed also by the captain of Moçambique, could muster 2,000 local natives for labour or for war. The stone fort contained seven or eight pieces of artillery. When Santos was there the town had a population of about 600 Christians, of whom about 40 were Portuguese, the remainder natives and Indians. The residents, with trade goods bought in Sena, travelled with their porters southwards and south-westwards into the lands of Monomotapa.

Tete, like Sena, was well supplied with cattle and sheep and goats; cheeses resembling those of the Alentejo; vegetables and fruit, beans and rice and other grains. Everything produced locally was cheap, but whatever had to be imported, such as wine, wheat flour, clothing and footwear, was understandably expensive. Currency in the Rivers consisted not in coins, but in small copper bars; small ingots of tin; coloured beads on strings; various kinds of cloth (the locally produced ones being known as *machiras*, the most popular and valuable those that came from Cambay); and gold, with the *mithqal* as the unit.[1]

There was little traffic across the Zambezi from Tete for, to the north-east and east, there were two cannibal tribes, the Mumbos and the particularly notorious Zimbas. Upstream from Tete lay the kingdom of Sacumbe, in which a cataract impeded navigation for a distance of twenty leagues—a reading

[1] A *mithqal* was worth 480 *reis* in theory, but gold was so plentiful in the Rivers that it was really equivalent to no more than 100 or 120 *reis* (Santos, I, pp. 192–3). Lima Felner calculated that in the middle of the sixteenth century a *mithqal* of Sofala weighed 4·83 grammes (*O Livro dos Pesos, Medidas e Moedas, por Antonio Nunes . . . 1554*. Lisbon, 1868, p. 55). This would be ·515 oz. fine, worth (at £12-10 an ounce) £1-18-9.

of Santos might have saved Livingstone much embarrassment in 1858 when he found that he could not steam past these Quebrabasa rapids. Above the rapids lay the kingdom of Chicôa, which was rich in silver. From Chicôa the Zambezi was again navigable, 'but nobody knows to where', added Santos. The fact that the lower river flooded when there was no local rain proved that its waters had come from afar. There was a belief that the river rose in a great lake in the interior, where a number of other great rivers also had their source.

The Zambezi was the highway to the lands of Monomotapa. As soon as a new captain of Moçambique entered the fortress it was incumbent upon him to send Monomotapa a present of cloth and beads worth 3,000 *crusados* to ensure free access for the traders who swarmed into the Paramount Chief's lands in search of gold. With the lands opened up by this payment, Santos declared, traders could travel about with their goods and their bags of gold more securely than if they were in Portugal. But if the captain did not pay this *curva*, as it was called, the Monomotapa would declare an *empata*, and order his warriors to seize the merchant's wares.

Portuguese traders from Sena and Tete frequented three fairs in the lands of Monomotapa: Luanze, Bocuto and Massapa. The nearest of these was Luanze, which was probably south of the Mazoe on the Southern Rhodesian side of the border with Moçambique.[1] Bocuto was further up the Mazoe, beyond its junction with the Nyadiri.[2] Massapa lay at the foot of Mount

[1] The site of Luanze has not yet been determined. According to a document signed by Filipe it was thirty-five leagues from Tete, between the Nyadiri and the Ruenya. Diogo do Couto repeated the distance of thirty-five leagues, and said it was between two rivers which joined to become the 'Nausovo'; but he added that it was ten leagues from each of these rivers which is possible only by an inclined route, since the maximum distance between the Nyadiri and the Ruenya is forty-five miles. Pedro Barreto de Resende and António Bocarro, in 'Livro do Estado da India' (*RSEA* II, p. 392) declared it to be forty leagues from Tete, and no more than a stockade. António Bocarro gave the distance from Tete as thirty-five leagues, five days' hurried journey; he added that it adjoined lands of Mocota. An informant told Mr Abraham of a Ruanje hill near Mount Chitomba, at the south-western corner of the Mkota Reserve; a hurried visit there by the writer in 1958 failed to find any remains.

[2] Filipe described Bocuto as being alongside the Manzovo, i.e. Mazoe river, on the opposite side and ten leagues from Massapa, forty leagues from

Fura—the modern Mount Darwin,[1] which rises to 4,950 feet, upwards of 2,000 feet above the surrounding countryside. Portuguese were forbidden to ascend this hill, according to Santos, because from its crest a great proportion of the lands of Monomotapa could be seen, and he feared lest their extent and beauty excite the covetousness of the Europeans. On the crest, Santos romantically but wrongly alleged, were fragments of old walls, built of stone and mortar, believed to be the remains of a factory of the Queen of Sheba.[2]

Tete, and between the Mazoe and the Nyadiri. Couto described it as being between small rivers which joined, two leagues from the bank of each, and forty leagues from Tete. According to Bocarro it was between two small rivers, forty leagues from Tete, and thirteen from Luanze crossways on the same range. During the 1958 search previously referred to, we came across a loopholed stone wall fortifying a low rocky bluff overlooking the Mazoe immediately above its confluence with the Nyadiri. The nearest natives told Mr Abraham that the wall was already there when their ancestors entered the area, which Mr Abraham calculated to be at the end of the seventeenth century. The site could be forty leagues from Tete; but it is sixty-five as the crow flies from Mount Darwin. Twelve miles further up the Mazoe we looked at the remains of two other loopholed forts, but they, according to the local inhabitants, were built only in the nineteenth century.

[1] 'Near the head of the Umkaradzi valley stands a lofty mountain, a splendid landmark for many miles round. The range of hills from which this peak rises is called Fura by the natives, but as we were now in a country in dispute between the British and Portuguese, and as I could not discover from the natives that any white subject of Portugal had ever travelled in this district, I had what some people will call the impertinence to name it Mount Darwin . . .'.

[2] On the crest are only some rough-piled stone walls, with no trace of mortar, which are certainly post-Sheba and are probably post-Santos. Massapa fair, according to Filipe, was very close to Fura. According to Couto it was fifty leagues from Tete, reached by way of the Mazoe. According to Bocarro it was four leagues from the Mazoe, ten from Bocuto, and fifty from Tete. Resende and Bocarro added (*RSEA* II, p. 393) that it was made of mud, with loopholes. Phelipe de Assumpção mentioned that it was in among stony hills. There are at least three circular loopholed dry-stone forts at the foot of Mt Darwin, visited by the writer in 1950–2 with Messrs K. Kirkwood, E. H. M. Chetwynd and C. P. Lewis (E. Axelson, 'Some loopholed forts in the Mount Darwin District', *Proceedings and Transactions Rhodesia Scientific Association*, Salisbury, 1956, pp. 1–6). More stone walling was reported by Mr Abraham in 1958. There are other forts on the Mazoe to the east and on Mt Tsawa. Despite persistent rumours of a ruined church near Mt Darwin no such remains have yet been discovered.

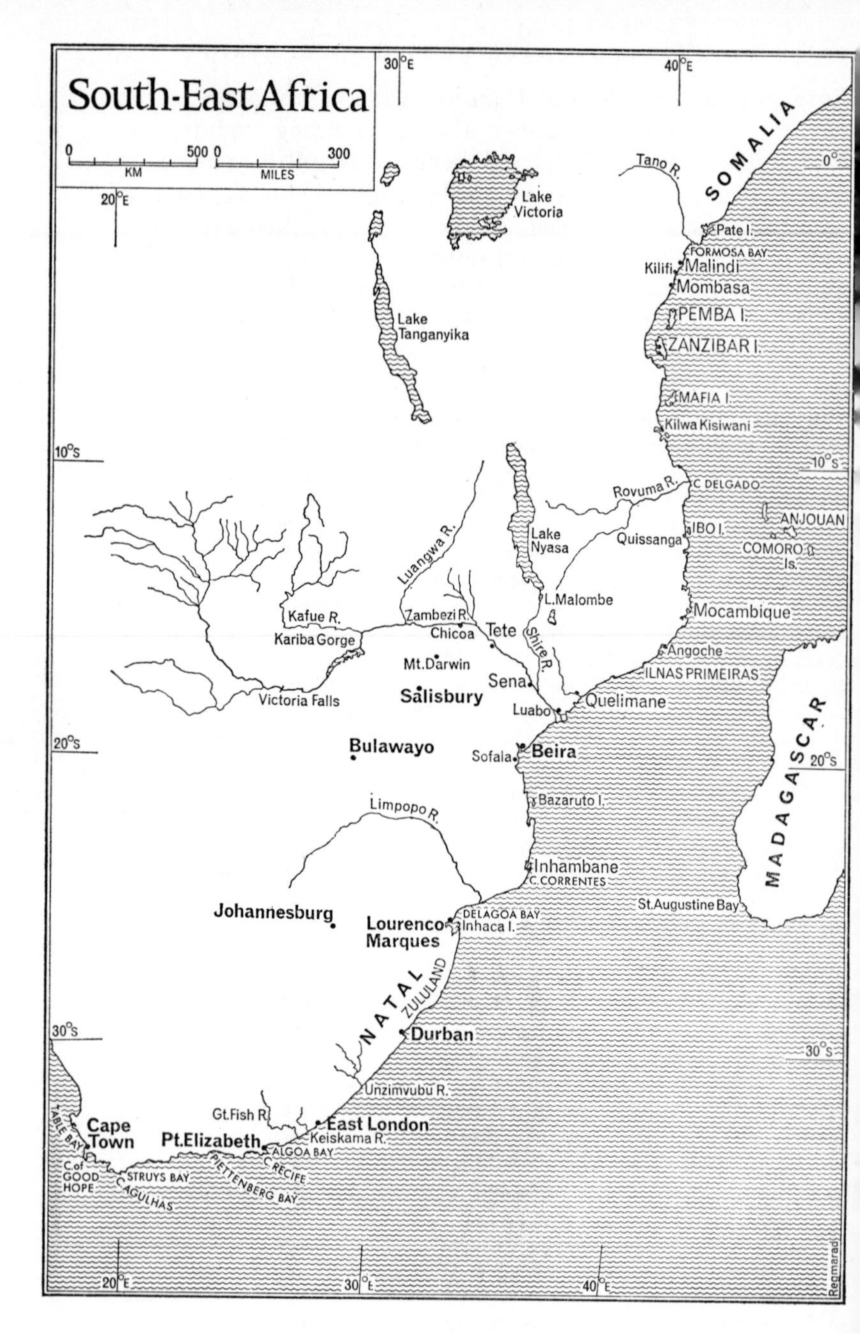

14. South-East Africa

The principal and richest of these fairs was Massapa. Its captain was nominated by the Portuguese but his appointment, which was for life, had to be confirmed by Monomotapa. He had absolute jurisdiction over all natives visiting Massapa, and over all Portuguese visiting the lands of Monomotapa. No Portuguese could pass beyond Massapa without the permission of this Captain of the Gates, or of Monomotapa. The captain collected on Monomotapa's behalf one roll of cloth in twenty from all incoming traders, who came to trade for gold.

The lands of Monomotapa were rich in gold. Natives obtained it by digging alongside rivers and washing the earth in great wooden bowls; by searching for nuggets during the rainy season; and by crushing ore. But the penalty for extracting gold from really rich mines was death, for Monomotapa feared that if the cupidity of the Portuguese were over-aroused they might try to seize his country. The country also produced much iron and copper, the iron used for weapons and hoes, the copper for the bracelets that adorned the arms and legs of both men and women.

The Monomotapa who was reigning at the end of the sixteenth century Santos considered to be called Mambo: but this was a title. The reigning Monomotapa in 1600 was Gatsi Rusere. The language spoken by him and his closest tribesmen was Karanga, which Santos regarded as the most polished of all the languages of south-east Africa; his subjects nearer the coast spoke Tonga.[1] From his head kraal, known as Zimbabwe,[2] Monomotapa ruled over lands which Santos estimated to be 200 leagues square. In reality the shape was more of a rectangle, some 400 miles long by 200 wide. To the south and west lay

[1] Santos, *Ethiopia Oriental* I, p. 223. 'They speake the Mocaranga Tongue, the best Language of all the Cafres; and whereas the Moores of Africa and Arabia, draw their words out of the throat as if they would vomite; these pronounce their words with the end of the tongue and the lips, that they speake many words in a whistling accent, wherein they place great Elegance, as I have heard the Courtiers of Quiteve, and Manamotapa speake. Their stile of speaking is by Metaphors: and Similitudes very proper, and fitted to their purpose.' (Purchas, p. 1550 and E. Axelson (ed.), *South African Explorers*. OUP, 1954, p. 47.)

[2] Usually spelt Zimbaoe in records of the time. Though used to denote the headquarters or court of the King wherever he might be (e.g. João de Barros, *Da Asia*, Lisbon, 1777–8, I–II, p. 378) Dzimbahwe properly meant the 'big stone house' at Chitako (Abraham, 'The Monomotapa Dynasty', p. 76).

Butua, which was also rich in gold, though the inhabitants did not extract much owing to their distance from Portuguese buyers.[1] To the north and north-east Monomotapa's lands were limited by the Zambezi. They touched the sea, between the Luabo and the Tendaculo. To the south-east and south they marched with the now independent kingdoms of Manica, Quiteve and Sedanda.

The Portuguese reached these last kingdoms through Sofala, the southernmost permanent settlement on the coast. Its square fortress still stood in good repair, its walls sixteen feet high, a round bastion at each corner, a tower two stories high, with adequate artillery. Its captain was appointed by the captain of Moçambique. Close to the fortress was the Christian town, with some 600 Portuguese, mulattoes and natives. Further away was the Muslim village, its 100 inhabitants poor and miserable, yet even so having to pay tithe to the church; some served as sailors, others helped the traders. Every six months one or two *pangãios* arrived from Moçambique with the customary trade goods of cloth and beads; they took away slaves and gold, ivory, pearls and dugong teeth, ambergris, honey, butter and rice.

Portuguese sovereignty extended no more than a league or two from the fortress. Every year the captain had to pay a *curva* of 200 rolls of cloth, worth some 100 *crusados*, to placate the neighbouring Quiteve. In return, traders were allowed to traverse the Quiteve lands freely, on payment of one roll of cloth in twenty. Their destination was Manicaland.

The Manica lived around modern Macequece and Umtali; their chief was known as Chicanga. They produced gold in the same ways as the Karanga, but Santos commented on the dangerous nature of their mining: they would sink shafts and drive galleries in pursuit of the vein, but in the absence of effective timbering there were many accidents. The mined gold was inferior in quality to the alluvial.

South of Manicaland lay the kingdom of Biri,[2] south of

[1] The reference is to the Que Que, Gatooma, Hartley goldfield. Santos would have us believe that Butua stretched to Angola, declaring a blanket from there had been bought in Manica (I, p. 199).

[2] This would not be the Biri in the Dande where António Fernandes saw in about 1511 or 1512 a dry-stone fort being built, but the offshoot whose descendants live in the Marandellas district today.

Quiteve the kingdom of Sabia, the chief of which was known as Sedana, and whose lands flanked the Sabi river and included the Bocicas, as the Bazaruto islands were called, and Inhambane. To Inhambane came each year a *naveta* or *pangãio* sent by the captain of Moçambique to trade for ivory, slaves, amber, honey, butter, rhinoceros horns and hooves, hippopotamus teeth and hooves, and pearls.

The southernmost outpost of Portuguese influence in south-east Africa was at the Bahia da Lagoa (corrupted by the English to Delagoa Bay), or the river of Lourenço Marques as it had come to be called. Here, to Inhaca island, the captain of Moçambique sent a *naveta* each year with the customary cloth and beads to be exchanged for the same goods as those obtained at Inhambane with the exception of pearls. Inhaca was also the goal of many parties of survivors from ships wrecked to the south. . . .

The Portuguese had long maintained a captain at Malindi, whose sultans had been allies of the Portuguese since the days of Vasco da Gama. In 1585 a Turkish adventurer, Ali Bek, had appeared on the coast, and with spectacular success had won the homage of local sultans and sheikhs as far south as Mombasa —with the exception of Malindi—due, according to Santos, to the scandalous behaviour of the Portuguese on the coast, and the irreconcilable antipathy of Islam to Christianity. The Portuguese were prompt to punish the main towns for their switch in allegiance, but in 1589 Ali Bek returned, and built a fort in Mombasa. A Portuguese armada arrived, and attacked the unfortunate Turks and Arabs while the Zimbas were storming their way on to the island from the mainland. To prevent further threats from the Turks, the authorities in Portugal agreed to the construction of a fortress at Mombasa; it was begun in 1593.

The southernmost town of interest to the captain of Mombasa, to which he occasionally sent a factor in search of trade, was Kilwa. But this was not the Arab capital of the coast whose noble palace, cupolaed mosques and extensive stone buildings had excited the admiration of the first Europeans who had gazed upon them a hundred years before. The loss of her Sofalan gold trade, Portuguese sackings, and Portuguese blockades of the coast had already reduced the town to near destitution when the Zimbas ate up most of the citizens in 1593. The town now lay in ruins, its sultan poor and powerless.

The island of Mafia had previously been famed as a producer of coir and copal, but apparently at this time the captain no longer maintained a factor there. The island of Zanzibar also, for all its fertility, does not seem to have been under direct Portuguese influence, though thirty years earlier its king had been forced to become a vassal of Portugal. The emerald island of Pemba had closer links. Santos eulogized its luxuriant vegetation, its streams, its fields, its herds, its orchards and its woods, which produced timbers fit for the construction of the largest ships. On the island lived many Portuguese; but they were not very vigorous, because of the local fevers and an excess of good living. At the turn of the century the island became even more unhealthy.

Pemba, according to the sultans of Malindi, fell under their jurisdiction until Francisco Barreto set up a puppet king with obligation to pay 200 *pardãos* as tribute a year. After this puppet's death the King of Portugal ordered Pemba to be restored to Malindi if the dead king had left no heir. He had, however, and the son gave great help to the Portuguese during their construction of the fortress at Mombasa, and again in 1595 when there had been the threat of a Turkish attack. Filipe now suggested that the son be converted and given the island, but the islanders poisoned him. He left no heir. Viceroy Francisco da Gama took his brother to Goa and offered him the kingship if he would be baptized and marry a Portuguese. When he procrastinated the Viceroy decided to bestow the island on the Sultan of Malindi. Filipe refused to confirm this, and ordered the island to be granted to the dead king's brother. The Sultan of Malindi continued to urge his claim to the island. The brother eventually submitted, taking the name D. Filipe da Gama, and he duly married an orphan from Portugal; the Viceroy presented the island as a dowry on condition that the youth paid tribute. He went to take possession, but his subjects revolted against him and the Portuguese and drove him out. The Viceroy attributed the rejection of the new king to his being a Christian, but Friar Santos held a different opinion. He declared that many of the Portuguese settlers, especially those who were ex-soldiers, extorted whatever or whomever they desired from the islanders, and that the islanders had simply turned against their oppressors and the king who was in alliance with them. The rejected king and numbers of Portuguese found refuge in Mombasa.

The fortress of Jesus, which commanded the entrance to Mombasa harbour, was still incomplete at the beginning of the seventeenth century. This harbour lay between the three-mile-long island and the point of the mainland to the east. To the west of the island lay the even deeper and more capacious harbour of Tuaca or Kilindini. The excellence of these harbours, and the fertility and comparative salubrity of the island, prompted periodic suggestions that Mombasa should become the main port of call of ships bound from Portugal to India. But these suggestions were not accepted in Lisbon, with the result that Mombasa never rose to major importance during the century, with a Portuguese population adequate to ensure its defence. It remained primarily an outpost to protect Moçambique and the Rivers from any Turkish or Arab attack; but it was also a trading station, for the purchase of ivory, coir, copal and other products of the coast.

At Mombasa the Portuguese had established a customs house; all trade goods imported for use anywhere along the coast were supposed to go through the customs and pay 6 per cent duty, plus a further 1 per cent for the construction and maintainance of the fortifications. Such an order could not help but cause resentment among the Arabs whose very livelihood depended on coastal trade. The only Arab to secure any advantage from it was the Sultan of Malindi who, as a reward for his allegiance to the Portuguese and the aid he rendered in establishing Fort Jesus, had been appointed to serve also as Sultan of Mombasa. The Sultan now claimed a third share of the customs revenue. He further asked that his vessels might pass freely to other Portuguese fortresses without payment of duty, and that he might send one a year without molestation to the port of Mecca. He asked that he be officially recognized as the judge of civil and criminal cases among the Muslims, and that the captain of Mombasa decide nothing of consequence without reference to him. He again asked that the island of Pemba be delivered to him; and he requested that he be acknowledged as the brother-in-arms of the Portuguese King. The authorities in

Lisbon granted him the third of the customs, but they wanted more information before granting his other demands, with all the delay that this involved. By such prevarications are allies turned into enemies. As it was, the sale of the captaincy did not suffice to pay the garrison, and the customs' revenues did not cover the other administrative expenses. However the captain himself could reckon on netting 30,000 *crusados* during his term of office.

The small but growing Portuguese town lay on the landward side of the fortress, between the fortress and the Arab town. Dominating it was the church constructed by Augustinian friars, to which Order had been entrusted all missionary enterprise along the coast.

Malindi was in decline at this time. Its harbour, open to the north-east monsoon, had always been inadequate during this season. By Barreto's day, encroachment by the sea had reduced much of the town to ruins. Tribal incursions, the transfer of its Sultan to Mombasa, and the establishment of the Portuguese customs house in that rival town, accelerated its decay.

The town of Lamu was still smarting from the execution of its sultan in 1589. The town of Manda had been razed to the ground by the same punitive expedition which had cut 2,000 coco-nut palms, and the Manda islanders were slowly re-establishing themselves at the turn of the century. Nearly equally pitiful was the plight of the inhabitants of Pate Island. On this low mangrove-lined island, fifteen miles long by a maximum of seven miles broad, had been three prosperous towns. The rulers of Pate town, in the south-easterly part, which had been especially famous for its weaving, had been executed by the same expedition, which had also ordered its stone fort to be broken down. Siyu, which lies up a west-facing creek in the middle part of the island, had its stone walls broken down. Only Faza, at the northern end of the island, had escaped. The Portuguese had then signed treaties of peace with the three towns. But there could be no lasting peace as long as the means of livelihood were denied these towns.

The jurisdiction of the captain of Mombasa extended in theory to Cape Guardafui, but the Portuguese exercised no authority over the Arab towns situated on the shores of Somalia.

Two main dangers threatened the Portuguese on the Mombasa

and Malindi coasts. One was the threat from the Arabs. With the gold trade of Mashonaland and Manicaland no longer available to them, the Arabs of the coast lacked the wealth to maintain their high standard of civilization. They could survive only by trade. But the Portuguese were doing all in their power to make such trade impossible. Dhows had to have passports to put to sea in the north-western Indian Ocean. It was often inconvenient or impossible for Arab masters to obtain such passports which in any case had to be bought, often by graft. Any dhow encountered without such a passport could be seized by any Portuguese vessel, the craft and its contents arbitrarily confiscated, its passengers and crew made captive or enslaved. This greatly reduced the volume of traffic between the Persian Gulf and India, and east Africa. The requirement that all imports had now to go to Mombasa to pay customs duties was not only regarded as an injustice, but it forced up the price of goods, and postponed the arrival of goods at towns north of Mombasa. The competition of the captain's factors, who bought ivory and slaves, copal and coir, amber and ambergris, wax and tortoiseshell, rice and maize, still further reduced Arab trade. The Portuguese no longer conducted a religious crusade against the Arabs; but as a result of their policy of extracting the utmost material profit from the coast the Arabs were reduced to desperate economic straits; it required only acts of particular injustice by individual Portuguese to precipitate rebellion and war.

The other threat came from the African tribes adjoining the Portuguese settlements. These tribes had come to accept the Muslim settlers, for Persian-Arab colonization on the coast had extended over 650 years. Muslim traders had served the tribes by bringing in cloth and beads, in return especially for their ivory and captives. Islam was an acceptable religion to many, particularly because it permitted plurality of wives, and there had been considerable intermingling of populations, with the result that Swahili had become the lingua franca of the coast. But even so, the Arabs had found it essential to site their cities on islands, or surround their mainland towns with powerful walls. The tribesmen with whom the Portuguese came into closest contact at the beginning of the century were the Segeju, a warlike people whose defeat of the Zimbas and of Kilifi and seizure of Mombasa had made it possible for the Sultan of

Malindi and the Portuguese to occupy that island. The Segeju had staged a meteoric rise to power. They had come from the north, probably under pressure from the Galla, and now possessed vast herds of cattle. Their food consisted largely of milk and blood from their cattle. The youths wore their hair done up with clay, five or six pounds in weight, which they polished until they resembled helmets, and which they wore until they reached man's estate. This they established by killing a man in war or fair fight; and as proof of their killings they displayed trophies from their victims—just such trophies as those with which David won Michal. Other tribesmen, called by the Portuguese the Mossungulos, identifiable with the Langulo, were nearing Mombasa at this time. Also warlike people, who fought with bows and poisoned arrows, they were soon to influence the affairs of that fortress. The Portuguese were not yet familiar to the tribesmen, many of whom doubtless regretted the disturbance caused by these new arrivals to the traditional Arab trade. The Portuguese might buy their friendship with cloth; but if this friendship were lost, they might ally themselves actively with the Arabs.

Such then was the position of the Portuguese in south-east Africa at the beginning of the seventeenth century. Probably never exceeding 400 in number (except when passing armadas temporarily swelled their strength) they held sway along a coastline of 2,100 miles, commanding the shores and coastal waters from their bases at Moçambique and Mombasa. Their only penetration into the interior was up the Zambezi and inland from Sofala. Only a few traders enjoyed the healthy uplands of Mashonaland and Manicaland. Otherwise the only Portuguese settlements were on the coast, or at low-lying Sena and Tete. Ill-health sapped the strength of the few settlers. Wars with Bantu tribes, and with Arabs in the north, presented constant threats, and there was the ever-present danger of attack by their enemies from Europe, the Netherlanders and the English. The position in Europe and in India made reinforcement difficult. But the greatest single factor prejudicing the welfare of the settlements was the impossibility for the captains to reconcile the conflicting demands of loyalty to the crown, whose interests centred on the fortresses, and their quest for personal profit which caused them to direct their energies more to the Rivers or to the offlying islands. In attempts to resolve this duality lies the crux of Portugal's problems in this region throughout the seventeenth century. . . .

The sieges of Moçambique were the first battles fought between Europeans on southern African soil; they were the most decisive military actions to be fought in this region in the seventeenth century. Had the Netherlanders gained the fortress, it is doubtful if the Portuguese, now on the defensive over so vast an area of the Atlantic and Indian Oceans and facing a critical shortage of manpower, could ever have assembled sufficient force to retake it: their possessions in the East would have been further prejudiced; and having lost their base they would have been forced to withdraw from the Zambezi. Had the Netherlanders retained Moçambique as a base they might never have been impelled to found a refreshment station at the Cape of Good Hope, and the whole course of south African history would have been profoundly different. As it was, the Portuguese victory ensured the continuance of their power in south-east Africa, and they were left free to continue their efforts to exploit the deposits of gold and silver in the lands of Monomotapa, the successful development of which was an essential pre-requisite to firm colonization. . . .

IX. EARLY PATTERNS OF TRADE

23. The great caravans

E. W. BOVILL *Caravans of the Old Sahara* Oxford University Press for Royal Institute of International Affairs 1933; pages 246–59

. . . In the subversive effects of the European occupation, now fast approaching, no sphere of human activity was more completely revolutionized than trade. That this should have been so was inevitable, for the European had always been rigorously excluded and only by right of conquest was he finally able to open new outlets to the coast and thus divert trade from the ancient caravan routes.

As long as the peoples of the interior remained masters of their own destiny trade continued to follow with little interruption the channels through which it had flowed since before the dawn of history. Moreover, because politics were seldom allowed seriously to disturb its course, the conditions of commercial life had probably changed very little since their stimulation by the Arab invasions. We shall do well therefore to take a brief glance at the trade of the interior as the great explorers found it, and while its general conditions remained much as they had been throughout history.

In the first half of the nineteenth century the greater part of the caravan traffic between Barbary and the Western Sudan was still concentrated on the three great trade routes which must be numbered amongst the oldest highways in the world—the Taghaza–Timbuktu road in the west, the Ghadames–Air road to Hausa in the centre, and in the east the Fezzan–Kawar road to Bornu. On each of these roads there were long waterless stages which heavily laden caravans could only cross at great peril. Nevertheless the test of time had proved them the safest routes for merchants, besides being also the shortest. Each represented about two months' journey for a camel caravan. Lesser roads came into use periodically only to be abandoned through failure of wells or pasturage, or through the hostility of the nomads. On the three ancient highways there was greater certainty of finding water where it was expected, and in the face of this compelling circumstance neither desert politics nor blackmail could force the toiling caravans of merchants permanently to forsake them. They had endured through the ages and were the channels along which culture reached the Sudanese.

The greatest of the three was the Taghaza–Timbuktu road, pre-eminent as a trade route, and still more important as a cultural highway. The destruction of Sijilmasa in the closing years of the previous century had deprived this road of its historic northern terminus. Its place had to some extent been taken by the neighbouring town of Abuam, but much of the trade had left Tafilelt and gone to In Salah, the capital of Tuat. The rest, and perhaps the greater part, of the old trade of Sijilmasa had been diverted westwards to Wady Nun, which was situated near the coast a few miles from Cape Nun.

Merchants trading from Wady Nun and Abuam with the Sudan travelled through Akka, which had inherited from Sijilmasa the business of fitting out and equipping the trans-Saharan caravans, and thence along the old road through Taghaza and Taodeni to Timbuktu. Instead of turning westwards at Taodeni to Walata (which was now in decay, like Wadan, though still noted for the skill of its goldsmiths) the road followed the more direct route through Arawan. Here it was joined by two other roads; one running from Tuat to Timbuktu through Mabruk; another coming from Sansanding on the upper Niger. Centuries of traffic had not lessened the dangers of this road. In 1805 a caravan of 2,000 men and 1,800 camels perished of thirst in the desert when returning from Timbuktu, not a man or beast being saved.

The Taghaza road, which was controlled by the Berabish Arabs, owed its long-continued prosperity to the unequal distribution of gold and salt in the interior. Medieval Europe knew that the gold of the Saharan caravans came from an unknown country in the Sudan which they called Wangara. We now know that this Wangara was the country which extends across the upper Senegal basin from the Faleme to the Niger and includes the provinces of Bambuk, Bure, Manding, and Gangaran, the last being a variant of the name Wangara. Alluvial gold is very widely distributed throughout this region which was the principal, but not the only, source of the gold which for so many centuries flowed freely northwards across the Sahara and not less abundantly, though for a shorter period, through the European trading factories on the western Guinea coast.

Some of this gold probably came also from Lobi on the Black Volta river where there are gold workings of great age. Farther south, moreover, there were the famous Ashanti goldfields. Since the fifteenth century the principal outlet for Ashanti gold has been the sea-coast, but before that much must have found its way into the Sudan, especially to Gao, by the roads which since very early times have been used by the kola nut traders.

But of all the districts which contributed to the Saharan gold trade Bambuk was the richest. Early in the history of the exploration of the coast reports of the wealth of this district had reached European ears. We have already seen that in the sixteenth century it had been visited by a band of Portuguese adventurers who had perished without turning their discovery to account. It was not till the first half of the eighteenth century that it was rediscovered by the French, then actively trading on the Senegal, but their repeated attempts to exploit the goldfields all ended in failure.

Neither Park nor Caillié nor the pioneers who had preceded them realized that these goldfields were the Wangara of history. So the discovery of the African El Dorado continued to exercise men's minds, exciting nearly as many conflicting theories as the problem of the termination of the Niger. In 1824 Dupuis, influenced and consequently misled by Leo, announced his opinion that the ancient Wangara extended along the coast from Ashanti in the west, across Dahomey, to the Cross river in the east. 'Wonderful as it may seem,' he declared, 'that we should have actually colonized the country for many ages past, without ever having known it even by name.' A year or two later Denham came to the conclusion in the course of his travels that there was no such place as Wangara. 'All gold countries,' he wrote, 'as well as any people coming from the gold country, or bringing Goroo nuts, are called Wangara.' This was half true, for Wangara is the name by which Mandingo traders, whose enterprise carries them very far afield, are widely known in the Sudan, especially to the Hausas. Even Barth failed to realize that Wangara was Bambuk. In one map he sought vainly to identify it with Lobi and Ashanti; in another he placed it with fair accuracy on the Senegal.

The comparative silence which followed the discovery of the Bambuk goldfields was in striking contrast with the keen interest which they had excited in Europe for so many centuries. This was not so much due to the failure of Europeans to recognize them as the famous Wangara, nor was it due to lack of gold, but rather to failure to exploit them profitably owing to their remoteness from the coast, the difficulties of transport, and the necessity of having to restrict work, as Idrisi had described, to four months in the year.

It is unlikely that so many centuries of trade had not reduced the richness of the Wangara mines. Nevertheless gold was, and still is, constantly being washed down from the highlands by the Faleme and its tributaries so that gravels which have been worked to exhaustion are found after three or four years' rest to have become rich again. This gave rise to the native belief that gold travelled mysteriously of its own accord; it may also be the origin of the legend, mentioned by Yaqut, that gold grew like carrots. After the seventeenth century we hear less about gold passing through Djenné and Timbuktu to Morocco; but the trade continued, though on an ever-dwindling scale, for the next two hundred years.

El Bekri's statement that the Ferawi used to exchange gold for an equal amount of salt was probably not a gross exaggeration. We find a similar statement about Mali on certain Jewish maps of the early sixteenth century, which may or may not have been a repetition of El Bekri. But less than a century ago a European traveller in these parts found himself so short of salt that he was fully prepared to make such a bargain. It is impossible for those who have not witnessed it to realize how intense is the craving for salt amongst those to whom an adequate supply is denied. In the Western Sudan it was universally a luxury which only the rich could regularly enjoy.

With the exception of the salt pans of the Dallul Fogha in Dendi, which were only capable of supplying the requirements of a very small area, scarcely any natural salt occurs in the Western Sudan. Where the natives were unable to import it they obtained it from the ashes of grasses, millet stalks, and shrubs, and also from cattle dung. But these inadequate sources of supply were never equal to the needs of the people.

Up to the end of the sixteenth century the countries of the middle Niger were almost wholly dependent on the salt pans of Taghaza for their supplies. It will be recollected that in 1585 the Songhai, driven out of Taghaza by the Moors, began to work the now famous deposits at Taodeni, which thereafter became the principal source of salt for the middle Niger. It was carried at least as far upstream as Bamako, which Park found being supplied from Taodeni and with sea salt from the Rio Grande. Salt was also obtained from Sebka d'Ijil in the north-west, which was known as Taghaza el Gharbie or West Taghaza.

Although Taghaza and Taodeni had inexhaustible stores of salt their customers often found them very unreliable sources on which to depend for this essential to the well-being of man. Being situated in the heart of the desert and defenceless against marauders, the salt pans were often the prey of raiders so that in times of turbulence there was grave risk of no salt reaching the Sudan. Moreover the labourers who dug the salt were wholly dependent for their subsistence on passing caravans whose comings and goings were necessarily very irregular. Their miserable lot at Taghaza was graphically described by Leo. 'Neither haue the said diggers of salt any victuals,' he wrote, 'but such as the merchants bring vnto them . . . insomuch that oftentimes they perish for lacke of foode, whenas the merchants come not in due time vnto them.' The passage of time does not seem to have brought much improvement. As recently as the year 1910 no less than fifty-six people died of starvation at Taodeni owing to the failure of a caravan to arrive in time to save them.

Timbuktu owed as much to gold and salt as did the great highway of which it was the southern terminus. Neither growing nor manufacturing anything, it depended on imports for its food and on foreign trade for its prosperity. It was essentially an entrepôt. The important position it had for so long held in the commercial life of the interior was chiefly due to its situation at the point where the Niger is most accessible from the Maghreb and its outpost, the oasis of Tuat.

Timbuktu was served by three important routes. Firstly the

waterway of the Niger from Sansanding and Djenné, the two markets on which the city depended for its supplies of rice and millet, and whence came gold and slaves and ivory and kola nuts; secondly the ancient Taghaza road; and lastly the Tuat road which led through Ghat to Ghadames, the merchants of which occupied a predominant position in the trade of the interior. In Barth's time Timbuktu was importing kola nuts from Tangrela, far away in the *hinterland* of the Ivory Coast, Manchester cottons and English cutlery from Mogador, and it was in touch with the trading factories on the Senegal and Gambia rivers through Sansanding and Bamako. Such was the imposing scale on which this desert city conducted its foreign trade.

The Ghadames–Air road is probably not less ancient than the Taghaza road. Where it passes over rocky ground the deeply worn tracks clearly indicate its immense age and the great amount of traffic it carried. The route it followed seems never to have varied. Between Ghadames and Ghat it was, in the first half of last century, controlled by the fierce Azger Tuareg. Between Ghat and Air, where it passes over one of the worst bits of desert in the world, it was controlled by the Kel Owi. Half-way it was joined at In Azawa, or Asiu, by the Tuat road to Air which passed through the Ahaggar massif and was controlled by the Ahaggar Tuareg. The main road entered Air at Iferuan. This was an important junction, for here the road was joined by the old pilgrim way from Timbuktu which entered Air at In Gall, passing thence through In Azawa, Ghat, Murzuk, Augila, and Siwa to Cairo. Agades, which dates only from the fifteenth century, lies off the main road, a few miles to the west. Owing to the country surrounding the city being unsuitable for heavily laden camels the road has never been diverted to pass through the capital. This road used to end at Katsina. But when, as the result of the Fulani *jihad*, Kano rose to occupy the predominant commercial position, the latter became the southern terminus of the road which was diverted eastwards through Zinder. Between Kano and Air it was controlled by the Kel Geres.

In the days when Gao was the capital of a rich empire, Agades occupied an important position, for it was the chief entrepôt for the gold trade between Gao and Tripoli. The capture of Gao by the Moors killed this trade and Agades consequently fell into decay. Politically it continued to occupy an important position and its situation close to the great trans-Saharan caravan road between Ghadames and Hausa always ensured it a certain amount of foreign trade.

What little prosperity remained to Agades in the nineteenth century was derived principally from the salt trade. The grazing grounds of Air were constantly thronged with camels and it was this abundant supply of transport which enabled the people of Agades to control the salt trade with Hausa. A remarkable feature of this trade was the gigantic caravan, known as the *Taghalam* or *Azalai*, which set out from Air every autumn to bring salt from Bilma, the chief town of the Kawar oasis. Probably nowhere else in the world could be found a commercial enterprise comparable with the spectacular scale on which the *Azalai* was conducted. As recently as 1908, when it was in its decline, it numbered no less than 20,000 camels.

Elaborate preparations preceded the departure of the *Azalai*. The assemblage of so many camels took a long time. They congregated at Tabello in central Air where there was sufficient grazing to condition the animals for the arduous journey before them. Although the round journey to Kawar and back took only three weeks, the endurance which it demanded was so great that the losses of camels were very heavy and vast numbers of skeletons marked the route of the *Azalai*. This immense caravan, moreover, was such a vulnerable body that it was frequently raided by those Tuareg who were not participating, and it sometimes suffered heavy losses at their hands. Most of the camels of the Azalai belonged to the Kel Geres and the Itesan.[1]

One of the principal duties of the Amenokal's vizier, the Sarkin Turawa of Agades, was to conduct the *Azalai* in person. It set out in October and carried, besides corn and cloth to barter for salt, immense quantities of forage, for there was no grazing in Kawar where the few local camels were fed on dates. Fachi, an outpost of Kawar, was reached in five days, and there the *Azalai* was joined by a caravan from Damagaram. It entered Bilma three days later. By a curious and unexplained phenomenon the 'singing' of a neighbouring peak used to give the people of Bilma two days' warning of the approach of the *Azalai*

[1] All the older and more remarkable buildings in Air are attributed to the Itesan.

or of any other exceptionally large caravan coming from the west.

The return to Air was made by the same route, the camels carrying a few dates besides immense quantities of salt. After a rest in Agades a large part of the *Azalai*, with the Sarkin Turawa still at its head, travelled south to Sokoto and thence to Kano where salt was sold for distribution all over Hausa and beyond. The camels returned from Kano to Air loaded with cloth and corn.

Kano was at this time by far the most important commercial city in the interior, not excepting Timbuktu. The population, predominantly Hausa, but with a large foreign element which included a rich colony of Tripolitan Arabs, was estimated by Barth at 30,000, but with the coming of the dry season and the opening of the trade routes this number was doubled by the influx of traders. Kano enjoyed the advantage of being the centre of a rich agricultural district which produced all the requirements of a teeming native population and a considerable surplus of corn for export. But the real foundation of its extraordinary commercial prosperity was the industry and skill of the Hausa craftsmen whose wares were in demand all over northern and western Africa. The most important trade was that in cotton cloth, woven and dyed in Kano, Katsina, Zaria, and neighbouring towns.

> The great advantage of Kano [wrote Barth] is that commerce and manufactures go hand in hand, and that almost every family has its share in them. There is really something grand in this kind of industry, which spreads to the north as far as Murzuk, Ghat, and even Tripoli; to the west, not only to Timbuktu, but in some degree even as far as the shores of the Atlantic, the very inhabitants of Arguin dressing in the cloth woven and dyed in Kano; to the east, all over Bornu, although there it comes into contact with the native industry of the country; and to the south it . . . is only limited by the nakedness of the pagan *sans-culottes*, who do not wear clothing.

The slave trade was a considerable item in the commerce of Kano, about 5,000 slaves being imported annually to Ghat, Fezzan, Bornu, and southwards to Nupe, whence some probably found their way to the Christian slave ships on the coast.

Most of the imports into Kano came down the Air road and the rest through Kawar and Bornu. They consisted principally of a coarse kind of silk from Tripoli and a wide range of European trade goods. The latter included cottons from Manchester, French silks, glass beads from Venice and Trieste, paper, mirrors, and needles from Nuremberg, sword blades from Solingen,[1] razors from Styria, besides quantities of spices, sugar, and tea. Kano was also the chief entrepôt in this part of the Sudan for the important trades in salt from Bilma, already described, kola nuts from Gwanja in the *hinterland* of the Gold Coast, and natron from Lake Chad.

The valuable trade in kola nuts, most of which came from Gwanja, was largely controlled by the people of Kano. This nut, known to the natives and the early Arab explorers as *goro*, had been in use in the Western Sudan since very early times.[2] The twin interlocking kernels were regarded as symbolic of friendship and no present was complete unless it included kolas. Consequently they acquired a kind of ceremonial importance and it became customary to swear oaths on a kola nut. The curiously bitter flavour not only appeals strongly to the palate of the native, but it has the property of making the foulest water taste sweet after chewing the nut. Kolas are undoubtedly very sustaining and they are widely regarded among the natives as a cure for impotency. They are transported immense distances, but they need great care for they perish easily if neglected and this always kept their price high. Nevertheless so greatly were they appreciated that from at first being only a luxury of the rich, they became virtually a necessity to a very large part of the population.

The kola nut was one of at least three articles which used to travel the whole distance from the coastal belt of Guinea to the shores of the Mediterranean, where the nuts were sold at a dollar apiece. Glass beads from Venice and unwrought silk from Tripoli found their way to Gwanja, where they were exchanged for kolas, and to Badagry on the Slave coast. The latter was the most important trading port on the west coast of Africa and had become the chief centre of the European slave trade. It was divided into British, Spanish, Portuguese, and French quarters

[1] Many of the sword blades still used in the Western Sudan bear such well-known Solingen marks as the 'wolf' and the 'orb and cross'.

[2] Leo seems to have thought that kola nuts were the fruit of the baobab tree.

and there was a large Hausa colony trading between Kano and the coast.

Between Kano and Badagry there was no single well-defined trade route. These two places were separated by a belt of dense bush and rain forest, peopled by Yorubas and many lesser pagan tribes, mutually hostile and constantly in a state of political instability. The tracks running through this belt were consequently liable to be closed to traders at frequent intervals. Instead of flowing freely along a well-known road trade tended to percolate along a variety of ill-defined tracks. It was this belt of pagan forest which for so many centuries proved an impenetrable barrier to Europeans trading on the coast.

In these disturbed regions, as in the Sahara, it was necessary for traders to travel together in large bodies for mutual protection. The caravans thus formed were sometimes several thousand strong with immense numbers of pack animals. The crossing of the Niger was a serious undertaking for such huge companies of traders and could only be accomplished where the necessary facilities existed. The riverain tribes had established ferries at suitable points and made large profits by levying tolls on the heavy traffic they attracted. The two principal ferries used by Hausa traders were at Rabba, near the modern Jebba, and at Komie (Wonjerque), just below Busa. There was a less important ferry upstream at Illo.

From the ferry at Komie one road ran north-east through Birnin Gwari and Zaria to Kano. Another well-known route followed the left bank of the Niger through Yauri into the north-western districts of Hausa, where it converged on an important kola route running in a north-easterly direction from Gwanja. The latter was an alternative route from the kola district to Kano, the crossing of the Niger being effected probably at Illo. These two, with a third coming from Wagadugu and Fadan Gurma, were the chief trade routes leading into Hausa from the west; they converged and met in the valley of the Gulbin Gindi, probably at or near Jega.

Barth tells us that Jega was 'the important place which . . . on account of its mercantile importance, had attracted attention in Europe a good many years ago'. Diligent search has failed to reveal how and when Jega came to attract attention in Europe at a period when so little was known of this part of Africa. It undoubtedly was an important place, but neither Clapperton nor Lander mentions it.

Jega occupied in Hausa and the surrounding country a commercial position second only to that of Kano. Like Bamako, Wagadugu, Fadan Gurma, Gaya, and Kano it was situated in very close proximity to the twelfth parallel of north latitude. It cannot be by mere coincidence that we find these six important markets and several lesser ones strung out along the same parallel. This line runs through the zone of parklands which separates the savannas from the forests. It roughly divides the *hyphaene* and date palms of the north from the oil palms of the south, and the humped from the humpless cattle. It approximately marks the southern limit of camel transport and the northern limit of the tsetse-fly. To the north of this line the population is predominantly Muhammadan, to the south mostly pagan.

Generally speaking this intermediate zone of parklands was peopled by tribes of mixed origins who made an outward display of Muslim culture, but at heart had strong pagan sympathies. The breadth and elasticity of their religious views generated in their towns an atmosphere favourable to trade between the slave-raiding Muhammadan and the hunted pagan. The necessity for trade, which transcended all considerations of race and creed and politics, had to be satisfied and it seems that the twelfth parallel offered exceptionally favourable advantages for the growth of the necessary entrepôts. Here kolas, gold-dust, and slaves were exchanged for salt and natron and European trade goods from the far-distant north.

The position of Kano was not comparable with that of the other important markets on the twelfth parallel. Owing to the elevation of the plain of which it is the centre, Kano belongs geographically to the savannas rather than to the parklands. Although the greatest entrepôt of the interior it was primarily a centre of production and its prosperity was based on the skill and industry of its people and on the fertility of its soil rather than on the accident of geographical situation to which Jega owed its importance.

All the conditions which made it desirable as an entrepôt were to be found in Jega. Being free from tsetse it could be safely visited by the animal transport of the savannas. Situated at the head of perennial navigation on the Gulbin Gindi it could at all times be reached from the Niger by water and on this account was exceptionally accessible from the forests. Its inhabitants, the Gimbanawa, were an unprogressive people who professed Islamism but had marked pagan sympathies. The exceptional prosperity which they enjoyed cannot be said to have been due to any special effort on their part, for the whole of the trade of Jega was in the hands of foreign brokers.

Jega enjoyed the further advantage of being close to the salt mines of the Dallul Fogha. Its situation also enabled it to tap the trade of Gwanja and Badagry and to profit by the political importance of the twin Fulani capitals. Sokoto and Gwandu were too frequently disturbed by the clash of arms and the marshalling of troops to generate the tranquil atmosphere so necessary to trade. The religious fervour of the Fulani, moreover, was definitely discouraging to the cosmopolitan hordes of small traders who throng the great markets of the Sudan. With fanaticism within and turbulence without there was little enough to attract trade to Sokoto and Gwandu. But as they gradually became the centres of a wealthy population there was a need for a large and easily accessible market where the foreign trade of the country could be handled. This need was largely satisfied by Jega.

The ancient Fezzan–Kawar road was the last of the three great desert highways leading to the Western Sudan. This was the old Roman road from the Garamantes to the Aethiopians and its route can have altered little since Septimus Flaccus and Julius Maternus first led their troops down it into the interior.

The caravan traffic on this road had always been subject to periodical interruption owing to the turbulence of desert politics. The road was nominally controlled by the negroid Tebu of Tibesti whose hereditary and bitterly hated enemies were the Tuareg of Air. Raids and counter raids were constantly taking place across the road and when the Tuareg failed to capture Tebu herds they not infrequently consoled themselves with robbing passing caravans.

Although the salt of Bilma played a part in its life the Fezzan–Kawar road was essentially a slave route. Every European who travelled this bloodstained highway was profoundly impressed by the thousands of human skeletons, mostly those of women and girls, with which it was strewn.

Until the intervention of Christian powers in the middle of last century there had always been a large demand for negro slaves in the countries of the North African littoral. They were partly required for local markets, but large numbers were exported to Egypt and Turkey. In the North African markets the highest prices were always paid for Hausa slaves on account of their good looks and their superior industry and intelligence. The Taghaza and the Ghadames–Air roads were both used by slave traders, but the part they played in the trade was small compared with the Fezzan–Kawar road; so much was this so, that in Denham's time foreign merchants trading with Bornu refused to accept payment for their trade goods in anything but slaves, which consequently became the chief currency of the country.

The slave merchants took care in their own interests that their slaves were in good condition before they set out across the Sahara. The men, mostly youths, were coupled with leg-irons and were chained by the neck, but the women and girls were usually allowed to be free. Only the most robust survived the desert march and these were little better than living skeletons when they reached Fezzan. Here they were rested and fattened for the Tripoli market where prime slaves were sold at a profit of 500 per cent. Appalled though we may be by the horrors of the trans-Saharan slave traffic they were not equal, in the opinion of those qualified to draw the comparison, to those of the trade which Europeans carried on between the coast of Guinea and the West Indies.

The traffic in eunuchs was a particularly hideous branch of the slave trade of the interior. In the Sudan there was always a good demand for eunuchs as harem attendants. Consequently it was customary for the healthiest boys and youths captured in a slave raid to be gelded, and in Mossi it was the punishment meted out to incorrigible thieves. Owing to the hopeless lack of surgical skill not more than 10 per cent survived.[1] The most noted sources of supply were Mossi and Bornu both of which enjoyed an international reputation in the trade. The Mossi

[1] Barth tells us that less than one in ten survived. A native of Kano once related to the author how he remembered a hundred Ningi pagans being gelded and ten surviving, which was considered as many as could be expected.

people were supposed to be especially skilled in the operation and kept their methods a carefully guarded secret. They and the Bornuese, besides supplying a considerable local demand, did a large export trade with Turkey and Egypt which, with the Barbary States, were the principal foreign markets. Perhaps it was a deal in eunuchs which brought an embassy from the Sultan of Turkey to Bornu in the sixteenth century. Leo once took part in this trade and tells us how he bought eunuchs from some wild tribes on the coast of Tripoli.

Repulsive though this trade seems we should remember before condemning the Sudanese for their barbarity that not only was it common throughout the Muhammadan world, but that it was long practised in Europe. During the Middle Ages large establishments, mostly under the direction of Jews, were maintained in France, notably at Verdun, for the supply of eunuchs to Muslim Spain. A still more deplorable example were the *Soprani* of the Sistine Chapel, 'the musical glory and the moral shame' of the papal choir. Although the *Soprani* were not finally abolished till late in the nineteenth century by Pope Leo XIII, the gelding of boys continued to be practised in Italy till even more recent times.

As the result of the enormous demand for slaves for export and for domestic use locally, the raiding of the hill and forest pagans became one of the principal dry-weather occupations of the Muhammadan tribes throughout the length and breadth of the Western Sudan. The young men and women would all be carried off to slave markets, but usually the grown men, who always commanded a poor price, and often also the aged and infirm, who were unsaleable, were massacred in cold blood. All this ruthless savagery was perpetrated in the name of religion. As Lord Lugard has truly said, 'It is the most serious charge against Islam in Africa that it has encouraged and given religious sanction to slavery'.

The abolition of the slave trade was one of the changes wrought by the coming European occupation which caused the decay of the trans-Saharan caravan routes. It was not that these roads relied so much on the traffic which the trade provided, but the oases depended on slave labour to hold back the encroaching desert which was always threatening to engulf them. It was the negro Haratin and Bella, not the nomads, who carried on the cultivation by which the oases were preserved. Consequently with the increasing difficulty of securing fresh negro labour the Sahara crept in and the oases began to disappear.

A more potent factor in the destruction of the caravan routes was the competition of sea-borne trade. Once the interior had been thrown open from the coast of Guinea the gold, ivory, and ostrich feathers which had been the principal exports across the desert were conveyed to the northern markets by the more circuitous but safer and cheaper sea route. At the same time European salt began to flood the Sudanese markets, and this further sapped the trade of the ancient desert highways.

This reversal of the course of trade profoundly affected the political situation in the Sahara. The modest attempts at agriculture in the oases had always been an important economic factor in the life of the Tuareg and one which they could ill afford to lose. As transport agents and as convoyers, blackmailers, and raiders of caravans they were also very dependent on the carrying trade of the Sahara for a part of their livelihood. When these resources began gradually to melt away the narrow margin which in the desert divides starvation from plenty quickly vanished.

When the local means of subsistence became inadequate desperate need compelled the people of the desert to prey on each other and on the sedentary tillers of the oases and of the peripheral areas. A period of chronic disturbance supervened and the roads became so insecure that what little remained of the carrying trade of the Sahara was completely destroyed. Oases dwindled, wells fell in, and water-holes silted up. Through human neglect the sterility of the Sahara became more profound than ever before, and the ties which for countless ages had bound Barbary to the Western Sudan were for ever broken.

24. Trade and politics

K. ONWUKA DIKE *Trade and Politics in the Niger Delta* Clarendon Press, Oxford 1956; pages 1–9

The history of modern West Africa is largely the history of five centuries of trade with European nations; commerce was the fundamental relationship that bound Africa to Europe.[1] This long period of trade divides conveniently into two sections. The first opened with the Portuguese advent and ended with the prohibition of the slave trade in 1807. The second section covers the years 1807–85. A review of the former will soon show its essential characteristics and the more permanent elements in its organization. It is important to emphasize the pattern of trade during these four hundred years in order to appreciate the depth and intensity of the revolution which occurred in it during the nineteenth century.

This trade fluctuated in accordance with European policies and demands. In the fifteenth and sixteenth centuries gold constituted the main quest.[2] During the seventeenth and eighteenth centuries the slave trade predominated. It must be admitted, however, that the total value of Portuguese trade with West Africa does not compare well with that of Asiatic commerce. A report included in the Cottonian MSS. of the British Museum shows that towards the end of the sixteenth century, whereas the eastern trade yielded an annual revenue of two million cruzados, the value to the Portuguese Crown of the entire trade of Guinea was only 280,000 cruzados. But the golden age of the Guinea traffic so far as Portugal was concerned ended about 1530. The report quoted above dealt with the trade of Portugal when her monopoly was on the wane. The discovery of the Cape route to India, therefore, did not mean the extinction of the African trade. The richer and vaster Asiatic commerce naturally demanded greater attention, but the West African trade did not die.

From 1510 Africans ceased to be mere curiosities in Portugal.

[1] Compare with the statement by J. Simmons in *Parish and Empire* (London, 1952). 'The British Empire was founded first of all upon trade.... It was trade, first and foremost, that took Englishmen to the West Indies, to Africa, to India and Malaya and the Far East. This is a fact, not open to dispute, and it is in my view very foolish of English men to feel in any way ashamed of it.'

[2] From all accounts this early trade paid handsomely. Azurara records that the highest returns were registered between 1450 and 1458. Pachecco estimates that 170,000 dobras of pure gold were carried annually to Portugal from Guinea after 1481. 'There are indications, in the correspondence of King John II of Portugal, that the Crown came to depend upon a regular supply of gold from Mina.'

At Lisbon in that year the first considerable number of African slaves for the West Indies were bought and exported. By 1539 the Portuguese were estimated to have been exporting between 10,000 and 12,000 annually. As is well known, this enforced movement of West Africans to the New World was accelerated by the European colonization of the Americas and Indies. In 1609 the English occupied Bermuda and by 1623 Barbados, the Leeward Islands, Nevis, Antigua, and Montserrat were considered English possessions. The French and English also settled at St Christopher in that year. In 1635 the French colonized Guadeloupe and Martinique, and Marie Galante in 1648. St Lucia and Grenada were occupied in the 1650s. The Dutch, in their turn, settled at Curaçao, St Eustatius, and Tobago around the 1630s. The Danes, who were late arrivals, acquired the small island of St Thomas in 1671. As the European colonization of the West Indies gained momentum so the exploitation of the Caribbean region increased the demand for African labour. In none of these islands did the slave trade assume importance until the introduction and development of the plantation method of sugar cultivation in the years 1640–50. This not only created a demand for labour greater than the system of indenture could supply, but also gave the planter a commodity—sugar—profits from the sale of which paid for the coveted Negroes. Meanwhile the position in Africa itself was changing. Portuguese monopoly of West African commerce collapsed when challenged in the sixteenth and seventeenth centuries because her military and naval defences were very weak. They could not withstand the naval might of England, Holland, and France. Henceforth West Africa from Cape Verde to the Bight of Biafra became the scene of European enterprise and rivalry. In the scramble for African slaves even small nations such as Denmark, Sweden, and Brandenburg fought for a share of the spoils.

During these two centuries none of the old staples of trade—gold, ivory, malaguetta, and Benin pepper—proved as permanent or profitable as the traffic in Africans themselves. This traffic in men was the principal item of African commerce and became important to the economies of the chief European nations engaged in it. It has been estimated that between 1450 and 1850 ten million West Africans—five to six million seems nearer the mark—crossed the Atlantic Ocean. This export of populations was at its height in the eighteenth century and averaged something between 70,000 and 80,000 a year. The part played by African colonists in the building of the New World is now being acknowledged. In the eighteenth century economists reckoned that the wealth of the Indies was one of the main supports of the contemporary British empire. This wealth was largely the product of African labour. It is now known that the triangular trade—that is the trade between Britain, West Africa and the West Indies—provided one of the many streams from whence emerged the capital that financed the industrial revolution. No aspect of West African history has received fuller treatment, and justifiably so, than the iniquitous trans-atlantic slave trade. Sir Reginald Coupland stated, with scarcely any exaggeration, that the treatment of Africa by Christian Europe in the period of the slave trade constituted 'the greatest crime in history'. . . .

In West African history the concentration of students on external factors[1] such as the suppression of the slave trade, the work of the Navy, the era of the explorers, the forts and settlements along the coast, the policies and personalities of the various Foreign and Colonial Secretaries, has tended to submerge the history of the indigenous peoples and to bestow undue prominence on the activities of the invaders. As yet no comprehensive assessment of the African middlemen's position in the Atlantic slave trade exists; few if any studies have displayed the real magnitude of the revolution brought about by the prohibition of the traffic from 1807 or the full effects of abolition on the existing native governments. As an instance, a major thread in West African history—the character of the association of the coastal kingdoms with the European traders—is treated, if at all, as merely incidental to the subject; yet without

[1] Blake, in *Transactions of the Royal Historical Society*, 4th series, xxxii, points out that Dr S. E. Crowe, in her *Berlin West African Conference, 1884–1885* (London, 1942), makes very little reference to the effects of Partition on the African peoples. He also calls attention to Sir Alan Burn's *History of Nigeria* (London, 1942), in which the author devotes 5 out of 25 chapters to population and physical features, 17 to the history of the country since 1851, and only 3 to the period 1481–1850. 'His sixth chapter on "the period of unrestricted slave trade, 1481–1807" exemplifies the submergence of the main pattern of African history by the concentration on the transatlantic slave trade.' The Gold Coast has been lucky in its historians.

knowledge of this association the position of power occupied by the African middlemen in the period of the slave trade cannot be appreciated.

British prohibition of this trade, a movement which in West Africa precipitated a radical change in the economic sphere—the trade was the economic mainstay of all the coastal principalities—soon wrought corresponding changes in the social and political planes. It is, of course, a truism that up to a point a profound change in the economy of any given community tends to bring about an unsettlement of and a readjustment in the social organization. Such a change did occur in nineteenth-century West Africa; in comparison with the three centuries that preceded them, the fifty years between 1830 and 1885 were an epoch of change and revolution; it was essentially a period of transition from a predominantly slave-trading economy to one based on trade in the raw materials of the West African forest. A cursory glance at the pattern of the early trade (1481–1807) is necessary not only for an understanding of its essential characteristics but even more for an appreciation of the depth and intensity of the revolution which swept away the old order in the nineteenth century. . . .

Portuguese rule, or whatever there was of it, was strictly limited to their fortified trading posts on the coasts or on the adjacent islands. Their four bases were Argium (an island situated in the bay formed by the arm of Cabo Blanco and the African mainland); Santiago Island (the largest island in the Cape Verde archipelago); São Jorge da Mina ('Mina' was a term vaguely used for the Gold Coast); and São Thomé Island, the base for the trade in the bights of Benin and Biafra. All these were founded before or about 1500.

They were never designed for launching expeditions into the vast interior, an impossible undertaking considering the multitude of Africans and the handful of Portuguese, the extensive coastline, and the limited and inadequate material equipment at the disposal of the merchant-adventurers. Whatever the original intentions of the Portuguese might have been, West African peoples and conditions confined their activities to trade and diplomacy and allowed them little scope for conquest and empire.

The forts and settlements occupied commercially strategic

areas. The Arguim base, for instance, was placed in a suitable position to divert towards the western coast the desert trade which for centuries had passed northwards by caravan across the Sahara to the ports of North Africa. São Jorge da Mina, their most important base in Guinea, defended the gold trade of Mina and its neighbourhood. That the Europeans came to think almost exclusively in terms of trade is evidenced by the fact that sections of the coast came to be known by the commodities they produced. Hence the Gum Coast, the Malaguetta or Grain Coast, the Tooth or Ivory Coast, the Gold Coast, and the Slave Coast.

One factor militating against their penetration of the interior was the African attitude to land. In strict West African customary law, tribal land was corporatively owned. The chiefs—protectors of the tribal heritage—could not sign away lands of which in reality they were merely trustees. This being the case the alienation of land to foreigners was out of the question and tribal leaders were in duty bound to oppose any encroachment on their preserves. That this practice was recognized even in the early stages of Portuguese trade is borne out by the fact that the ground on which their most important base in West Africa was built—the Castle of São Jorge da Mina—was 'leased' from the Fetu and Comani peoples. The African chief, Caramansa, who negotiated this 'concession', suspicious of Portuguese motives for desiring to build a fort, left the white invaders in no doubt of the outcome of duplicity on their side.

To maintain the safety of their settlement the Portuguese courted the favour of the Fetu and Comani people; customary 'presents' were made to the rulers of the tribe and even interior potentates received their share of the 'gifts' in order to encourage the flow of trade between the hinterland and the coast. To hold their own against the vast superiority of the natives the Portuguese, when it suited them, exploited inter-tribal jealousies, and only in extreme cases did they resort to armed intervention. Other methods such as conversion to Christianity, intermarriage, and treaties of friendship were used to maintain good relations. . . .

It became a recognized fact that the sovereignty of the African states was unimpaired by the presence of Europeans. On the whole the political power of the African states reigned supreme over aliens and natives, for the strong and despotic governments provided by the coastal principalities suited the semi-military society of the time. Under these governments the slave trade throve amazingly. Moreover, through their administration of the forts the European governments had come to learn of the dissipation of energy and capital consequent on territorial responsibility and regularly warned their subjects to keep to trade and avoid entanglement in African politics. It followed, therefore, that so long as the existing indigenous governments served their trade interests well, white men were prepared to work through them and to endure whatever hazards and inconveniences this entailed. In recognition of this fact European governments deprecated activities other than trading, such, for instance, as developing gardens and plantations, on the grounds that the land occupied by the European was only leased from the natives. In 1752 the Board of Trade forbade the Committee of the Company of Merchants to introduce cultivation in the Gold Coast on the plea that 'in Africa we were only tenants of the soil which we hold at the goodwill of the natives'. Writing from Gambia in 1678 the local chief agent of the Royal African Company recommended that all trading should be conducted from sloops, 'for a factor once settled ashore is absolutely under the command of the king of the country where he lives, and is liable for the least displeasure to lose all the goods he has in his possession, with danger also to his life'. When in 1799 the Governor of Sekondi, going one evening to visit a neighbouring Dutch governor, was seized, stripped, and beaten by the natives, the Council of Cape Coast Castle merely commented that he had no business to be paying a call so late!

On the slave coasts this abstentionist policy was most pronounced. Here European forts such as those on the Gold Coast were not tolerated. At Whydah, a 'free port for all Europeans', the king disallowed the erection of anything stronger than a mud fort at the safe distance of three miles from the shore. In the Niger Delta the merchant-adventurers made their sailing ships their home and, with the exception of the baracoons (warehouses erected on the shore for slaves and barter goods), they had no foothold on African territory. These characteristics were commonplaces at the time and were emphasized by the most reliable of contemporary writers. 'There is no small number of men in Europe', wrote William Bosman of the Gold Coast in 1721, 'who believe that the Gold Mines are in our power; that we, like the Spaniards in the West Indies, have no more to do but to work them by our Slaves: though you perfectly know that we have no means of access to these Treasures.' . . .

25. Streams of trade in Guinea states

ROLAND OLIVER and J. D. FAGE *A Short History of Africa* Penguin Books 1962; pages 107–11

. . . The two main southward-flowing streams of influence from the Sudan corresponded in historic times with two major systems of long-distance trade linking the Sudan to Guinea. The dominant traders in the east were the merchants of the Hausa states, whose activities were supplemented towards the south-west by the Yoruba. In the western half of West Africa, Mande merchants were dominant. The two trading systems met at the edge of the forest, north of the Gold Coast, and some idea of their antiquity may be gained from the traditions relating to the trade with this region. It would seem that Mande merchants were already visiting Bono, primarily for gold, about the middle of the fourteenth century, that is to say, about a century later than the foundation of Djenne, the metropolis for the trade of the western Sudan with the lands to the south. The trade from the north-east seems to have developed slightly later, with Hausa merchants beginning to go to Gonja, just east of Bono, in the fifteenth century.

Before the appearance of Europeans on the scene, there was thus a network of trade routes linking towns and villages throughout almost the whole of West Africa between the Sahara and the coast. Regular markets were held, often arranged in daily cycles so that neighbouring markets would not compete with one another. Although much trade was doubtless purely local in character, for example the exchange of foodstuffs for local manufactures within a particular area, the operations of the Mande, Hausa, and Yoruba merchants were truly international.

TAET

It is evident that this long-distance trade was closely connected with the existence of organized states. The regions untouched by the itinerant traders were for the most part difficult country such as marshland and mountain, in which simple kinship groupings had escaped the attention of the state-builders. By far the largest of these regions seems to have been the particularly difficult and thinly populated forest of what is now Liberia. However, the correlation between long-distance trade and statehood was positive as well as negative. The staples of the trade were for the most part luxuries rather than necessities. In the first place, most West African communities could grow or manufacture enough to supply their own basic needs. Secondly, the cost of transport was high. This was particularly so in the forest, where head-loading was the rule because animal transport was inhibited by the lack of fodder and the presence of tse-tse. It was therefore economic to carry over long distances only commodities whose value was high in proportion to their bulk. A demand for luxuries, of course, implies the existence of a wealthy class. This first existed in West Africa in the shape of kings and their courts, and the specialized professions—administrators, soldiers, artists, metal-workers, court musicians, remembrancers, and the like—which they were able to support from their control of the surplus wealth produced by their subjects. This surplus flowed into each court essentially in the form of tribute, and it was doubtless accumulations of tribute in such widely desired commodities as gold or kola-nuts which made the initiation of international trade possible when outside demands arose.

Generally speaking, as we have seen, states developed in the Sudan before they did in Guinea, and this explains the dominating position in the Guinea trade of merchants from the Sudan. The Mande and Hausa merchants doubtless first moved southwards in response to demands coming from the north, across the Sahara, which their own states were able to satisfy only inadequately or not at all. But trade breeds wealth, and so more trade, and Sudanese merchants were soon trading to Guinea to satisfy the demands of their own growing wealthy class, of which, indeed, they themselves were becoming significant members. Nor was this all. The Guinea states also began to trade for their own enrichment, though—with the possible exception of the

Yoruba—their trading remained for the most part a royal enterprise. Their merchants were at least as much agents of the kings as members of an independent class doing business on its own account.

The principal exception to the long-distance trade in luxuries alone was the trade in salt, carried into the forest both from the sea and from the Sahara via the Sudan. There was also a trade in cattle and in horses, from the Sudan into Guinea. The principal Guinea exports were gold-dust, which reached the Sudan and ultimately the Mediterranean from workings in the Gold Coast region and the earlier workings in Wangara; kola-nuts, one of the few stimulants tolerated by Islam and therefore valued throughout the Sudan, which also reached the Maghrib; and ivory, though the ivory trade was nothing like as important as it became in European times, when part of the Guinea coast west of the Gold Coast became known as the Ivory Coast. Goods which travelled mainly in the other direction, from north to south, included—besides horses and cattle and some of the salt—beads, trinkets, and other small items of metalware such as cutlasses; scarce and therefore valuable base metals such as copper and its alloys; cloth; and cowrie shells. These last, brought all the way from the Indian Ocean via Egypt, serve to remind us that West Africa had well-developed systems of money, as also of weights and measures. In addition to cowries, gold-dust, blocks of salt, and pieces of iron, of copper, or even of cloth were also recognized mediums of exchange. Not all the beads and cloth traded in Guinea, however, were imports. Some or perhaps most of the cloth had been woven in the Sudan or in North Africa, and some of the beads came from the Mediterranean region; but there was also trade in stone and glass beads and in cloth which had been manufactured in Guinea itself; Yorubaland in particular seems to have exported both.

In view of later developments, there is one striking omission from the list of commodities featuring in the early Guinea trade, namely slaves. Domestic slaves certainly existed in Guinea, particularly in the more developed communities, as retainers and agricultural labourers of the kings and other prominent men, while the porters in the trading caravans, too, were doubtless slaves. But trade in slaves, at least on any great scale, seems to have been a late development. References to a regular export to North Africa of Negro slaves, many of whom must have come from south of the Sudan, do not appear in the Arabic sources before about the twelfth century. It seems likely that this trade really began to develop only after the growth of Islam in the western Sudan which followed the conquest of Ghana by the Almoravids. In the Guinea coastlands it seems clear that it was only with the growing European demand, from the sixteenth century onwards, that the large-scale slave trade developed. The other trades, however, were already well developed by the time of the European arrival on the coast. Thus, when Europeans reached the Gold Coast towards the end of the fifteenth century, they found that Mande merchants were already there, and that among the goods in local demand were Moroccan cloth, and beads and cloth exported from Benin and probably of Yoruban manufacture.

It was this universality of trade in cloth and other luxuries which, together with the largely urban pattern of settlement, chiefly distinguished the Guinea region from all other parts of Africa south of the 'Sudanic' savanna belt, at least during late medieval and early modern times. In the whole of Bantu Africa, imported cotton cloth was known at the time of the first Portuguese contacts only in the urban settlements of the eastern seaboard and in a very limited inland region around the gold-producing area south of the Zambezi. But at the same period in Guinea practically every village was linked by trade of some sort with the Muslim civilization of the Sudan and of North Africa. And when Europeans arrived on the Guinea coast by sea, they accordingly found a fertile field for their commercial activities. In time, however, the entrance of long-distance trade to West Africa from the south was to bring radical changes both to its economy and to the balances of power among its states. . . .

26. The slave trade (i)

J. D. FAGE *An Introduction to the History of West Africa* Cambridge University Press 1955; pages 80–7

. . . The buying and selling of slaves on the coast was a complicated business. In the first place, where African political authority extended over Europeans, slaves could usually not be bought or sold without the permission of the African chief. For example, the chiefs of the tribes at the mouths of the Oil Rivers would not allow trade to begin until duties had been paid. At Whydah on the Slave Coast, European factors were required to purchase a trading licence for each visiting ship. They were then required to buy the king's stock of slaves at a price well above the current market price before they were allowed to complete their cargo with slaves bought from private merchants. In addition, the king levied a tax on the purchase price of every slave bought. Even where the Europeans were not subject to African authority, trade was usually impossible unless the European traders gave substantial and frequent presents to the local chiefs and elders.

There was no trading currency in common use throughout the coastal districts. On the Windward Coast, slaves and European imports were commonly valued in relation to bars of iron; on the Ivory Coast, to pieces of cloth; on the Gold Coast, to gold dust; between Accra and Keta, to cowrie shells; on the Slave Coast, to both iron and copper bars; in the Oil Rivers, to brass basins; in the Cameroons, to pieces of cloth. Iron and copper were used by the Africans for making tools and utensils, and were imported from Europe in standard size bars. It was accepted on the Slave Coast that one iron bar was worth four copper bars. Similarly, Europeans imported cloth in standard lengths. Now, except for cowrie shells and gold dust, these media of exchange were all commodities which could be consumed, and their value varied in accordance with the extent of the need for them. As a consequence, the process of bargaining in the slave trade was apt to be unduly complicated and lengthy. An example may help to make this clear. Let us say that on the Slave Coast a European trader who wanted slaves was doing business with an African who wanted guns. They had to agree on the value of a slave and of a gun in terms of bars, and to do this they needed to take into account not only the relative scarcity or abundance of slaves and guns on the coast at the time, but also the relative scarcity or abundance of iron and copper bars. Where the large trading companies were strongly established, possessing depots in which they kept adequate stocks of the imports most in demand, they tried to fix prices, saying, for example, that the price of a certain kind of gun was so many bars. But these prices could easily be upset by the arrival on the coast of an interloper whose trading might result in a temporary glut either of guns or of bars. In addition, the maintenance of stocks was apt to be a chancy business because African tastes for European goods were apt to change. For example, in one year blue cloth might be in great demand on one part of the coast and quite unsaleable on another only a few miles away, while a year later, for no reason apparent to the Europeans, the position might be reversed.

Once acceptable prices had been agreed upon, the slaves on sale were inspected by a surgeon from the ship or factory, and the old and infirm slaves weeded out. In general only about one-third of the slaves taken by Europeans were women. This was partly because less women were offered for sale, partly because the effects of child-bearing meant that the ages between which women could be considered fit for plantation slavery were more narrowly limited than for men. Men were usually taken between the ages of ten and about thirty-five; women usually only up to the age of twenty-five. The selected slaves were then usually branded with the mark of their purchaser and shipped, or confined within forts or factories awaiting shipment.

Because the supply and demand varied from time to time and from place to place on the coast, and because of the complicated system of trading, it is not easy to give representative examples of the prices paid by Europeans for slaves in West Africa. However, at the beginning of the eighteenth century, the equivalent of as little as £3 might be paid for a fit male slave in the prime of life; at the beginning of the nineteenth century perhaps as much as the equivalent of £25 would be paid. But it must be remembered that the purchase price of a slave was paid in goods the value of which on the coast might bear little relation to their cost in Europe.

The goods brought to West Africa by the European traders varied slightly according to the period, the nationality of the traders, and the place where they were trading, but the following commodities found a pretty steady sale: textiles (woollens and linens manufactured in Europe, cottons manufactured mostly in India until the nineteenth century, and silks manufactured either in Europe or in Asia); all kinds of firearms, powder, and shot; knives and cutlasses; many kinds of European-made ironmongery and hardware; iron, copper, brass, and lead in bar form; spirits (rum, brandy, or gin, according to the country of origin of the trader); and many kinds of provisions.

The volume of the slave trade

We do not have enough information to be able to state exactly how many African slaves were carried across the Atlantic to America. However, on the basis of the information we do possess, it seems likely that the number of slaves imported into America, from the time the trade began in the sixteenth century until it was eventually brought to an end in the nineteenth century, was at least fifteen million, and unlikely to have been much greater than twenty million. It should be noted that these figures are for the slaves *landed in America*. The number *leaving Africa* must have been considerably greater, since it was rare for a slave ship to complete a voyage without the death from disease of at least a part of its human cargo. It seems reasonable from what we know of the mortality on slaving voyages to assume that *on an average* at least a sixth of the slaves shipped from Africa never lived to see America. On occasions the mortality was very much higher than this. Thus in all probability, somewhere between eighteen and twenty-four million Africans were carried away from West Africa by the European slave trade.

It has been stated earlier that the number of slaves imported into America in the sixteenth century was at least 900,000. The subsequent growth of the demand for slaves on the plantations, and the intensive competition between European traders to supply this demand, soon made the sixteenth-century trade seem insignificant. In the seventeenth century the number of slaves reaching America was more than three times as great, at least 2,750,000, or an average of 27,500 a year. The eighteenth-century trade was on an even greater scale, at least 7,000,000 slaves reaching America, or 70,000 a year on the average. During the nineteenth century, the demand for slaves continued to increase at first, and it did not finally cease until by the 1880s all the American nations had at length abolished the status of slavery. The efforts made to stop the trade prevented a steady expansion as in the previous centuries; nevertheless, by the time the trade had finally come to an end, a further 4,000,000 slaves had arrived in America.

Slaves were taken from almost the whole length of the western coast of Africa, from the Senegal in the north to Angola in the south. Some were even taken to America from the east coast. We are concerned in this book only with the slave trade north of the Cameroons. However, with the exception of the Portuguese trade from Angola and São Thomé to Brazil, the European trade in slaves from the coast south of the Cameroons became important only during the course of the eighteenth century, and it was extended to East Africa only in the nineteenth century. Even as late as the end of the eighteenth century, it seems that at least two-thirds of the slaves carried across the Atlantic were taken from the coasts which concern us between the Senegal and the Cameroons.

The trade north of the Gambia was insignificant, amounting probably to less than a thousand slaves a year at the end of the eighteenth century. At the same time, the number of slaves being taken each year from the Windward Coast between the Gambia and Sherbo Island was about 3,000; from the Grain and Ivory Coasts between 4,000 and 5,000; from the Gold Coast about 10,000; from the Slave Coast about 9,000; from Lagos and Benin about 3,500; and from the shores of the Gulf of Guinea to about as far as the Cameroons, about 18,000. These figures refer only to a particular period, and of course the proportionate contributions of the different parts of the coast did not remain fixed throughout the whole period of the trade. However, the contribution of the Gold Coast to the total was great throughout the period from about 1640 to about 1820, and that of the Slave Coast from about 1680 to about 1860. When the European powers with bases on these coasts began to be active in their attempts to stop the slave trade, there tended to be a corresponding increase in the activities of the slave-traders in the Gulf of Guinea and on the Grain and Ivory Coasts.

General effects of the slave trade on West Africa

At first sight it would seem that the most outstanding effect of the slave trade upon West Africa must have been the loss and destruction of population caused by the trade. In addition to the slaves actually exported to America, the slave trade caused the loss of countless other lives to West Africa. There were those killed in the wars caused by the trade; those killed by slave raids, or wounded and left to perish because they were too old or infirm to be of value as slaves; those who died from the hardships of the march to the coast or of their captivity while awaiting shipment; finally there were those unfortunates who were condemned by the European buyers of slaves as unfit for purchase, many of whom, if they were not left to die, became victims of the practice of human sacrifice which was greatly stimulated by the slave trade and its wars. In all it has been suggested that for every African who became acclimatised to plantation slavery in America, at least one other African lost his life through the operations of the slave trade. Thus during the whole period of the trade, somewhere between thirty and forty million souls must have been lost to West Africa.

Although this figure represents an amount of man-made human misery and suffering almost without parallel, a number of factors must be taken into account before we can state with certainty that this loss of population seriously affected West African life. In the first place, the loss ought to be considered in relation to the total population of West Africa. Unfortunately we have no means of knowing what the population of West Africa was during the period of the slave trade. Today it is upwards of forty million, and would seem to be increasing fairly rapidly. This would suggest that the population of West Africa during the slave-trade period is unlikely to have been more than twenty million at most. Since the total loss was spread over more than 300 years, this suggests that the average loss of population to West Africa as a result of the slave-trade was less than 1 per cent a year of the total population. Such a rate of loss need not necessarily have been a crippling one for a healthy society.

But the effects of the slave trade were not evenly distributed in time and space. When the slave trade was at its height, clearly the rate of loss of population was much higher than the average for the whole three and a half centuries, while we also know that some parts of West Africa contributed many more slaves to the trade than did others. In addition, the slave trade tended to take away the young and the fit men and women and to leave behind the old and the infirm, thus making it more difficult for the West African peoples to replace their losses by new births. Consequently there must have been times and places in West Africa when the loss of population caused by the slave trade must have had a very damaging effect, not only on the size of population, but also on its health and virility. Yet it is interesting to note that those parts of West Africa which might be assumed to have suffered most from the trade—the Gold and Slave Coasts and what is now southern Nigeria—are today some of the most advanced and densely populated regions of the country. Even when the slave trade was at its height, these regions were remarkable for the density of their population and for their elaborate political organisation. There is evidence that trade with Europeans, even, in certain circumstances, the trade in slaves, acted as a stimulus to the growth of population and the development of political institutions.

Even if in general the slave trade tended to reduce the population of West Africa in an unhealthy manner, we still cannot say with any certainty that, had there been no slave trade, the population of West Africa today would have been larger, or very much larger, or even that it would have been of a higher physical standard. We do not know whether African methods of farming would have developed sufficiently and rapidly enough to support a larger population. The increase of population in recent years has clearly tended to strain the ability of West Africa to feed itself, even though methods of food production have been improved through contact with Europeans, a contact which in many cases began with the slave trade.

We can, however, be quite certain that the slave trade acted generally as a factor retarding orderly progress and development in West Africa. The dominant economic activity for many peoples became trade, and a peculiar kind of trade which discouraged rather than stimulated agricultural and industrial production, which indeed discouraged constructive work of any kind. It became cheaper and easier for West Africans to buy tools and clothing and all sorts of manufactures from the Europeans rather than to make them for themselves. Many arts and skills which they possessed, such as iron-working, the making of pottery, of cloth, of brass and copper ware, deteriorated or even died out. And the West Africans paid for the European-made substitutes, not by any productive endeavour in other fields, but by the economically negative and destructive work of waging wars and capturing and selling men, the labourers whom they needed for the achievement of sound prosperity.

The slave raids and the wars occasioned by the slave trade brought even more disastrous results than the continual wastage of labour and energy that might have been put to productive use, or the continuing destruction of the physical assets of the country such as crops, herds, villages, and towns. The constant threat of slave raids and wars produced a chronic state of uncertainty in which it was pointless to produce more than the minimum amount of food needed for domestic consumption, or to build houses and towns more elaborate than the minimum needed to provide elementary shelter from the elements. There was no point in expanding production, in planning and building for the future. Tomorrow all might be destroyed, and the builders and planners might be enslaved or killed. Life could only be lived in the present. Society could not progress because fear and uncertainty were ever stronger than the desire for improvement. . . .

27. The slave trade (ii)

J. W. BLAKE *European Beginnings in West Africa* Imperial Studies Series, Vol. XIV, Longmans for Royal Commonwealth Society 1937; pages 84–9

. . . The trade of malagueta, however, had a much longer life than that of Benin pepper, and was pursued throughout the sixteenth century. A Portuguese historian has assembled valuable figures to indicate the quantity of the traffic. Between 1498 and 1505, 2,000 quintals of malagueta were consigned to the chief Portuguese factor at Antwerp, an average of 250 quintals per year. Only 75 quintals of Benin pepper were annually consigned to the factor over the same period. The quantity of malagueta was probably greater than that of Benin pepper throughout the twenty years before 1506. Moreover, 454 quintals of malagueta was the average figure for the years 1509–14. In 1537 King John III sold 400 quintals at the rate of 12 cruzados per quintal, and this would suggest that there had been no appreciable fall in the annual amount of malagueta imported since the beginning of the century. If this be a correct surmise, it is also a remarkable one, for French traders in Guinea often carried away a part of the available malagueta after 1530, and their intrusion must surely have had a detrimental effect upon the value of the Portuguese trade.

After an early boom, profits from the malagueta trade seem to have fallen. It would appear that the negro merchants soon grasped the value of their wares and raised their prices. Pacheco illustrates this price revolution in a passage about the trade of the Rio dos Sestos: formerly, one alquier of malagueta could have been bought for one pewter manilla, but, when he wrote (*c.* 1505), the negro merchants demanded 5 or 6 manillas for the same measure of Guinea pepper. The black merchants would carry their pepper in baskets out from the mainland in their canoes, which they called *almadias*, and would haggle with the Portuguese traders until they should have made a satisfactory bargain. Probably, interlopers were partly responsible for the acumen of the natives. However, the fall in profits on the Guinea Coast was paralleled by a similar fall on the Antwerp bourse. One pound of malagueta fetched 12 dinheiros in 1511, but only half that sum in 1517. A recovery occurred later in the century, so that in 1578 one pound was priced at 28 dinheiros. These price fluctuations were incidental to the main importance of the trade, its value to the crown. Malagueta remained a royal monopoly throughout the sixteenth century.

The slave trade between West Africa and Portugal began in 1441, when Antam Gonçalves brought the first cargo to Lisbon. This was the beginning of a steady flow of slaves to Portugal for two generations. The Arguin factory was the original centre for the trade on the West African coast, but, as more land was found, the commercial centre of gravity tended to move southwards. Senegambia became a valuable field for slave-raiding; so, later, did the Rio de Casamansa, the Rio de Case, Cape St. Anna, the Rio dos Sestos and, ultimately, all the coast of Benin. It is probable that the slave trade of Upper Guinea was flourishing by 1470, but that of Benin was not opened up until 1486, when the factory of Gató was built. During the sixteenth century, thousands of slaves were obtained on the coast of the Kingdom of Angola, and Loanda, which was founded in 1578, grew to be the largest sea-port of that province, and became the centre of a very flourishing commerce. The fortunes of Angola were thereafter largely dependent upon the Portuguese colony of Brazil, because of the slave trade between them. It was, however, the island of São Thomé which first came to be the centre of the slave traffic in the Gulf of Guinea. Negroes were taken to São Thomé from Benin and from many places on the coast between Benin and Cape St. Catherine, while slaves from Angola, called Angolares, were also carried to the island. Most of these unfortunate captives were shipped either to Portugal or to Pernambuco in Brazil. The trade expanded considerably during the century, so that, by 1602, a number of slave marts had been established by the Portuguese all round the coast of the Gulf. It would seem, indeed, that permanent factories were actually maintained in one or two places, like the earlier one at Gató.

The negro merchants raised the price of slaves, as of malagueta, after only a few years of trading. It was possible to buy eighteen Moors for one horse at Arguin in 1455, but half a century later, a horse would only purchase twelve negroes near the Senegal. A similar change occurred at the Rio dos Sestos, where the price of one slave rose from two shaving basins to four or five. The native merchants of Porto d'Ali demanded a horse for six slaves in 1505 and, by that year, the former slave trade six miles south of Cape Verde had even been abandoned.

This evidence suggests that, towards the end of the fifteenth century, the slave trade declined. An examination of the figures for slaves, imported into Portugal, at first sight tends to confirm the decline. Cadamosto recorded that in his day 700 or 800 slaves were annually carried to Lisbon. The researches of Lucio de Azevedo show that 448 slaves, belonging to the crown alone, were imported annually between 1486 and 1493, and an average of 500 during the years 1511–13. Now all these figures seem to indicate that fewer slaves were imported after the generation of Cadamosto. Moreover, this conclusion is specially attractive, because it confirms the theory of a decreasing volume of traffic just before the opening up of the market in the new world for West African negroes. But, how unreliable such casual estimates can be is revealed by collating Cadamosto's evidence with Pacheco's reckoning that, 'when the trade of Upper Guinea was well-ordered, in each year more than 3,500 slaves were drawn from it'. His statement appears to be irreconcilable with the rest of the evidence, except it be considered a gross exaggeration. Nor can we ignore the probable effect of the discovery of Benin in 1486, for the Benin slave trade must surely have augmented the total volume of the traffic. Probably, the number of imported slaves varied from year to year, and a tendency to decline was checked, firstly by the opening up of Benin and, secondly, by the demand for native labour in the new world.

The first batch of negroes was purchased in Lisbon for the West Indies in 1510, and the licence system was inaugurated three years later. Thereafter, the revenue from the slave traffic was an important royal asset, but it was soon found necessary to restrict the purchase of negroes. An edict of 15 March 1518 regulated the price of slaves, and forbade merchants to penetrate into the interior of Guinea to get them. Some of the Santiagians, who enjoyed special privileges in Senegambia, seem to have penetrated up country to trade, while there were renegades and degraded whites who mixed with the inland native tribes, and negotiated trade between interlopers and negro merchants to the crown's disadvantage. Later writers refer often, and generally with scorn, to these men, against whom the law of 1518 was directed. A royal pardon was offered to those who would return at once, provided they should surrender up one-half of the wares which they had already bought. Behind the law would seem to be the fact that the demand in the West Indies for blackamoors was growing, and on every licensed shipload of slaves, which came to Portugal, the king imposed a freight charge. It is patent how an increase of interloping traffic, or a consequent fall in prices, was liable to deprive the crown of revenue.

The number of slaves exported from West Africa rose rapidly after the opening up of the transatlantic market. In the four years 1513–16, more than 700 slaves were carried annually to Portugal and Spain from Santiago alone. The island of São Thomé flourished, since it was the centre of the African slave trade until 1578. By 1540 the export of slaves, in some years, may have reached 10,000. In the middle of the century, slaves were transported directly to the West Indies from São Thomé. Some have wondered whether it was not the general rule for slaves to be taken first to Portugal, and then reshipped for Brazil and the West Indies. This may have been so, but some slaves were carried straight across the Atlantic, for King John III, in one of his letters, refers to 'the slaves which go from the island of São Thomé to the Antilles'. The end of the century saw an amazing expansion: in 1595, when the *asiento* was leased to Gomez Regnal, it was stipulated that 4,500 slaves should be imported to the new world annually for nine years. Although many of these slaves were secured in Congo and Angola, the number is sufficiently high to indicate how far the Guinea slave trade had expanded.

The slave trade was in many ways the most important branch of the traffic of Guinea. It was the earliest to prosper; it proved to be more reliable than others, like gold and malagueta, which tended to decline after 1530; and it provided a greater source of income for the crown, which continued to draw revenue from it for over two centuries.

Of the ivory trade there is strangely little evidence. Martin Boviage held the right to purchase all the ivory brought from Guinea in 1469, so that Fernão Gomes was unable to exploit it. When Pacheco wrote his *Esmeraldo*, elephants' teeth could be bought at many places along the coast of Upper Guinea, ivory collars from the Teymenes at the Rio de Case, and a good deal of ivory in the Kingdon of Benin. The absence of any references to trade along the modern Ivory Coast suggests that this region was unfrequented by the Portuguese. Pacheco asserts that the negroes were untrustworthy: 'Seven villages are to be met with from the Rio de Laguoa forward for seven leagues', he writes, 'and here there is no trade and the negroes are treacherous'.

Yet the evidence of Pacheco can only be taken as accurate for the early sixteenth century. Long before 1600 the Portuguese had begun to trade off this part of the coast, and at the end of the century the Hollanders began to displace them. Moreover, English interlopers purchased ivory there as early as 1555, securing a considerable quantity of 'teeth' at a village, which was situated thirteen leagues east of Cape Palmas. Accordingly, it may be assumed that the Portuguese opened up a valuable ivory trade on the Ivory Coast before the middle of the century. This did not lead to the abandonment of the older, if smaller, trades, for Portuguese merchants were still working the traffic at the Rio de Nuno and in northern Sierra Leone in 1594. Unfortunately, no exact evidence has been found of the value of the ivory trade. It was not converted into a government monopoly, and this would suggest that the crown attached less importance to it than to malagueta. . . .

28. The slave trade (iii)

C. R. BOXER *Salvador de Sá and the Struggle for Brazil and Angola* Athlone Press of the University of London 1952; pages 223–7, 229–34

Angola 'The Black Mother'

Although some seventeenth-century Europeans with experience of labour conditions in tropical America thought that Amerindians made better slaves than did African Negroes, the weight of contemporary evidence is the other way. The superiority of the Negro to the Brazilian Indian, as a slave, has been accepted on the whole by all modern historians; although there is more doubt as to the Negro's servile value compared with that of more advanced Amerindian races.

The stone-age culture of the wandering forest tribes of Brazil made adjustment to a life of slavery much more difficult for them than for the Negro, who was used to some form of bondage in his native Africa. The Amerindians, on the whole, were more vulnerable to the diseases imported by the white man than were the Negroes, particularly when they were herded together in large numbers. They died fast in captivity, and this applies not only to the Brazilian savages enslaved by the Portuguese, but to the more advanced Mexican and Peruvian Indians who were forced to labour for the Spanish settlers in the mines or in the *encomiendas*.

In the last quarter of the sixteenth century Antonio de León calculated that only a third of the sixteen thousand Indians who were recruited yearly for the forced labour corvée (*mita*) of Potosí returned to their native villages at the end of their term in the mines; while the Caribs of the Antilles were virtually extinct by this time. As regards Brazil, some fifty years later Father Antonio Viera wrote that over two million Indians had been exterminated by the Portuguese. Nor was it only the Jesuits who complained that the Portuguese exceeded the Spaniards in their cruelty to the Amerindians. An important contributory reason for the demand for Negro slaves was the Jesuits' opposition to the enslavement of the Amerindians. The Society of Jesus was supported in its stand by the kings of Spain and Portugal, whereas neither the Society nor the crown raised any objection against Negro slavery. The preference for African slaves first showed itself, and was always most marked, in hot low-lying areas; but by the early seventeenth century Negroes were in demand even for mining at Potosí in High Peru. Thus there existed a big, growing, general demand for Negro slaves from West Africa, which the Portuguese by virtue of their position were the people best able to supply.

Originally, the bulk of West African slaves came from Guinea, but by 1600 the chief slave-producing areas were the regions then known as the Congo and Angola. These regions were but vaguely defined; the old kingdom of Congo may be taken as the region bounded on the north by the river Zaire (or Congo), on the south by the river Dande, on the west by the sea, and by the river Kwango on the east. Angola may be taken as the area between the Dande and Longa rivers, with a hinterland stretching several hundred miles into the interior. Its native name was Ndongo; the Portuguese called it Angola, from the name or title of its ruler (Ngola) when first they visited it. Its chiefs formerly owed allegiance to the king of Congo, whose suzerainty was shaken off about the middle of the sixteenth century, the king only keeping possession of Luanda island and its valuable cowrie fishery.

Estimates of the total number of slaves exported annually

from the region of Congo and Angola in the early seventeenth century suggest that this was a round figure of fifteen thousand in an average good year. Their distribution between Spanish and Portuguese America, in times of peace and normal trade, may be taken as approximately the following:[1]

Pernambuco	4,400
Bahia and Rio	4,000
Spanish Main and Antilles	5,000
Buenos Aires and Rio de la Plata	1,500

The profits to be made in the slave-trade between West Africa and South America were immense, as all foreign visitors to Brazil and Peru noted. Negro slaves exported to the Spanish possessions fetched even more than those sold to supply labour for the expanding Brazilian sugar industry. One of the principal —if illegal—aspects of this trade was the importation of Angola slaves into Buenos Aires, either direct from Luanda or via Brazilian ports. Most of these Negroes were intended for sale in Potosí and High Peru, but a fair number remained in Tucumán and in the Rio de la Plata region.[2] Slaves who were sold for a few squares of palm-cloth in Angola fetched from four to six hundred pesos in Peru, according to age and condition.

The human reservoir which the Portuguese were tapping for slaves in Congo and Angola was inhabited by Bantu peoples in a rudimentary stage of civilisation. They were not, however, savages, with the possible exception of the Jagas who will be described shortly. They knew how to work metals, including iron and copper, how to make pottery, and weave raffia tissues of palm-cloth. They had domesticated several animals—pigs, sheep, chickens, and in some districts cattle. Maize, mandioc, sweet potatoes and other plants introduced by the Portuguese

[1] The figure of 15,000 Negroes exported yearly from Luanda is given in the Dutch letters narrating the capture of the city in 1641, and published in English translation, *A Little Forraine Newes*. Cf. also Taunay, 'Subsídios para a história do tráfico africano no Brasil', pp. 35–42; Correia Lopes, *A escravatura*, pp. 87–91; Pastells, *Historia*, i., p. 298; Mello, neto, *Tempo dos Flamengos*, pp. 208–14 and sources there quoted.

[2] For the prices fetched by Angola slaves in Tucumán during the first half of the seventeenth century, cf. Lizondo Borda, *Documentos coloniales*, ii., pp. 59–60, 152–4, iii., pp. 15–16, although Negro slaves in this region were not so much for field work as 'para el honor de las personas'.

were cultivated in the native villages. They lived, for the most part, in huts or kraals constructed of flimsy materials, sometimes conical and sometimes rectangular in shape. They did not know the art of writing and seem to have had no contacts with the far more advanced races on the upper reaches of the Niger, where there was a flourishing university at Timbuktu in the fifteenth century. Tribal law and custom regulated their daily lives, many offences being punishable by torture, death or slavery. The authority of the tribal chiefs (called *sobas* or *sovas* in Angola) was very great, and in some cases, absolute.

The ruler of the old kingdom of Congo claimed supremacy over the neighbouring kingdoms of Matamba, Ndongo and Loango, etc., but the effectiveness of this suzerainty varied very widely. The ruler of Congo had been baptised by the Portuguese in the fifteenth century, and the king and his court were superficially Christains and aped European ways. Many Portuguese missionaries and traders settled in the Congo capital of Mbanza Kongo, or São Salvador, one of whose native names was *ekongo dia ngungo*, 'the town of the church bells', from its numerous and European-style religious buildings. Christianity was only skin-deep in most regions and fetichism and animism were the real beliefs of the mass of the natives, Angola not being affected by Christianity at all. The principal Congolese chiefs received the title of Dom, and in some regions the rank of Count; nobles of both sexes usually had baptismal Christian names.

The civilisation of the tribes who were not so closely affected by Portuguese influence as was the old kingdom of Congo, displayed the following characteristics which are typical of the so-called Zimbabwe or Rhodesian cultural group:

(*a*) absolute authority wielded by the king or chief;
(*b*) presence of one or more influential women of very high rank in the ruler's entourage;
(*c*) four or six councillors in attendance on the ruler;
(*d*) a very small ruling class;
(*e*) presence of the following sacred objects: knife, bell, chest containing ancestors' bones;
(*f*) lion or leopard as totems.

The most striking example of female influence among these tribes in the seventeenth century is that of Queen N'Zinga, ruler of one of the cannibal hordes known as the Jagas who infested the region of Matamba in the east of Angola. The origin of the Jagas is uncertain, nor are modern anthropologists agreed as to whether they were identical with the cannibal Zimba (Muzimba) hordes who ravaged vast regions of East Africa in the last quarter of the sixteenth century. The Jagas were true cannibals, eating human flesh not merely as a ritual sacrifice but as a matter of habit, convenience and conviction. Unlike the other Bantu tribes, they kept no flocks and indulged in no agricultural pursuits. They were purely nomadic robbers. They killed all their own children, and kept the choicest of the youths and maidens whom they captured in war, bringing them up in the 'law of the Jagas'. They were, therefore, rather a collection of wandering hordes than an ethnic tribe. They were greatly dreaded by their less warlike and more sedentary neighbours, some of whom acknowledged their suzerainty rather than that of the king of Congo. . . .

Slaves were obtained by the Portuguese in various ways, by war, by tribute or by barter. Under normally peaceful conditions, slaving agents called *pombeiros or pumbeiros* (from a native word meaning 'hawker') roamed the interior regions, purchasing slaves from the local chieftains and taking them to Luanda for transportation to Brazil. The pombeiros were mulattoes, or often pure Negroes, who would be sent out by their Portuguese masters at Luanda with anything up to a total of a hundred and fifty Negro slaves as carriers to transport the palm-cloth, cowries, wine and other merchandise for which slaves were purchased in the interior. These pombeiros would stay away from one to two years before either sending, or bringing back to the coast, chain-gangs of five or six hundred slaves. Although usually very loyal to their European masters, it was not unknown for them to default on their employers and to make off with the slaves and the merchandise. Some of the most trusty pombeiros did not return to Luanda for years on end, but stayed up-country and received periodically merchandise from the coast in exchange for slaves. The original form of currency had been a kind of cowrie shell known as *njimbu* or *zimbo*, which was found on the island of Luanda, and imported extensively from Brazil. The *zimbo* was gradually supplanted by the use of *panos* or palm-leaf cloth, and by rock salt, brandy, gunpowder and other European commodities of relatively small intrinsic value. Slaves could thus be had very cheaply, whether from the Jagas, or from the *sobas* (*sovas*) or chiefs of the other tribes.

A *soba* who had sworn allegiance to the governor of Angola was entrusted by him to a Portuguese soldier or official.

This soldier seeth that he have no wrong; and the lord [*soba*] acknowledgeth him to be his master; and he doth maintain the soldier, and maketh him rich. Also, in the wars he commandeth his master's house to be built before his own, and whatsoever he hath taken that day in the wars, he parteth with his master. So that there is no Portugal soldier of any account, but he hath his Negro sova or Lord.

The Portuguese conducted their campaigns in the interior with flying columns composed of a few hundred (or less) Europeans and mulatto soldiers, accompanied by the *guerra preta* of several thousand native auxiliaries and carriers who were recruited through these loyal or vassal *sobas*.

Slaves destined for export from Luanda were kept in large buildings or barracoons, pending embarkation. They usually arrived in very bad condition from the interior, having marched sometimes hundreds of miles with very little food, and the Portuguese took good care to fatten them up at Luanda, feeding them well and giving them palm-oil to grease their skins. Sick slaves were placed in quarantine apart from the healthy ones. If no ships were available, they were employed during the day-time on agricultural work, particularly in planting and cutting mandioc. On the day they were due to embark, they were taken to a nearby church, or other convenient place, and there baptised by a parish priest in batches of hundreds at a time. The ceremony did not take very long. The priest said to each slave in turn, 'your name is Peter, yours is John, yours is Francis', and so on, giving each man a piece of paper with his name written on it, putting a little salt on his tongue, and sprinkling holy water over the crowd with a hyssop. Then a Negro interpreter addressed them as follows: 'Look you people are already children of God; you are going to the land of the Spaniards [or Portuguese] where you will learn things of the Faith. Don't think any more about where you came from, and don't eat dogs, rats, or horses—now go with a good will.'

The confusion and misery of the subsequent embarkation has often been described. The suicide rate was high, many Negroes preferring to jump overboard and drown, rather than to reach America as slaves. In order to prevent this, the hatches were battened down and the Negroes kept below decks even when the ship was still in port. It is not surprising that many died in these fetid and insanitary conditions. On embarkation at Luanda, slaves were classified by a standard measurement known as the *peça de Indias*, by which was meant 'a Negro from fifteen to twenty-five years old; from eight to fifteen, and from twenty-five to thirty-five, three pass for two; beneath eight, and from thirty-five to forty-five, two pass for one; sucking infants follow their mothers without accompt; all above forty-five years, with the diseased, are valued by arbiters'. A bonus was paid to the crown for each *peça* exported to Brazil, and twice that sum for each *peça* exported to Spanish America.

The crossing averaged about thirty-five days from Luanda to Recife, forty days to Bahia, and two months to Rio de Janeiro. According to Father Antonio Vieira, the slave-ships were popularly called *tumbeiros* (undertakers), an aptly sinister designation. These vessels at this period were usually small ships or caravels of under 200 tons, with cargoes of anything up to 600 slaves. As these slave-ships were often very lightly manned, sometimes with only ten or a dozen Europeans aboard, the Negroes were seldom allowed on deck for occasional exercise and fresh air, for fear lest they would either mutiny or commit suicide.

The resultant conditions in the crowded holds below deck are better imagined than described, but even so, the Portuguese had a relatively high reputation as efficient slavers among their foreign competitors. Pieter Mortamer, the first Dutch Director of Luanda, took this view in an official report on the slave-trade which he drew up in September 1642:

The Portuguese succeed better in bringing over five hundred slaves in a caravel, than we do with three hundred in a large ship. This is because the Portuguese look after and feed them better, which brings them a two-fold return at the time of sale. They wash down the deck every other day with bad vinegar; they cook warm hot-pot for their slaves twice daily, once with African beans, the next time with maize, and all well-cooked with a good big spoonful of palm-oil mixed therein, together with a little salt, and sometimes a large hunk of dried fish in each dish. During the day, they have always a little *farinha* and some water, while they have a little nigger-wine especially on hand for the sick, and give every slave two or three pieces of old cloth wherewith to cover himself.

Mortamer also recommended the construction of barracoons at Luanda for the housing of slaves awaiting shipment,

like each Portuguese has attached to his private dwelling, and thus the slaves will come fit on board, remain fit on the voyage, and if the crossings are quicker, they will fetch half as much again in the market; nor will one then hear so much of their dying or jumping overboard, or killing themselves as they do now.[1]

This report has often been cited by historians (myself included) as indicating that the Portuguese, owing to their long experience in the slave-trade, were, relatively speaking, more humane than most other European slavers, if only because they were more efficient. The contemporary Dutch writer, Olfert Dapper, in his previously quoted description of Africa, also alleges that the Dutch never managed the slave-ships so well as did the Portuguese. Subsequent research has led me to doubt the validity of this assertion, and in any event there is not sufficient documentary material for the seventeenth century available in print to decide the matter one way or the other. Mortamer's eulogy of the Portuguese as slave-traders, although confirmed by Dapper, may be offset to some extent by a Jesuit eyewitness' description of the condition in which the Angola slaves arrived at Buenos Aires in 1631. He alluded to their heavy mortality on arrival, 'both because the climate is very unfavourable to them (being quite contrary to their own) as because they are landed stark naked and living skeletons, being ordinarily ill-treated by their masters'. It may be added that despite this, the Jesuit stated that 'all the cities of these Indies are full of Angola Negroes'.

On reaching their port of destination, the surviving *peças de*

[1] Mortamer apparently acted on his own suggestions; in five Dutch ships which arrived at Recife from Luanda between 4 October 1644 and 14 January 1645, only 99 slaves died on the crossing, out of a total of 1,778 embarked in Angola. Letter of the Council at Recife, 13 February 1645, in JHMS.

Indias were registered and marketed 'like any other merchandise', the majority being destined for work in the sugar-plantations. Prices naturally varied in accordance with their age, sex and physical condition. Tribal origins also affected their market price. At one time, the slaves of Sudanese origin from Upper Guinea were highly valued on account of their superior strength and intelligence. But these slaves, many of whom were Moslems, did not forget that they had once been free, and they were usually to the fore as leaders of slave rebellions, particularly in the eighteenth and nineteenth centuries. For these and other reasons, the Bantu Negroes from Angola were the most sought-after in Brazil during the whole of the seventeenth century. Less independent, less reserved, more loquacious and more adaptable than the Sudanese, they readily accepted Christianity (or the outward form thereof) and imitated Portuguese ways more easily than did the proud-spirited Moslems.

The Brazilian *engenho*, or sugar-plantation with its mill and boiling-house, of this period is vividly described by Richard Flecknoe who visited Rio de Janeiro and its neighbourhood in 1649.

Now for their sugar, thus it grows, and thus 'tis made. Their sugar-canes are pruned to the height of standing corn; nor need they other culture, but every second year to cut them close by the roots, as we do osiers, when against the next year they never fail to spring up again, the flags of which canes are of a pleasant green, and show afar off just like a field of corn; which being ripe about the month of June, they joint them in pieces some feet long, and carry them to the mill, turned by oxen, or water, consisting of two round cylinders, about the bigness of millposts, plated with iron, which turning inwards, and joining as close together as they can meet, so squeeze the canes in passing through them, as they come out on the other side all bruised, and dry as cakes, which were all liquid before; which liquor is conveyed by troughs to certain cauldrons, where it is boiled, still retaining its amber colour, till poured out at last into their forms or coolers, with a certain lee 'tis rendered white. And in these mills (during the season of making sugar) they work both day and night, the work of immediately applying the canes into the mill being so perilous as if through drowsiness or heedlessness a finger's end be but engaged between the posts, their whole body inevitably follows, to prevent which, the next Negro has always a hatchet ready to chop off his arm, if any such misfortune should arrive.

The dependence of these sugar-plantations on Negro slave labour was almost complete, except in the few areas where Indian slaves were still available. The *senhor do engenho*, or proprietor of a large sugar-mill, needed between a hundred and a hundred and fifty slaves; a small mill (*engenhoca*) needed a minimum of forty; while the *lavradores* or copyholders, who did not own a mill but sent their cane to the mills for grinding, required about thirty. The slaves were wanted to clear the land for cultivation in the first place, and then to plant, trim and harvest the sugar-cane. They were needed to build, maintain and repair the mills, water-wheels, canals, etc. which enabled the engenho to function; as also to manage the oxen and to row the boats used for transporting the sugar to market. Furthermore, they were employed as carpenters, potters, tile-makers, blacksmiths and domestic servants of every kind. They fully deserved their popular appellation of being 'the hands and the feet' of their white employers.

Not for nothing was Brazil described by a Portuguese seventeenth-century writer, Don Francisco Manuel de Mello, as a 'paradise for mulattoes, a purgatory for whites, and a hell for blacks'; nor can all the twaddle which is written nowadays about the absence of a colour-bar in Portugal and Brazil alter the fact that life for a slave was essentially a hell on earth. . . .

X. ETHIOPIA

29. The kingdom of Aksum

MARGERY PERHAM *The Government of Ethiopia* Faber & Faber 1948; pages 10–12, 13–16, 17–19, 37, 38–43, 44–5, 47

The history of Ethiopia may be said to begin in Arabia. The people who, at some time during the first millennium before Christ, crossed the Red Sea to colonize the highlands of the African horn were an off-shoot of the Semitic Savaean civilization which flourished in the south-west of Arabia. Though its first coins are from the sixth or fifth centuries B.C. and its historical records run from about 150 B.C. to A.D. 350, this civilization had probably taken shape some 1,000 years B.C.

The emigrant Semites landed in a continent of which the north-eastern part appears to have been inhabited by the eastern group of Hamites, often called Cushites, who also include the Gallas, Somalis, Danakil, and Kaffas. The Hamites had probably already pushed most of the earlier negro groups back to the fringes of the modern Ethiopia. Since the Ethiopian civilization which resulted from this contact of Hamites and Semites was like the marriage of members of the same family, something must be said to explain their relationship. The words Semitic and Hamitic are, of course, linguistic terms and can only be applied to races with the knowledge that since language, like other cultural traits, can overflow the boundaries of race, these terms can never be exact. If, however, allowance is made for a large and variable margin of error, language can be taken as a rough guide and is, indeed, sometimes the only one available. The Hamitic and Semitic language groups show so many affinities that it is generally accepted that the races speaking them branched from a common stem. Authorities differ as to whether this race, grandparent to the Ethiopians, originated in Africa or Asia.

Both groups are Caucasian and thus belong to the same branch of the human race as the great majority of Europeans. For this reason the Hamites are sometimes called Eurafrican. The further term Cushite is derived from the ancient name applied to parts of north-east Africa. The Hamites supplied pre-dynastic Egypt with its population, and remarkably pure representatives of this group are found today among the Beja and Beni Amer tribes who are neighbours to Ethiopia in the Anglo-Egyptian Sudan and Eritrea. Both of these peoples, and especially the latter, with their light and graceful physique, wavy hair, fine eyes, and features which are clear-cut without being too sharp, appear, by our own European standards, strikingly beautiful types. Among other Hamites are the Berbers of North Africa and two more groups closely associated with Ethiopia on the east and south, the Somali and the Galla. Thus the basically Hamitic Ethiopians are largely surrounded by other Hamitic groups. To put Ethiopia in relationship with the rest of Africa, it must be remembered that successive waves of Hamites moving south and west have mingled with the negro peoples of Africa to produce the Bantu and other variations of Eurafrican-negro fusion which fill most of eastern, central, and southern Africa. The Ethiopian physical type, where it has not been modified by mixture of negro blood, is fairly tall, with the lower half of the body more developed than the trunk. The nose is generally well cut, the hair curly, the head long, and the general appearance Caucasian, the colour varying between brown and black.

The Semitic branch from the common stem seems to have flourished first in south-western Arabia. Its most important extensions from here were represented by the Akkadians of ancient Babylonia, the Assyrians, the Canaanites, the Phoenicians, the Hebrews and, of course, the closely associated Sabaeans and Arabs. It is even claimed that Semites were responsible for the great Egyptian culture, but, even without this distinction, their record in the history of civilization is noble. All the Semitic languages show a closer kinship with each other than can be traced amongst the probably older Hamitic languages.

The Sabaean civilization began to develop in the south-west corner of Arabia just as the first known Arab kingdom, the Minaean, which had its focus further north, was in decline. Its rise can be traced by coins and inscriptions of the sixth and following centuries B.C. Its prosperity seems to have been founded largely upon trade, especially upon the trade in myrrh, cinnamon, and cassia, and above all in incense, the valued produce of that undistinguished little tree which grows on the coasts of the two continents where they approach each other in this region and which became a necessity to the worship of the Egyptian temples. Though Saba, which is probably the Sheba of the Bible, gave its name to the civilizations of this group of tribes, no single state gained lasting supremacy and power found successive centres. The most famous, perhaps, was Ma'rib, 4,000 feet high in the south-western hills, renowned for a great sluiced dam for water storage and irrigation.

It is important to realize, in tracing the origins of the Aksumite kingdom, that the Sabaean was a high civilization for its period and one which, even allowing for some exaggeration, stands out in Greek records for its architecture, its economic resources, and the wealth and luxury of its aristocracy. The connection with Ethiopia can be traced by the relics of Sabaean settlements with their inscriptions and architectural and decorative forms which, crossing the sea, mark a route which can be clearly traced from Adulis on the coast to Aksum, a bare hundred miles away in a straight line, but 7,000 feet high in the mountains. Two Semitic tribes living on the opposite coast may have bequeathed their names to Ethiopia—Habashat, from which springs the Arab term Habash. This is still to be heard, generally in hostile terms, from the lips of the Somalis: while the Ethiopians themselves use the term Habasha. Its European form is Abyssinia. The Agaziyan or Ge'ez tribe gave its name to the Semitic language which, developed from Sabaean by the emigrants, became the classical tongue of the new kingdom.

We do not know the exact date or the circumstances of this fruitful emigration. To judge by its astonishing achievements in what appears to have been a savage land it must have taken place when the Sabaean civilization was in its prime, though it may have begun earlier. There are, indeed, archaeological remains which suggest that there were civilized emigrants in the region as early as 1000 B.C. Time must be allowed for the occupation of a sufficient area of what are today the highlands of Eritrea and Tigre to build up the conquering power and civic splendour of Aksum when it is first revealed to us in the opening centuries of our era. . . .

The word Ethiopia—the land of the people with the burnt

faces—was applied with the vagueness of geographical ignorance to the region immediately beyond the Egyptian frontier which was for long the frontier of civilization. There is evidence from Egyptian hieroglyphs of the seventh, twelfth, and eighteenth dynasties that caravans had reached the Blue Nile, but neither in them nor in Nubian, Assyrian, or Hebrew sources is there any evidence about the Aksumite kingdom. To Homer, the Ethiopians are simply the uttermost of men, the swarthy but blameless men who live beyond Thebes on the borders of the ocean stream. To Herodotus they live 'towards the rising of the sun'. Diodorus, Pliny, and Strabo, like Herodotus, all applied the name Ethiopia to Nubia. They do not seem to have known of the high tableland where Aksum had been founded. The first inscription of the Aksumites, as we shall see, shows that they themselves applied the word Ethiopia to the territory on the middle Nile. Lying south-east of Ethiopia, they alone were in a position to be clear about the southern boundaries of their neighbour. Elsewhere the geographical vagueness was still apparent in the middle ages. Great difficulty was found in locating the realm of Prester John and it was even possible for some later writers to use the word Ethiopia when referring to India and other parts of Asia. Had not Vagie found the source of the Nile in India? 'Abash', Marco Polo recorded confidently, 'is a very large province and constitutes Middle India.'

These were later vagaries. The true Nilotic Ethiopia, stimulated as we have seen by Egyptian influences, began to develop more historical identity of its own before the end of the ancient era and the names of Napata and Merowe came into use along with the general term, Ethiopia. As the nucleus of power and wealth moved south from the Egyptian border to Merowe, the cultural standards of Ethiopia showed signs of decline, though there was some recovery in the third century B.C. when friendly relations were established with the Ptolemies in Egypt, and Greek influence followed Egyptian up the Nile and reached the heart of the country. When the Romans took over the control of Egypt after the death of Cleopatra, hostilities broke out and in 23 B.C. Augustus sent down an expedition under Petronius which utterly destroyed Napata. This was the limit of a conquest which was not retained though Nero sent what must have been the first of those official geographical missions, which became so common in the nineteenth century, to discover the source of the Nile, a mission which enabled Pliny to give an account of Queen Candace in Merowe.

Candace appears to have been the generic title of the queens of Merowe and from this kingdom must have come the earnest eunuch, 'a man of Ethiopia' who, while studying Isaiah in his chariot, picked up Saint Philip by the wayside. The first century was, however, one of decline. The civilization bequeathed by Egypt was threatened by negro infiltration from the south. The archaeological remains show a rapid descent in art and technique and little pyramids that are still to be seen appear the very poorest relations of the great piles at Gizeh. Today, in the treeless flats of the Butana plain, which the writer has traversed, can be found the traces of the dying civilization running along one of the two routes which made hazardous links between the Ethiopia of the past and that of the future. By the fifth century A.D., probably as the result of the spread of the black Nuba from Kordofan, this region came to be called Nubia. The process of decline continued. The Nuba from the south-west, the Beja from the east, and, as we shall see, the Aksumites from the south, all ravaged the island of Merowe. Communications between Ethiopia and Aksum must often have been broken. In the sixth century—two centuries later, it is interesting to note, than Aksum—Nubia became at least partially Christian, the most outstanding state now being that of Dongola. In the fourteenth century the last Christian kingdom of Nubia was overrun from the north by the Arabs whose expansion over this region in Muslim tribal units meant an almost complete obliteration of the Ethiopian-Nubian civilization.

It was easy for the successors of the kingdom of Aksum, to whose country the word Ethiopia was already sometimes applied, to appropriate exclusively for themselves the word Ethiopia which they had begun to use some time after their own conversion. It was probably the immigrant Syrian monks who translated the Bible from Greek into Ge'ez who first applied Ethiopia to Aksum. The rulers and their clerks were naturally quick to seize upon such references to Ethiopia as they could find in ancient and holy writings which knew nothing of Aksum or Habashat, and these appropriations were duly entered into the canons and chronicles which they began to write about the fourteenth century. From then onwards travellers and writers could take their choice between the words Abyssinia and Ethiopia when referring to the mountain kingdom. The Latin writers generally chose the second form and those of Anglo-Saxon countries the first. In 1941, however, after the British reconquest of the country from the Italians, the Emperor decreed officially that the name was to be Ethiopia. This word has therefore been used throughout this book, except in this section of the historical introduction when the ancient Ethiopia was still in existence and the forerunner of the modern Ethiopia was still the kingdom of Aksum. We may note that there has in recent years appeared in Ethiopia a tendency to extend the historical larceny of the medieval clerks and to endeavour to exalt the country by appropriation of the new historical and archaeological knowledge of Nubian Ethiopia as they appropriated the biblical references. . . .

Aksum, for all its nearness to their trade routes, was in little danger of conquest by Greece or Rome. The traders and sailors of Ptolemaic Egypt found it no more necessary to occupy the lands surrounding an emporium than did the seventeenth-century Europeans who established their trading stations on the west coast of the continent some eighteen centuries later. Rome made even less impression upon this region than Greece. She did not even succeed in making herself the full legatee of the Greek trade with the east though it was partly with this object that Augustus sent a costly expedition in A.D. 24 into Arabia. The remnants of this force turned back exhausted from the Sabaean commercial centres to find their way again through the desert to their ships.

These, then, were the meagre contacts which the Sabaean outpost in the African mountains made northwards with the civilized world as represented by Arabia, ancient Ethiopia, and Egypt. To the south and south-west was a vast, unpenetrated region of savage tribes and kingdoms, Hamitic and negro. It is only in the first century A.D. that Aksum makes historical entry into the ancient world with two pieces of evidence to which approximate dates can be given. The first evidence is drawn from inscriptions in Arabia and Aksum which show that, about the same time as the Roman expedition into Arabia, the

Aksumites were already re-crossing, as aggressors, the Straits of Bab-el-Mandebe over which they had come as emigrants. They had accepted an invitation from the Sabaean King of Sana to make war upon his neighbours of Saba and Raydan.

The second piece of evidence from this century contains the first known reference by name to the kingdom of Aksum and the first historical name of a king. It comes from the Periplus, which described the Ptolemaic trading stations. The Greek author, who was writing a navigator's description of the coast for sailors, speaks of the port of Adulis and then goes on to state that eight days' journey into the interior lies the capital of the kingdom of Aksum through which came the ivory from the other side of the Nile—by which he probably meant the Takkaze—for export to Rome. From the islands around Adulis came tortoise-shell. The King was one Zoscales, who was 'miserly in his ways and always striving for more, but otherwise upright and acquainted with Greek literature'. Thus the kingdom which was the forerunner of the modern Ethiopia first enters history, not gradually from the modest beginnings of a barbarian tribe, but as an established power sharing in the commerce and culture of the ancient world. It may be noted, as the first point in the long and controversial story of the Ethiopian claim to the Red Sea coast, that, though the Greek sailor ascribes a long strip of this coast to the government of Zoscales, yet ships were bound to anchor off the island of Adulis to escape the attacks of the barbarous natives of the mainland. Presumably at this time, as for most of the succeeding centuries, the highlanders were unable to incorporate or even subject the lowlands, so that trade between the mountain kingdom and the coast was a hazardous proceeding, only to be achieved by strong caravans. . . .

It has been said that Ethiopia was cut off from the world from the time of the Muslim advance of the seventh century to the beginning of the sixteenth. This is true as a rough generalization. There were, of course, occasional contacts in addition to that with Alexandria. Interest was directed to a fictitious letter supposed to have been written by the ruler Prester (Priest) John to the Emperor Manuel Comnenus in 1165. There was another letter which must have been meant for the Negus written by a Pope in 1177 and addressed to 'John, the illustrious and magnificent king of the Indians'. In 1441 another Pope, in contact with Ethiopia through Alexandria, thought he had secured the adherence of the country to the Roman church, a claim which appears to have been unknown to Ethiopia. Ethiopians also went to Jerusalem where they had been given some religious privileges by Saladin. . . .

In 1520 the Portuguese sent their famous embassy which carried the chaplain Father Francisco Alvarez, who afterwards recorded the story. We have from two men on the expedition a fuller account than his of the dramatic meeting on the shore at Massawa. Here the Portuguese found the Moors holding the island of Dahlak, while the Christians under the great lord of the northern province, the Bahr-Nagash (King of the Sea), were on the mainland. Both parties fled as the ships approached. Then some men were seen coming out in a canoe up to the brigantine to ask who had come.

'Christians,' was the answer, 'vassals of the King of Portugal.' Very great was the joy of the two of them and they kissed their feet when they heard this, and kept saying nothing but 'Christian, Christian, Jesus Christ, Son of Saint Mary', kissing their garments and begging them to take them to the Captain Major.

It was, indeed, a great moment in Ethiopian history when these long-isolated Christians of Africa met these Christians from another world coming in power to help and comfort them. As Gibbon drily remarks: 'In the first moments of their interview the subjects of Rome and of Alexandria observed the resemblance, rather than the difference, of their faith. . . .' It is sad to reflect how soon the happiness of the meeting was to be lost in sectarian hatred.

Some fifteen Portuguese were detached to go into the interior. Among them was Alvarez, whose description of the country, based upon a six years' visit, is one of the best accounts of Ethiopia ever compiled. He appears to have been a quiet, tactful man, deeply versed in ecclesiastical practice but wholly without narrowness or intolerance. He brought to Ethiopia an open mind and he writes with quiet common sense, neither seeking nor finding any very dramatic contrasts between this remote African kingdom and his own Portugal. He describes the country as it was at the end of the middle ages and as, especially in many of its institutions, it remained with very little change almost until our own day. He thus occupies an intermediate position of great value to the historian who wishes to look either backwards into the medieval period or forwards into the coming centuries. It is this which makes his book so useful, especially for those studying the origin and character of Ethiopian institutions. This use of Alvarez must not, however, be anticipated in this section, which must be confined to an outline of political events.

Alvarez reveals Ethiopia to us as it was, on the very eve of the most destructive of the Muslim invasions, and probably at the highest point of civilization and prosperity that it has reached since the decline from the impressive if narrowly based achievement of Aksum; it was certainly the highest point relatively to contemporary standards of European civilization.

The embassy went over the mountains through the country of the Bahr-nagash, which appears to have been more fully populated then than it is now, and into Tigre. Everywhere in this northern region they saw churches and multitudes of priests and monks; they passed through 'well-tilled fields of wheat, barley and millet, pulse, lentils, and all other sorts of vegetables', and 'with tillage and fallow as in Portugal, there were fine herds of cattle, horses, mules and fowls'. The travellers admired the antiquities of Aksum: they passed on through the lordships of nobles, princes, and princesses of the church and of the Emperor himself; they saw one of the great feasts of raw meat on plates of bread, and, finally reaching Shoa through Angot, they approached the Emperor (whom they call the Prester, though he was not, of course, a priest) in his vast, moving capital of tents. There are magnificent descriptions of this, with its central portion curtained off for the king. Within this, or nearby, were tents for the queen; for the treasury; for two churches; for the royal wardrobe; for the court of justice; for the prison; for the pages and the kitchens. Every great lord and the Abuna had his own group of tents, each like a small town. There was a market place in which the Moors handled all the trade except that in food. The king was surrounded with all the splendour and luxury possible under such conditions and served by hundreds of courtiers, dressed in beautiful muslins and silks from the east. Even the horses wore diadems and plumes, and four lions bound in great gold chains were paraded. The envoys were treated to 'an infinite quantity of bread and wine and many dainties of meat of various kinds and very well arranged and a calf whole in bread, that is to say, in a pie, so well dressed that we could not get tired of it'.

Their welcome was not, however, one of undiluted cordiality. The king frequently put off seeing them and pestered them for presents like any petty African chief. Once, however, the meeting had taken place, Lebna Dengel and his courtiers showed their dominant interest in ecclesiastical matters in prolonged talks with Alvarez, during which they questioned him closely and eagerly about the history, doctrine, and ritual of his church. The Emperor gave him a church-tent of brocade and Mecca velvet, and himself attended matins and mass in it and approved highly the Frankish forms of service.

Alvarez did not penetrate into the west of the country; from Amhara he went south into Shoa. From his description we learn that during the medieval centuries the Ethiopian kingdom had been greatly extended southwards and had assimilated the Hamitic-speaking peoples of what is now central Ethiopia. The great provinces of Tigre, Amhara, Gojjam, and Shoa had, of course, taken shape long before. In the south were the Hamitic border kingdoms of Enarea, Gurage, and Kaffa, all independent of the Emperor. At the same time the Muslim peril was growing in the east and it was upon their mutual fear of this threat that Portugal hoped to find common ground with this Christian nation which held a citadel right upon the Muslim frontiers. The Emperor's lordship went no further north than Massawa and even the immediate hinterland here was largely Muslim. The Danakil were independent. The kingdoms of Fatigar and Adel, of which the latter was much the more important and dangerous, lay close to Ethiopia on the east, while in the north-west the last remnants of Nubian Christianity were disappearing under the advancing Muslims who, in this period, established the kingdom of Sennar near the fringes of Ethiopia on the middle reaches of the Blue Nile. The Ethiopians had little to fear from the pagan blacks on the western side or from the old Hamitic kingdoms still surviving in the south. . . .

After six years the Portuguese envoys at last took their leave, extricating themselves with difficulty from the tenacious hospitality of the Ethiopians. The Emperor, in a letter to the king of Portugal, paid a tribute to Alvarez, whom, with perfect accuracy, he called 'a just man and very truthful in speech'. The Portuguese reached home safely and Alvarez wrote the book which, published in 1540, at last dispelled Europe's ignorance about Ethiopia.

The Muslim enemy had, however, realized the danger which this mission represented. The Ottoman Turks were on the move and new vigour and fanaticism were running through the Muslim world. It was essential to them that their Portuguese enemies should not link up with this Christian outpost in Africa. They set to work to cut off such contacts as Ethiopia still had with the sea. By agreement with Cairo it had been possible to send regular pilgrimages to Jerusalem, but soon after the Portuguese mission arrived in Ethiopia a large party of pilgrims was massacred by the Muslims in north-eastern Tigre. This was a grim warning. In 1527, soon after the Portuguese left Ethiopia, the armies of Adel attacked. They had two great advantages. They were under the command of a very able leader, Muhammed Gran (the left-handed) the governor of Zeila, who had entered into an alliance with the Turks. Secondly, they possessed firearms, new and terrifying weapons in those parts. These were carried by trained Turkish soldiers, and the army was also reinforced from Arabia. The result was the most dreadful disaster Ethiopia had ever suffered. The Muslims gained an easy victory and proceeded to reduce and ravage the whole country. It is impossible to estimate how much of its civilization, represented in the stone buildings, churches, and monasteries and all the other accumulated treasures of the middle ages, including the manuscripts, was destroyed. The king became a fugitive in the mountains and it is said that the majority of the people accepted the faith as well as the yoke of the Muslims. . . .

The Portuguese had been tardy in giving help to Ethiopia but their great impulse of imperial energy had not yet passed and they acted vigorously. Penetrating the screen of sea-power the Turks had thrown over the Red Sea, the son of Vasco da Gama, Christopher, landed at Massawa in 1451, with four hundred men with matchlocks. Grañ, however, borrowed 900

Turks from those holding Arabia and destroyed the bulk of the European force and killed da Gama. It was now that the Portuguese showed their true metal. The remnants of the force, in co-operation with Lebna Dengel's son, Galaudeiros, built up a new army in the mountains, equipped with firearms which had been held in reserve and using gunpowder which one of them succeeded in making from local materials. In a surprise attack in 1543 on Gran's camp they killed this formidable enemy and gained a complete victory.

This meant the end of the direct threat by the Muslim armies from Adel. The Muslim tide ebbed back as quickly as it had come. This was fortunate indeed, as the Turks now dominated the whole coast line and had completely seized Massawa, thus cutting Ethiopia off from further external aid. The new king Galaudeiros set to work to build up the royal power and restore the ravaged country and its church. He had some success, but the attacks from Adel had opened the way to another enemy, of whom we shall hear much. East and south of Shoa a number of pastoral, Hamitic tribes, pagan except where they were beginning to come under Muslim influence, had collected after migrating, it seems, from Arabia and the Somali coast. Though they had no unity they were known collectively as the Gallas, or Oromo. . . .

The theme of the attempted conversion of Ethiopia to Roman Catholicism is, of course, given from the point of view of the missionaries, and since it left little behind it but dislike and suspicion towards their church, it may be very quickly summarized.

The attempt began, as far as serious evangelization is concerned, in the reign of Galaudeiros (1540–59), when Andrea de Oviedo and several priests arrived in the country in 1557. Their teaching had no effect upon the vigorous and theologically effective Galaudeiros, or upon his brother Minas (1559–63), who tried to stamp out the beginnings of the Roman faith which the Portuguese soldiers had, in limited and scattered fashion, begun to introduce. Minas's son, Sarsa Dengel (1563–1596), was, however, more tolerant, even though, in a reign of constant wars with the Gallas and with Adel, he gave no credence himself to the new faith. Oviedo was succeeded by another Jesuit, Paez, who, after he had, with wonderful patience and diplomacy, worked his way in through the Muslim barrier, set himself with great skill to earn the respect of the Ethiopians as a schoolmaster, an expert in both their languages, and a craftsman. Working himself as a designer and master-mason, he built for the Emperor a two-storied palace near Lake Tana, much to the astonishment of the Ethiopians who, having no name for such a phenomenon, called it 'a house upon a house'. He succeeded in converting the Emperor Za Dengel, but this ruler's efforts to extend the religion by the use of his royal power stirred the chiefs and the church to a rebellion in which he was killed.

His successor Susenyos (1607–32) was also converted by Paez and, after first attending to wars with the Agaus and Gallas, he proclaimed his conversion. Unfortunately for the Jesuits, Paez upon his death was succeeded by the intemperate and rigid Mendez, who found his way in across the land of the Danakil. There followed some wretched years of reiterated rebellions against the king, and this at the very moment when the Galla menace demanded unity. At last, wearied by the misery of his kingdom and impressed by the tenacity with which his people fought for their national church, Susenyos abandoned his policy and abdicated.

He was succeeded by his son Fasilidas (1632–67), who decreed the suppression of Roman Catholicism and the banishment of the Jesuits. Some of these, led by Mendez himself, took refuge with the Bahr-nagash who, in the tradition of his office, was in revolt against the Emperor. He was coerced, however, into giving them up. He sold them to the Muslim governor of Suakim from whom they were ransomed by the Spanish Government. Those who were still hiding with Ethiopian converts were hunted out and executed with their hosts.

Rome could not at first accept defeat and several attempts were made to send new missionaries to this obstinate people. They were killed by the Muslims who guarded all the approaches and who were even encouraged by Fasilidas to act in this way. In the reign of his son two small parties of friars did manage to reach the country, but, as soon as they were detected, they were stoned to death. The Ethiopians, inaccessible, conservative, and tenacious in their ancient faith, thus defeated the revived and militant Roman church in its attempts which lasted for more than a century, and which enriched the roll of martyrs.

Fasilidas was a firm ruler. He waged constant war against the Gallas in the attempt to stem the tide of their advance. He restored the great church at Aksum which the Muslims had partially destroyed, and he used Gondar in Bagemdir as his capital. His son John maintained the prohibition against the entry of Europeans and was mainly taken up with disputes with the native theologians 'whose languid faith', according to Gibbon, had been 'inflamed by the exercise of dispute' with the Roman Catholics. The reign of his son Yasus (1682–1706) was marked by two abortive attempts by Louis XIV to open up relations with Ethiopia. Yasus was an able administrator and reformer and stands out all the more because he was the last strong king before a prolonged period of confusion and decline....

This barren and squalid period of Ethiopian history can be summarized very shortly here. The eighteenth century saw Yasus the Great succeeded by his son Takla Haimanot, who was very shortly murdered by conspirators. After another brief reign of his uncle in 1709 the line of Solomon was deposed and the lord of Tigre was set up as Emperor. This interregnum lasted only five years, at the end of which, such was the strength of Ethiopian royalty, the line of Solomon was restored in the person of Dawit, called the Inexorable. He showed this character by massacring the monks of the famous Shoan monastery of Debra Libanos because they disagreed with him upon a theological point of great refinement. After five years, in 1729, he died, leaving behind an infant son Yasus II (1729–53) who, after a long minority, grew up to be a weak and vain young man, wholly unable to control a kingdom that was rapidly going to pieces before the rivalries of the nobles and turbulence of the Gallas, large numbers of whom were now strongly established inside as well as just outside the frontiers. In 1753 Yasus II was succeeded by his young son Yoas. The Gallas now seized their chance. Dawit had raised a Galla to be his chief minister and governor of Damot, and this man's son Fasil seized the succession to this office by force and his Galla army became a power to be reckoned with. Meanwhile, Yoas's mother was a Galla and she brought all her relations into high office. The Ethiopian nobility raged at the elevation of people whom they regarded as semi-barbarians. Midael, the able and ruthless governor of Tigre, put himself at their head, murdered Yoas and set up another Solomonian puppet whom he discarded in turn and poisoned after a brief tenure, replacing him by his son Takla Haimanot II.

Most of these characters come to vivid and dramatic life in the pages of James Bruce, the Scottish explorer who arrived at this time, 1769, in Gondar. It is disappointing that such a full and able narrator should have been given such a sorry story to tell. For the whole of the two years that he spent in the country as a courtier and, indeed, an official of the friendly young monarch and his terrible master, Ras Midael, he can describe little besides wars, conspiracies, treacheries, and bloody reprisals: men were massacred, tortured, chopped to pieces, flayed alive. The picture is relieved only by his admiration for individual Ethiopians and his friendship with them. At last, sickened as he says with the perpetual bloodshed—'I at last scarce ever went out, and nothing occupied my thoughts but how to escape from this bloody country'—he at length succeeded in leaving and returned safely to Scotland. He wrote, years later, those enthralling volumes which are almost our only external evidence for the eighteenth century and he brought back a most precious collection of Ethiopian chronicles and other documents. His record, even though it deals with a period of decadence, provides us with much valuable evidence about Ethiopian institutions.

Bruce maintains that the Shoan princes deliberately admitted the Galla flood into Wallaga so as to increase their independence by cutting themselves off in this way from the control of decadent Gondar. Yet—a striking tribute to their loyalty to the reigning branch of the royal dynasty to which they also claimed to belong—they did not attempt to break away from their allegiance and sent troops to Gondar when required. The Emperor on his side always showed 'great tenderness and distinction' to the people of Shoa, since from this kingdom his own dynasty, protected from the Zagwe usurpers, had been restored by the efforts of the great Shoan and national saint, Takla Haimanot.

The period that follows is, if anything, even more dismal and confused than the preceding years. The country did, indeed, fall to pieces. At the beginning of the nineteenth century there appeared at one time to be no less than six men claiming to be Emperor. The great provinces became practically independent. The Gallas had now come between Shoa and the other provinces, and the ambitious dynasty of Shoa, which claimed Solomonian descent, had built up there a position of de facto independence. In the north emperors were made and unmade, the imperial rulers now being puppet kings in the hands of the lords of the great provinces. By the middle of the nineteenth century the main contestants were Ras Ali of Gondar, a mayor of the palace of Galla blood, the Ras of Tigre, and the ruler of Shoa. It was at this moment that an adventurer who had built up for himself a private army by successful brigandage along the north-western frontier suddenly emerged. Ras Ali, having failed to put him down, temporized, giving him his daughter in marriage. After Ras Ali's death this man, Kassa, in 1855 coerced the Abuna into crowning him Emperor under the name of Tewodros, which may be translated here into its European form of Theodore, by which he is well known. The character of the man and still more the renewed contacts with the outside world which now took place make the beginning of his reign a proper point at which to begin the modern history of Ethiopia.

30. The conversion of the kingdom

A. H. M. JONES and ELIZABETH MONROE *A History of Ethiopia* Clarendon Press, Oxford 1960; pages 26–9

. . . The story of the evangelization of Abyssinia is thus told by Rufinus:

One Metrodorus, a philosopher, is said to have penetrated to further India in order to view places and see the world. Inspired by his example, one Meropius, a philosopher of Tyre, wished to visit India with a similar object, taking with him two small boys who were related to him and whom he was educating in humane studies. The younger of these was called Aedesius, the other Frumentius. When, having seen and taken note of what his soul fed upon, the philosopher had begun to return, the ship on which he travelled put in for water or some other necessary at a certain port. It is the custom of the barbarians of these parts that, if ever the neighbouring tribes report that their treaty with the Romans is broken, all Romans found among them should be massacred. The philosopher's ship was boarded; all with himself were put to the sword. The boys were found studying under a tree and preparing their lessons, and, preserved by the mercy of the barbarians, were taken to the king. He made one of them, Aedesius, his cupbearer. Frumentius, whom he had perceived to be sagacious and prudent, he made his treasurer and secretary. Thereafter they were held in great honour and affection by the king. The king died, leaving his wife with an infant son as heir of the bereaved kingdom. He gave the young men liberty to do what they pleased but the queen besought them with tears, since she had no more faithful subjects in the whole kingdom, to share with her the cares of governing the kingdom until her son should grow up, especially Frumentius, whose ability was equal to guiding the kingdom—for the other, though loyal and honest of heart, was simple. While they lived there and Frumentius held the reins of government in his hands, God stirred up his heart and he began to search out with care those of the Roman merchants who were Christians and to give them great influence and to urge them to establish in various places conventicles to which they might resort for prayer in the Roman manner. He himself, moreover, did the same and so encouraged the others, attracting them with his favour and his benefits, providing them with whatever was needed, supplying sites for buildings and other necessaries, and in every way promoting the growth of the seed of Christianity in the country. When the prince for whom they exercised the regency had grown up, they completed and faithfully delivered over their trust, and, though the queen and her son sought greatly to detain them and begged them to remain, returned to the Roman Empire. Aedesius hastened to Tyre to revisit his parents and relatives. Frumentius went to Alexandria, saying that it was not right to hide the work of God. He laid the whole affair before the bishop and urged him to look for some worthy man to send as bishop over the many Christians already congregated and the churches built on barbarian soil. Then Athanasius (for he had recently assumed the episcopate), having carefully weighed and considered Frumentius' words and deeds, declared in a council of the priests: 'What other man shall we find in whom the Spirit of God is as in thee, who can accomplish these things?' And he consecrated him and bade him return in the grace of God whence he had come. And when he had arrived in India as bishop, such grace is said to have been given to him by God that apostolic miracles were wrought by him and a countless number of barbarians were converted by him to the faith. From which time Christian peoples and churches have been created in the parts of India, and the priesthood has begun. These facts I know not from vulgar report but from the mouth of Aedesius himself, who had been Frumentius' companion and was later made a priest in Tyre.

There is no doubt that this romantic story is authentic, for Rufinus lived in the latter part of the fourth century and may well have spoken with Aedesius, then an old man. The story is, moreover, supported by other pieces of evidence which prove that Rufinus' 'India' is Abyssinia, and that the king who took Frumentius and Aedesius into his service was Ella Amida, and that the prince for whom they executed the regency was Aeizanas. The first confirmatory piece of evidence is a letter, cited by Athanasius, directed by the emperor Constantius to 'his most precious brothers' Aeizanas and Sazanas (who is mentioned in Aeizanas' trilingual inscription), dynasts of the Axumites. Frumentius, it will be remembered, had been consecrated by Athanasius, the champion of the Nicene faith, shortly after he became patriarch of Alexandria in 328. Since that date the tide had turned in ecclesiastical affairs; the Arian faith now triumphed under the patronage of Constantius, and Athanasius had been expelled from the chair of Alexandria. The object of Constantius' letter is to urge Aeizanas to send Frumentius to Alexandria to be examined in the faith by George of Cappadocia, who supplanted Athanasius as patriarch of Alexandria in A.D. 356. The emperor's attempt to make Frumentius subscribe to the Arian faith does not seem to have been successful.

The second piece of evidence is the already mentioned inscription of Aeizanas commemorating the conquest of the Nubians. In this inscription he no longer styles himself 'son of the unconquered Mahrem' but simply 'son of Ella Amida, the unconquered', and he attributes his victories not, as heretofore, to his tutelary god Mahrem, but to 'the Lord of the Heavens who has power over all beings in heaven and earth'. This phrase is not perhaps quite explicit evidence of Christianity, but the coins of Aeizanas show that it is to be interpreted in a Christian sense. His early coins bear the pagan symbol of the crescent and the disk, his later coins bear the cross. It appears then that Frumentius, on his return to Axum as bishop, succeeded in converting the king to Christianity, not immediately, for the majority of Aeizanas' inscriptions and coins are pagan, but towards the end of his reign. The fact that this, Frumentius' crowning achievement, is not mentioned in Rufinus' story is good evidence of its authenticity. Aedesius, Rufinus' informant, could tell him of the part of Frumentius' career which he himself had witnessed; of his later evangelical work he had only the vaguest reports.

The Abyssinian story of their own conversion agrees substantially with Rufinus' account. A slight difficulty is caused in the Abyssinian account by the fact that they have applied to themselves, with all the other biblical references to Ethiopia, the famous story of Philip and the eunuch. Queen Candace as a matter of fact ruled in Meroe and was queen of Nubia and not of Abyssinia. The author of Acts, furthermore, never states that she was converted, and in point of fact Nubia remained pagan some two centuries after Abyssinia was converted. Abyssinian tradition, however, asserted that the eunuch whom Philip baptized had evangelized Abyssinia in the apostolic age. This was embarrassing, for it left Frumentius very little to do. The difficulty was successfully circumvented. The Abyssinians, it appears, received the true faith from the eunuch of Queen Candace, but, since he had never been consecrated bishop, they lacked the priesthood and the sacraments. Frumentius, or as he is more commonly called in the Abyssinian stories, Abba Salama (the father of peace), finding them already orthodox, had only to introduce to them the sacraments. . . .

31. Medieval civilisation

A. H. M. JONES and ELIZABETH MONROE *A History of Ethiopia* Clarendon Press, Oxford 1960; pages 63–7

. . . The official title of the King of Abyssinia was, and still is, Negusa Nagast, or king of kings, of Ethiopia. His grandiloquent title is justified by the fact that he ruled over an agglomeration of petty kingdoms. Some of them were ruled by hereditary kings, tributary vassals of the king of kings. This applied especially to the outlying pagan and Moslem kingdoms to the south and east. The king endeavoured to attach these subordinate royal families to himself by marrying their daughters; the polygamy which this policy involved was to a certain extent atoned for by the conversion of the princesses to Christianity. The policy was by no means always successful. Alvarez states that the wars of Lebna Dengel's reign were caused by his having refused to marry the daughter of the king of Hadya on the ground that she had projecting front teeth; having been converted to Christianity she could not be restored to her Moslem father and was married to one of the Abyssinian nobility, an insult which was deeply resented. The policy also led to the curious result that the daughter of a Moslem king might be regent of Abyssinia; for during a minority the queen-mother ruled. In fact Helena, who first opened negotiations with the Portuguese, was daughter of the Moslem king of Doaro. No evil effects seem to have followed from this; Helena indeed was an excellent ruler.

In the central parts of the kingdom the tributary kingdoms had long been reduced to provinces. They were still called kingdoms. Some of the governors, the Bahrnagas, for instance, or Kings of the Sea, who ruled the maritime province, were still styled kings. But they ruled at the king's pleasure; during Alvarez's stay four successive governors ruled the maritime province. The same applied to the subordinate governors to whom Alvarez gives the titles of ras and shum. They were not allowed to leave their lands save on a summons from the king, and if a summons came they went to court carrying their families and possessions with them, for they did not know if they would return. On arrival at court they encamped on the outskirts and awaited a message from the king. They might wait ignored for several months. In the meanwhile they went about stripped to the waist. On receiving their summons they presented themselves, still stripped to the waist, and having at last learned for what purpose they had been summoned and whether they were to be confined in their governments or dismissed, they resumed their normal clothes. According to Alvarez changes were very frequently made and the power of the king was absolute.

Each ras and shum was responsible for the military contingent of his district. When Alvarez was at court he constantly saw them arriving with bodies of troops and being dispatched to the seat of war. The governor was responsible for the tribute of the whole province, each subordinate governor paying his quota to him. Alvarez witnessed the payment of the tribute of the kingdoms of Gojjam, Tigré, and Bahrmedr (the maritime province). The kingdom of Gojjam had belonged to the queen-mother Helena and, as she had recently died and no governor had been appointed, one of the Favourites, the principal ministers of the kingdom, collected and delivered the tribute. He presented himself stripped to the waist a little way from the king's tent and cried three times, 'Sire!' The reply came, 'Who are you?' He answered, 'I who call am the smallest of your house, I am he who saddles your mules and bridles your baggage mules, I serve you in whatever you command. I bring you, Sire, what you commanded me.' The reply was given, 'Pass on', and he advanced followed by the tribute. First came three thousand horses, then three thousand mules. There followed three thousand men each carrying a heavy cotton cloth, such as were used as blankets, then three thousand men each carrying ten light cotton cloths. At the end came three men each carrying a tray covered with green and red cloths; on them was the gold tribute, which was thirty thousand ouquias. The whole procession took ten days to pass. The tribute of Tigré and Bahrmedr was presented in similar form. It consisted of horses and silks and stuffs. This pageant was no doubt arranged to impress the Portuguese embassy and it produced the desired effect. Alvarez comments indeed on the very poor quality of the horses and mules, but the quantity and richness of the stuffs amazed him. It may be noted that there was no currency in Abyssinia. The tribute was collected in kind. For purposes of trade blocks of salt, and in some districts lumps of iron, were still used as they had been in the days of Cosmas.

The king's revenue greatly exceeded his expenditure. His expenditure was very small. His army consisted of bodies of men at arms provided by the governors, rases, and shums at their own expense. The troops in so far as they did not live on the country brought their own provisions with them when on campaign. The governors of all grades lived on the tribute of certain villages in their governments which were assigned for their maintenance. The great officers of state were similarly maintained by fiefs granted to them by the king. The abuna and the churches and monasteries were supported by other villages and lands; these were held in perpetuity and not like the fiefs of the secular lords at the king's pleasure. All the rest of the land belonged to the king and paid tribute to him. The only regular expense which fell on the king was the maintenance of himself and his immediate entourage. He was of course expected to reward his officers with lavish gifts from time to time. He also sent gifts to neighbouring kings periodically, but in this way he normally got as much as he gave; the only unreciprocated gifts were those sent to the patriarch of Alexandria and the sultan of Egypt, for which the king got nothing in return save a new abuna. The king constantly made lavish donations to the Church, building new monasteries and churches and enriching those that already existed with gold and silks and stuffs. But a large surplus remained which was hoarded in pits and caves scattered about the country or in impregnable ambas. Peter de Covilham assured Alvarez that in one of these caches, which was near his own house, there was enough gold to buy the world; every year he had seen a large quantity put in and he never saw any taken out.

The exact extent of the territory ruled by the Abyssinian king at this date is rather difficult to determine from Alvarez's account. Bahrmedr stretched according to him to the neighbourhood of Suakim—he is not clear whether it included this town or not. On its way to seek the king the embassy passed through the kingdoms of Tigré, Amhara, Angot, and Shoa. Later Alvarez paid a visit to the court when it was in the kingdom of Fatigar, and passed an Easter on the borders of Goragé, which was an unsubdued pagan district. Alvarez never visited the western half of the Abyssinian dominions and he is rather vague about these regions. He heard of the important kingdoms of Begamedr and Gojjam and Damot, the last only partly converted to Christianity, and beyond Damot he heard vague stories of Gafat, a pagan country still apparently unsubdued. He does not mention the rich kingdom of Dambya around Lake Tsana, but he heard of the existence of Christian Nubians northwest of Abyssinia. The Christianity of Nubia was at this time in its final agony. During the stay of the Portuguese embassy the Nubians sent an embassy to the king of Abyssinia begging him to send them priests; for they had lost touch with Egypt, whence they got their bishops. The king in a rather uncharitable spirit refused, saying that he got his abuna from Egypt, how then could he give priests since another gave them to him? It was about this time that the Moslem kingdom of Sennar was established on the north-west frontier of Abyssinia. . . .

32. The Moslem invaders and the Portuguese

EDWARD ULLENDORFF *The Ethiopians* Oxford University Press 1965; pages 71–8

The reign of Lebna Dengel (1508–40), Na'od's son, began under the regency of the Empress Helena, who continued her cautious and generally successful policy. At the same time, she was shrewd enough to realize that the tense but 'peaceful co-existence' with the Muslim strongholds on the Red Sea coast could not last for ever. She therefore acted upon a suggestion, first advanced by Pedro de Covilham, to enlist the aid of Portuguese naval forces in the dislodgement of Muslims from the Red Sea littoral. The arrival of a Portuguese exploratory mission was, however, much delayed, and it did not, in fact, reach the country till 1520 by which time the general situation had undergone profound changes.

Lebna Dengel had meanwhile assumed the reins of government and found himself opposed to the prudent course steered by the Empress Helena. The period of Lebna Dengel's rule is marked by two events of transcendent importance to the history of Ethiopia: the climax of the Muslim struggle with the Christian Empire culminating in the virtual occupation of the Abyssinian highlands, and Ethiopia's entry into relations with Europe in general and Portugal in particular.

While the Portuguese were still considering Helena's request for help, the Adalite incursions had become more audacious under the leadership of the Emir Mahfuz, the Governor of Zeila. But Lebna Dengel was ready when, in 1516, the Muslim armies moved against the foothills and highlands. He stationed his troops on both sides of the mountain gorge through which the enemy had to pass, and when he struck, the Christian success was complete: the Adalites were killed or routed and Mahfuz himself was slain. Lebna Dengel exploited his victory to the full; he invaded Adal, burning villages and fields and destroying the Sultan's castle at Zankar, a place not yet properly identified. Meanwhile a Portuguese fleet under Lope Soarez had come upon Zeila at a time when its garrison was away fighting under Mahfuz. Zeila was occupied and burnt by the Portuguese crew.

Abyssinia was overjoyed, and the young King had a hero's welcome on his return. The Ethiopian chronicles vividly describe the elimination of the Muslim menace and the confident expectation—not unreasonable at the time—that Islam in Abyssinia was *hors de combat* for ever: 'tranquillity and peace now reigned in all the dominions of the Negus'. It was in these circumstances of recent military success and renewed prosperity that the Portuguese Embassy under Rodrigo de Lima (of which we possess Alvarez's most valuable account) arrived in Ethiopia in 1520. When finally the members of the Embassy were admitted into the Imperial presence, they offered precious gifts of silk and velvet instead of the expected firearms. The King was half-hidden behind curtains like a deity; earlier requests for a Portuguese alliance were now disclaimed, and the policies once pursued by the Empress Helena were merely a dim recollection of a remote past. Six years were spent in desultory negotiations (punctuated by disagreements among members of the Mission) about a possible Portuguese occupation of the principal Red Sea ports, thus shielding Abyssinia from a threatened Turkish assault. But no agreement had been reached when the Portuguese left in 1526.

Meanwhile the sultanate of Adal was convulsed by internal struggles. The recent defeat had done grave harm to the prestige of the Walasma dynasty, whose authority was now constantly challenged by the Emirs and military commanders. The Sultan Abu Bakr had transferred the capital to Harar, possibly to extricate himself from the persistent pressure exerted by the generals who drew their principal support from the Dankali and Somali peoples. Chief among those forceful military commanders was Ahmad ibn Ibrahim (nicknamed Grañ, 'the left-handed') who soon became the effective master of the Muslim possessions in Ethiopia and assumed the title of Imam. We are fortunate in possessing a detailed eye-witness account of the Muslim conquests of the sixteenth century, with the Imam Ahmad as the central figure, written by Shihab ad-Din (*Futuh al-Habasha*, ed. by R. Basset).

Grañ had first made sure of the strength of his position in Adal and had then welded the Danakil and Somalis into a formidable striking force, inspired by the old ideal of the *jihad* and lust of conquest and plunder. He initially concentrated on limited objectives, raids and incursions into the plains and foothills, before venturing upon the distant and difficult highlands. But in 1529, three years after the departure of the abortive Portuguese Mission, he struck and inflicted a major defeat on Lebna Dengel. He was, however, unable to drive home this advantage, as his armies disintegrated, drunk with victory and booty. It was only two years later that he was finally ready to begin the great conquest and invasion which inundated nearly the entire territory of traditional Abyssinia, burning churches and monasteries and forcibly converting large numbers of Christians. Dawaro and the Shoa province were conquered in 1531, and Amhara and Lasta followed two years later. At the same time Bali and Hadya as well as the Gurage and Sidama regions fell into Grañ's hands.

The holocaust enveloped most parts of Ethiopia and brought in its train misery and murder, ruin and devastation. Much of the literary and intellectual heritage of Abyssinia was irretrievably lost, and the barbarism and brutality had an effect far transcending that age. To Ethiopians a good deal of their hard-won civilization was destroyed, while to the historian and *éthiopisant* precious documentation and irreplaceable evidence perished for ever.

When, in 1534, Grañ and his hordes reached the Tigrai, they received at least some temporary checks and setbacks, for the Tigreans were proud, courageous, and combative, and their country mountainous and inaccessible. Yet the Muslim impetus had not yet spent itself. Meanwhile, Lebna Dengel sought refuge in the unoccupied parts of the Tigrai; from there he went to Begemder and Gojjam. But both provinces were overrun by the Muslim armies and shared the common fate of spoliation and pillage. Lebna Dengel then recognized the wisdom of the policies initiated by the Empress Helena and that, having dallied for six years with the Portuguese Embassy, it might now be too late to establish his good faith with the Portuguese.

The expedient which then occurred to him was little short of ingenious, for—if our sources serve us well—he now attempted to bring the monophysite Church, without changing its character or doctrine, under the supreme jurisdiction of the Church of Rome. By this move he hoped to enlist the sympathy and active support of Portugal and other Christian powers. The tool he used for this purpose was João Bermudez, a detained member of the Portuguese Embassy, whom the King had apparently had consecrated as Abuna and then, in 1535, despatched to Europe to summon help. But before such assistance came Lebna Dengel died in 1540, exhausted, harried, and convinced of the doom of his country.

The accession to the then tottering throne of his son Claudius (Galawdewos) could not have occurred at a more inauspicious moment in the history of Ethiopia—yet within less than two years the situation had radically changed, and the final *dénouement* came so unexpectedly and with such speed that every true Ethiopian could not but see in this the outstretched arm of the God of the Old Testament, who had come to deliver his chosen people. And the deliverance came from the sea. The 400 men under Christopher da Gama had disembarked at Massawa in 1541 and, aided by the valiant Bahr Negash Yeshaq, who had held out at Debaroa, set out on their epic march into the interior. When the Portuguese contingent met the Imam Ahmad, they were successful in two encounters, but could no press their victory home. Meanwhile, Grañ asked for and obtained reinforcements from the Turkish Pasha, with which he prevailed over the Portuguese and their leader, who was put to death. But the remaining 200 Europeans had not been demoralized; they managed to join forces with the remnants of Claudius' armies and, near Lake Tana, fought what was probably—at least until recent days—the most decisive battle in the long and chequered history of Ethiopia. They smote the Muslim troops and slew Grañ himself.

Though there still followed some skirmishes, with the death of Grañ the serious Muslim menace to Ethiopia had been removed for ever. Assisted by the soldiers of a Christian country from Europe, the Ethiopians had finally saved their ancient Christian Kingdom and heritage. But the salvation had come at a very late hour: Ethiopia lay prostrate and exhausted; many of its churches and monasteries existed no longer; its clergy was weakened, and its people were either Islamized—however superficially—or terrorized and in urgent need of moral and material succour.

Adal, though greatly enfeebled, continued with harassing operations against the Ethiopians. A nephew of Ahmad Grañ moved against the plateau, but he was beaten by Claudius, who subsequently advanced on Adal and wrought much devastation. Harar was now the main Muslim stronghold in Ethiopia, and it was from there that another attack was launched which, in 1559, led to the death of the Emperor Claudius.

But despite such isolated successes the Muslims no longer constituted a serious danger to the Abyssinian Empire. By the middle of the sixteenth century the prospect of an Islamized Ethiopia had become very remote. A new threat now arose which was, at least in part, unleashed by the upheavals of recent years and which was equally damaging to Christians and Muslims: the great Galla migrations, which were to become the dominant feature during the next three centuries. The Gallas had been pushed towards the centre of the country by persistently exerted pressures from Somalis and, to a lesser extent, Danakil. The vacuum created by the long-drawn wars between Muslims and Christians and the consequent weakening of both enabled the Gallas to scale the mountain chains in the east and south of the great plateau. Some isolated Abyssinian victories scarcely stemmed or even affected the gathering momentum of this tidal wave which, by sheer force of numbers, was utterly irresistible. Abyssinians fled once again from their homes or were swallowed up in this vast immigration. Ethiopian territory became increasingly constricted, and the ethnic composition of the population underwent notable changes. The Gallas swamped most parts of the Shoa province, reached Amhara and extended to the southern and eastern regions of Lasta. They settled all along the outer fringes of the plateau in an immense semicircle, leaving untouched only the northern highlands, the area of the old Aksumite Kingdom.

The Muslims fared no better. The Gallas invaded the Harar region and settled everywhere—except in the city itself. The Imam transferred his seat to Aussa, and continued to exercise a measure of authority over Harar till the middle of the seventeenth century. The independent Emirate of Harar then continued till Menelik's conquests at the end of the last century.

The Gallas had nothing to contribute to the civilization of Ethiopia; they possessed no material or intellectual culture, and their social organization was at a far lower stage of development than that of the population among whom they settled. They were not the only cause of the depressed state into which the country now sank, but they helped to perpetuate a situation from which even a physically and spiritually exhausted Ethiopia might otherwise have been able to recover far more quickly.

Claudius' successor, Minas, had only a brief reign of four years which marked the nadir of Ethiopian power. But his son, Sarsa Dengel (1563–97), was a great warrior in the old tradition of Amda Sion. Oddly enough, he turned his major attention first to the north-west, Agaw-Falasha country, which had not been effectively subdued. His battles against the Gallas occupied almost his entire reign, but the buoyancy of this great mass of people was such that every success was purely ephemeral and brought no lasting relief to the hard-pressed Ethiopians.

In the north-east the Turkish occupation of Massawa had not been a serious embarrassment until the Turks sent a military force into the Eritrean highlands and took possession of Debaroa, the headquarters of the Bahr Negash. When the Bahr Negash Yeshaq, who had previously stood so firm in the struggle against Grañ, deserted and joined the Turks, Sarsa Dengel moved against the Ottomans and defeated them in 1578, killing both the Turkish Pasha and Yeshaq. With that the Turkish venture on the plateau collapsed; they still remained at Arkiko and Massawa in a sort of token occupation undertaken on their behalf by a local notable styled *na'ib* ('deputy').

Sarsa Dengel's forceful rule, which had brought a small

measure of recovery, was followed by the short and insignificant reigns of Ya'qob and Za-Dengel. When Susenyos (1607–32) acceded to the throne, he ushered in another era of turbulence —but this time commotion of a rather different nature.

After the victory over Grañ 100 or 150 Portuguese soldiers, the remnant of da Gama's contingent, had stayed in the country and become an integral part of the Ethiopian population. They had brought back with them João Bermudez, who still claimed to be the lawful Archbishop of the Ethiopian Church. He was, however, too uneducated to impose the Roman faith by argument and persuasion. Instead, he relied on his spurious authority, and by constant bullying and gross tactlessness made himself so obnoxious that he had to be exiled. The Society of Jesus then despatched a 'genuine' Latin Bishop, Andrew de Oviedo, together with a small mission. The Emperor Claudius explained to them that he already had a monophysite Abuna and that he had no intention of severing his ties with the See of Alexandria or of abandoning Ethiopia's ancient monophysite faith. More positively, Claudius composed a document which is known under the name of 'Confession of Claudius'. The first part is a formal exposition of the monophysite doctrine, while the second half is a defence of the special character of Abyssinian ecclesiastical customs. In this latter part Claudius is particularly anxious to rebut the Jesuit charge of the Hebraic mould of the Abyssinian Church. The value of the 'Confession' has to be judged in the light of the polemical literature of that time, which was a product of the monophysite-Catholic controversy.

The Spanish Jesuit Pero Paez, who reached Ethiopia in the first decade of the seventeenth century, was by far the most tactful and successful of Roman Catholic missionaries. He had studied the languages and customs of the country, and by his courtesy and knowledge he attained a position of high prestige. The Emperor Susenyos showed him much favour and became more and more susceptible to the influence of Paez's teaching. He relaxed prohibitions against the Roman Church, permitted proselytizing, and discouraged the observance of the Sabbath. When Paez finally induced him to be received into the Roman faith, the King no longer resisted. At that time Paez was replaced by Alphonse Mendez, who, in 1626, accepted the

Negus' formal oath of obedience to the Roman Pope. But Mendez forced him to link this personal act of submission with a general abjuration of monophysitism for his whole people. There followed an outcry, especially as Mendez had tied this conversion to an abolition of the entire Ethiopian ritual: baptism, circumcision, fasts and feasts, ordination of deacons and priests, etc. The opposition was not confined to the clergy, but included members of the Imperial family and, above all, the ordinary Abyssinian, who had no interest in, or knowledge of, doctrinal matters, yet whose life, in every phase, was deeply anchored in the national ethos of the monophysite Church and the expression it gave to the special character of people and country.

The popular commotion had been so spontaneous and the upheaval so serious that, in 1632, Susenyos was forced to revoke the Roman adherence and to proclaim the return to the old faith of the nation. He himself abdicated in favour of his son Fasiladas, who re-established the age-long union of State, Church, and Monarchy, expelled the Jesuits, and thus severed relations with the European power whose interference in the country's religious affairs was construed as an attack upon Ethiopia's independence. We now enter a period of long isolation, of suspicion of Europeans, and the growth of xenophobia. . . .

XI. EGYPT

33. Ottoman Egypt and the French invasion

S. J. SHAW *Ottoman Egypt in the Age of the French Revolution* Harvard University Press 1964; pages 3–8, 10–13

In Egypt, as elsewhere in the Ottoman Empire, the people were divided into two great classes, the ruling class of Ottomans ('Osmânlîlar), to whom the special appellation of 'Egyptians' (Mişirlîlar) was also applied, whose duty was to defend and exploit the wealth of the Sultan in order to support and maintain themselves and their master, and the vast majority of 'subjects', the Rayas, whose main function in life was to produce wealth by trade, industry and agriculture for the benefit of the Sultan and his ruling class.

At the end of the eighteenth century, the Ottoman ruling class in Egypt was organized in two interrelated hierarchies in order to carry out its functions, the official 'Ottoman hierarchy' in which the government was organized and the unofficial 'Mamlûk hierarchy' by which it actually was directed and carried out.

The Ottoman structure of government in form remained little changed from that established subsequent to the Ottoman conquest of Egypt in 1517. The powers and functions involved in fulfilling the basic duties of the ruling class were divided among four institutions of government which were parallel to those into which the Ottoman ruling class in Istanbul divided itself for similar purposes.

The functions of coordination, supervision and execution, carried out in Istanbul by the Sultan and his Grand Vezirs, were given in Egypt to a Governor, called Vâlî by the Ottomans and Pâşâ by the Egyptians, who was appointed from the Sultan's corps of Vezirs and sent to Egypt for a term of two years to represent the Sultan in the process of government. It was the duty of the Governor to transmit and diffuse the orders and decrees of the Sultan, and to supplement these with his own when they were necessary. As the representative of the Sultan, the Governor had to supervise the activities of the financial, military and religious officials of the Ottoman hierarchy in the country, to make certain that they acted in accordance with the laws (Qânûn) of the Sultan in carrying out their duties, and to punish them if they violated those laws in any way. This was accomplished mainly in the meetings of the Imperial Council (Dîvân) of Cairo, which he alone could convoke and dismiss, and whose decisions only he could legalize by issuing the necessary orders to those who had to carry them out. The Governor represented the Sultan in all official functions, and thus demonstrated both the latter's continued rule and suzerainty and the subordination of all the members of the Egyptian ruling class to him.

The military functions of government, the tasks of defending the roads and lands from attack of desert bedouins, of keeping security in town and country, of enforcing the laws of the Sultan and decrees of his Governor, were entrusted to the Ottoman military garrison in Egypt, which itself was organized in a series of military corps, the Janissary and 'Azab corps, who were the infantry, the Gönüllüyân (Cameleers), Tüfenkçiyân (Riflemen) and Çerâkise (Circassians), who moved both by foot and on horseback in pursuance of their duties. In essence, the latter two were the servants of the Governor and were instituted to carry his decrees to all parts of the land and collect taxes from the subjects into his treasury. The first two were the servants of the Imperial Council itself, as the embodiment of government in Egypt, forming the army of Egypt when required, and policing its cities and countryside in times of peace. The cavalry corps served the Governor's representatives in the countryside, the provincial governors, whose primary duties were to make sure that the lands were cultivated, the taxes collected, and the bedouins kept in their desert homes far from these sources of wealth.

The financial and administrative functions in Egypt, all the duties involved in exploiting its wealth and making certain that the revenues of the state were used in the ways decreed by the Sultan and his Governor, fell to the administrative class of Efendis and scribes, who organized their activities in the Treasury of Egypt, the instrument through which the basic objectives of Ottoman government were carried out and thus the object for which the Governor and the Military Corps were instituted and directed in their activities. It was for the scribes of the Treasury to make sure that all the sources of wealth in the domain of the Sultan were exploited; that the land was cultivated to its utmost degree; that the life-giving waters of the Nile were gathered, stored and used to the maximum extent in making the lands fertile and productive; that the artisans and traders of the cities worked their trades and exchanged their goods and created profits which could be exploited for the benefit of the state; and to exploit it—to tax each source of wealth as much as possible; to determine how much each of the Rayas should pay; and to organize the most efficient and least expensive way of collecting the Rayas' dues as taxes for the Imperial Treasury.

By the end of the eighteenth century, it was mainly through the tax farm (Iltizâm) system that the Treasury accomplished this function. Over each source, or combination of sources, of wealth a tax farm was superimposed. The tax farmer (Multezim) had to make sure that the lands were cultivated and that trade and industry were carried on as they were supposed to be. It was for the tax farmers to collect taxes and deliver them to the Treasury; and in return for this essential service they were allowed to keep a portion of their collections for themselves, as reward for their diligence and efficiency, as the equivalent of the salary which the Treasury would otherwise have had to pay to accomplish these functions. So in exploiting the wealth, the main activity of the Treasury was assigning tax farms, making certain that the tax farmers carried out their functions as they were obliged to do, and receiving the fruits of their labours. And then it was for the Treasury to take the fruit of the Sultan's wealth and to expend it in those ways which he and his Governor decreed; to pay the soldiers who defended the imperial wealth; to pay for essential services in Egypt—the maintenance of the irrigation-system—the collection of taxes—provision for the poor and the indigent as well as for all the charitable and pious services which abound in an orthodox and Muslim land; to pay the scribes themselves and the Governor and all the other officials of the state who were not rewarded by tax revenues or others given to them by the Treasury. But this was not all. Egypt was not ruled merely to support itself. Egypt was established as the granary of the Ottoman Empire as it was for the empires which previously ruled in the eastern Mediterranean. A great portion of the collections of the Treasury was used to purchase the wheat, rice and lentils which Istanbul and the western part of the Empire consumed, and also to provide the supplies and provisions which the pious and indigent inhabitants of the Holy Cities needed for survival while pursuing their noble activities. And the great annual pilgrimage to the Holy Cities, composed of pious Muslims striving to fulfil one of the principal obligations of their faith, also was supported by the Treasury of Egypt. Its food was provided, its path was protected from the bedouin inhabitant of the desert, its direction and organization was supplied by the Treasury of Egypt, and the men paid by it.

The land of Egypt was a great tax farm of the Governor. To the Sultan he paid a purchase price (câ'ize) in the same way that the tax farmers under his jurisdiction paid a price to the Treasury in return for their farms. He exploited its wealth through the Treasury just as each tax farmer exploited the cultivators and the artisans over whom his farm was superimposed. He collected its revenues and paid its expenditures just as they did. He was obliged to deliver to the Treasury of Istanbul a fixed annual amount coming from the surplus of Treasury revenues over expenditures, just as the tax farmer had to produce a surplus of tax revenues over expenses of cultivation and exploitation, and he was able to keep the balance of his collections as profit (fâ'iz) for himself in the same manner as the lowest of his tax farmers. And so the Governor of Egypt owed to his master, the Sultan, an annual 'remittance' (Irsâliyye) of money and supplies in addition to those which were sent as part of the Treasury expenditures before the surplus was determined every year. It was this 'remittance' which made the austere court of the fifteenth-century Sultans into the lavish splendour of the age of Suleyman the Magnificent and his successors after the lands of Egypt were brought under their sway. It was the wealth of Egypt produced by its governors which preserved the appearance of strength in the Ottoman Empire long after its internal structure had begun to decline, and it was to the production and exploitation of this wealth that the Sultans looked to more and more as the sole functions of their agents in Egypt.

And then, as in the Porte, there was the religious function. The law of the Sultan (Qânûn) had to conform to the principles of the religious law (Şarî'a), and the latter had to be enforced in the cases where it applied. For this, the fourth institution of the Ottoman ruling class in Egypt was composed of the learned men, the 'Ulemâ, who knew the law and the Muslim sciences to all their extent. The law was applied in courts by Qâḏîs, it was taught in schools by Müderrises, it was expounded and studied by jurisconsults (Müftîs) here as elsewhere in the Empire. And here, too, the principal offices were filled by the men of the Sultan, learned in the Ottoman way, loyal to the Sultan, determined to make certain that his other officers fulfilled his civil (Qânûn) law as well as the religious (Şarî'a) law, and themselves participating in the functions of local government to an extent which is only just becoming apparent.

Here, then, was the Ottoman structure in Egypt when Napoleon Bonaparte came upon the scene; organised to exploit the land and produce wealth for the Sultan. But there was more. While the 'Ottoman hierarchy' was maintained and controlled by officers sent from Istanbul during the sixteenth and seventeenth centuries, this had abruptly changed in the century which followed.

Throughout the eighteenth century, the bulk of the Ottoman ruling class in Egypt was in fact composed of locally based and locally trained slaves (Mamlûks) and former slaves, who organized themselves into the 'Mamlûk hierarchy' of Egypt. Composed of Armenians, Circassians, Abkaziens, Mingreliens, Georgians, Russians, Poles, Hungarians, Germans, Spaniards and Maltese, and of negroes brought from the depths of Central Africa and enslaved and trained in the same way as those who had ruled the Mamlûk Empire vanquished by the Ottomans three centuries before, this new Mamlûk hierarchy had first arisen in the middle of the seventeenth century when the Ottoman officials began to purchase and train their own slaves to fortify their authority and to enable them to better carry out their duties and responsibilities. Now the slaves had become masters and filled most of the positions in the Ottoman hierarchy. The leaders of the Mamlûk hierarchy held the Egyptian title of Emîr and the Ottoman rank of Bey with the right to display two horsetails (Tûğ) as signs of their importance. Each Emîr had his own house (Beyt) composed of slaves and freedmen who performed in his service under the direction of his Kâşif, his chief subordinate, the ablest and most skilful of his freed slaves.

Slaves were usually brought to the great markets of Cairo and Asyût by slave merchants (Cellâbûn) who transported their human chattels in caravans through the mountains of eastern Anatolia and the deserts of Syria and Sinai from Transcaucasia, and into the western and southern deserts of Egypt from the legendary lands of Sennâr and Dârfûr, in the south of the modern Sudân. Each Emîr purchased as many of these slaves as he could to enhance the strength and prestige of his house. Once entered into the entourage of an Emîr, the new slave (called Serrâc) was trained in his new religion and way of life as well as in the military and scribal arts in the same way that the Devşîrme slaves were trained as Acemî Oğlân in the palace of the Sultan in Istanbul. It was the Kâşifs, the executive officers of the Emirs, who supervised this training and conversion of the young slaves into useful servants. They were treated not as despised chattels, as were slaves in the West, but as members of the family of their master, whom they called Seyyid or Ustâz. They were accepted as his sons, and they served him in the same way as a page in the palace of a great European king or lord. They regarded each other as brothers (H̱ôşdâş) not rivals, and worked together to expand the fortunes of his house as well as their own. During and after this period of education, the Serrâc slaves were paid by their master from the treasury of his house, of which they were now integral and active parts. Led by the Emîr and the Kâşif, they formed the army of his house; they fought its battles; they attacked its enemies; they did all they could to enhance its power and prestige. . . .

So by the end of the eighteenth century, almost all the positions in the Ottoman hierarchy were held by members of the Mamlûk houses, locally maintained and locally supported, who used these positions and their revenues for their own benefit and that of their house, rather than for that of the Sultan. The leader of the strongest of the Mamlûk houses was elected as their leader, the Şeyẖ ul-Beled (Chief of the City), who thus became the real ruler of the country. By the time Bonaparte stepped on to the shores of Egypt for the first time, it was with the Şeyẖ ul-Beled he had to fight in order to conquer the land, rather than with the Ottoman Governor. For in such a situation what was the Ottoman Governor? What was the entire Ottoman hierarchy which he was supposed to direct? Only when there were a number of relatively equal Mamlûk houses struggling for predominance could the Governor have any voice at all by playing them off and throwing his support to the party which promised the most in return. Usually these promises took the form of the Governor's giving the triumphant Mamlûk houses the legal right to seize the positions and properties of their vanquished rivals in return for their payment to the Porte of the Ḥulvân 'inheritance tax'. By this device, the Porte in fact turned over to the Şeyẖ ul-Beled and his friends in the Mamlûk houses all power and authority in its structure of government in Egypt. Since the Sultan lacked the military power to enforce his presence, to back up his Governor in any more forceful activity, he ceded the Ottoman hierarchy which he had created to the Mamlûks and turned to other means to accomplish the objectives for which it had been created, the exploitation of the land, the delivery of revenues to the Porte. And during much of the eighteenth century, despite the fact that the Mamlûk houses ruled supreme in Egypt and the Ottoman governors were no more than ambassadors to the councils of the Mamlûks, by skilfully playing off the various Mamlûk houses, by collecting large payments of Ḥulvân in return for assisting and legitimizing the triumph of those Emîrs who promised the most, by letting the Mamlûks take over the whole structure of Ottoman government in Egypt and exploit it for their own benefits, and by then skimming off the cream of their profits when they died, the Porte in fact was able to secure more cash revenue from Egypt than it had been able to do during the seventeenth century, when its officials ruled as well as reigned, but in an imperial system becoming increasingly inefficient and unable to accomplish its essential objectives.

But in the end, this policy was self-defeating. The Ottoman governors could benefit from Mamlûk divisions only when several relatively equal Mamlûk houses fought for power. When one Emîr combined unusual ability with this Ottoman support, eliminated his rivals, took over their houses and properties and revenues, and ruled supreme with no opposition, then the governors had little power and the Ottomans no revenue. Increasingly in the eighteenth century this became the case, with the virtually independent regimes of 'Alî Bey el-Kebîr between 1768 and 1774, and of Murâd and Ibrâhîm Beys in the years preceding the French occupation being the outstanding examples. In these cases, the Mamlûk Şeyẖ ul-Beleds were able to make themselves independent of the Porte, to cut off all revenues including the Ḥulvân, to rule as emperors, as the Mamlûk emperors had ruled Egypt in the past. Only in such cases was the Porte stirred to more direct military action to cow the Mamlûks. The rebellion of 'Alî Bey was ended when the Porte was able to get 'Alî's chief Kâşif to betray and kill his master, and thus restore the Mamlûk divisions of power. In 1785, the dictatorial rule of Murâd and Ibrâhîm Beys and, even more important, their refusal to send Ḥulvân or anything else to the Porte led to a new Ottoman conquest of Egypt, led by the Admiral of the Ottoman fleet (Qapûdân Pâşâ), Gâzî Ḥasan Pâşâ. But even after he drove Murâd and Ibrâhîm into Upper Egypt and assumed rule in Cairo, he did not even try to restore direct Ottoman rule as it had existed in the sixteenth century. Instead, he restored the multiple Mamlûk houses so they could be manipulated by the Governor for the profit of the Porte. In the end, however, Ḥasan Pâşâ and his army were recalled to Turkey in 1786 to meet the threat of a new Russian war before he was able to complete his work. So it did not take long for Murâd and Ibrâhîm to reconstitute their house, restore their power, and rule Egypt as independently as they had before. In the last decade before the French occupation, they did indeed rule Egypt as its masters, they kept its revenues for themselves, with the weakening Ottoman state no longer able to take the direct military action needed to restore the situation. Bonaparte, in fact, was able to say he came to Egypt not only to save it from Mamlûk tyranny, but also to restore it to the control of the Sultan, whose rule had been in name only in the previous years.

XII. THE SPREAD AND INFLUENCE OF ISLAM

34. Islam and the modern world

I. M. LEWIS *Islam in Tropical Africa* Oxford University Press for International African Institute 1966; pages 76–91

(a) *The Colonial Era*

Our main purpose here will be to consider the effects of the colonial situation on the character of the relations between Muslim and non-Muslim peoples and, despite (or sometimes because of) the association of colonization with Christianity, the further consolidation and spread of Islam during this period. It need scarcely be added that this is an extremely broad question. In seeking to deal with it we shall find, as in other aspects of the development of Islam in tropical Africa, a similar range of apparently contradictory responses and reactions which reflect the diversity of circumstances and conditions in different regions and at different times during the colonial era. Notwithstanding this, however, certain broad generalizations will emerge.

The immediate effects of colonial rule naturally varied with the policies and attitudes of the colonizers, both official and unofficial, towards Islam. As well as by larger imperial concerns, these have inevitably been influenced by the degree and character of the attachment of the administering powers to Christianity, and even more significantly in practice, by the exigencies of local circumstances. Consequently, it is scarcely surprising that policy and practice should have varied considerably both among the colonial possessions of a single metropolitan power and within the same colonial territory at different periods and phases of its existence. These contrasts reflecting a necessarily pragmatic response to differing conditions are especially apparent in the early stages of colonization. Compare, for example, Leopold's initial alliance with the Arabs in the Congo with later events; or the use by Britain of Zanzibar's tenuous claims to the East African coast, with British opposition to Islam in Buganda and Central Africa.

One of the clearest and least ambiguous instances of a colonial power's direct encouragement of Islam, and not merely as a religious force, is seen in the history of the Italian colonies of Eritrea and Somalia. In these territories once the work of pacification had been completed the local administrations sought to use Islam as a means of furthering the metropolitan government's aggressive ambitions against Christian Ethiopia. Here, in fact, to a large extent, and particularly in Somalia, which was in any case solidly Muslim, the colonial situation represented a continuation, and in some respects an intensification, of the pre-colonial political circumstances. In her North African colonies, and especially in Cyrenaica, where she had Senusi nationalism to contend with, Italy's enthusiasm for Islam was more restrained. At the other extreme in the Belgian Congo, once the Arab flirtation had outgrown its utility, the administration's attitude was one of uncompromising hostility towards Islam. This, of course, was in part the result of Leopoldian clericalism, as well as the need to limit Arab trading competition, and the authorities' intolerance of Islam in this case virtually halted the spread of the new faith in an area where it had just begun to make a tangible impact.

In the British sphere, although the Kenya coast and Zanzibar have some claim, northern Nigeria and the Northern Sudan probably afford the best examples of territories where administrative sympathy and support for Islam was strongly expressed. Once the initial resistance to British control had been overcome in northern Nigeria, the agreements establishing the authority of the new rulers forbade all Christian proselytization in the Emirates, and left the field clear for further Muslim consolidation. Moreover, the incorporation of many elements of the traditional Muslim political organization in the new administrative system of indirect rule naturally enhanced the status of Islam and encouraged its wider dissemination. In the Anglo-Egyptian Sudan, after the storms and tribulations of the Mahdia were safely over, much the same position was reached.

On a much smaller scale a comparable degree of administrative partiality for the Muslim Somali of the Northern Province of Kenya (similar to that displayed in British Somaliland) led to the preferment of these nomads in their conflicts with non-Muslim Galla Boran, and helped to convince those Boran who were cut off from their traditional ritual centres that the best passport to success lay in their adopting Islam on the Somali pattern. In quite other circumstances and with different effects, where administrative attitudes towards Muslim minorities were not so favourable, the Ndendeuli of Tanganyika provide an instance of a people to many of whom Islam seemed more attractive than Christianity, since they identified the latter religion with their traditional enemies the Ngoni.

In the French West African territories the establishment of colonial rule involved widespread conflict with Islam, for in the circumstances of the extensive influence of Haji 'Umar's Tijaniyya brotherhood it was, as Richard-Molard has put it: 'the world of the *torobe* (clerics) that it was necessary to dominate entirely, or nothing at all'. While this naturally fostered the continuance of the tradition of revivalist holy wars and their redirection against the Christian colonizers, a combination of strong measures with a later practical tolerance of Islam did not prevent the eventual attainment of harmonious relations between the two sides. Official French policy towards Islam vacillated considerably, but even at its most hostile made little difference to the situation on the ground. As Gouilly has aptly remarked: 'The same men, who at Bamako or Dakar elaborated directives destined to confound "The Peril of Islam", in practice took measures which were designed to strengthen it.' And in any case, unlike the position in Leopold's Congo, many of the French officials held strongly secular and anti-clerical views which left little room for any religiously grounded intolerance of Islam. Others had come from Algeria.

If, then, official French policy was from time to time, and particularly in the first two decades of this century, deliberately concerned to restrain Muslim proselytization and ever watchful of foreign Muslim infiltration, this did not prevent the local administrative officials from reaching something of the same sort of practical understanding with their Muslim subjects as was generally achieved under British rule. Thus, even such an initially intransigent movement as that of the Muridiyya in Senegal, formed at a time when orthodox Islam supported the colonial system, later lost its militancy and devoted its energies to the intensive cultivation of ground-nuts with the benevolent approval of the French authorities. Likewise, in Britain's small

Somaliland Protectorate, where Shaikh Muhammad 'Abdille Hassan's twenty-years' *jihad* (1900–20) against the Christian Ethiopians and British affords one of the clearest instances of a Muslim protest movement which arose directly in circumstances of Christian colonization, the end of this turbulent period led eventually to a new understanding with the Administration in which Islamic institutions were respected and supported and all Christian proselytization was prohibited.

Thus, in general in those colonies where Islam was already strongly entrenched, whatever the character of the initial colonizing action, and whether or not traditional Muslim rulers were retained, as in most British possessions, or displaced, as was often the case with the more direct system of French administration,[1] the new authorities did not seek to disestablish Islam. Nor, indeed, except in the Congo, did the colonial administrations succeed in preventing proselytization or the further spread of Islam. On the contrary, the overall effect of colonization was rather generally conducive to a new expansion of the faith. And while the exclusion of Christian proselytization from the most ardently Muslim areas under British rule did not, of course, cordon these off completely from Christian influence, since, as in Northern Nigeria, Christians were frequently employed in the administrative services, almost universally the colonial administrations helped their Muslim subjects to build mosques and schools, and often directly subsidized pilgrimage to Mecca or facilitated its organization. Here administrative action was largely determined, irrespective of the official policy in vogue, by the inescapable fact that in Islam Muslims possessed a bridge mediating between the narrow particularism of traditional society and the wider impulses and requirements of modern life and economic interests.

Significantly, it was precisely in those regions where Islam was not already available to provide this vital service that the adherents of traditional African religions turned with enthusiasm to Christianity as the means to an effective participation in the wider world opened up by colonization. This was generally the situation in East Africa behind the Muslim coastal belt, and on the West African coast. In both these regions Africans

[1] The practical effects of French and British administrative policy must not, of course, be contrasted too strongly.

achieved positions of prominence in the wider supra-tribal society, not so much as in Muslim areas by success as traders and soldiers, as in the Christian Western occupations of teacher, clerk, and government official.

In areas in which both religions were represented the dichotomy between Muslim and Christian occupations was most marked where the British pattern of Indirect Rule had entrenched conservativist Islam and the young aspiring men of modernist outlook issued from the schools of the Christian missions. This division seems to have been less marked in the Sudan Republic, where British rule was more direct. The contrast was also much less striking in the French and Italian territories, where the system of administration and the 'civilizing mission' of the colonizers exerted a powerful levelling effect. These provisional generalizations, however, certainly require more detailed testing, and a comparative study of the cultural and religious backgrounds and school careers of officials and politicians in the different territories would be illuminating.

In British, French, and Italian territories a further important effect of administrative action directly favourable to Islam was the considerable, though varying, authority allowed to the Shari'a under colonial government and the widespread appointment of official *qadis* and Muslim courts whose jurisdiction was by no means restricted only to suits between professing Muslims. Moreover, in many regions the use made of the Quran for swearing witnesses has exerted a notable influence. Where the unconverted have been offered the choice of swearing on the Quran, or on the Bible, or by some 'fetish', the general tendency has been to adopt the Muslim practice.

More widely still, irrespective of particular colonial policies and administrative procedures, the *pax colonica* itself created conditions which greatly encouraged the dissemination of Islam. Prior to colonization, as we have seen, Islam had spread most successfully in circumstances of social change, of tribal interaction and dislocation, and of the extension of economic and political frontiers. With the new opportunities for trade and commerce and the greatly improved and more secure communications, both within countries and between them, it is scarcely to be wondered at that a new era of Islamic expansion should have been ushered in. The trend now, moreover, was towards individual conversion, the very personal character of which is seen in the presence of Muslims, Christians, and the adherents of traditional religions within the bosom of the same families and kinship groups.

Increased travel and trading activities, migrant labour and movement, the development of administrative and commercial towns, all these played a vital part in throwing together Muslims and non-Muslims of different tribal and ethnic groups in circumstances in which co-religionists displayed an impressive solidarity despite their differences of origin. Nothing could more persuasively demonstrate the supra-tribal character of the community of Islam, and the many advantages open to its members. Christianity, of course, and Church and other Christian associations, offered similar benefits, but not, it would seem, on the same scale or as readily.[1]

At the same time the local expansion of Islam received renewed stimulus and encouragement with the arrival of new Muslim immigrants from the Middle East and India and Pakistan, and the introduction of dynamic modern missionary movements such as the Ahmadiyya sect in West Africa and the Isma'ili and other sectarian organizations in East Africa. Although these often gave rise to new lines of division and conflict, they also brought welcome new blood.

Finally, it is essential not to overlook the obvious consideration that, especially in areas subject to dual missionary activity, the association of the colonizers with Christianity usually tended to give Islam a special appeal as the religion of resistance and independence, and this effect was enhanced by the readiness with which Islam, unlike Christianity, adapted itself to local conditions and imposed few, if any, restrictions on the formation of a local indigenous clergy. Despite some tendencies towards unorthodox developments in Islam, it is perhaps this above all which accounts for the very small number of Muslim separatist movements in Africa, in contrast to the multitude of Christian separatist churches, and explains the remarkable unity of Islam throughout tropical Africa.

Thus, the total effect of the *pax colonica*, as much involuntary as intended, was to promote an unprecedented expansion of

[1] There would seem scope here for a comparative study of the functions and success of Muslim and Christian associations.

Islam. And, as Professor Froelich justly observes for West Africa, and this also applies to a lesser extent in the other areas surveyed in this book, in half a century of European colonization Islam progressed more widely and more profoundly than in ten centuries of pre-colonial history. In this short space of time it seems probable that the number of Muslims in tropical Africa had at least doubled.

This rapid expansion has naturally not been completely uncontested, least of all by the Christian missions themselves. And, as we have seen, attachment to Christianity has furnished an important alternative avenue into the new world of larger allegiances and interests, and also another means for the expression of traditional hostilities and conflicts. This is especially evident in the contrasting cases of Ethiopia and the Sudan Republic. In the first, national integration has been pursued through the medium of the Christian culture of the dominant Amhara and the Amharic language, in opposition to the conflicting claims of scarcely less numerous but less powerful Muslim interests. In the second, it is the Muslim culture of the dominant north which has become associated with national integration at the expense of the south, where a separatist tradition was fostered under British rule and found expression through Christianity.

Conflicting religious attachments, and not merely between Islam and Christianity but also within Islam itself, have thus sometimes served to entrench traditional differences, leaving many denominational conflicts to be resolved after independence. Yet they have, at the same time, also pointed to wider loyalties and interests, and have helped to override traditional tribal particularism. From the point of view of the secular needs of the new states, this is certainly a most significant contribution; and what is perhaps most remarkable is the mutual tolerance and restraint which Muslim and Christian proselytizers have frequently displayed.

(b) *Nationalism and Independence*

The history of the role of Islam in the development of African nationalism has yet to be written. There are few studies, even in particular territories, of the political activities and alignments of Muslims, or of the influence of Pan-Islamic propaganda from Egyptian and other sources, far less any general examination of this important topic as a whole. Hence we can only conclude this brief survey by suggesting some points of comparative interest concerning the political positions associated with Islam in the growth of national movements, and the place of this religion and of its adherents in the newly independent states.

It will be apparent that the same factors which enabled Islam to act as a bridge between tribalism and the wider system of relations established under colonial rule might also be expected to give African Muslims an initial advantage over their non-Muslim countrymen in the initiation and organization of nationalist movements directed towards sovereignty and independence. Thus, particularly in West Africa, as the heirs of a commercial and partly urban tradition concerned with long-distance trade and the pilgrimage, with at the same time a fund of Muslim knowledge and some command of a written language and administrative experience in both the pre-colonial and colonial régimes, as well as often of resistance to the colonizers, local Muslims clearly possessed a unique heritage which could be applied to the development of modern nationalism. Their special advantages, moreover, lay not only in the field of ideas, organization, and communication but also in the crucial realm of finance.

These resources, of course, could only be expected to be unreservedly harnessed to modern nationalist endeavour where this aimed at goals which were fully acceptable to the interests of the Muslims concerned. Where the attainment of independence was regarded as being likely to prejudice Muslim interests, the same organizational resources and skills could equally easily be applied in a manner which radical African nationalists would regard as conservative. The manner in which the Muslim factor has operated in the growth of African nationalism, therefore, has depended very largely upon the special circumstances of Muslim interests in different territories at different times.

The recent political histories of Mali, Senegal, and also Guinea probably afford the best examples of the general coincidence of Muslim and popular nationalist aims in West Africa, while this is seen even more unequivocally in the rather different circumstances of Somaliland[1] and the Sudan Republic. On the other hand, in territories where former ruling Muslim dynasties were preserved, or immigrant Muslim communities (such as the Arabs in East Africa) were assigned a specially privileged position by the colonial administrations, they naturally tended to adopt a more conservative ideology and position. Consequently, as in Zanzibar and northern Nigeria, such specially favoured Muslim groups resisted the appeal to a wider nationalism, except when they were in a position to espouse a type of nationalism which seemed compatible with the advancement of their own particularist aims. The contrast here can perhaps be seen when the success of popular 'radical' nationalism in Mali is compared with its failure (at least up to the present) in northern Nigeria, following the French destruction of traditional Muslim power in Mali and its preservation by the British in northern Nigeria.

Nevertheless, although this distinction appears to have some value, and not least in suggesting lines along which further analysis might profitably be directed, it must not be maintained too rigidly. There is a sense, for example, in which it may be argued that nationalism in the Sudan Republic, despite its early Muslim Dinka direction, may be regarded as concerned with the conservation of northern Muslim political control. And the case of Somaliland is so unusual that it merits further brief mention.

The roots of modern popular Somali nationalism lie in the traditional cultural nationalism of this ethnic group, in which Islam has always been a vital component. From the beginning, Somali nationalism has aimed at the creation of a sovereign Somali state embracing the entire Somali population, and has consequently sought the re-unification of those parts of the nation dismembered by the colonial partition.[2] Hence, although two parts of the nation (the former British and Italian Somalilands) are now joined in the Somali Republic, the struggle to unite with the remaining three parts in French Somaliland, Ethiopia, and northern Kenya still continues. This, of course, is

[1] This term is used here to include all the Somali territories—those under Ethiopian and Kenyan jurisdiction, as well as those in French Somaliland and the Somali Republic.

[2] Prior to colonization, however, despite their strong cultural nationalism, the Somalis did not form a united political group.

the reverse of the general trend elsewhere in Africa, where the movement is not from nation to state, but from state to nation; and parallel phenomena are only found in the particularistic tribal divisions within states.

Given the particular advantages which the Somali enjoy, although they remain as yet not fully realized, it might be thought that in other new states, with their patchworks of tribes and language groups, Islam might be regarded as an aid to national integration. So far elsewhere, however, Islam seems rarely to have been viewed in this light, except in the Sudan Republic and, more questionably perhaps, to some extent in Mali and Senegal.

As far as actual Muslim participation in nationalist movements is concerned, in all areas where the religious orders were strongly developed they played a significant role. In Senegal the Muridiyya movement's change of position from militant anti-French activity to quietist co-operation was followed subsequently by pressure-group activity in favour of the *Section Française de l'Internationale Ouvrière* and later by support for Senghor's *Bloc Démocratique Sénégalais*. Again in Senegal during the crucial period between 1958 and 1960 the Muridiyya and the Tijaniyya (almost three times as strong) both aligned themselves with those who favoured the retention of strong ties with France. But the Hamallist reformist branch of the Tijaniyya developed in the years between the two world wars in the Soudan (i.e. Mali) and neighbouring French territories as a proto-nationalist vehicle of popular protest against colonial administration and Muslim compliance. It appealed most to submerged social groups, and with such a following it helped to prepare the ground for the emergence of the *Rassemblement Démocratique Africain* after the Bamako conference in 1946.

In the Sudan Republic, as might be expected, recent political developments have been more strongly influenced by the activities of the religious orders. Here the critical factor is the association between the Khatmiyya *tariqa* and the Ashiqqa party, on the one hand, and that between their rivals the Ansar (led by the Mahdi's son) and the Umma party, on the other. The *tariqas* have also similarly played an important role in Somali politics, although in this case, with the overriding strength of clan ties, their political connexions are less clear cut.

If the religious orders, by their very nature as organizations dedicated to promoting a wider sense of communal identity than that based on tribalism, have facilitated the growth and achievement of modern nationalism (and, incidentally, pointed to wider territorial regroupings of African states), where they have come to be of importance in modern politics their inter-denominational rivalries have also necessarily exerted a significant force. This is evident, as we have seen in the competition between the Khatmiyya and Ansar in the Sudan Republic, and is also apparent in West Africa in the rival attractions of the Qadiriyya and Tijaniyya. Thus, in strongly Muslim countries the *tariqas* have not only contributed in various ways to the development of nationalism as such but have also markedly affected the character of internal politics in the pre- and post-independence phases. Detailed comparison of their political roles with those of Christian organizations in areas of mixed religious affiliation would be of considerable interest.

Passing now to Islamic education, we find that traditional forms of religious teaching and schooling, while showing remarkable resilience, have naturally tended to be weakened in competition with imported forms of Western secular education. Consequently, the products of the former system, malams, shaikhs, and *qadis*, etc., have generally only identified themselves strongly with the new nationalist movements in territories such as Mali, Senegal, the Sudan Republic, and the Somali Republic (and in different circumstances in northern Nigeria), where nationalist aims and aspirations have been couched, at least partly, in Muslim terms by parties under predominantly Muslim leadership or seeking Muslim support. And even then, although their co-operation has been important, they have seldom played a leading role. Their sustained allegiance has probably been most crucial in such countries as the Sudan and Somali Republics, where Islam is a fundamental part of local culture and where the rise of modern nationalist movements was at the beginning, at least, largely independent of any large-scale economic development and trade-union activity.

By contrast, those who have had experience of the modernist centres of Muslim higher education in Egypt and North Africa seem generally to have played a more active and critical role in the generation and diffusion of nationalist ideas and also in the organization of local independent Muslim schools as instruments of educational and social reform.[1] Equally, pilgrimage to Mecca, with greatly increased participation from such outlying areas as West Africa, and the growth of local interest and involvement in such organizations as the Islamic Congress[2] fostered the wider dissemination of reformist anti-colonial ideas from the Arab World, to say nothing of the extremely significant impact of the Arab Press and Radio, particularly from Cairo.

Faced with such a militant modernist interpretation of Islam, with its ready accommodation to the secular requirements of nationalism and the modern state, the old order of clergy has tended to become a conservative force wedded to traditional forms of religious education and opposed to the extension of modern secular schooling. Hence, even in predominantly Muslim countries, despite the deep commitment of the political *élite* to Islam, this old guard has naturally not been immune from criticism and attack. Friction similarly arises over the traditional activities of holymen and the custodians of saints' shrines where these are seen as profiting from the ignorance and unsophistication of the populace. This conflict between the guardians of traditional Islam and the new more secularly orientated political leaders is highlighted by such controversies as that over the status of Arabic and the Arabic script in countries such as the Somali Republic.

At the level of ideology itself the conceptual scheme of Islam (especially in its reformist modes), if secularized sufficiently, can readily be transposed into that type of modern nationalism which is the moving spirit of Pan-Africanism. Thus, the leaders of Sekou Touré's *Parti Démocratique de Guinée*, much influenced by their experience of trade unionism and the theory of Marxism, could claim in 1954 that '. . . we are in

[1] Cheikh Touré's *Li takune mu'minan. A fin que tu deviennes Croyant* (1957) provides an interesting statement of the reformist position in Senegal at this period. Here the faithful are exhorted to join the struggle against colonialism and capitalism and against the obscurantism and extortions of venal *marabouts*.

[2] The Sixth World Islamic Conference met at Mogadishu in the Somali Republic in December 1964. Egypt and Algeria did not attend.

the pure line of Islam, conquering because humane and charitable'.[1]

In this accommodation to new circumstances and needs, in which, up to a point, the resilience of Islam is again demonstrated, the *jihad* becomes the struggle against colonialism (or neo-colonialism), the reformers become 'freedom fighters', as in Algeria, *dar al-Islam* becomes the body of sovereign African states, and *dar al-harb* those which have yet to shake off the colonialist yoke. And, stretching the analogy yet further, the unity of the community (*umma*) may be seen as the unity of the African or Afro-Asian peoples. The ideal universal state, ruled according to the precepts of Islam in which justice, equality, and brotherhood shall prevail, is transposed into the model African union organized according to the principles of 'African socialism'. These and other conceptual equivalences would seem to give the popularist ideology of Pan-Africanism (at least in the local context) a special appeal, actual or potential, among Muslim communities with a tradition of reformist or Mahdist ideas.

Once this has been said, however, it must immediately be added that these theoretical correspondences, however persuasive, have not so far been realized in any stable wider political association, despite several abortive attempts, between the Muslim and non-Muslim states of Africa and Asia. Pan-Africanism and Pan-Islamism remain two distinct, sometimes over-lapping, but never fully interlocked spheres of interest and attachment, and are both encompassed in that larger, vaguer, and even more fluid circle of alignments represented by the Afro-Asian block. And this seems likely to continue as long as a distinction is drawn within Islam between Arab and non-Arab. For those African Muslims who once vaunted their putative Arab connexions are now increasingly claiming that they are Africans.

The difficulties involved in any wider political identification are perhaps most acutely revealed in the external policies of Egypt, which sits uncomfortably athwart both worlds and aspires to a position of leadership in each. And here, of course,

[1] Quoted from *La Liberté*, 28 December 1954, by Ken Post, *The New States of West Africa*, Penguin Books, London, 1964. Sekou Touré is, of course, himself a Muslim.

the traditional attachment of states such as Ethiopia, and of many of the new African leaders to Christianity, would seem destined to help to maintain these distinctions. In inter-African affairs the real importance of these cleavages is evident in the uneasy relationships between Egypt, the Sudan, and Ethiopia, to say nothing of the problem of Somali unification, on which the often vigorously voiced support of those Muslim states outside Africa has fallen upon deaf ears as far as those of their co-religionists who live in the continent itself are concerned.[1] The understandable interest of the latter in the preservation of their own sensitive frontiers and territorial prestige, and their natural fear of comparable particularist movements at home, have restrained such sympathy as they might perhaps otherwise have felt for a cause which to Somali nevertheless appears as a positive contribution both to African and Islamic unity.

At the same time, it must also be remarked that those African countries which are officially constituted as Muslim states seem in African, as in wider extra-African, affairs to have shown little identity of interest or purpose. Often, indeed, they have adopted contrary positions on international issues (as, for example, in their attitudes towards Israel) and fallen into opposed camps in their larger allegiances, other principles of common interest exerting a greater attractive force than the bond of common adherence to Islam. Nor could it be said that their various constitutions conform in any sense to a common 'Muslim' pattern. The extent to which Islam has in any constant fashion moulded the character of their political processes, save in superficial aspects, is equally open to question, although, admittedly, this is a topic which requires much more intensive research before a considered judgment can be given. Nevertheless, the presence of Islam as a unifying culturo-religious force might be supposed to endow these states with a sufficient sense of cohesion

[1] At the same time, however, it must be remarked that at the Sixth World Islamic Conference in Mogadishu in 1964 all the African Muslim countries and communities represented (including those from West Africa) pledged themselves to support the Somali struggle for unification. Although it would be premature to assess the significance of the Conference's resolutions on this or other wider issues (such as hostility towards Israel), it seems reasonable to suggest that the mounting of the meeting itself should be seen as a Muslim attempt to emulate the Addis Ababa Pan-African Summit Conference of 1963.

to permit the existence of democratically competing political parties without danger to their national solidarity. This potential, if it is such, has so far seldom been realized very effectively, except in the Somali Republic, where there is an unusually high degree of cultural homogeneity and national cohesion.

Finally, if everywhere in tropical Africa Islam is today on the march, the wider political consequences of any great new expansion of Muslim influence and Pan-Islamic solidarity seem likely to be tempered by the increasing secularism of modern Muslim states and the general recognition that secular aims and policies are more important in the modern world than common religious interest. Moreover, today in states of mixed denomination all religions are honoured, and at state ceremonies the Muslim, the Christian, and the traditionalist join together in offering prayers and libations, each according to his fashion. As with Christianity in the West, Islamic civilization is being gradually detached from its religious roots, and the gulf between the spiritual and the secular spheres of life is widening. While, as elsewhere in the Muslim world, continuing to influence deeply the private lives of individuals, it is thus at least questionable whether Islam can be expected in the future to exercise the profound political effect it has had in earlier periods of African history.

Thus, although Islam may be regarded as a distinctive mode of life and religion, as a historical heritage, or as a general ideology of universal applicability, or, indeed, as all of these, it is increasingly on the first two, rather than on the last of these that the emphasis falls today. And the paradox is that Islam is gaining its greatest following in the history of tropical Africa at a time when its wider influence seems to be diminishing.

35. Islam in East Africa

J. SPENCER TRIMINGHAM *Islam in East Africa* Clarendon Press, Oxford 1964; pages 65–8, 70–5

. . . Islam is an *oecumene*, an intercultural system which has always sought to expand and consequently embraces all sorts of different peoples. In its response to local geographical, racial, social and political forces Islam developed clear regional sub-cultures, yet all the different regions retain a recognizable Islamic stamp. A traveller like Ibn Baṭṭūṭa traversing the whole Islamic world remained in a relatively familiar world in spite of regional differences. This unity is provided by the law, and it was the ascendancy of the law which moulded life and institutions and gave identity and continuity to the culture. As the type and nature of the people, their land, culture, and the historical conditions of Islamic penetration have given special characteristics to the Islam of the Maghrib, West Africa, Eastern Sudan, and Ethiopia, so that of East Africa also reflects historical and environmental peculiarities.

Formation of an African-Islamic Regional Culture. The process may be expressed thus:

Islam→Bantu Culture=creative tension=synthesis in the Swahili Culture.

The key to appreciation of how this culture was formed lies in understanding the relations between the thin layer of immigrants and the Bantu with whom they were associated. African culture was the passive element, and Islam brought the vital cohesive element. This always remained dominant, yet the resistance of the passive element to dominance by Islamic institutions was strong and the effect of the interaction upon the different strata of the Swahili varies considerably.

In spite of the strength of the connexion with Arabia the culture was formed independently of full Arabization. The immigrants adopted a basically Bantu language as their means of expression, mainly differentiated as kiSwahili from the languages of Nyika tribes by a vast importation of Arabic words which tended towards unification though expressed in many dialectal forms. Swahili as a literary language was cultivated by the Afro-Arabs, hence it has a greater proportion of Arabic words than the spoken language.

The process of interaction which took place was a dynamic one in that the influence of South Arabian Islamic and Bantu cultures was reciprocal. Islam dominated the life of the settlements, but the Bantu in turn modified the character and life of the community. From Islam stemmed a view of life and society which created a new community. The culture retained the decisive stamp of its South Arabian birthplace, especially in law, but in the new environment, and through intermarriage with Bantu much was absorbed from African life. Absorptions were selective and remoulded to harmonize with the basic assumptions of Islam. Elements which could not be absorbed because contrary to Islam, but which the community needed, were allowed to exist parallel to the Islamic system of life, though even these (e.g. spirit cults) developed new forms in the process.

This Islamic sub-culture stretched from the Bajun of the Banadir coast to Mozambique, and across the sea to the Comoro Islands and the northern coast of Madagascar. The community was largely static since it was only reinforced by the coming of individuals from Arabia, on the one hand, and the absorption of individual *mahaji* on the other, but did not seek to expand the range of its culture by spreading its distinctive ethos among Bantu societies.

One feature of this sub-culture is of special interest. Islam spread through the accidents of historical necessity. We do not find the same pattern exactly reproduced throughout the Islamic world, for the formation of a Muslim community like the Swahili or, and this is more general, the transformation of an existing community through its adoption of Islam, comes about through the interplay of the aggressive culture, as expressed by Muslims from particular culture areas, upon people who had been moulded in very different ways. The dynamic tension between Islam and African culture, however, finds expression in the remarkable unity of African Islamic culture. So it comes about that, although the historical aspects leading to its formation are quite different from those leading to the formation of the Islamic culture of the Sudan belt, in that Islam did not penetrate existing communities but created a new community, the resultant Afro-Islamic culture pattern is, however, much the same as in West Africa. Islam brought the same institutions which modified African life, and it was around the Islamic institutions that retained or kindred African institutions coagulated. This statement will need to be substantiated in detail in another study. In the meantime one may guard against misapprehension by pointing out that the differences between east and west African Islam are evident. These are due, from the Islamic aspect, to differences between the regions from which the influence came (South Arabia and North Africa) and, from that of the basic cultures, to differences between the local environments (Bantu and Sudanese).

The culture formed reflects both the strength and the weakness of the *sharī'a*, the equivalent of the Church as the preservative of Islam's uniqueness and distinctive ethos. It is stronger than customary law only in certain spheres. Its rigidity gives rise to parallelism. In some spheres traditional rites have been almost completely obliterated, death rites for example; in others traditional rites dominate as with marriage as a transitional rite, though with marriage as a legal institution Islamic regulations are paramount.

Parallelism. When the development of the mainstream of Islamic culture was arrested there arose the phenomenon of parallelism. Pressure of human needs led to elements of past experience which had no direct relevance to Islam or were inharmonious with its world view having to be retained. Such elements might be either neutralized or allowed to exist parallel to the orthodox system. Sufism, ultimately admitted among the Islamic sciences, was neutralized thereby, but institutional mysticism (the Sufi *ṭawā'if*) had to be allowed to exist, though frequently under attack. These, together with the associated saint-cult, represent the sub-strata of the religion of ordinary people. Orthodox religion, not providing for a pastoral office or agencies for intercession and emotional outburst, had insufficient to offer to people's deeper needs, and all this remained parallel to the orthodox institution.

When Islam spread in Africa its forms were inflexible and

therefore African religious beliefs and institutions continued alongside the new religious features. The result is a fusion in life but not a true synthesis, the unyielding nature of the Islamic institutions precluding this. The parallel elements bear the mark of their indigenous origin. Everywhere the traditional world remains real and its emotional hold vivid. The dualism this brings into religious life is evident to anyone in contact with Swahili society. Religious life rests on a double foundation, the Bantu underlayer and the Islamic superstructure. The degree to which the life of the different Swahili social groups rests upon each primary culture varies. The most evident contrast is between town and countryside (Zanzibari Arabs and waHadimu) and between classes (e.g. Arab and waZalia). On the island of Zanzibar the life of the waHadimu rests more on the old foundation, whilst that of the people of the stone town is dominated by Islam. . . .

The Swahili variant of Islamic culture was the result of the impact of a religion based on historical revelation upon African 'natural' religion. The historical character of Islam from which its unique culture derives differentiates it sharply from African religion which is timeless and natural in that it derives from nature, that is, the interaction of man and divinity is manifested in the world of nature, not, as in Islam, from the action of God in history.

Islam came with a written law from which deviation was theoretically impossible, though it did have a mythology based on *ḥadīth* and other Islamic legends which proved useful in providing a means of instruction, reconciliation and justification for Islamic practices. The religion of nature and Islam were in dynamic relationship during the years when the Swahili culture was being formed in a dialectal process in which Islam could only triumph either through assimilating African institutions like the bride-price into a corresponding Islamic institution, or, when assimilation was impossible as in possessive spirit practices, by accepting them alongside Islamic institutions. As elsewhere the Sufi *ṭawā'if* and saint veneration were a recognized part of Islamic culture. Each supplied something the community needed.

Equilibrium was attained between the Islamic and African elements in the resultant pattern of life. In this process, though social institutions remained basically African, Islam revolutionized the inner man; the repudiation of large spheres of Islamic law being in no wise incompatible with full loyalty to Islam. We have noted that the culture shows a basic similarity with other African Islamic cultures, and this is so, even though Islam came to west Africa after it had received its definitive form, whereas the Swahili communities, though marginal, grew within the general pattern of Arab Islamic culture.

By adopting Islam the African entered into history; even time changed since the Islamic calendar is not natural like the agricultural year, and parallel calendars existed, one for agriculturalists related to the sanctions underlying African institutions and the other related to those underlying Islamic institutions. The two elements making up Swahili culture are thus manifest in every sphere of life.

Acculturation was succeeded by assimilation. Such a pattern of Muslim-Swahili culture, once solidified, could not easily be disturbed. New human acquisitions from African societies added nothing, and henceforth pagans were assimilated into that culture.

Although East African Islamic culture was retarded and marginal it was successfully maintained around the unmodified core of Islam without being extinguished by assimilation. Their Islam was preserved through the maritime link which not merely brought immigrants and cultural elements, but reinforced their consciousness of belonging to another world. Later immigrants, 'Umani Arabs as well as Indians, maintained their ethnical identity. This was due in the case of the 'Umanis to racial pride and sectarianism, whilst the cultural differences between Indians and African Muslims, although not all Indians were sectarians, was too wide to be bridged.

The problem of the spread of Islam among Africans, and above all its assimilation, arises from the nature of those who should have been its chief agents. The coastalists built their Islam into a defensive cultural barrier which cut them off from Africans. They did not settle among them in the countryside, nor send out Qur'ān teachers. The later groups in interior settlements were often almost isolated, worshipped in their own mosques, and had little social intercourse with Africans. This accounts for the superficiality of conversions in the interior.

It seems evident that Arab immigrants sought to reproduce their own way of life without fundamental changes. To a considerable extent they succeeded in maintaining an Arabic-based culture. Few immigrant families continued to speak Arabic in their daily life yet they continued to think of themselves as Arabs and were dedicated to the study of Arabic as their culture language. In this they were helped by the place of Arabic in Islamic life and close links with their Hadrami homeland. It is rare for the Hadrami woman to leave her country, so obviously the immigrants, who belonged to the country and urban and not bedouin classes, became African in physical characteristics within a few generations. Also the life of the settlers was based on slave labour and their interaction with Islamized household slaves, identified with the stronger culture of their masters, yet with the Bantu linguistic environment basically stronger than Arabic, formed the Swahili-Islamic sub-culture. The 'Arabs' of the present day still strive to keep their separateness. Here there is a difference between the descendants of the older groups and the more recent immigrants. The older groups are now Swahili-speaking; the oldest have no knowledge of their tribal origins, the tribal names they claim being made up, generally east coast place names. The hereditary religious families are in a dual language situation, and they remain conscious of their Hadrami origins, in some cases keeping up relations with their kinsmen in Arabia.[1] Their distinctness is also maintained through the continual slow emigration, thus the tendency for settlements and quarters to derive from particular South Arabian clans or towns. With the 'Umanis Arabism is a matter of superior social and political status.

Although there is a complex of cultural elements in Swahili culture the Islamic predominates and within that the culture of Hadramawt. The religious detachment of the 'Umani 'Ibāḍīs, for whom 'Ibāḍiyya is their tribal religion, accounts for their

[1] Whilst new Hadrami immigrants maintain ties with their homeland to which the majority return, for those who stay, generally those who entered Zanzibar government service and those who have obtained some economic stake in the country and marry local wives, the ties become very tenuous. W. H. Ingrams writes that, 'It is estimated that over 90 per cent. [of the Hadramis in Lamu] have permanently severed their connexion with the Hadhramaut'.

lack of influence, but Arabs from Hadramawt, especially the Tarīm-Saiwūn region, established a religious ascendancy which they retained through the ʿIbāḍī political ascendancy. This is shown in such aspects as the prevalence of the Shāfiʿite *madhhab*, methods of teaching and manuals used, the derivation of the content of Swahili narrative and didactic poems, traditional hereditary clans of religious leaders, respect for *sharīfs*, and many aspects of material culture.

The people embraced by the Swahili culture comprise many separate groups, divided on status-class criteria, following the same monochrome Islam, yet exhibiting great diversity, for there are various levels of Swahili cultural consciousness. The oldest is the Shirazi; then there are the northern 'Arabs', the Manga Arabs, and the various assimilated people from the mainland. The true Swahili culture is that of the first two which developed in southern Somalia and northern coastal Kenya. The assimilation of the others varies because complete assimilation can only be achieved through intermarriage, and the extent to which this can take place varies. Some Manga have been wholly absorbed and have abandoned ʿIbāḍism. Immigrants from the mainland were assimilated haphazardly, the result of irregular immigration and individual settlement, and did not acquire internal cohesion (whereas individuals who were more closely integrated through marriage became members of an established group), fusing amorphously with the resident community as segments without being integrated with it. On the other hand, the former slave population was more integrated, having a recognized social position, wherever they maintained links with their social masters. Then there is an outer group of Swahili colonies who had lost their language and features of their culture who yet retain full awareness of their tribal origins (Makua, Yao, Zaramo, etc.) and maintain distinctive traditional traits.

Each Swahili centre and each group has its own religious outlook compounded from the parallel action of Islam and the spirit world upon their lives. Each centre, each quarter, each social class, has its own recitals of *qaṣīdas* and *maulidis*, its own dances, music, and amusements; in short, its own special atmosphere.

Apart from the insular and coastal communities this culture

is found in its fullness in the interior only at Ujiji on the shores of Lake Tanganyika. Groups of Swahilis in other centres maintain it, of course, but the position is different since they form only one element in the midst of diversification. We have shown that Islam spread inland only during the last hundred years. Large numbers of Muslims in the interior are fringe Muslims or Muslims by association; only in certain groups and in towns has Islam brought about deep changes. The reason for this seems to be that in the interior, as on the coast, its spread has been mainly by individual conversion; not through the absorption of individuals into an Islamic society, but through its adoption by individuals who continued to live in their own communities where an attempt to change tribal institutions would be resisted. This meant that the power of Islam to change was weakened. New converts adopted mainly the religious elements of Islam. It meant also that the same Swahili terminology is used everywhere. Islam, in other words, was not translated into the local idiom. The weakness of the *sharī'a*, even in communities where the cumulation of individuals has led to a large proportion of the population becoming Muslim, is due to the weakness of the follow-up by clerics with their Qur'ān schools, largely confined to towns. An intelligent and well-trained *faqīh* met in Ujiji confirmed that Islam needs an urban centre if it is really to root itself. It has had considerable influence upon the indigenous law and custom of the waJiji, but the heterogeneous nature of the waJiji accounts for this. The shaikh said that though Islam was strong in some of the nearer villages, the farther one got from the town the weaker its influence became. Though there were twelve Qur'ān schools in Ujiji town there were none in the countryside.

Sectarianism is an aspect of East African Islam which immediately strikes the visitor and contrasts with West Africa. Although the monochrome Islam we have described is that of the African Muslims whom we shall study, immigration, especially from the Indian sub-continent, has introduced Islamic sectarianism in closed groups. The Asiatic Muslims have been only slightly modified by their changed environment and unlike the Arabs have not adopted the Swahili language and culture nor married African women. They have influenced African Muslim society only slightly. In East Africa each

Islamic group lives a common social life little impinging upon that of the others. They have separate religious festivals or stress them differently. We find at Zanzibar, for example, a series of different mosques according to either sect or race: mosques for the various Shī'ī sects, the two types of Arab colonizers, and numerous mosques for African Muslims. . . .

36. Maghribi Islam: rigourism and bewilderment

ROGER LE TOURNEAU *Unity and Variety in Muslim Civilisation* (edited by von Grunebaum) Chicago University Press 1955; pages 231–9

. . . Of the establishment of the Muslim religion in North Africa, it must be confessed that we know almost nothing. The first conversions of the inhabitants cannot have been prior to the foundation of Kairouan (Qairawân) by "Uqba b. Nâfî', the generally accepted date of which is A.D. 670. The chroniclers assert, on the other hand, that in 711, when the Muslim troops left for the conquest of Spain, the Islamization of the Maghrib was practically completed; in fact, the Berber contingents, furnished especially by the tribes of northern Morocco, formed a good part of the army of Ṭâriq b. Ziyâd, and then even of Mûsâ b. Nuṣair himself. We also know that, up till the nomination of Mûsâ b. Nuṣair to the government of Ifrîqiya, the resistance of the Berbers to the Muslim conquest was very vigorous. The date of Mûsâ's nomination is controverted: at the two extremes, some place it in 698, others in 705 or 706; if it is accepted that Mûsâ took over his command right at the start of the eighth century, it must have been in barely ten years that he made Islâm triumphant in the whole Maghrib. Now we know exactly nothing about this crucial period, or about the procedures which Mûsâ followed to obtain these massive conversions, or about the doctrinal instruction which was given to the new converts. We may nevertheless suppose as entirely probable that the new believers of the tribes were very ill-instructed in their new religion: there would have to have been a veritable army of specialized missionaries to preach the doctrine appropriately, and these missionaries would have had to speak Berber and get themselves accepted by the tribes—just so many practically insurmountable difficulties. It was a different matter in the urban centres created or revived by the Muslim occupiers; there they were in some number and could easily indoctrinate the local population. Thus, from the time of the appearance of Islâm in North Africa, we see it dividing into branches completely distinct from each other—the Islâm of the cities and that of the tribes.

The first is hardly to be distinguished from the Islâm practised in the east. It was drawn from a good source, since it was often spread originally, if not by the companions of the Prophet themselves, at least by their 'followers'. Nevertheless, a few superstitions certainly remained, especially in the less-educated urban circles. By reason of circumstances it was the Mâlikî school which soon took root in North Africa, and it very soon produced illustrious masters such as the famous *qâḍî* Suḥnûn, one of the most brilliant doctors of the Mâlikî school as a whole. The light soon went out from Kairouan to illuminate other Muslim cities of the Maghrib; the Mosque of the Olive at Tunis was founded in the first half of the eighth century and probably very quickly became an important centre of study. It is not to be doubted that these hearthfires of Muslim learning sent out their rays round about and that the neighbouring tribes underwent their influence, but for a long time the cities were few; until the foundation of Fez, one can hardly find any to mention in Morocco except Tangier and Ceuta, which were quite untypical, and Walîlâ, the ancient Volubilis, a Berber hamlet rather than a real city, if one is to believe the *Rawḍ al-Qirṭâs*; in the present Algeria between Tlemcen, still very unpretentious, and Constantine there was an almost completely empty space. Ashîr, Médéa, Miliana, and Algiers were not to be born or reborn till the second half of the tenth century, under the impulse of the Zîrids; the Qal'a of the Banû Ḥammâd was not to rise from the earth till the beginning of the eleventh century. Only Ifrîqiya had a relatively great urban density. Later, when the cities became more numerous, the habits had been established and the tribes continued to live apart, in the religious sphere as elsewhere.

It is not surprising, then, that the Islâm of the tribes was very little influenced by the Islâm of the cities and that it presented very different characteristics. Having little learning, it was for long very unstable: the Khârijite doctrine was early to take the place of Sunnism in a large part of North Africa; later, Shî'ism, with the missionary Abû 'Abd Allâh, was to spring up in the confederation of the Kutâma, north of Sétif; in Morocco, as early as the middle of the eighth century, a Berber deformation of the Muslim religion, about which we are imperfectly informed, was to spread through the whole of the important confederation of the Barghawâṭa, between the Bû Ragrag and the Umm al-Rabî'. It is certain, moreover, that very strong traces of the old Berber beliefs persisted alongside or, rather, under the cover of a not very particular Islâm, as they had persisted in the time when the Maghrib was in part Christian. Unfortunately, we are reduced to conjectures on this point as on many others, for the Muslim authors do not broach these subjects, which they consider improper. We do not know, therefore, exactly what these beliefs were or to what degree they were influenced by the Muslim religion. Nevertheless, on the basis of what exists at present, it can be affirmed that there has been no lack of superstitions since the beginnings of Islâm in the Maghrib.

What also deserves to be noted is that, however uncertain, however impure it may be, this Islâm of the tribes took root immediately. It is within the framework of the Muslim religion that all the various forms of belief which have just been mentioned appeared: Shî'ism and Khârijism were Muslim—there is no need to prove it—and even the religion of the Barghawâṭa, so far as we know it, was only a counterpart of Islâm, with its Koran, its prophet, its fasts, etc; nowhere is there a return to the former paganism, even less to Christianity. The famous text of Ibn Khaldûn on the many apostasies of the Berbers applies only to the period preceding the activity of Mûsâ b. Nuṣair. We are confronted, then, with a faith very variable in its mode of appearance, very poor in point of doctrine, but very tenacious and vital from the beginning—the unquestioning faith of the poor.

For that matter, the Islâm of the tribes did not always remain unconscious of its weaknesses and its inadequacies. It must not be forgotten that the great reforming movements of the Maghrib were born in the tribes and were propagated by them: the Almoravid reform sprang up in the western Sahara and developed among the Ṣanhâjian tribes of those regions before it was carried by them to Morocco, as far as Algiers, and then to Spain; the Almohad reform saw the light among the Maṣmûdian tribes of the Upper Atlas and was propagated by them in the whole of the Maghrib and Muslim Spain. That these movements quickly took a political turn is not what matters here; what is important for us is that the Islâm of the tribes came to feel its deficiencies and to try to remedy them.

With this desire to do better, to behave better in the eyes of God, must be connected the Maghribî mystical movement. Everything proceeded as if the tribes, tired of seeing reform turning inescapably to politics, had sought elsewhere the satisfaction of their religious needs. They found it in people obsessed with the problems of the other world (*ahl al-dîn* in contrast to *ahl al-dunyâ*), unattached to the goods and the affairs of this world (*fuqarâ'*), and initiated, often on the occasion of trips to the east, into the Muslim mysticism which had long since come into existence. It could not be said, of course, that Maghribî mysticism was the monopoly of the tribes; many city people adhered to this movement, and many mystics of the Maghrib were townsmen and scholars, like the famous Sîdî Bû-Madyân revered at Tlemcen. This did not prevent the mystical movement from having spread widely across the countryside of the Maghrib, as witnessed by the rapid multiplication of the *zâwiya* and the success of the brotherhoods, especially from the fifteenth century on; is it not reported that the brotherhood of Muḥammad al-Jazûlî (*ṭarîqa jazûliyya*) numbered twelve thousand members at the death of its founder (about 1465)? Now his domain was essentially the region which stretches between the present localities of Safi, Agadir, and Shishâwa, where there then existed no city worthy of the name. If certain mystics, like al-Jazûlî, studied in a thoroughgoing manner the traditional theology, others were simple countrymen who, with hardly any contact with the learned of the cities and without having studied the doctrine thoroughly, arrived through prayer, the meditation of Koranic texts, and a sort of inward illumination at the religion of the heart which they set about preaching around them or, better, into which they *initiated* the simple folk among whom they lived. A hagiographical collection like the *Dauḥat al-nâshir* of Ibn 'Askar (third quarter of the sixteenth century) is full of facts which support the principle which has just been laid down. It is probable, although we have very vague information about him, that the famous Moroccan mystic, Sîdî 'Abd al-Salâm b. Mashîsh (beginning of the thirteenth century), was one of these country mystics: no one tells us that he went to study in the east or even at Fez; he is shown to us simply as living at the top of a mountain, the Jabal 'Alam to the south of Tétouan (Ṭiṭṭâwn), separated from this lower world and devoting his days to meditation and prayer.

Finally, though the descendants of the Prophet (*shurafâ'*) were everywhere the object of a special esteem, they enjoyed a veritable veneration in the Maghribî countryside; the success, first of Idrîs b. 'Abd Allâh among the Aurâba Berbers, then of his son Idrîs b. Idrîs in a part of the present Morocco, does not seem explicable except by the fact that they were descendants of the Prophet. Even more, when the Shî'ite missionary, Abû 'Abd Allâh, settled among the Kutâma, he asked them to embrace the cause of a person of whom he could speak only in vague terms, since he did not know him himself, but, since it was a matter of a descendant of the Prophet, the Kutâma let themselves be won for the cause of this unknown man; it is thus that 'Ubaid Allâh gained power in Ifrîqiya. There is, then, to be found very early among the Berber population of the Maghrib a sort of anthropolatry with regard to the members of the Prophet's family.

The slow infiltration of the Bedouin tribes—Banû Hilâl, Banû Sulaim, and others—and their coexistence with the pastoral Berber tribes might, it would seem, seriously have modified the features of the Islâm of the Maghribî tribes. It did not do so at all. For one thing, the first Bedouins did not arrive in North Africa till the middle of the eleventh century, when the Berbers had long since formed their Muslim habits. Further, it appears that the Bedouin tribes let loose upon the Maghrib by the Fâṭimids of Egypt were very little preoccupied with religious matters. It can even be thought that they were influenced by their new neighbours, the Berbers, in point of religion. If the Hilâlian migration constituted a decisive factor as concerns the Arabization of the Maghrib, the same cannot be said of its Islamization.

The Turks did not play any more important a role. As is known, they did not occupy all the Maghrib, since Morocco always escaped them, and they made their presence felt in southern Algeria only in a sporadic manner. Besides, the Anatolian peasants and the renegades of various origins who made up the greater part of the Turkish occupiers were not zealots in religious matters, if they even practised the faith at all, so that the only trace in the religious sphere of three centuries of Turkish occupation is the existence of the Ḥanafite rite (*madhhab*) alongside the Mâlikî rite in the few administrative centres where the Turks were in sufficient numbers.

The presence of a dense Western population since 1830 in Algeria, 1881 in Tunisia, and 1912 in Morocco and Tripolitania, has been much more significant. Certainly the Western powers which established themselves in these countries in virtue of various treaties, whether Spain, France, or Italy, all proclaimed their respect for the Muslim religion and their express intention not to harm it in the least. The same formulas, or very nearly, are to be found in this regard in such different texts as the proclamation of Marshal de Bourmont after the capitulation of Algiers, the treaty of Le Bardo between the French government and the Bey of Tunis in 1881, and the treaty of Fez by which the Sultan of Morocco accepted the French protectorate in 1912. The sincerity of those who signed these diplomatic documents in the name of the Western governments cannot be doubted, any more than the good faith of those who applied them. In Algeria the Catholic Church tried to get conversions in Kabyle circles but, meeting with very little success, gave it up; it can even be said that at the present time it accepts only after thorough inquiry and mature reflection a few very rare conversions of Muslims to Catholicism. The attitude of the Protestant missions is nearly the same. It can be affirmed, then, that neither on the official level nor on the religious level nor even, aside from very rare exceptions, on the individual level have the Westerners in North Africa carried out any concerted and conscious action against Islâm.

Some Muslims complain of the way their cult is administered in Algeria, where a non-Muslim government appoints and pays the officers of the Muslim cult. It must be mentioned that these complaints are few, very recent, and inspired by considerations which are as much political as religious; it is known, besides, that the officers of the Muslim cult have nothing in common with a consecrated clergy and that, consequently, the conditions of their appointment are much less important than in the case of priests. If on the level of principle it constitutes an anomaly that a non-Muslim government should take charge of the Muslim cult, it must be admitted that in fact the Muslim community of Algeria accepted this situation without difficulty and that the officers of the cult appointed under these conditions suitably discharge their functions. Besides, it is known that the Algerian Assembly is at present considering a bill for the separation of the Muslim cult from the state.

Finally, in Algeria and elsewhere, the Western governments which were masters of the situation did not content themselves with showing regard and honour for the representatives of Muslim learning and with assuring an absolute respect for religious buildings and ritual ceremonies; they have caused the mortmain goods to be profitable, as in Tunisia or in Morocco, where the yield of the *ḥabûs* properties has considerably increased in absolute value since the establishment of the protectorate, and have restored or built a number of mosques. Recent mosques are numerous in Algeria, for example, the vast Mosque of Laghouat; I have also seen at Murzûq a very beautiful mosque built by the Italian government alongside the old Turkish mosque. It is appropriate to point out also the considerable work undertaken in Morocco by the office of historical monuments, in co-operation with the vizierate of the *Ḥabus*, to restore to their ancient splendour several mosques or madrasas of Fez, Rabat, Salé, Marrakesh, etc.

In spite of this respect for the Muslim religion which has been announced and practised, it is not in doubt that the simple presence of hundreds of thousands of non-Muslims and of non-Muslim administrations in the Maghrib is pregnant with consequences for Maghribî Islâm.

To begin with, the frequent personal contacts, often on a basis of trust, with Westerners have led the Muslims of the Maghrib to open their eyes to the outside world, which they had scarcely done till then. This country, turned in for centuries upon itself and its convictions, has suddenly discovered—in the cities at first and now in many corners of the *bled*—another world of ideas and beliefs. This discovery has led some into doubt; many others, without going so far, have come nevertheless to temper the traditional rigourism of Maghribî Islâm. The contact of the civilizations, so fruitful in so many other spheres, has also had its effects in the religious domain, not so much as concerns the doctrine itself as with regard to the relations between adherents of different beliefs.

Further, the presence of Europeans has brought to life in some Muslims the tendency to Muslim reform: the reactions of the Westerners in the presence of the practice of Maghribî Islâm, whatever direction they took, have convinced certain ardent believers of the necessity for a religious reform. 'The Europeans must not', they thought, 'be able to make fun of the crude ritual of such-and-such a brotherhood or of the charlatanism of such-and-such a marabout, nor must an informed Islamist be able to point out heterodox practices here and there; the only way to escape such reactions is to return to the pure Islâm of the Koran and the sunna.' Others have believed that the European influence was harmful to the believers (women's dress, cinema, drink, mingling of the sexes) and have reacted against it by recalling the essential precepts of Muslim morality.

In another field, the substitution of European administrations for, or their superimposition upon, the traditional Muslim administration has had its consequences in the strictly religious sphere. It has happened that essentially religious officials, like the *qâḍî* and the *muḥtasib* in Morocco, have been deprived of an important part of their functions, not because the administration of the protectorate desired to suppress them, but because it envisaged their role from a purely administrative angle, not a religious one. Of the *qâḍî*, who was formerly the principal religious figure in the city, controlling the *ḥabûs* properties and the religious instruction, that is, all the intellectual life, enjoying a prestige greater than that of the governor (*'âmil* or *qâ'id*), it has made a simple judge of questions relating to personal status; as for the *muḥtasib*, censor of morals and supervisor of the traditional economic life, he has been transformed into a quasi-parasite, simply a liaison agent with the ancient guilds, and authorized, by virtue of this, to receive as formerly a title in money or goods from those under his jurisdiction. These transformations are to be explained by the fact that the European administration, judging matters from its purely practical point of view, without any spiritual concern, saw in the *qâḍî* a judge charged with applying the Muslim law just as a French judge applies the civil code, and in the *muḥtasib* a sort of provost of tradesmen, a temporal head of the guilds. It left to the one only his judicial functions, not realizing that a judge could be at the same time administrator of sometimes considerable properties and the inspector even of religious instruction; it left to the other his economic functions, without taking account of his moral role, which, it must be emphasized, had dwindled some time before the establishment of the protectorate; and, as little by little the artisan activity has entered willy-nilly into the general economic cycle of the country, the technical organizations charged with economic questions have taken artisan affairs under their charge, so that the activity of the *muḥtasib* has gradually diminished almost to nothing.

Furthermore, the European administration, with all the respect that it had for the Muslim religious life, noticeably upset its development. There is an official holiday on the day itself and sometimes on the morrow of the great religious solemnities (*'Îd ṣaghîr*, *'Îd kabîr*, *Maulid*, *'Âshûrâ'*), just as the Catholic holy days of obligation give the right to one or two free days (Christmas, and then Easter Monday, the Monday of Pentecost, and All Souls' Day). Now, the Maghribî custom was that the Muslim holidays were the occasion of several days of family rejoicings. If the Western administrations have greatly facilitated the Pilgrimage, they have, on the other hand, greatly interfered with celebration of the fast of Ramaḍân. Formerly this had been a month of greatly slackened activity, which permitted the believers to fulfil the hard obligations of the Muslim fast in the normal course of things. Certainly the administrations or the European enterprises allow some accommodations to the Muslims they employ; even so the practice of the fast becomes a very arduous ordeal for them, which many do not have the courage to face.

Education has completely changed in character. Leaving aside some timid attempts like the foundation of the Ṣâdiqî

College at Tunis in 1875 or the organization of a school of engineers at Fez (*madrasat al-muhandisîn*) under Maulây 'Abd al-Raḥmân, it can be said that traditional Maghribî education was only religious; sciences like grammar, history, and astronomy were only, as a matter of fact, auxiliary to the only science that counted, that of divine things. The Europeans have introduced to the Maghrib a modern education, provided in the same spirit as it had been in Europe, that is, in a secular spirit. That this secularism was almost always respectful of religious doctrines my North African experience allows me to affirm; it is nonetheless true that in modern education God does not hold the place which He held in the traditional education. In the territories controlled by France, at least (I do not know exactly what has been done elsewhere), a corrective to this secularism has been introduced: Franco-Muslim institutions have been founded in Algeria, in Tunisia, and in Morocco. As their name indicates, they provide not only an Arabic but an Islamic education: theology, law, and ritual have their place in it. But they are not there alone; by their side mathematics, natural sciences, etc, are taught in a Western spirit. Such an education, however respectful the European teachers are of the beliefs of their students, cannot fail to form young minds in a way very different from the past and to bring about important consequences in the spiritual field.

On the other hand, the development of modern means of communication has greatly facilitated relations between the Maghrib and the Arab countries. The reknitting of these ties, which had been so strong at the start of the Arab conquest and which had much relaxed from the eleventh century on, has had its effect on the political level but also on the religious level. Maghribî reformism has been influenced by eastern theorists like Muḥammad 'Abduh and Rashîd Riḍâ; the prestige of the University of al-Azhar and of King 'Abd al'Azîz Ibn Sa'ûd is in fact undeniable.

In short, one cannot insist too greatly upon the importance of the presence of the Europeans in North Africa.

37. Islam and national movements in West Africa

THOMAS HODGKIN *Journal of African History* Vol. 3, No. 2, 1962
Cambridge University Press; pages 323–7

The question around which these lectures were constructed might be stated as follows—What has been the influence of Islam on national movements (defined roughly as 'movements seeking to modify or transform the colonial situation') in West Africa, and on political institutions and ideas in modern West African states? The region of West Africa with which I am primarily concerned is the *bilād al-sūdān* from Senegal to Chad. My purpose in raising this question is partly a general one: to explore the connexion between the pre-colonial history of the region (in the light of the work of Urvoy, Rouch, Mauny, M. G. Smith, Charles Smith, Hiskett, Bivar, Fage, Hampaté Ba, Boahen, and others to whom I am much indebted) and its modern political movements and institutions (which are being studied on an increasing scale by the political scientists).

The following propositions attempt to summarize, very provisionally, my conclusions:

The Almoravid movement, and its short-lived ascendancy in the Western Sudan, though simply an episode in the process of Islamization by methods of peaceful penetration during the eleventh century A.D., was of significance for the later history of the region in at least three ways. (i) It assisted the development of communications with the Maghrib and Andalus. (ii) It checked the possibility of the spread southwards from the Maghrib of 'deviant' forms of Islam, and transmitted to the emerging Muslim states of the Western Sudan its own particular conception of 'orthodoxy'—Maliki rigorism, respect for the *fuqahā'*, hostility to *kalām*. (iii) It created a precedent for later reforming movements seeking to bring about a total transformation of society in accordance with the prescriptions of the Sharī'a.

The relatively rich documentary sources for fourteenth-century Mali provide some basis for judging the extent to which, by this period, the impact of Islam had modified indigenous, pre-Islamic institutions: e.g. as regards court ritual, the observance of Ramadan and the 'Īds, the employment of *qāḍis* (in the towns), the establishment of Koranic schools, the use of foreign specialists (associated with the diversification of external relations, to include Egypt and the Hijaz as well as Morocco).

The assumption of power in Gao by Muhammad Askia at the end of the fifteenth century, and the century of Askia rule over the Songhai Empire which followed it, were associated with certain new developments and policies, in particular. (i) The creation of a more centralized system of government and a more complex bureaucracy. (ii) The growth of the numbers and political influence of the *'ulamā'* (with an increased tendency for the monarchy to depend upon the support and collaboration of the *'ulamā'*). (iii) The development of centres of higher education and research in the Islamic sciences (Timbuktu, Djenné), concerned with the training of *'ulamā'*. (iv) The application of a more positive policy of Islamization within the Empire.

More work will have to be done on the history of the region, and its relations with the wider Muslim world in the seventeenth and eighteenth centuries, before it will be possible to attempt an adequate historical explanation of the nineteenth-century reforming movements associated with 'Uthmān dan Fodio, Shehu Aḥmadu, and al-Ḥājj 'Umar al-Tāl. The following factors appear, however, to have been contributory. (i) The general decline, relatively to Western Europe, in the power and prosperity of the Muslim world—of which there was evidently some awareness in the Western Sudan in the late eighteenth century—and, connected with this, the decline in the trans-Saharan trade. (ii) Comparing the situation in the seventeenth and eighteenth with the situation in the sixteenth century, a relative weakening in the power of Muslim states (Gao, Bornu), and a relative strengthening of pagan power (Segu, the Kororafa) or of governments whose loyalty to Islam was doubtful (Gobir). (iii) The special role throughout the region of the Fulani *'ulamā'*, as the inheritors of the 'Timbuktu tradition' of scholarship, and their tendency, given suitable opportunities, to move over from educational and missionary functions to political action (Futa Jallon, Futa Toro, in the eighteenth century). (iv) The revival of the *Qadirīyya* (with which the dan Fodio family was closely connected) under the leadership of

Shaikh Sīdi al-Mukhtār al-Kuntī (1729–1811), as a carrier of reformist ideas.

(The question of external influences—Wahhabist or other—on these reforming movements requires special consideration.)

Thus these nineteenth-century movements can be variously interpreted as. (i) An effort of the (predominantly Fulani, or Fulfulde-speaking) *'ulamā'* to reassert their claims to power, on a basis similar to that which they conceived had existed under the Askia Dynasty in Gao. (ii) An effort to establish a genuine Islamic polity on the model of the early Caliphate (or of the ideal constructions of the Abbasid jurists), and to root out or transform such traditional institutions as were incompatible with this model. (iii) An effort to extend the frontiers of *dār al-Islām* at the expense of *dār al-kufr*, through the establishment of a large system, transcending local and ethnic particularisms, held together by a common loyalty to its religious-political head (*Imām* or *Amīr al-mu'minīn*, not *Sultān*), common observance of the Sharī'a, and a common Islamic ideology.

It would seem that the extent to which effective reform of social and political institutions, in the light of these dominant ideas, was in practice achieved was markedly greater in Masina under Shehu Aḥmadu's régime than in the Sokoto Empire under 'Uthmān dan Fodio's—where, though the pre-Fulani systems were modified in a number of particulars, new Fulani *amīr* tended to become old Hausa *sarki* writ large.

What Gouilly has called the *empires combattantes* of the last quarter of the nineteenth century—of which the most significant were Samory Touré's in the western, and Rabeh Zubayr's in the central sector of the Sudan—have not yet been adequately studied. They appear, however, to have presented certain interesting new features, in particular. (i) The emergence, during a period in which established systems and dynasties were tending to disintegrate under European pressure, of a number of 'upstart' political-military leaders, 'new men', whose claims to leadership depended primarily upon their personal abilities. (ii) The provision within the new political-military structures, within limits, of a career open to talents (e.g. Samory's *sofas*). (iii) The use of Islam (combined, in varying degrees, with 'national' sentiment) as an ideological basis for resistance to European penetration: hence a new phase of

Islamization (reflected in the setting up of Koranic schools, etc.), and—partly as a consequence of (i) and (ii)—an emphasis upon the egalitarian, as well as the activist, aspects of Islam.

I know of no comparative study of French and British policies in relation to the former Muslim states which they included within their respective colonial systems and in regard to Islamic institutions in the region. In a superficial way it is clear that among the effects of both types of administration and policy were: (i) The loss by these states of their sovereignty (combined in some cases—e.g. the Fulani emirates of Northern Nigeria—with the preservation of a considerable measure of internal autonomy). (ii) The weakening of the historical connexions of *bilād al-sūdān* with the Maghrib and the Muslim world, and its reorientation—particularly as regards economic relations—towards the coastal ports and the West. (iii) The development—on a very restricted scale in most areas—of Western, predominantly secular, systems of education; with the survival, but gradual decline, of Islamic forms of education. (iv) The formation of political alliances between colonial administrations and elements within the Muslim community favourable to a policy of collaboration—whether fief-holding nobility, traditionalist *'ulamā'*, or *ṭarīqa*-leaders; administrative support for quietist, and opposition to activist (e.g. Mahdist, Reformist, Modernist) interpretations of Islam. (v) Hence a tendency to arrest processes of social and political change taking place in pre-colonial Muslim society—with the preservation in a more or less modified form, within the colonial administrative and legal framework, of *qāḍi*-administered Maliki Law. (vi) As a consequence partly of the development of communications and trade, processes of urbanization, etc., associated with the colonial epoch, a new phase in the dissemination of Islam (regarded as a system of observances and social practices rather than as a set of moral imperatives).

The foregoing paragraphs attempt to indicate the kind of historical context within which it is possible to discuss the question regarding the impact of Islam on modern national movements referred to at the beginning of this paper. (It should be made clear that in raising this question one is not committed to an instrumental view of Islam, nor to any presuppositions about the forms of organization, types of leadership, methods, objectives, ideologies, etc., which national movements may adopt.)

Among *Islamic institutions (and ideas) which have tended to retard the development of national movements* in the West African context, the following might be included. (i) '*Ilm*, in the sense of education in the traditional Islamic sciences, with particular emphasis on Maliki *fiqh*—in so far as this scholastic tradition has tended to produce an attitude of mind that is resistant to the ideas both of Muslim reformism and of secular nationalism. (There are, however, exceptions to the generalization that the '*ulamā*', trained in this tradition and concerned with its maintenance, have on the whole been unsympathetic to reformist and nationalist beliefs.) (ii) The *ṭarīqas* (particularly the *Qādirīyya*, but also the *Tijānīyya* in some of its aspects), in so far as these have developed the kind of characteristics criticized by the reformists, and labelled 'maraboutism'—emphasis on the total submission of the *ṭālib* to his shaikh or *muqaddam*; anti-rationalist attitudes and practices (use of amulets, gri-gris); 'sectarianism', in the sense of putting loyalty to the *ṭarīqa* above the wider loyalty to the Muslim '*umma*; collaboration with the colonial authorities, in return for a protected and privileged status. (iii) In certain areas (e.g. that covered by the former Sokoto Empire), where pre-colonial social and political institutions have been preserved with the minimum of modification and pre-colonial dynasties of an authoritarian type have survived, the tendency to identify Islam with this particular framework of institutions (and, especially, with dynastic power). Hence national movements at some stages have been resisted: (*a*) as intrusions from outside the system; (*b*) as seeking to disturb the existing social-political structure.

Among *Islamic institutions (and ideas) which have tended to assist the development of national movements* should be included the following. (i) The activist *ṭarīqas*: e.g. the *Muridīyya*, in Senegal, under the leadership of Amadou Bamba (*c.* 1850–1927), particularly during its early phase; the *Hamallīyya*, in former French Sudan (Mali) and adjacent territories, under the leadership of Shaikh Hamāhu'llāh (1886–1943), during the period between the two wars; in some respects the *Tijānīyya*, in particular Shaikh Ibrāhīma Nyās's connexion, in the period since World War II. (ii) The reforming movements, which have emerged mainly in the period since World War II, as a result partly of internal stimuli (the younger generation of Muslim intelligentsia, outside the Muslim 'Establishment' of dynasties, office-holders, traditionalist *'ulamā'*, *ṭarīqa*-leaders, etc., asserting a causal connexion between the colonial situation and loss of *Imān*, Faith); partly of external stimuli, particularly the University of al-Azhar (through the influence of its West African graduates), the *Salafīyya* (the reforming ideas associated with Muhammad 'Abdu and Rashīd Rida', transmitted mainly via the Maghrib), and Wahhābi influences (operating partly through the *hāj*). In their political aspect these movements have been essentially anti-colonial, anti-traditionalist, and anti-maraboutic; in their practical aspect they have laid special stress on the development of a reformed and modernized type of Islamic education. (iii) At the level of ideas: (*a*) awareness of Muslim West Africa as an integral part of *dār al-Islām* as a basis for rejection of assimilationist policies (particularly in French territories); (*b*) reference back to major pre-colonial Islamic states (both medieval and nineteenth-century), and late nineteenth-century movements of resistance to European penetration under Muslim leadership, as support for modern radical nationalist, or 'Pan-African', ideologies. (iv) Mahdist movements, during the early colonial period (these, though deserving attention, have been for the most part of minor and local significance).

Finally, it seems possible to pick out certain continuing factors in the political history of Muslim West Africa which have some relevance for the new states, for example. (i) Relationships with the Maghrib (and, more remotely, Egypt)—determining the form in which Islam was initially presented, and a recurrent source of new stimuli. (ii) The succession of reforming movements, from the Almoravids to modern times, seeking a total reconstruction of the social and political order in the light of the principles of Islam (however interpreted), each having to come to terms, in varying ways, with the actual structure of West African society. (iii) Partly associated with (ii), the Empire-building tendency, and the use of the universalist conceptions of Islam to promote political cohesion and weaken the various centrifugal forces (ethnic and other) operating within an imperial system (as against this, ideological conflicts within the West African Muslim community have also played a part in inter-state conflicts—e.g. Sokoto-Bornu, Dingiray-Masina). (iv) The tendency of the institutions of Islam to be modified and adapted in relation to the cultures and social needs of particular West African peoples, countered by the efforts of the *'ulamā'* to preserve the purity of Islam (interpreted in terms of Maliki Law by the Traditionalists, as a body of ethical-political imperatives by the Reformists). (v) The importance (since the late eighteenth century at any rate) of the *ṭarīqas* as agencies for the dissemination of Islam—capable of wide variations as regards their social and political attitudes: quietist in some contexts; channels of reforming and protest movements in others; operating, in some modern systems (e.g. Senegal), as powerful pressure-groups within, or on the periphery of, political parties.

XIII. SPREAD AND INFLUENCE OF CHRISTIANITY

38. Christian missions in West Africa

VIRGINIA THOMPSON and RICHARD ADLOFF *The Emerging States of French Equatorial Africa* Stanford University Press 1961; pages 301–8

. . . In 1490 the King of Portugal first sent a few Franciscan and Capuchin missionaries to the Kongo kingdom, where they and their successors were extraordinarily successful for about 250 years. They were centred in Angola, and it was not until 1663 that they founded at Loango the only mission in what later became French territory. Concentrating on the conversion of the king and the upper classes of the Bakongo tribes, these early missionaries did not try to win over the population in general, although the Capuchins made some attempts to establish hinterland posts. They did not trouble to learn the local languages, and for many years they preached and heard confessions through an interpreter. Moreover, they made remarkable concessions to local custom, including the toleration of polygamy and pagan practices among their converts, though occasionally some of the more zealous priests tried to destroy fetishes. The 'Christian' rulers of the Kongo, for their part, used the missionaries and the religion they brought as a means of reinforcing kingly authority, and they included the cross among the royal insignia as the symbol of their judicial power. Later the cross, statues of saints, and some of the church ritual were absorbed into animist practices to such a point that, in the Loango region, the cult of the Virgin Mary became almost indistinguishable from that of the local earth goddess.

This process of absorption and adaptation went so far that by the time the second wave of Catholic missionaries reached the coast of central Africa in the late eighteenth century they found it almost impossible to enforce strict Christian practices among their African converts. Frenchmen predominated in this group of missionaries, members of the Order of St Esprit, and they were accompanied by nuns of St Joseph de Cluny. In the late nineteenth century one of their number, Father Augouard, worked closely with Brazza in opening up the Congolese hinterland, and he founded two mission stations at Linzolo and Brazzaville that were to become the most important in Moyen-Congo. A network of missions was set up in the heart of the Balali country, owing to the zeal of Augouard and his aides, who besides being priests, were explorers, builders, and managers of farms and workshops. They trained Africans to become carpenters, masons, and blacksmiths, and even tried to raise meat animals so as to wean their converts away from cannibalism. Under Augouard's successors, mission posts—to which primary schools were added—multiplied in the lower Congo basin, and others were founded in the Likouala and Haute-Sangha regions.

During the seventeenth century, Italian Capuchin missionaries had tried intermittently to evangelize the tribes of coastal Gabon, and in 1775 they were joined by two French priests, but none of these early missionaries left lasting traces in the country. Two French fathers of the St Esprit Order, who had been forced to leave the Ivory Coast, went to Gabon in 1843, and were persuaded by the French naval officers stationed there to remain in the country rather than return to France. One of them, Bessieux, began work on a dictionary of the local language, and his companion, Le Berre, wrote the first grammar of any Gabonese language. Both missionaries tried to penetrate the hinterland, but because of the difficulties of communication and the hostility of the tribes there, they retired to the coast and made their headquarters at newly founded Libreville. They were soon joined by other missionaries and nuns. In 1861–2 they constructed a large mission compound, comprising a chapel and a school, that became the model for other concentrations of Catholic missionary enterprise in Gabon. Le Berre, after he succeeded Bessieux as bishop of Libreville, made a second and more successful effort to evangelize the rural Fang, and in 1878 he founded the missions of N'Gounié and Okané. Even more than in Moyen-Congo, mission posts in Gabon became economic enterprises, in which the raising of food crops was as vital to their survival as was the establishing of schools to attract Africans and make converts.

For many years Catholic missionary activity in AEF remained within Moyen-Congo and Gabon, and only in the twentieth century did it spread to the north. By 1909 the evangelization of Oubangui had reached the point where its capital was made an apostolic see. Mission work in that colony was confined to the Bangui area until about 1925, when it started pushing into the M'Baiki and Bambari regions and radiated as far as the Sara country of southern Tchad. In 1938 the missions at Bangassou, Doba, and Bozoum (with headquarters at Berbérati) were reorganized as an apostolic vicariate, distinct from that of Bangui, and entrusted to the Capuchins who had come to AEF from Ethiopia after the Italian conquest of that country. In Tchad, except for the Moundou area, mission work spread even more slowly than in Oubangui. A Jesuit military chaplain began trying to evangelize the tribes living on the banks of Lake Tchad in 1934, but it was not until 1947—when eastern Tchad was detached from the Khartoum vicariate—that the Vatican asked the Jesuits to organize a mission in that territory. At that time, the rank of an apostolic prefecture was conferred on Tchad, except for the south-western zone, which remained a part of the Berbérati vicariate.

The ecclesiastical organization of the Catholic missions in AEF kept pace with the growth of their activities, and both increased rapidly in the years that followed World War II. At the end of the nineteenth century there were only three ecclesiastical circumscriptions—at Loango, Brazzaville, and Libreville—to which that of Bangui was added in 1909. Between 1927 and 1947 the arrival of the Capuchins and Jesuits led to the creation of two more, at Berbérati and Fort Lamy. By 1956, however, the federation boasted nine distinct jurisdictions, of which two were archbishoprics (Brazzaville and Bangui), two were apostolic prefectures, and five were major dioceses. Of these nine jurisdictions, six were in the hands of missionaries of the St Esprit, two were in those of the Capuchins, and one was entrusted to the Jesuits. Ministering to the faithful were 300 European missionaries, 248 being French and the balance divided among six other nationalities, and 38 African priests.

The small proportion of African priests, both absolutely and in relation to the number of European missionaries, is striking, especially in view of the attention that was given to training Africans during the first years of missionary enterprise in AEF. Yet the situation in 1956 represented an improvement over that which had existed six years earlier, when there was a total of only six African priests. The sole African priest in the Fort Lamy apostolic prefecture was not ordained until 1957, and this was considered an event of such importance that it was attended by two archbishops, three bishops, and the head of the Papal Delegation for French Black Africa, who came from Dakar expressly for the ceremony. For some years after the war, the Catholic missionaries of AEF, apparently discouraged by the turn taken by two African priests whom they had regarded as shining examples, had not pushed the training of an African clergy. Because of the lack of secondary-school facilities in AEF until the mid-1950s, politically ambitious young Africans, such as Boganda and Youlou, naturally had been attracted to the priesthood as the only way of acquiring the higher education they needed to rise in the world. This trend became accentuated in 1955 when the Vatican initiated a policy of consecrating as rapidly as possible Negro bishops who could take over from the missionaries the management of churches in French Black Africa. Today, more than 30 Africans are studying at the Grand Séminaire of Brazzaville and 241 in the small territorial seminaries of M'Bamou, Mayumba, Libreville, Berbérati, and Fort Sibut.

The relations between the Catholic missions and the administration were never so marked by distrust as in French West Africa, and they have improved considerably in recent years. Most of the French naval officers who first governed Gabon came from conservative, strongly Catholic families, and they welcomed the missionaries as warmly as did their counterparts in Cochin China. Moreover, the missionaries rendered vital services to the government, by actively helping to open up the hinterland, acting as intermediaries with tribal chiefs, and even quelling revolts (notably that at Lastoursville in 1897), and also by spreading French influence by means of their schools. Passage of the Metropolitan anti-clerical laws in the early twentieth century, however, even though they were not promulgated in AEF, led to less cordial relations between the missionaries and civilian officials. The latter tended to believe that the missionaries were trying to create a state-within-a-state and their own zone of influence, and that they were weakening native society by their attacks on polygamy and their support of the emancipation of youths and women from traditional authority. The European lay community in general was inclined to judge harshly the African products of mission schools, holding the instruction they received there responsible for the Africans' aspirations for greater freedom as well as for their lapses from honesty and truthfulness. Basically the antagonism among European officials and merchants alike toward African Christians was based on the latter's insistence on being treated as a privileged group and their resistance to performing tasks they considered menial. Many seemed to forget that for years the missions had provided almost all African interpreters and clerks for the administration and trading firms.

With the growth of the Messianic cults, relations between the Catholic missionaries and French officials became more co-operative in the face of what they both regarded as a common danger. If the missionaries denounced the new cults as a resurgence of fetishism, they saw in them also a revolt against their ecclesiastical as well as against lay authority. In a sense, the missions, cooperating with the government in trying to suppress the new cults in Moyen-Congo and Gabon, virtually declared a war of religion on the aberrant Negro churches. Conversely, the missionaries were surprised and shocked by the hostility displayed by some African parishioners toward them during the fiftieth-anniversary celebrations of the founding of the Linzolo mission. Although even the most fanatical adversaries of the Catholic mission then feared to make an open attack on it, they apparently hoped to isolate and weaken the missionaries fatally by refusing to provision them.

Whereas the administration and Catholic missions were drawn closer together during the interwar period by their common fear of the Messianic sects, quite the reverse was true of the attitude of most French officials toward the Protestant missions. American Presbyterians had been the first Protestants to come to Gabon, as early as 1844, and six years later they founded a post at Libreville. In 1871 a Protestant Church was built at Baraka, in 1874 a small post at Balambila on the Ogooué, and in 1882 another at Talagouga. In the mission schools they founded, these Protestants taught Africans in the vernacular, and when the government issued regulations in the

1880s forbidding this, 'they were not prepared to teach in French, nor did they show any desire so to prepare themselves'. Highly placed French officials, including Brazza himself, pleaded successfully with the Paris Société des Missions Evangéliques to lend French teachers to the Presbyterian missions. But this proved to be only a palliative and relations between the Presbyterians and the government became increasingly strained, with the result that they ceded their work in Gabon to the Paris society in 1892. Protestant activity spread progressively to the rural areas, where they built dispensaries, primary schools, and vocational training institutions, the most outstanding of which were the agricultural station of Samkita (founded in 1909) and the forestry station and sawmill of Ngomo (in 1913).

At about the same time, Swedish Protestants of the Svenska Missionsförbundet came to Moyen-Congo and founded a station at Madoua in the Kinkala area. There they built their first primary school in 1911, which was subsequently cited as a model by the territorial education service. Their work was particularly successful in Boko district, where they soon acquired a following among the Bakongo and thus aroused the hostility of the Balali Catholics, who were in the majority there. The Swedish stations multiplied to the number of 12 in Moyen-Congo, and subsequently another Swedish organization, the Orebre Missionsförening, established three posts in Oubangui. In the latter territory they were joined during the interwar period by some American Protestant groups, notably the Sudan Mission and Mid-Africa Mission, which later extended their work to Tchad.

In both northern territories, the going is hard for all the Christian missionaries because they lack facilities for reaching the tribes scattered over immense areas, and because of the fact that most of the federation's Muslim populations are to be found there. The situation was very different, however, in the south, where the Africans were highly susceptible to Christian proselytizing and the means of communication were comparatively good. This was particularly true in the conventional zone of the Congo, where, under the provisions of article 11 of the treaty of St Germain, 'missionaries have the right to enter, circulate, and reside there, with facilities to pursue their religious work'. The signing of this treaty in 1919 opened the way not only for the established Protestant denominations to create as many posts as their resources would permit, but also for the advent of two new evangelical organizations, the Salvation Army and Jehovah's Witnesses. In recent years both have taken root in AEF, particularly the former in the Niari region of Moyen-Congo.

During the interwar period, the movement started by the Salvation Army spread rapidly through the region served by the Congo-Ocean railroad, where some villagers even abandoned their homes and fields to participate in the ceremonies organized by its agents. In fact, the Army's officers were disconcerted by the sudden success of their efforts, because of the aberrations to which they gave rise. Their African auxiliaries, fascinated by the uniforms, regalia, and hymns of the Army, increased greatly, and, poorly trained, they enthusiastically spread distorted doctrines. This led to the celebration of mystical rites that were strangely akin to the practices of the traditional secret societies. This did not become a widespread phenomenon, but elsewhere and in other ways the Salvation Army contributed to the development of some of the most extreme aspects of the Messianic cults, and its centres in Moyen-Congo served as places of refuge for a number of their leaders who were sought by the police.

The Watch Tower movement of Jehovah's Witnesses did not gain a foothold in AEF until after World War II. Their influence has extended to Oubangui, but it is mainly felt in the towns of Brazzaville, Dolisie, and Pointe Noire, where the Watch Tower is called Kinsinga. The extremist doctrines preached by the Witnesses resemble those propagated by the radical fringe of the Messianic cults, but the methods they use have alienated a segment of the African population. In 1956 the authors were told by a high French official that a fight had recently broken out between African Catholics, Protestants, and Witnesses in Oubangui because in some areas the Watch Tower propagandists had taken advantage of the temporary absence of the men from their homes to visit their wives and give them 'instruction'.

Although the policies of the Salvation Army and Jehovah's Witnesses in AEF have been inimical to the French administration, the orthodox Protestant denominations have taken no such stand and have closely collaborated with the government in the field of education. The administration in turn has granted as many favours to Protestant as to Catholic missionaries, even though most of the former are foreigners whereas the latter share the faith of most French officials and in great majority are of French nationality. During World War II, when the Protestant missions were cut off from their parent organizations, they received generous grants from French public funds. After eight of the Protestant missions came together in 1941 in a Fédération des Missions d'AEF, the government called upon its members for advice in formulating policy on social questions. In the post-war years, the Protestant missions have been treated on exactly the same basis as those of the Catholics in respect to official subsidies and representation on educational advisory boards.

Nevertheless, there is little doubt that the administration, for purely secular reasons, has preferred to see African converts enter the Catholic rather than the Protestant fold. Although Catholic missions at times have been considered by French officials to be an overly independent and socially disruptive force, as well as one that aroused the antagonism of some of the African elite, Catholic priests have been far more diligent than have Protestant pastors in supervising and often controlling the activities of most of their converts. Moreover, AEF was one of the very few French-speaking countries in Black Africa where the Vatican's prelates apparently were not instructed in 1955 to come out openly in favour of African self-determination, and where the Holy See has not forced the pace of creating African bishops or of replacing French missionaries by Catholics of other nationalities.

No overtly subversive activities on the part of the Protestant missionaries can be held responsible for having aroused the administration's mistrust of their sincerity or purposes. Nevertheless, the mere fact of the presence of their numerous denominations in AEF—which has broken the united Christian front and caused antagonism between African Christians—has been held mainly responsible for the development of the Messianic sects, with their dangerous doctrinal deviations. Because the basic Protestant creed of individual responsibility fitted in with their yearning for emancipation, the Africans adopted it and interpreted it to mean that they no longer owed obedience to the lay authorities but only to God. Furthermore, the majority of Protestant missionaries were linked neither by nationality nor by religion to the colonial regime, and the Swedes in particular were able to acquire a political influence far greater than might be inferred from the number of their converts. Reportedly the Swedish pastors in Boko district were not disconcerted by the spread of Kimbangism among the Bakongo there but, rather, considered it only the natural consequence of their teachings. Though they rarely participated directly in Moyen-Congo's postwar politics, it is interesting to note that a Swedish missionary was among the candidates for election to the Ouesso municipal council in November 1956.

Although the Protestants' success with dissident African elements naturally cannot be duplicated by the Catholics, who must perforce be intolerant of any movements that threaten their claim to universality and insistence on unity, both missionary groups have encountered much the same obstacles to their work in AEF and drawn many similar conclusions from their long experience there. Among the common handicaps to their progress are the discouraging results of working with the unstable, cosmopolitan, and easily distracted urban populations; the increasing difficulty of recruiting African catechists, because of the attraction of better-paid jobs; and the amount of time and energy devoted by missionaries to economic enterprises not directly related to their main task of evangelization. On the other hand, positive lessons have been derived from their common experience: both Catholics and Protestants have learned to concentrate their mission activities in a few large complexes rather than in numerous small posts; both have become increasingly convinced that they must train their African auxiliaries better and in larger numbers in anticipation of the prospective transfer of their churches to native management; and both have found schools even more effective than hospitals as a means of attracting and influencing the Africans.

Where Protestant and Catholic policy has mainly diverged is in the methods used to win converts. To build their church on as broad a foundation as possible, the Catholics have striven for mass conversions, and to this end have sent out catechists to live in the villages and try to win over their inhabitants en bloc. The Protestants, on the other hand, have placed their primary emphasis on the individual, and they have been reluctant to baptize any African who has not given proof of good conduct. Both policies have been successful in vastly increasing the number of their respective African converts, and though there are now more than twice as many native Catholics as Protestants (about 484,000 compared with some 218,000), the latter's relative numerical weakness has been offset—at least in Moyen-Congo and Gabon—by the influence in depth exerted by the Protestant missions. Since World War II, the Catholic missions have been trying to regain their hold over the elite by sponsoring the Christian trade-union movement and organizing *Action Catholique* groups, one of whose activities has been to publish the weekly paper *La Semaine de l'AEF.*

39. Development of Christianity in East Africa

ROLAND OLIVER *The Missionary Factor in East Africa* (2nd edition) Longmans 1965; pages 207–15

. . . The fact that Islam was able, without the assistance of professional missionaries, to expand, if not at the expense of Christianity, at least side by side with it, is in itself a reason for qualifying the assertions of a later generation of missionaries that Christianity was 'the natural sublimation of African animism'.[1] It may perhaps be argued that both Christianity and Islam found a *point d'appui* in the notion of a Supreme Being, which lay in the dim background of most of the tribal religions of East Africa. But it is more probable that, had the element of monotheism been in fact a considerable one, African beliefs would have offered a stouter resistance than they did. Evidence concerning the nature of the Christian expansion shows rather that it was the parochialism of tribal religions which proved their undoing—the fact that the basic monotheism had been so overlaid by the cult of tribal ancestors and the sanctification of tribal customs, that belief was shattered by the first impact of wider-than-tribal government.

[1] The phrase is that of Bishop Gresford Jones.

Moreover, if missionaries found that belief in Christian doctrines came easily to Africans, they soon discovered also how difficult and foreign was the practice of Christian morality. 'When the white man brings him so much knowledge that is obviously superior to anything he has so far met with, he is ready to believe that most of what is taught is true. . . . But the holiness of God is a strange novelty.' This was a fact which had scarcely come to light in the days when handfuls of Christians lived in isolated communities round the mission stations, or under the conditions of persecution endured by the infant churches of Mackay and Lourdel. The period of deployment through African catechists into villages far from the mission centres, however, brought a flood of disciplinary issues among baptized Christians, which well illustrated the difficulties of transition from a communal to an individual code of morality. It is recorded that Bishop Weston heard 500 cases of marriage offences during a single visit to Masasi, and again that in 1911 he interviewed more than 1,000 people who had been disciplined for moral offences, only about half of whom could be received back into communion. In 1910 no less than 73 out of 1,087 Moravian Christians had been placed under the lesser excommunication; and two years later the figure stood at 166 out of 1,557. Subtracting the numbers resident in the mission villages, the casualty rate at the outstations must have been something like one in four. No other society was courageous enough to publish the statistics. The Leipzig missionaries, however, reported in 1910 that a majority among them had become convinced that 'an African who had passed the age of puberty and who was left in his accustomed environment could never become more than a nominal Christian (Scheinchrist)'. Anglican missionaries in Uganda also complained of nominal Christianity during the early years of the century. Bishop Tucker was no disciplinarian, but in 1906 he judged the situation serious enough to hold a 'Mission' similar to that inaugurated by Pilkington in 1893. Bishop Willis found it necessary on his accession to institute a searching inquiry into the state of Christian morals and to introduce the threat of excommunication at the Synod of 1913. There is little evidence about Roman Catholic experience during the same period. The White Fathers always maintained strict rules of probation and pre-baptismal training; and as early as 1893 Bishop Hirth found it necessary to limit still further the number of baptisms at certain stations in order that the missionaries might have time to hear confessions properly. At a conference of Roman Catholic bishops at Dar-es-Salaam in 1912 it was decided that candidates for baptism must spend one year in the 'Hearers' Class', followed by at least two more in the formal catechumenate, during which their observance of the externals of Christian morality would be carefully watched.

The problems of discipline raised by the rapid diffusion of Christianity called the attention of most missions to the social and economic facts of African life, and set them to probe solutions preventive rather than punitive. In particular, both medical and educational work came to be viewed, no longer as rather dubious auxiliaries of evangelism, but as means of consolidating the Christian life among those who had already been baptized. There had of course been missionary doctors in East Africa since the days of Livingstone. The most prominent of the Presbyterian pioneers, both in Nyasaland and in British East Africa, had been ordained doctors. The C.M.S. had employed doctors in East Africa since 1875. Hine, Bishop of Nyasaland from 1896 till 1901 and of Zanzibar from 1901 till 1908, was a doctor. But the idea of a medical mission as something existing in its own right developed only with the growth of a Christian community, to which the work of a doctor could be related. It was not until 1885 that the C.M.S. appointed a sub-committee to consider the place of medical missions; and even then this body reported that they were useful 'where the Gospel could not easily be preached by ordinary evangelists, or among aboriginal and uncivilized people likely to be impressed by the kindly influence of medical work'. The old idea of the missionary doctor was symbolized by Bishop Tucker taking Dr Albert Cook on his pioneer journeys in Ankole and Acholiland, in order that the preaching of the Word might be reinforced by signs and wonders. But as the Churches grew, and as increasing numbers of baptized Christians had to be disciplined on charges of witchcraft and polygamy, it came to be realized that the medical mission was necessary as a social institution of the Christian community. If the witch-doctor was to be eliminated, with all that he symbolized of sub-Christian fears and hatreds, the missionary doctor must abandon his evangelistic itinerations, stay in his hospital and train African nurses and medical assistants to replace the sorcerer in village life. And equally, if the children of monogamous marriages were to survive in sufficient numbers to compensate for the renunciation of polygamy, then maternity work, child welfare and infant dietetics must all come within the missionary's sphere.

Again, as the Christian community increased, education began to outgrow its avowedly evangelistic beginnings. The first schools at the central stations of both Catholic and Protestant missions had been designed to train catechists. When Protestant missions later made literacy the normal test for baptism, it was intended as a test of sincerity rather than of education.[1] In essence there was little difference between their out-stations and those of the Roman Catholics, where teaching was usually oral. These out-stations or 'bush schools' survived for many years—indeed they still survive—as the normal instrument of Christian expansion. Above them, however, there gradually developed a hierarchy of more regular schools, often self-supporting through fees, and concerned not primarily with religious instruction but with the consolidation of the Christian community. In Uganda both Catholic and Anglican missions were aware of the advantages they had reaped from the stratification of African society: Buganda was perhaps the classic example of conversion from the top. It was natural therefore that both missions should have sought to maintain their initiative with the upper classes by establishing 'schools for the sons of chiefs'. The most exclusive of these institutions, the Eton and Downside of Buganda, were the King's School at Budo[2] and St Joseph's College at Kisubi; but the idea of the chiefly boarding school spread far and wide, to Ngora in Teso, to Maseno in

[1] 'Large numbers were coming forward and asking for baptism. Of their life we knew nothing. "Very well," was our answer, "we don't know you. We must test you. We must see that you have an intelligent knowledge of the way of salvation. Here are the Gospels. We will teach you to read them, and when you have read them we shall expect you to give an intelligent answer to the questions which we shall then ask you."' Tucker, *Eighteen Years in Uganda and East Africa*, London, 1908, p. 234.

[2] Budo, founded in 1903 by A. G. Fraser, later of Trinity College, Kandy and Achimota, was attended by the young Kabaka Daudi Chwa, and in 1908 charged the considerable fee of £7 a year.

Kavirondo, to Ushirombo in the Vicariate of Tabora, to both Catholic and Lutheran missions among the Chagga of Mount Kilimanjaro.

Another idea, which was possibly more prominent in theory than in practice, was that of Industrial Education. Whereas literary education developed out of the school for catechists, industrial education sprang from the mission buildings, the mission church, the mission press and the mission estate. As such, it was more characteristically a feature of Catholic missions, who aimed to be nearly self-supporting and who recruited and trained regular orders of lay-brothers to undertake these secular tasks, than of Protestant missions, who relied almost entirely on the salaries they received from the home constituency and who always found the greatest difficulty in recruiting European artisans. Nevertheless, as the expanding Churches suffered increasing disappointments from within their ranks, the minds of Protestant missionaries turned partly to economic remedies. 'I do not see', Archdeacon Farler had written, 'how you can raise man's spiritual life unless you raise his bodily life to correspond.' This was possibly a counsel of despair from a man who was shortly to retire from missionary work on grounds of ill-health; but it reflected a growing opinion that successful adherence to a new faith might involve the adoption of certain new economic and social standards. If the African Christian was to abandon his place on the old ladders of economic prosperity and social prestige by practising monogamy, he must be compensated by learning a trade or new methods of agriculture which would open the way to new ambitions. If his children were to sleep at home and live a Christian family life, he must have a house with two rooms instead of one. If he was to read his Bible, his house must have windows to admit the light, and therefore its shape must be square and not conical; nor could he afford to rebuild it every five years to meet the needs of shifting cultivation. If his children were to be educated, he must learn to do without their services on the farm and yet earn enough to pay their school fees. Again, to pay the government tax and his Church tithe he must have ready money; and, if he was not to leave his family to work on a railway or a plantation, he must produce not only for himself but for the market.

And so, during the period of consolidation after the first

great deployment, the 'pious industrial superintendents', so contemptuously dismissed by Dr Cust, so strongly advocated by Sir Bartle Frere, began to figure in the plans of the most evangelical missions. Berlin I engaged an agriculturalist to try to solve the economic problems of their converts. Berlin III reported experiments in new crops which their adherents could grow and sell for cash. The Church of Scotland Mission and the C.M.S. taught printing, smithing, carpentry and brick-making. In 1904 Mr Victor Buxton, a member of the C.M.S. Committee, founded the Uganda Company and East African Industries Ltd in order to provide employment for the mission's industrial trainees. It is difficult to assess just how far missionary initiative at this period was responsible for economic developments in East African society, how far, as distinct from other factors, it influenced peasant agriculture or helped to produce a class of artisans. What little evidence there is suggests that industrial education too often lifted Africans out of their own society only to enmesh them in the web of European economic enterprise. Certainly technical education did not, like literary education, develop into a mass movement, in which the pupils of the European missionary themselves became teachers, supporting themselves directly or indirectly on indigenous contributions. Indeed it is probable that the greatest service of the industrial movement to the Christian community lay less in the material enrichment of its individual members than in the churches and cathedrals with which it began to adorn a landscape too little tamed by human arts. . . .

40. Christian missions and the making of Nigeria

J. F. AJAYI *Christian Missions in Nigeria* Longmans and Northwestern University Press 1965; pages 1–5, 269–73

Some people see religion as a limited set of personal beliefs about God and worship which can be isolated from a person's general culture and can be changed without necessarily upsetting that person's culture or his world-view. Others see it as an affair of the community so intimately bound up with its way of life that a change of religion necessarily involves a change of culture and the development of a new conscience.

With their emphasis on law, orthodox Muslims generally take the latter, comprehensive view of religion. But in considering conversion to Islam they think of a progression from the limited to the comprehensive view of religion as a growth from the minimal impact to a fuller realization of the faith. When Islam was introduced into Bornu and the Hausa states in the fourteenth and fifteenth centuries, it spread informally at first as a set of ideas about God and worship, accommodated within the converts' monarchical and social customs. It was rather like a fashion associated with the courts and the military, mercantile and literate classes. Yet the elements of this fashion, the learned mallam as teacher, political or medical adviser; the widely travelled Muslim trader as customer or informant; even immaterial things like charms and amulets, court music, styles of dress and architecture as symbols of status and power, all seemed to lead back to Islam. And the spread of these led to the spread of the religion, down the Niger into Nupe and Igalla, and across the Niger into Yoruba. Then at the beginning of the nineteenth century, with Usuman dan Fodio's *jihad* in the Hausa states, there was a formal attempt to convert Islam from the level of personal beliefs to one of communal law, an attempt to shake off the remnants of traditional customs and to create a theocratic empire where Islamic laws and practices would prevail. Bornu successfully resisted being incorporated into this empire only because its administration as well as its Islamic faith were reformed by El Kanemi. But even areas which had felt only the minimal impact of Islam were also incorporated. In Nupe there was a disputed succession; at Ilorin there was a quarrel between the military governor and his sovereign at Old Oyo; and two Fulani mallams took advantage of these to convert Ilorin and Nupe into southern outposts of the Fulani empire.

Within Christianity, on the other hand, the element of theology has always been more important than that of law, and priests and kings have by no means always seen eye to eye. As long as the Church was united, Christianity tended to take the view that religion was an affair of the community, and most aspects of life were regulated by religious laws. But the Reformation, the disputes between Catholics and Protestants and between different Protestant denominations, further emphasized theology and the element of personal belief and personal commitment. For a while the communal view survived in the sixteenth century dictum of *cuius regio, eius religio*, in which the Capuchin missionaries who tried to introduce Christianity into Benin placed so much confidence. But Christianity was by then already reflecting the increasingly individualized society of Western Europe. More and more aspects of life were being regulated by ideas and beliefs outside the purview of religion. The European conception of religion became limited in the sense that it was seen as a personal and not a communal affair and that it was confined to only a special area of a man's life.

This development explains at least in part the ineffectiveness of the Christian missionaries in Benin and Warri. The Oba of Benin himself had asked for Portuguese missionaries, but when they arrived in August 1515, he was away fighting the Idah War. He summoned them to join him on the battlefront, asking meanwhile that lessons on religion be postponed 'because he needed leisure for such a deep mystery'. He returned after a year and asked that one of his sons and others of the chiefs be baptized and taught to read. He was soon back at his wars and presumably the missionaries returned home. When three other missionaries arrived in 1538, they found the Oba no longer interested. Portuguese trade in Benin had declined and the missionaries were unwilling to supply ammunition as requested by the Oba. Thereafter the missionary effort in Benin was fitful and intermittent, and it failed completely to displace the traditional religion.

In the middle of the seventeenth century, Spanish and Italian Capuchins made a determined effort. But they held on to the belief that because the Oba was 'adored' by his subjects with 'fear and unbelievable reverence . . . if he were converted to the Faith, the rest of his subjects would easily be won over'. They were given rooms in the palace, but denied free access to the Oba. They saw him only twice in ten months. They were denied the services of interpreters, and when in August 1651 they tried to disturb a religious festival involving human sacrifice, they were thrust out by an angry mob and subsequently deported. A number of missionaries tried to re-enter Benin through Warri, but without much success. In a moment of grave constitutional crisis in 1709–10 apparently one Oba invited the Capuchins back in the hope that their support might be useful, but he did not live long enough to give them a foothold.

In Warri, however, it did appear in the 1570s as if the Portuguese had successfully planted their religion there, since the Olu, anxious to maintain his independence from Benin, decided to enlist Portuguese support. He welcomed Augustinian missionaries from São Tomé and allowed his crown prince to be baptized as Sebastian. This prince later sent one of his sons, Domingos, to Portugal to be educated, and he came back with a Portuguese wife. The son of Domingos by this marriage, Dom Antonio Domingos, when he became the Olu, carried on this tradition of close Portuguese and Christian connections. Indeed, for about a century and a half, 1570–1733, the Warri rulers became well known as professing Christians. But the European religion did not spread beyond the court. Even at court its hold was recognized to be shaky.

> True Christianity [said the Bishop of São Tomé in 1620] is almost wholly confined to the king and the prince; the rest only call themselves Christian to please the king. They take their children to baptism only with the greatest reluctance, believing that a baptized child will die immediately. The majority of them take wives without the sacrament of matrimony, they circumcise their children and practise superstitious rites and sorcery.

Catholic baptism means little without the sacraments, and the Warri rulers could not even ensure a regular supply of resident clergy to administer them. Eventually the traditional religion reasserted itself at court, and from 1733 onwards the ruling family began to turn against Christianity. In the eighteenth century, the missionary enthusiasm of the Catholic countries of Europe declined; the Protestant countries showed none, and therefore few missionaries came to Warri. By the beginning of the nineteenth century there was little to show for the earlier missionary endeavours: only a few relics like the huge cross in the centre of old Warri, a few church decorations surviving among the traditional shrines, a few memories reflected in oral tradition and in the ritual of traditional gods.

There were, no doubt, other subsidiary factors hindering the Christian missionaries: difficulties of language, of transport, of health; inadequate numbers of missionaries and opportunities. Compared with their Muslim counterparts, the Christian missionaries laboured under great disabilities. The Muslims were usually fellow-Africans who, like the Fulani, could settle down or travel regularly with relative ease to the main centres of Islam not only in the Sudan but also in the Middle East and North Africa. The Christians were a few ailing Europeans, struggling to keep alive in the swampy creeks and depending on sailing vessels for communication with their bases in Europe. But the roots of their failure went deeper than this. After all, European traders working under similar disadvantages did not fare so badly in comparison with North African and Sudanese traders. The real problem was that to the people of Benin and Warri religion meant one thing, and to their Christian teachers quite another thing. To a people for whom religion was co-extensive with life, the Europeans presented trade and religion as two separate institutions, championed by two separate sets of people and guided by two different sets of principles. The missionaries were dependent on the traders for their transport and provisions, but they could not convincingly reconcile their teaching with the Atlantic slave-trade and slavery as practised in the New World. Ultimately, as the Dutch said, the two were incompatible. Thus the missionaries concentrated only on the aspect of personal belief and forms of worship, and consequently paid inadequate attention to education. For the same reason, they failed to understand the society they were dealing with. They saw in traditional religion no more than fetishes, idolatry and juju. The people of Warri, said a Capuchin in 1710, were 'obstinate, idolatrous and given to witchcraft and all sorts of abominable vices'. As Dr Ryder has said, not one of the Christian missionaries for all their devotion 'came near an adequate understanding of the complex religious system they were trying to displace'.

The essential point about the complex religious system was that it was not so much a matter of personal beliefs as the culture of the whole of the community. Religion, it has been said, was 'the cement of good-will and fear that kept the family as a unit and the village as a distinctive community'. The welfare of the individual, the family, village or larger community was believed to depend on the members severally and collectively maintaining the right relationships with the ancestors, gods and other unseen powers through a complex system of ritual observances. There were beliefs, of course, about the organic philosophy of the community, the proper relationships between the gods, between them and man, man and woman, the living and the dead; beliefs about the mysteries of life, sickness and death, good and ill fortune, and so on. But there was really no theology in the sense of dogmatic tenets. The traditional religion was an attitude of mind, a way of explaining the world, a way of life. It was expressed in laws and customs hallowed by time and myth as being essential for the well-being not just of the individual, but of the whole community. To the problems of life to which these customs tried to provide an answer, a catechism that was no more than a set of beliefs necessary for personal salvation must have appeared irrelevant. . . .

The way Bishop Crowther had been ousted showed that the transmutation of Europeans from guides to rulers was complete in the Church as it was becoming complete in the administration of the country, and that the earlier policy of encouraging the growth of an African middle class was completely overturned.

This change of policy was fundamental, though it did not lead to so complete a break with the past as men like Brooke and Robinson hoped. For they themselves died, Robinson in July 1891, Brooke in March 1892. With them died, too, much of the sensationalism of making a complete break with the work of the African missionaries. As soon as the missionaries who succeeded them got down to the not very romantic aspects of making Christianity appeal to other people, and doing so on a limited budget, they began to find many things they approved of in the policy of Crowther and his men.[1] Indeed, as roads and railways

[1] Archdeacon Dobinson, the only survivor of the Sudan Party, later apologized openly in Freetown and Lagos for his part in the 'Great Purge'. He said he had been 'hurried along in unknown depths of fierce-flowing river. . . .' He showed more appreciation of the local customs he previously despised and pleaded for more educated Africans to work on the Niger, as they did most of the work even if Europeans supervised.

and British political power penetrated the country and created in parts of the interior as much demand for education as Crowther found in the Delta in his time, the European missionaries, not only of the C.M.S. but of other missions as well, began generally to adopt Crowther's policy of evangelization through the village school. Like Crowther, they had to talk about the material advantages of having schools in the community. And just as in Crowther's time Sierra Leone had supplied teachers and evangelists, so after him, Lagos, Brass, Bonny, Calabar, Abeokuta, and to some extent Ibadan and Ogbomoso began to supply agents to the new centres of missionary work both on the coast in Benin and Ijebu and in the interior in Ekiti, Arochuku and other parts of Iboland. In this way the labours of the missionaries, African and European, in the fifty years before 1891 provided abundant fruit for the Church in the fifty years after.

It is also possible to argue that much of the later harvest was made possible precisely because the earlier missionaries had placed so much emphasis on education and civilization, and because this continued to affect the work of the later missionaries who would have liked to see much less emphasis placed on these things. But for the effects of the earlier policy in the older mission centres, people in the areas of Southern Nigeria being penetrated by missionaries in the later period might have taken less readily to mission schools, and might have been less ready to pay for them. As it happened, their demand for schools was so persistent that the choice of missionaries in the matter of whether to build schools or not was severely limited. Government officials who wished to maintain the delicate balance of the Indirect Rule system and wanted only children of chiefs to go to school, did not hide their distrust of mission schools, which continued indiscriminately to accept children of chiefs and commoners. Many missionaries were inclined to agree with the government officials about the bad effects of mission schools. Some of them, as it were, smote their breasts and pleaded guilty to the sins of their predecessors in fostering an allegedly idle middle class with no roots in and no love for their own country, good for nothing except imitating European vices. Yet it was precisely at this period that missionaries built more purely literary schools and embarked on far fewer schemes of industrial and technical education. In spite of the new emphasis on hospitals, it was through the village school that the Church was spreading rapidly in the later period. It may also be mentioned that the political officers contributed to this. Though they declared that the installation of a Government Agent from whom henceforth the local rulers had to take orders was an unimportant change that left the people's life unaffected, it had in fact created so great a psychological revolution in the people's attitude that they tended to rush to missionaries with less hesitation and less reserve than was the case in the earlier period. It was only with the coming of the District Officer that things began to fall apart.

The ousting of Crowther from the Niger did not stop the growth of the class of educated Africans, but it meant that until they became strong enough to demand more rights and privileges, their fortunes were severely limited. They were discredited in the eyes of the new European ruling class. Little that they did received favourable comment. Even when Samuel Johnson completed his *History of the Yorubas* in 1897 the C.M.S. showed no enthusiasm to publish it.[1] Their advancement in commercial houses and the civil service was curtailed, since all the important jobs came to be regarded as specifically 'European' jobs to which only rarely favoured Africans could be admitted. Their economic opportunities declined. They took little part in the commercial expansion that resulted from the railways and the introduction of cash crops. It was the peasants who, as the philanthropists had always wished, cultivated the crops, but it was the European firms, not the educated Africans, who had the resources and the facilities to export

[1] The book was completed in 1897. The C.M.S. said it was too long and were interested in a short history suitable for use in schools. Apparently Johnson refused to cut it down and sent it through the C.M.S. to an English publisher. Nothing more was heard of the manuscript. The author's brother, Dr O. Johnson, on a visit to England in 1900, was told that it had been mislaid. Within a year after that the author died and it had to be rewritten by Dr Johnson from Samuel's notes and earlier drafts. The new version was sent to England in 1916, but owing to enemy action during the war did not reach England till 1918 and owing to shortage of paper was returned to await the end of the war. It was finally published by Routledge & Son in 1921. By 1937 the C.M.S. were anxious to publish a second edition of the book.

them. Above all, their opportunities in the Church also became limited. The missions continued to rely on their African staffs, but highly educated pastors were not encouraged, and the highest posts were reserved for Europeans. After Crowther there were assistant bishops, but no diocesan bishop till 1953, when the constitutional changes in the country occasioned constitutional changes in the Church. It was not till 1946 that the Methodists appointed the first African Chairman of the District.

Some of the educated Africans for a while sought political careers as advisers to the local rulers in the interior, or as their agents in the capital. One effect of this may be seen in the fact that it was the centres where missionary work had been most successful in the earlier period and where the educated Africans were most influential that saw some of the most determined efforts to negotiate agreements to limit the rights of the British rulers. The Royal Niger Company had the greatest difficulty at Onitsha in its effort to obtain treaties on which to base its political privileges, and far more difficulty at Egga and Bida than at Sokoto. It was at Calabar and Bonny that the British Commissioner received the most specific conditions under which British rule would be accepted. Above all, Abeokuta, where the educated Africans came nearest to political power, managed to resist British annexation till 1914, having in the meantime evolved the Egba United Government in which educated Africans continued to hold important executive posts. But even that was temporary. Law and medicine, which afforded a chance of private practice and success independently of the new ruling class, became the goals of the educated Africans.

This eclipse of the educated Africans in one way delayed the full development of the Church, and in another hastened it. It delayed it because, as Venn always argued, as long as Europeans retained full control of the Church it could be no more than an exotic institution. Only the Africans themselves could make it a national institution. It is interesting to observe, for example, that little adaptation in the usages of the Church took place for many years after 1891. Venn had suggested that such adaptation should be made not by European missionaries but by the most highly accomplished and gifted of the African pastors themselves. From 1891 until quite recently, such pastors received little encouragement even in the missions sufficiently well established to produce them.

Yet this fact itself helped the development of the Church in another way by diverting the energies of many Africans towards the formation of an African Church where African usages and practices would be welcome. After some initial hesitation people began to take the United Native African Church formed in 1891 a little more seriously. In 1901 a 'major' secession in the Anglican Church in Lagos led to the foundation of the African Bethel Church. Elsewhere suppressed political feelings went into Prophet movements and revivalist organizations. The African Church movement, consisting of people brought up in different denominations, was bedevilled by differences over doctrine and conflicts over leadership. In particular there was conflict between those maintaining the congregational view of the minister responsible to the congregation, and those who believed in the sacerdotal view of a priesthood with apostolic succession and a hierarchy. There were compromises and schisms. In 1907 it was agreed that the head of the new African Church would be 'Superintendent, or in other words, Ecclesiastical or Presbyterian Bishop in contradistinction to Prelatical or Historical Bishop'. Some of those dissatisfied with this very obvious compromise broke away in 1908 and formed the African Salem Church.

But in spite of such schisms and of much bitterness of feeling the movement as a whole gathered strength. It showed that there were Africans who felt sufficiently deeply about the new religion that they were willing to try to express its spirit in their own way and to compete with the mission-supervised churches in spreading the Gospel to other parts of the country. It was a major outward sign that the Church had become established in Nigeria and was unlikely to die out again.

The African Church movement has another significance that should be noted in conclusion. It provides a link between the educated Africans of Crowther's age and the nationalists of our day who have re-emphasized the mid-nineteenth-century doctrines about the importance of an African middle class for the development of the country, and the distinction between the expansion of trade controlled by foreign European firms and economic development as a factor of social and economic change in the country.[1]

[1] J. F. Ade Ajayi, 'Nineteenth Century Origins of Nigerian Nationalism', *Journal of the Historical Society of Nigeria*, vol. ii, no. 2, 1961. cf. Herbert Macaulay, a grandson of Bishop Crowther, regarded as Father of Nigerian nationalism. In 1942, when the Methodists were celebrating the centenary of Freeman's arrival in Badagri, Herbert Macaulay was using the platform of the African Church to deliver a nationalist address, welcoming the missionary movement, but condemning European imperialism. *The History of the Development of Missionary Work with Special Reference to the United African Church*, Printed Pamphlet, Lagos, 1942.

XIV. AFRICAN RELIGIOUS MOVEMENTS

41. African religious developments

J. W. FERNANDEZ *Journal of Modern African Studies* Vol. 2, No. 4, 1964 Cambridge University Press; pages 534–42

. . . If we compile a list of types of African religious movements we recognise at once that we are confronted with too broad and redundant a typology. A partial compilation would include prophetism, faith healing, prophet healing, Bible church, Ethiopian, Zionist, messianic, millenarian, separatist, contra-acculturative independent, syncretist, and nativist, to go no further. It is a considerable challenge to reduce this plethora to the four basic types we propose—reformative, separatist, nativist, and messianic—because the various regions of Africa have become attached to the typologies that have grown out of original local research. Thus Sundkler's typology, Ethiopian-Zionist, has currency in Southern Africa. Yet, as Parrinder points out, it is not really satisfactory elsewhere. For one thing, other areas do not have the same racial problems as South Africa. These have been a dynamic factor in separatism there and are expressed in the term Ethiopianism. For another thing, all areas have not had the same close contact with New World revivalism and millenarianism: this contact was primarily with the American Negro separatist churches such as the African Methodist Episcopal Church in the United States or the various Negro Baptist Churches. Pentecostal revivalists such as the Christian Catholic Apostolic Church of Zion Illinois, the Adventists, and especially the Jehovah's Witnesses, whose watch-tower doctrines have had such an impact on Central Africa, were also important. No one can deny, within the framework of South African history, that Sundkler's two terms are appropriate in typing the religious movements that occurred there. We must seek for terms, however, that are less bound to a specific area and a specific history.

The classic typology for movements of the kind we are considering here remains that of Ralph Linton, made in his paper on 'Nativistic Movements'. By such movements he means 'any conscious organised attempt on the part of a society's members to revive or perpetuate selected aspects of its culture'. Linton discusses two sets of criteria—whether the movements are perpetuative or revivalist, and whether they are magical or rational. He combines these sets into the four theoretical types—revivalistic-magical, revivalistic-rational, perpetuative-magical, and perpetuative-rational. A recent and particularly cogent criticism of Linton by Worsley points out, however, that practically all religious movements are ready to adopt new elements, invent new ritual or reinterpret the old, and hence the categories perpetuative and revivalistic suggest a state of affairs so delimited as to be uninformative. Worsley also criticises the term rational, pointing out that it risks evoking an old argument as to logical and pre-logical mentality. What looks magical to us may be perfectly rational in another less sophisticated frame of reference with other premises. Reason should not be after all a function of range of awareness.

Nevertheless movements do differ as to the degree to which they perpetuate the old or incorporate the new. The clue to a more appropriate set of characteristics to which to refer a typology is found in Linton's statement that 'what really happens in all nativistic movements is that certain current or remembered elements of culture are selected for emphasis and given symbolic value'. If this is true, the question arises, whence does the particular movement obtain its symbols? From its own cultural tradition, or from the culture of the society or societies with which it is in contact? We find ourselves thus on a continuum, or a continuous series of gradual stages between movements which exploit primarily their own tradition, and movements which are largely committed by acculturation to the symbols of the contact culture. The continuum thus lies between the two poles of a traditional or an acculturated symbolism.

But the larger question remains as to how these symbols are used: whether instrumentally or expressively. This suggests a second dimension, which may be defined as follows. An instrumental type of religious movement chooses the elements for symbolic use in a realistic and goal-minded fashion and with a view to perpetuating them under existing conditions. We find fairly pragmatic attempts to compensate for the deprivations and other frustrations involved in the situation of subordination, without endangering the continuity and survival of the religious group, since it is seen as the only institution that can achieve its goals. In an expressive type of religion the emphasis is upon escape by symbolic displacement from the situation which is causing frustration. This is done by means of symbolic forms in ritual and ceremony, song, drama, and dance. Intense involvement of the participants in these activities draws their attention away from the frustrations and deprivations of their everyday situation. In such movements the group as an entity is not all-important. It and its activity are but means to this symbolic displacement.

In an expressive movement there is no calculated attempt to deal with a difficult situation directly. Rather the frustrations involved often spontaneously produce supernatural and visionary experiences in persons of charismatic qualities.[1] These movements rely on intense evocation of the supernatural and are given over to enthusiastic religious behaviour. Their emotional tone is high and they count heavily on ritualisation. Their leaders are preoccupied with internal concerns and not with representing the group to the larger situation of which it is a part. Moribund elements of culture may be revived, not in anticipation of practical advantages, but as part of a magical formula which will miraculously change a frustrating environment and return it to a pristine condition. In all cases these movements exhibit an unrealistic reliance on their ability to create and constitute their own universe through expressive symbolism.

In summary, then, movements whose emphasis is primarily instrumental keep enough cognisance of the total situation to which they are reacting to remain adapted to it and thus guarantee their survival. They are exocentric—well aware of their place in a larger field. Movements whose emphasis is expressive institute kinds of behaviour which compensate the individuals for the deprivations they feel at the moment; but

[1] The expressive-instrumental continuum is basic in the work of Talcott Parsons. He says of the expressive orientation: 'The essential point is the primacy of "acting out" the need disposition itself rather than subordinating gratification to a goal outside the immediate situation.' *The Social System* (Glencoe 1951), p. 348.

they remain preoccupied with these compensations, their symbolic gratification, without reference to the outside world of time and place, of which they are a part. They are not so much concerned with their group survival as they are with directly reducing the frustrations and anxieties with which they are living.[1]

We have some examples of what we mean in the Gabon religious cults studied by the writer. These cults, ordinarily typed syncretist, are in two different places along the expressive-instrumental continuum. Those concerned with expressive satisfactions insist on ritual procedure regardless of administrative disapproval of certain practices such as use of the corpse or ritual flagellation. Other cults, more instrumental in orientation, attempt to modify their practices to some extent to accord with the directives of the government and local administration. It is the latter who have had, quite naturally, greater survival value, but they have not provided the range of symbolic satisfactions available in the former. For example the expressive groups have always freely taken the alkaloid stimulant, *eboga* (Tabernenthes Eboga), an important guarantee of a satisfying ritual experience. The instrumental-type cults have been, because of their awareness of administrative disapproval, more sparing in the use of this drug, denying thereby some ritual satisfactions to their members for the sake of the survival of the group. The price of survival has been the pain of accommodation.

We may now locate the four types of religious movements proposed earlier in relation to our two bi-polar continua. Nativist movements are those oriented towards a *traditional* symbolism, which they manipulate *expressively*. Messianic movements generally employ an *acculturated* symbolism, which despite their acceptance of historic time they manipulate *expressively*, conjuring up millennial satisfactions. Separatist movements employ an *acculturated* symbolism, which they tend to manipu-

[1] It should be repeated that this is an analytic distinction; no religious movement is exclusively instrumental or expressive, nor could it be. We are concerned with the relative primacy of one mode or another of action. Knowledge of the relative primacy is of value in assessing the order of priorities in a movement's economy and is useful in predicting its capacity to survive.

late *instrumentally*. Reformative movements find their base in a *traditional* orientation, with which, because of their *instrumental* orientation, they deliberately and creatively combine an acculturated symbolism. This theoretical placing of the four types may be indicated in a diagram using two co-ordinate axes.

	Acculturated	
Separatist		Messianic
Instrumental	—	Expressive
Reformative		Nativist
	Traditional	

We now turn to individual cases. Every concrete movement may be located in a particular position on the co-ordinate system of the diagram, though there are difficulties caused by overlap and interpenetration.

Separatism. Most of the movements within this category have the organisational characteristics of a church. They place, in fact, heavy emphasis upon the social organisation and co-ordination of the membership. They are concerned with the group's status in the larger society and think usually, though not necessarily, of improving that status.[1] Usually they separated from European-dominated parent organisations for non-religious reasons. In respect to Christian symbols, religious belief, and ceremony, they continue to adhere very closely to the practices of the parent organisation and they remain therefore fairly orthodox in liturgy and theology. The separation from the parent body was designed to make possible greater status in church organisation, which was achieved. Members of the best examples of movements of this kind, the African Congregational

[1] Such separatist movements as the *Apostolowa Fe Dedefia Habobo* (the Apostolic Revelation Society) in Ghana, as described by C. G. Baëta, *Prophetism in Ghana* (London, 1962), pp. 77–93, have many of the instrumental characteristics of improvement associations. On the other hand South African separatist churches, though sensitive to their relationship to the larger society, strongly support apartheid and the social *status quo*. Sundkler, however, makes it clear that this support is strongest from those movements of a Zionist, that is, messianic, disposition.

Church and the Bantu Methodist Church in South Africa, are very conscious of their social status within the larger community, and are anxious that their religious behaviour should be instrumental in promoting or maintaining it. Many of the African churches which are classed as Ethiopian by Sundkler would fall fully into this category, as would all of the native churches recognised by the South African Government. If, for reasons of continuing frustration or weak leadership and organisation, fission occurs in a separatist church, and Sundkler testifies to the extent of this, it is likely that the newly formed groups will forget their concern with orthodoxy, and tend more and more to a syncretism and perhaps eventually to nativism. Also, continuing frustrations may lend importance to visionary experiences and give the movement substantial qualities of messianism. The dynamism of these movements has been amply portrayed by Sundkler, to whom the problem of orthodoxy is a main concern.

Other examples of this type of movement may be mentioned. One is the Church of the Lord Aladura, which had its beginnings among the Yoruba in Lagos in the twenties, and has since spread to the other three regions of Nigeria, and to Ghana, Sierra Leone, and Liberia as well. Here again we are dealing with founders who were all bona fide members of the Church Missionary Society affiliates in West Africa, but who claimed to have become dissatisfied with the immorality of European Christianity as evidenced by the foolishness of World War I and compounded by succeeding metropolitan barbarities. Nevertheless the leaders of this movement have been resistant to the symbolism of traditional African religion, and greatly desire to be accepted by the Christian community. Evidence of their concern with Christian orthodoxy has been their habit of enrolling their leaders in a two-year course at the Missionary Bible Institute in Great Britain.[1] The African Methodist Episcopal Church of South Africa and Rhodesia, the Watchtower Society of Jehovah's Witnesses (as opposed to any

[1] Recent research by R. L. Mitchell shows a preoccupation with alleviating the physical and spiritual sufferings of members by expressive techniques. His insistence that the Aladura movement must be studied from 'the perspective of the Protestant religious system' confirms in our view, however, its separatist character.

of the Kitawala or Watchman offshoots), and John Chilembwe's Providence Industrial Mission, all fall within the separatist division, though at rather different positions.

A final example of the separatist type is the African Greek Orthodox Church in Uganda, founded by Reuben Spartas in the twenties in dissidence and protest against the paternalism of missionary Anglicanism. At first linked with the Marcus Garvey movement and the African Orthodox Church in the United States, the remarkable thing is that by a long series of skilful negotiations Spartas finally gained in 1946 corporate acceptance by the Greek Orthodox Church. Thus, as Welbourn points out, both Romans and Anglicans in Uganda are faced not with a purely local schism, but with a recognised branch of a world church in their midst. What is demonstrated in this course of events for our purposes is the goal-minded, instrumental, and acculturated orientation of the movement, which eventually resulted in a full return to orthodoxy.

Nativist movements contrast in every way with separatist movements. In so far as they begin in the context of Christian colonisation, they express a fundamental disaffection with Christian symbolism and with the way Christianity confronts the supernatural. These movements turn to tradition for effective ritual and more penetrating belief. They are, like messianic movements, often preoccupied with directly healing or easing the multitude of physical and spiritual ills that afflict Africans, and they do this by ecstatic techniques and highly emotionalised ritual. In a purely nativist movement the sources of these techniques and rituals should be exclusively traditional. But, as Worsley has indicated, this is rare in the situation of culture contact which gives rise to religious movements. We almost always have a syncretism. Thus churches which Sundkler calls 'Zionist' in South Africa would seem to fall into this category, although a good many traditional curing practices have been prohibited.

Moreover, in the type-movement of South African 'Zionism', the *ama Nazaretha* or Nazarene Church of Isaiah Shembe, there is a patent search for a new messiah, partially made out in Shembe himself. Though the nativist orientation is strong here, so also is the messianic tendency. An indication of the strong traditional orientation is seen in Shembe's construction of an old-type Zulu village, Ekuphakameni, in order that his followers might worship and be cured in appropriate surroundings. The kinds of conditions created by European cities and farms could only further sicken his people. Another example of a nativist movement with overtones of messianism was Mau Mau in Kenya and, before it, Maji Maji in southern Tanganyika. The various modern anti-witchcraft movements which have been so abundant in Africa in recent years, and the Congo 'Holy Water' movements discussed by Kopytoff, also fall in this category.

Reformative movements are those which have preserved a strong sense of the viability of the traditional African religious attitude with its associated symbolism. However, these movements have been inescapably aware of Christianity and the attractiveness of some of its symbolism, and have therefore made calculated attempts to integrate Christian elements into their beliefs and ritual. A prime example of this type of movement is Bwiti in Gabon; a marginal example is *lalouisme* or the Abadice Cult in the southern Ivory Coast. The air of calculated recreation in all these movements is reflected in the name Abadice—coined from ABC—as well as their susceptibility to the obvious advantages of western civilisation. In the case of Bwiti we find, over time, the gradual reinterpretation and creative elaboration of an ancestor cult, Bieri, in the presence of Christianity. The orientation remains traditional, with the purposeful accretion of Christian elements. We may mention, as a movement marginally reformative in the direction of separatism, the National Church of Nigeria and the Cameroons, which was organised by Azikiwe's N.C.N.C. as its religious wing—mainly, to be sure, for instrumental political purposes, but also with the purpose of preserving a denigrated African tradition.

A better example of reformatism from Nigeria would be the Reformed Ogboni Society among the Yoruba. This traditionally had important social and political functions as a secret society, which have been much reduced, while its religious dimensions have been carefully syncretised with Christian elements. The Reformed Ogboni Society indicates in its very name the important feature of these movements—their sense of continuity with African tradition and, at the same time, their readiness to reform themselves by appeal to acculturation.

Messianic movements are commonly seen as those that arise out of intense xenophobia—in most cases the hated object is European and colonial domination. The prophet or black messiah, responding to visionary experiences, which confirm his election and provide him with charismatic personality, works upon this emotion in expressive ways. A *Weltanschauung* is created, irrespective of the actuality in which the movement exists, and the prophet guarantees for his followers either a return to the golden age of African culture, or the coming of a future millennium. The unrealistic promises and expressive practices of these movements reduce the frustrations of social domination and cultural deprecation by elaborating a compensatory universe. It is of interest, and may be due to African pragmatism, that a pure example of this type of movement is rare, though many African religious movements have moved through a messianic stage. It is of further interest that messianic movements characteristically reject a good portion of their own traditional religious practice. This is true of *kimbanguisme*, which in its early form was a messianic movement largely influenced by missionary protestantism. Other movements which through their expressive character and acculturation fall into this quarter of the diagram would be the Society of the One Almighty God in Uganda, with its adamant reaction to medicine of all kinds; and the Elliot Kamwana and Bamulonda movements in Rhodesia and Nyasaland. As marginally messianic we would include Alice Lenshina's Lumpa Church, and the Musama Disco Christo Church of Ghana. It is clear that the expressive orientation and messianic qualities of the Lenshina movement encouraged the fanaticism to which it succumbed in its recent confrontation with the Government. Because of the heightened emotion characteristic of these movements, the unrealistic expectations they create in their followers, and their neglect of the larger situation of which they are a part and to which they have reacted but remain unattuned, they are usually short-lived. Their organisational thrust is customarily expended in ritual and cosmological elaborations, and not in more viable social and political forms.

Select Bibliography

ARKELL, ANTHONY JOHN *The History of the Sudan from the Earliest Times to 1821* London 1961

AXELSON, ERIC *The Portuguese in South-East Africa, 1600–1700* Witwatersrand 1960

—— *South East Africa, 1480–1530* Witwatersrand 1940

BELL, H. IDRIS *Egypt from Alexander the Great to the Arab Conquest* Oxford 1948

BIVAR, A. D. H. 'The Wathiqat ahl al-Sudan: A Manifesto of the Fulani Jihad' *The Journal of African History* Vol. II, 1961, pp. 235–43

BIVAR, A. D. H. and HISKETT, MERVYN 'The Arabic Literature of Nigeria to 1804: A Provisional Account' *Bulletin of the School of Oriental and African Studies* Vol. XXV, 1962, pp. 104–48

BLAKE, J. W. *Europeans in West Africa, 1450–1560* Oxford 1942

BOVILL, E. W. *The Golden Trade of the Moors* London 1958

—— *Caravans of the Old Sahara* Oxford 1933

BOXER, C. R. *Salvadore de Sa and the Struggle for Brazil and Angola, 1602–1686* London 1952

BRIGGS, LLOYD C. *Tribes of the Sahara* Oxford 1960

CARY, MAX OTTO and WARMINGTON, ERIC H. *The Ancient Explorers* London 1929

CHITTICK, H. NEVILLE 'Kilwa and the Arab Settlements of the East African Coast' *The Journal of African History* Vol. IV, 1963, pp. 179–90

CLARK, J. DESMOND *The Pre-History of Southern Africa* Harmondsworth 1959

COLE, SONIA *The Pre-History of East Africa* Harmondsworth 1954

CUVELIER, J. and JADIN, L. *L'Ancien Congo, 1518–1640* Brussels 1954

DELCOURT, ANDRÉ *La France et les Establissements français au Sénégal, 1713–1763* Dakar 1952

DIKE, K. O. *Trade and Politics in the Niger Delta* Oxford 1956

DUFFY, JAMES *Portuguese Africa* Harvard 1959

DUNGLAS, ÉDOUARD 'Contribution à l'histoire du Moyen-Dahomey' *Études Dahoméennes* Vols. XIX–XXI, 1957–8, *passim*

EMERY, W. B. *Archaic Egypt* Harmondsworth 1961

FAGE, JOHN D. 'Ancient Ghana: A Review of the Evidence' *Transactions of the Historical Society of Ghana* Vol. III, 1957, pp. 77–98

—— *An Introduction to the History of West Africa* Cambridge 1962

—— *Ghana: A Historical Interpretation* Modisan 1959

FAIRSERVIS, WALTER A. *The Ancient Kingdoms of the Nile and the Doomed Monuments of Nubia* New York 1962

GAUTIER, ÉMIL FÉLIX *Les Siècles Obscures du Maghreb* Paris 1927

GERMAIN, GABRIEL 'Qu'est-ce que le *Périple* d'Hannon? Document, amplification littéraire ou faux intégral?' *Hespéris* Vol. XLIV, 1957, pp. 205–48

GRAY, RICHARD *A History of the Southern Sudan, 1839–1899* London 1961

GSELL, STEPHANE *Histoire ancienne de l'Afrique du Nord* (4 vols.) Paris 1920–1

HISKETT, MERVYN 'An Islamic Tradition of Reform in the Western Sudan from the 16th to the 18th Century' *Bulletin of the School of Oriental and African Studies* Vol. XXV, 1962, pp. 577–96

HODGKIN, THOMAS (ed.) *Nigerian Perspectives: A Historical Anthology* London 1963

HOLT, PETER MALCOLM 'Funj Origins: A Critique and New Evidence' *Journal of African History* Vol. IV, 1963, pp. 39–55

JONES, A. H. M. and MUNROE, ELIZABETH *A History of Ethiopia* Oxford 1955

JONES, GWILWYM IWAN *The Trading States of the Oil Rivers: A Study of Political Development in Eastern Nigeria* London 1963

JULIEN, C. A. *L'Histoire de l'Afrique du Nord* (Vols. I and II) Paris 1951

KIRWAN, L. P. 'The International Position of the Sudan in Roman and Mediaeval Times' *Sudan Notes and Records* Vol. XI, 1959, pp. 23–37

LEWIS, BERNARD *The Arabs in History* London 1950

MARSH, Z. *East Africa Through Contemporary Records* Cambridge 1961

MCBURNEY, C. B. M. *The Stone Age of Northern Africa* Harmondsworth 1960

MAUNY, RAYMOND A. *Tableau Géographique de l'Ouest Africain au Moyen Âge d'après les sources écrites, la tradition, et l'archéologie* Dakar 1961

MURDOCK, GEORGE P. *Africa: Its Peoples and Their Culture History* McGraw-Hill 1959

NIANE, DJBRIL TAMSIR *Soundjata, ou l'épopée mandingue* Paris 1960

NICKERSON, JANE S. *A Short History of North Africa* New York 1963

OLIVER, ROLAND and MATHEW, GERVASE *History of East Africa* Oxford 1962

PARRY, JOHN H. *The Age of Reconnaissance* Weidenfeld & Nicolson 1963

PIRENNE, JACQUELINE *Le Royaume sud-arabe de Qatabân et sa datation d'après l'archéologie et les sources classiques jusqu'au Périple de la mer Erythrée* Louvain 1961

PERSON, YVES 'Les Ancêtres de Samori' *Cahiers d'Etudes Africaines* Vol. 4, 1963, pp. 125–56

PRIESTLEY, MARGARET and WILKES, IVOR 'The Ashanti Kings in the 18th Century: A Revised Chronology' *Journal of African History* Vol. I, 1960, pp. 83–92

PRIESTLEY, MARGARET 'The Ashanti Question and the British: 18th-Century Origins' *Journal of African History* Vol. II, 1961, pp. 35–60

ROUCH, JEAN *Contribution à l'histoire des Songhay* Dakar 1953

SHAW, STANFORD S. *Ottoman Egypt in the Age of the French Revolution* Harvard 1964

SMITH, H. F. C. 'A Neglected Theme of West African History: The Islamic Revolutions of the 19th Century' *Journal of the Historical Society of Nigeria* Vol. II, 1961, pp. 169–85

STRANDES, JUSTUS *The Portuguese Period in East Africa* East African Literary Bureau, Nairobi 1961

SUMMERS, ROGER *Zimbabwe: A Rhodesian Mystery* Johannesburg 1963

TRIMINGHAM, J. SPENCER *A History of Islam in West Africa* Glasgow 1962

URVOY, YVES *Histoire des populations du Soudan Central* Paris 1936

—— *L'Histoire de l'empire du Bornou* Paris 1949

VANSINA, JAN *L'Évolution du royaume Rwanda des origines à 1900* Brussels 1962

WALKER, ERIC A. *The History of Southern Africa* Longmans 1959

WARMINGTON, B. H. *Carthage* London 1960

—— *The North African Provinces* Cambridge 1954

WILKES, IVOR 'The Rise of the Akwamu Empire, 1650–1710' *Transactions of the Historical Society of Ghana* Vol. III, 1957, pp. 99–136

—— *The Northern Factor in Ashanti History* Legon 1961

WRIGLEY, CHRISTOPHER C. 'Speculations on the Economic Pre-History of Africa' *The Journal of African History* Vol. I, 1960, pp. 189—203

Chronological Table

The following list of dates is intended only as a guide and is not exhaustive. In order to facilitate an understanding of comparative trans-continental developments the following events have been listed in chronological order rather than by country or region.

c. 3–5000 B.C.	Middle Stone Age proper evolved from Sangoan and Fauresmith times
8–10000 B.C.	End of Middle Stone Age (close of Pleistocene)
5500–2500 B.C.	Makalcian (wet) phase. Free exchange between Mediterranean and Negroid populations
146 B.C.	Carthage finally taken and destroyed. End of pre-Roman period in North Africa
150 B.C.–A.D. 642	Period of Roman-Byzantine domination in North Africa
146	Septimius Severus born in Tripolitania
192–211	Reign of Septimius Severus. Summit of Roman rule in Africa
211 (February)	Death of Septimius Severus in York, England
642	Invading armies from Arabia cross Egyptian frontier and enter Cyrenaica
708	All North Africa (except one garrison in Ceuta) in Muslim hands
c. 734	First unequivocal mention of Western Sudan (by Ibn Abd Al Hakam 803–870)
734–750	Umayyads attack Ghana
c. 790	First mention of Ghana (by Al Fazari)
c. 850	Proto-Vakarange leave Lake Tanganyika, migrating south
920–*c.* 1040	Anarchy among Sanhadja Berbers
920–1050	Apogee of Sarakole empire of Ghana

961–971	Tin Yeroutan (a Berber) king of Aoudaghast
969	Mu'izz, fourth Caliph, conquers Egypt at fourth attempt (Fatimid period)
990	Ghana conquers Aoudaghast, subjugating the Middle Senegal, and the bend of the Niger
1035	Abdullah commences conversion of Berbers to Islam
1036–1094	Reign of Caliph Mustansir. Peak of Fatimid period in Egypt, covering North Africa, Sicily, Egypt, Syria and Western Arabia
1042 (trad.)	Abdullah ibn Yasin unites Godala, Lamtuna and Masufa, under Almoravids
1042	Abdullah commences conversion of western Sahara
1050	Beginning of the Mali Empire
1054	Abdullah reconquers Aoudaghast
1054–1055	Almoravids (under Ibn Yasin) take Aoudaghast
1058	Death of Abdullah (after conquering Spain)
1062	Almoravids occupy Fez
1076	Almoravids sack Ghanaian capital. Rise of second period of Muslim prosperity in Aoudaghast
1076	Abu Bekr defeats Ghana
1090–1150	Territorial expansion of Kanem begins. Dunama I of Kanem
c. 1120	Tekla Haymanat declares himself first Zagwe ruler of Axum
c. 1150–1225	Sultan Ali bin al-Hasan, first ruler of Kilwa
c. 1190–1225	Lalibela of Axum
1204	Establishment of island-state of Pate by Nabhani family from Muscat
c. 1224	Oualata founded
1235–1240	Sundiata, king of Mali, captures Sussu provinces, destroys capital of Ghana
1240	Mali, under Sundiata Keita, destroys Ghana

1250–1440	Proto Sotho/Tswana clans infiltrate from north to escape the Kalahari
c. 1250	Djenné founded
c. 1260	Vali, successor to Sundiata, makes first pilgrimage to Mecca
c. 1260	Emergence of Mamluk Sultanate (to rule Egypt and Syria to 1517)
1260	Mansa Uali makes Za Assibai his vassal
c. 1270	Yekuno Amlak regains Axum throne for Solomonoid dynasty. Capital moved to Shoa
1275	Ali Kolon flees from court of Mansa Maghan
1312–1337	Mansa Musa (Kanburi Musa), chief of Mali
1314–1344	Reign of ‘Amda Seyon in Ethiopia
1324	Mansa Musa visits Mecca
1328–1329	Muslims finally defeated by Christians in Axum, ‘Amda Seyon becoming first Emperor of Ethiopia
1325–1433	Malinke of Mali dominates Timbuctoo, Gao and Middle Niger
1332	Collapse of Kilwa Mosque
1337–1341	Maghan I of Mali
c. 1341–1360	Sulaiman king of Mali. Restores peace
1349–1385	King Yaji of Kano
1352	Ibn Battuta’s voyage to the Sudan
1360	Beginning of decline in Mali prestige
1360–1373	Maria Juba II of Mali
1374	Musa II accedes to Mali throne (puppet of Mari Diota)
1380	Foundation of state of Bornu (from Kanem)
1383	Beginning of succession of Mamluk Sultan, achieved by strongest commander
1391	Kanem builds new capital at Koka
1392	Death of Imam ’Ali Si’id in Abyssinia. Muslim Gradabūrse clan’s founding ancestor
c. 1400	Karanga nation established

1400	Sack of Mali by Sonni ma Dau
1400	Mosi lay waste to Debo region
1415	Portuguese conquer Ceuta
1415	Muslims routed in Abyssinia. Ruler Said ad Dīn martyred
1431	Tuaregs capture Timbuctoo
1434–1468	Reign of Zar' a Ya'qob in Ethiopia
1434	Gil Eanes rounds Cape Bojador
c. 1440	King Chibatamatosi sends emissaries in search of salt
c. 1440–1450	Karanga kingdom expands northwards, extending into kingdom of Mwene Mutapa
c. 1440–1473	Ewuare the Great, king of Benin. Height of Benin power
1441	Nuno Tristao and Antao Gonçales begin exportage of slaves from Africa
1441	Slave trade between West Africa and Portugal begins. Antao Gonçales brings first cargo of slaves to Lisbon
1444	Nuno Tristãs discovers mouth of the Senegal. Dinis Dias reaches Cape Verde
1445	First purchase of Africans by Portuguese
c. 1450	Maçina secedes from Mali
1452–1463	Arrival of Peul scholars from Mali
1454–1456	Papal bulls granting Prince Henry of Portugal sole right and duty of converting Guinea
1460	Pedro da Sintra sights mountains of Sierra Leone
1463–1499	Muhammed Rimfa, the greatest pre-Fulani Kano king
c. 1464–1492	Sonni Ali, king of Songhai
1464 (6 November)	Opening of reign of Sonni Ali (Ali Ber). Attack on Mosu, siege of Djenné
1465–1467	Attack on Dogo. Decimation of Peul tribes of Bandiagara
1468 (30 January)	Sonni Ali enters Timbuctoo. Tuareg chief flees to Oualata

1468	Sonni Ali captures Timbuctoo
1468–1591	Songhai kingdom
1469	Afonso V leases Guinea to Fernão Gomes
1469	Sonni Ali leads expedition against Tosko and attacks Tuaregs
1470	Foundation of Ngazargano in Bornu
1471	Sonni Ali destroys the Mosi. Enters Djenné
1472–1476	Sonni Ali pacifies the lake region, founds province of Dirma
1473–1480	Olua, son of Ewuar
1474–1489	Portugal and Castile in war of succession
1475	Isabella formally authorizes her subjects to engage in African trade
1477–1478	Mossi armies ravage central Mali
1479	Treaty of Alcaçoas, ending of war
1481–1504	Ozolua, *oba* of Benin
1482	Portugal factory fort of São Jorge de Mina built by Diogo d'Azambuja
1482	Diogo Cão crosses Equator and reaches Cape Santa Maria, after leaving four emissaries to Nzinga Nkuwu, king of Kongo
1483	Sonni Ali routs Mossi
1484	Sonni Ali attacks Dogan of cliff region
1485	Wolof take over Tekrur
1486–1488	Sonni Ali persecutes Moslems of Gao region
1486	Slave trade of Benin begins with building of factory at Gató
1487	Bartolomeu Dias doubles Cape of Good Hope
1490	First Christian missions sent by king of Portugal (to Angola)
c. 1490	Birth of Leo Africanus (El Hassan ibn Mohammed el Wezzan) in Granada
1492	Death of Sonni Ali
1493	Muhammed Ture overthrows Abu Bekr Da'o, 'pagan' successor to Sonni Ali, at Battle of Angao
1497 (25 December)	Vasco da Gama discovers and names Natal

1498	Muhammed plunders the Mossi kingdom of Yatenga and invades the Mali province of Diara
1498	Vasco da Gama rounds Cape of Good Hope. Beginning of Portuguese threat to Mamluk state
1499–1507	Mali over-run by Songhai
1500	Arrival of first European (Portuguese Pedro Cabral) at East African city-states
1500–1600	Foundation of second Luba Empire and the Lunda states (from pre-existing states of the Kaniok, Mutombo, Mukulu, Putu and Songhai)
1504–1550	Esigie, *obo* of Benin, sends ambassador to Lisbon
1505	Sofala becomes Portuguese
1505–1543	Afonso, first Christian manikongo (king of Kongo)
1506–1543	Imam Ahmad Ibrahim al Ghazi, Muslim leader
1507	Moçambique becomes Portuguese
1507–1529	Idris ibn Ali Katagarmabe reconquers Kanem
1508–1540	Reign of Lebna Dengel in Ethiopia
1510	In Lisbon, first African slaves for West Indies bought and exported
1513	Muhammed invades Hausa city-states; controls route to Aïr
1515	Muhammed captures Agades from the Tuareg
1516	Foundation of State of Kebbi by the *kanta* (ruler)
1517	Ottoman Empire defeats Mamluk Empire
1517	Ottoman conquest of Egypt
1520	Portuguese send embassy to Ethiopia (Fr. Francisco Alvarez); he remains six years
c. 1522	Foundation of Baguirmi Empire

1522–1536	Reign of Birni-Bessé, a chief from the Yemen, over the Baguirmi Empire. Conqueror of Fulani, the Massas and the Arabs; founder of Massenya, first Sultan
1527	Ottoman Turkish Muslim army, under Muhammed Gran, attacks, defeats and ravages Ethiopia
1528	Abdication of Muhammed following defeat at hands of three of his sons
1531–1537	Muhammed Bengan Korei, ruler (*askiya*) of Songhai
1538	Muhammed dies in exile
1539–1549	Ishaq reign; partially revives Songhai power
1540–1559	Galauderos, Emperor of Ethiopia, conqueror of Muslims
1541	Christopher da Gama lands Portuguese force of 400 men at Klasama. Bulk of force, including da Gama, destroyed by Gran
1542	Emperor Galauderos of Abyssinia routs Muslims at Lake Tana
1543	Portuguese remnant, with Galauderos (1540–1549), defeats Gran in surprise attack
1548–1568	Malo III, conqueror of Moito
1549–1582	Reign of Da'ud. Invader of Yatenga, conqueror of Maçina
1557	Andrea de Oviedo arrives in Ethiopia with several priests
1560	Gonçalo da Silveiro enters kingdom of Nogomo Mupunzagato, king of Mwanamutapa
1563–1596	Reign of Sarsa Dengel in Ethiopia. Converted to Roman Catholic Church
1568	Fortress of San Sebastião begun
1568–1598	Abdullah IV, the first usurper. Real founder of Baguirmese state. Islam becomes official religion

1570–1610	Reign of Idriss Alauma of Bornu
1576	First unquestionable evidence of existence of Accra
1577	Muslim capital of Abyssinia moved from Harar to Aussa
1578	Port of Loanda founded
1580–1617	Idriss Alauma. Unifies Bornu by attaching Kanem. Imposes protectorate on Baguirmi
1584	Annihilation of Moroccan army in Sahara
1585	Songhai, driven out of Taghaza by the Moors, begin to work salt deposits at Taodeni
1588–1591	Reign of Ishaq II, *askiya* of Songhai. Confrontations with Morocco
1591–1599	Struggle of the Dendi against the Moroccans
1591 (30 March)	Jouder (Spanish renegade) arrives with 3,000 armed men at Niger
1591 (12 April)	Jouder defeats Songhai army at Tondiki
1591 (17 August)	Mahmoud arrives at Timbuctoo
1591 (14 October)	Mahmoud defeats Songhai under Askia Issihak at Bemba
1591	Tuaregs fire Timbuctoo
1593	Fortress of Mombasa founded by Portuguese
1594	Death of Mahmoud
1596	Death of Mansur
1599	Nuhu, *askiya* of Songhai, deposed
1599 (25 March)	Jouder is recalled to Morocco
c. 1600	Foundation of Imbangala Cokwe, Luena and southern Lunda states
c. 1600	Islam introduced to Baguirmi
c. 1600–*c.* 1700	Height of Oyo power, between reigns of Obalokun Agana Erin and Onisile
1603–1604	Za Dengel, Emperor of Ethiopia
1607–1632	Susneyos, Emperor of Ethiopia
c. 1620	Mbo settle in Natal

c. 1624	Collapse of Mogadishu's Mudaffer dynasty
c. 1625	Baguirmi dynasty is converted to Islam
1630	Kingdom of Mogadishu ruled by puppet Mavura. Portuguese settlement begins
1631	Yusuf bin Hassan proclaims independence of Mombasa
1632	Yusuf abandons Mombasa
1632–1667	Fasilidas Emperor of Ethiopia. Decrees suppression of Roman Catholic church, banishes Jesuits
1635–1665	Burkomanda I—VII. Conqueror of Kanem, Borku and Khenga
1637	Death of Yusuf bin Hassan
1640–1650	Introduction and development of plantation method of sugar production in West Indies
1640–1820	Height of slave trade from Gold Coast
1642	French forces occupy Bourbon (Réunion), and establish base on Madagascar
1642–1677	Badi Abu Duqn, *makk* of Funj sultanate of Sennar. Zenith of Funj power
1644	Dutch East India Company occupies Mauritius
1650	Rise of Akwamu Empire
1650–1675	Baguirmi comes under sovereignty of Bornu
c. 1650	Foundation of Lozi state
1651	All shaikhs of East African littoral in arms against Portugal
1652	Dutch settle in Cape Town
1652	Dutch East India Company first use Cape of Good Hope
1652	Arrival of Riebeeck in Cape Peninsula—introduction of slavery
1663	Mission station established at Loango
1667	Tuaregs besiege Ngazargamu
1670	Sultan of Oman pillages Moçambique
1677–1681	Akwamu conquest of Accra
1680–1860	Height of slave trade from Slave Coast

c. 1680–1715	Badi el Ahmar, *makk* of Funj. Decline of Funj
1682–1706	Yasus, Emperor of Ethiopia
1693	Akwamu capture Christiansborg castle
1697	Ashanti Federations of Akan tribes
1698	Sultan of Oman captures Fort Jesus
1698	Arab forces establish themselves at Mombasa
1700	Juabe state absorbs all provinces
c. 1700	Foundation of Lunda states of the Kwango Kasai
1709–1714	Line of Solomon deposed
1712	Death of Osei Tutu, king of Asantahene
1713	Treaty of Utrecht
1715	France annexes Mauritius (Île de France)
c. 1720	Kwena of Sechele secedes from Bantu cluster to settle in Batswanaland
c. 1721–1750	Opuku Ware, ruler of Ashanti
1722	Dutch mission to Ghana
c. 1723–1761	Badi abu Shelukh, last *makk* of Funj
1724	Adja invaded by Agadja, king of Fon
1724	French capture Arguin and Mauretania
1727	Fon people conquer kingdom of Hueda
1729–1753	Yasus II, Emperor of Ethiopia
1733	Akim defeats Akwamu
1743	Funj defeat Ethiopia
1744	Opuku defeats Regonba and Gonja
1747	Funj conquers Kordofar
c. 1750	Foundation of Kazembe state on Luapala river
1750–1764	Kusi Obodum king of Ashanti
1751–1758	Hadji XV Emperor of Ethiopia
1753	Yoas murdered by Mikael. Takla Haimanot II succeeds
1754	Uthman dan Fodio Fulani leader. Battle of Ondumman

1755	Shaikh of Mombasa attack on Zanzibar fails
1764–1777	Osei Kojo, king of Ashanti, conqueror of Akim
1765	Senegambia becomes the first British African colony
1769	James Bruce arrives in Gondar
1769	*Jihad* begins against Fulani and Moors in Western Sudan
1769–1770	Governor of Moçambique attempts unsuccessfully to reconquer Mombasa
1772	Abolition of slavery in British Isles
1775	Fulani dynasty overthrown, replaced by Torodo imams
1775	Birth of Seku Ahmadu
1783	Great Britain cedes Arguin, Gorée, Saint-Lions and the Sénégal littoral to France (Treaty of Versailles)
1784	Zanzibar is conquered by Imam of Muscat
1785	Ottoman reconquest of Egypt, led by Gâzï Hasan Pâşâ
1785–1808	Abd er Khamane Gaurong I, XVI. Start of Baguirmese decadence
1786	Hasan Pâşâ recalled to Turkey. Murâd and Ibrâhïm Beys return to power
1787	The Province of Freetown experiment begins; party of 401 sails from England
1788	Formation of African Association in London
1790	The Province of Freetown experiment ends by the dispersion of the settlement by the Temme
1792	Sultan Salim III introduces Nizam Jidid reforms in Ottoman Empire
1792	Re-establishment of Granville Town

Index

DATE DUE

FE 25 '70			
MR 5 '70			
AP 27 '70			
MY 11 '70			
SEP 28			
OC 5 - '70			
DE 14 '71			
Nov. 5 1:00			
12/6 8:00			
8:00			
NO 06 '07			

GAYLORD PRINTED IN U.S.A.